St IVES ART pre-1890

THE DAWN OF THE COLONY

~

DAVID TOVEY

~

ABOUT THE AUTHOR

David Tovey was born in 1953 and was educated at his father's preparatory school, Tockington Manor, near Bristol, and at Clifton College, before reading Jurisprudence at Pembroke College, Oxford. After twenty years as a solicitor, he returned to University in 1996 to read History of Art and is now an independent art historian, specialising in Cornish Art. His particular interest in St Ives art derives from the fact that his great-grandfather, William Titcomb, was one of the early settlers in the colony. Since 2000, he has curated a number of exhibitions and written several books on Cornish art. In particular, he published in 2003 a history of the first 25 years of the St Ives Society of Artists (1927-1952), entitled *Creating A Splash*, which is already in its third print run, and curated the resultant exhibition, which toured six venues during 2003-4 and attracted over 80,000 visitors. He lectures widely on Cornish representational art, particularly to members of the National Association for Design and Fine Arts Societies. His previous books include:-

George Fagan Bradshaw - Submariner and Marine Artist - and the St Ives Society of Artists
(Wilson Books, 2000 ISBN 0 9538363 0 4)

W.H.Y.Titcomb : A Newlyner from St Ives, dealing with the years 1858-1908
(Wilson Books, 2003 ISBN 0 9538363-2-0)

W.H.Y.Titcomb : Bristol, Venice and the Continental Tours, covering the years 1909-1930
(Wilson Books, 2003 ISBN 0 9538363-1-2)

Creating A Splash - The St Ives Society of Artists - The First Twenty-Five Years (1927-1952)
(Wilson Books, 2003 & 2004 ISBN 0-9538363-4-7)

What the critics said about *Creating A Splash*

"Tovey provides fascinating biographical information on each [of the major artists associated with the Society] and a well-researched history of the ups and downs of the Society. However, perhaps the most important aspect of this remarkable book is the concise and informative entries on the lesser known members, many of whom were capable of producing mini-masterpieces of great subtlety and sensitivity. These works frequently come up on the market and the lack of biographical information on the artists who painted them is a constant frustration. Tovey is clearly aware of this and has filled his book with an amazing amount of original research, ensuring the book will be highly valued as an essential reference source for many years to come.......This book is not only recommended to all interested in the history of British art, but would be my personal nomination for the most useful art book of the year." - Brian Stewart, Curator of Falmouth Art Gallery, Kent on Sunday

"Terrific reference on Cornish art, including entries which are the most complete summaries known on an artist, plus plenty of illustrations." - Joan Porter, Antiques Trade Gazette

"Taken together, exhibition and book add up to an informative, fascinating, not to say formidable double act... David Tovey's book, which is encyclopaedic in scope, really does include all you ever wanted to know - but were afraid to ask - about art in St Ives". - Frank Ruhrmund, Art Critic, The Cornishman

---

First published in 2008 by
WILSON BOOKS
11-13 Mill Bank, Tewkesbury, Gloucestershire, GL20 5SD
(01684 850898) Email : dwt4@talktalk.net

A catalogue record for this book is available from the British Library.

ISBN for this paperback edition ISBN 9780953836352

Printed and bound in England by Rowe the Printers, Hayle, Cornwall, TR27 4QZ

ST IVES ART pre-1890 — THE DAWN OF THE COLONY

CONTENTS

INDEX OF TABLES

INDEX OF SPECIAL FEATURES

ABBREVIATIONS

BAPFA	Bristol Academy for the Promotion of the Fine Arts
NEAC	New English Art Club
RA	Royal Academy
RCPS	Royal Cornwall Polytechnic Society
RI	Royal Institute of Painters in Watercolours
ROI	Royal Institute of Oil Painters
RWS	Royal Society of Painters in Watercolour
SBA	Society of British Artists
SWA	Society of Women Artists
WCAU	West Cornwall Art Union

COVER ILLUSTRATIONS

Front cover: Helene Schjerfbeck, *View of St Ives*
(Private Collection, Helsinki)
(Photo: Central Art Archives/Hannu Aaltonen)

Back cover: William Trost Richards, *Fishing Boats at St Ives, Cornwall*
(William Vareika Fine Art)

AUTHOR'S NOTE

Early St Ives art has suffered the most appalling neglect. It really is astonishing that the early years of Britain's premier art colony, which has flourished since 1885, have not previously been the subject of any exhibition or of any detailed research, other than Marion Whybrow's ground-breaking book on the St Ives Arts Club published back in 1994. This is despite a huge surge in interest in late Victorian Cornish art following the seminal exhibition, *Artists of the Newlyn School*, nearly thirty years ago in 1979. Furthermore, the four Royal Academicians, who made their initial reputations in St Ives during the 1890s - Adrian Stokes, Arnesby Brown, Julius Olsson and Algernon Talmage - have also not been the subject of any exhibition or even of any monographs, notwithstanding that Julius Olsson was considered, in his day, to be Britain's premier seascape painter, whilst Arnesby Brown was hailed as "the greatest English landscape painter since Constable".

The overlooking of the early history of this colony is perhaps all the more extraordinary given that the Tate Gallery established a branch in St Ives in 1993. However, Tate St Ives, until now, has concentrated its attention on modernist art of the post-1939 period and on seeking to ensure that St Ives remains a vibrant centre for art production, and has considered that the first fifty years of the colony is not a part of its core remit. Until recently, it has also made little attempt to research or review this early period, even for context purposes.

It is regrettable that there is currently nowhere in St. Ives where quality early St Ives paintings are permanently on public display, and that neither the St Ives Museum nor the St Ives Town Council go out of their way to publicise the examples that they own. The sad result of this disinterest is that much that has been written about early St Ives art is based on erroneous or incomplete information, and myths and half-truths have grown up and been perpetuated.

In the course my research, I have been endlessly surprised by quite how much new information of considerable significance I have been able to unearth and, accordingly, my intended single volume history has had to be expanded into a series of publications. These attempt to set out, once and for all, the extraordinary story of early St Ives art in considerable detail, so that the full extent of its astonishing achievements can finally be appreciated. I hope that they will not only prove enjoyable reads but also essential reference points for many years to come for curators, historians, dealers, collectors and all with any semblance of interest in Cornish, or indeed, British art. The ramifications from this research, though, go far beyond Cornwall to America, Canada, Australia, New Zealand and Scandinavia, for artists from these and other countries were greatly touched by their experiences in St Ives.

The first two volumes in the series will be published in May 2008 to accompany two exhibitions that will be held in Cornwall that summer - the first ever exhibitions devoted solely to early St Ives art.

This first volume, *St Ives Art pre-1890 - The Dawn of the Colony*, looks at the work of the visitors to St Ives in the period prior to the formation of the colony in 1885 and at the initial success of the colony, particularly in Paris, in the years up to 1889 and has been published by myself to coincide with the exhibition at Tate St Ives in the summer of 2008, entitled *Dawn of a Colony : Picturing the West (St Ives 1811-1888).*

The second volume, *Pioneers of St Ives Art at Home and Abroad (1889-1914)* - Wilson Books, Tewkesbury ISBN 0-9538363-6-3, deals with the major paintings by British and foreign artists working in St Ives, which were exhibited in the years 1889-1914 in London, Paris and Pittsburgh, and looks at how St Ives became a world-renowned centre for both the practice and teaching of landscape and marine painting. This book is intended to link in with the exhibition *Dawn of a Colony : Lyrical Light (St Ives 1889-1914),* which commenced at Penlee House Gallery & Museum, Penzance in June 2008. The term "Pioneers" has been used, as there is only space in the book to deal with the best works by the most successful artists. It has not been possible, therefore, to deal with all artists working in the colony.

The third volume, provisionally entitled *Early St Ives Art (1885-1927) - The Artists and the Community*, is likely to be published in 2009-10. This looks at the impact that the artists had on the town in a myriad of different ways. It discusses their backgrounds and how they inter-reacted with the locals. It looks at the effect that they had on business in the town, on tourism and on town planning and on sporting and cultural activities. It tells the story of their homes, their studios, their training at the local art schools and their social life. It also gives me the opportunity to discuss some of the lesser artists, who nevertheless played important roles in the community. I will also highlight the best art produced in the years 1914-27.

I have also been asked to prepare a Dictionary of all artists known to be working in St Ives prior to 1927, which, at the time of writing, may or may not come to fruition, although the research has been done.

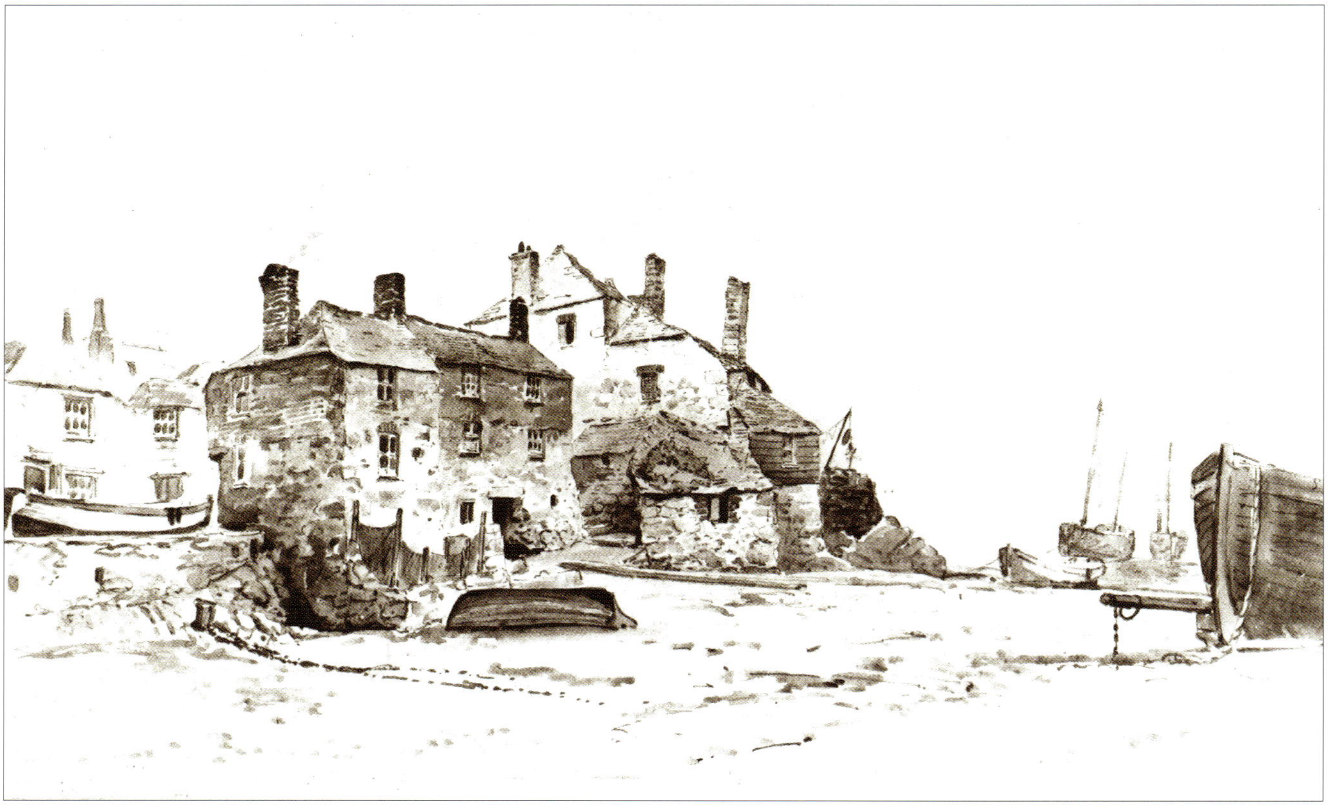

Fig. 0.1 Anon *St Ives before Smeaton's Pier* (David Lay, Penzance Auction House)
This work clearly does not date from the eighteenth century and so is merely a speculative reconstruction.

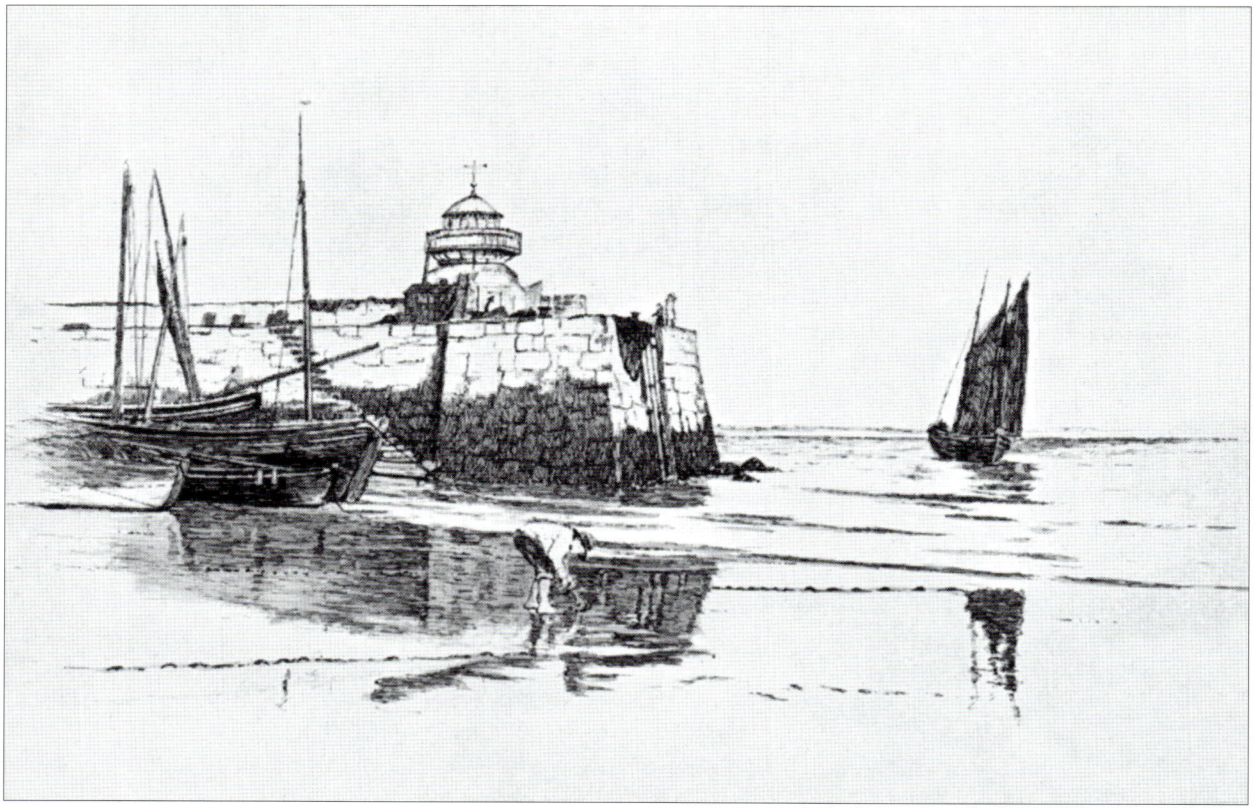

Fig. 0.2 William Henry Bartlett *Old Lighthouse, Smeaton's Pier, St Ives* (*Art Journal*)
This drawing is likely to pre-date 1888 for, in the years 1888-90, Smeaton's Pier was extended and another lighthouse erected at its end. The distinctive 'pepperpot' lighthouse, now in the middle, was retained.

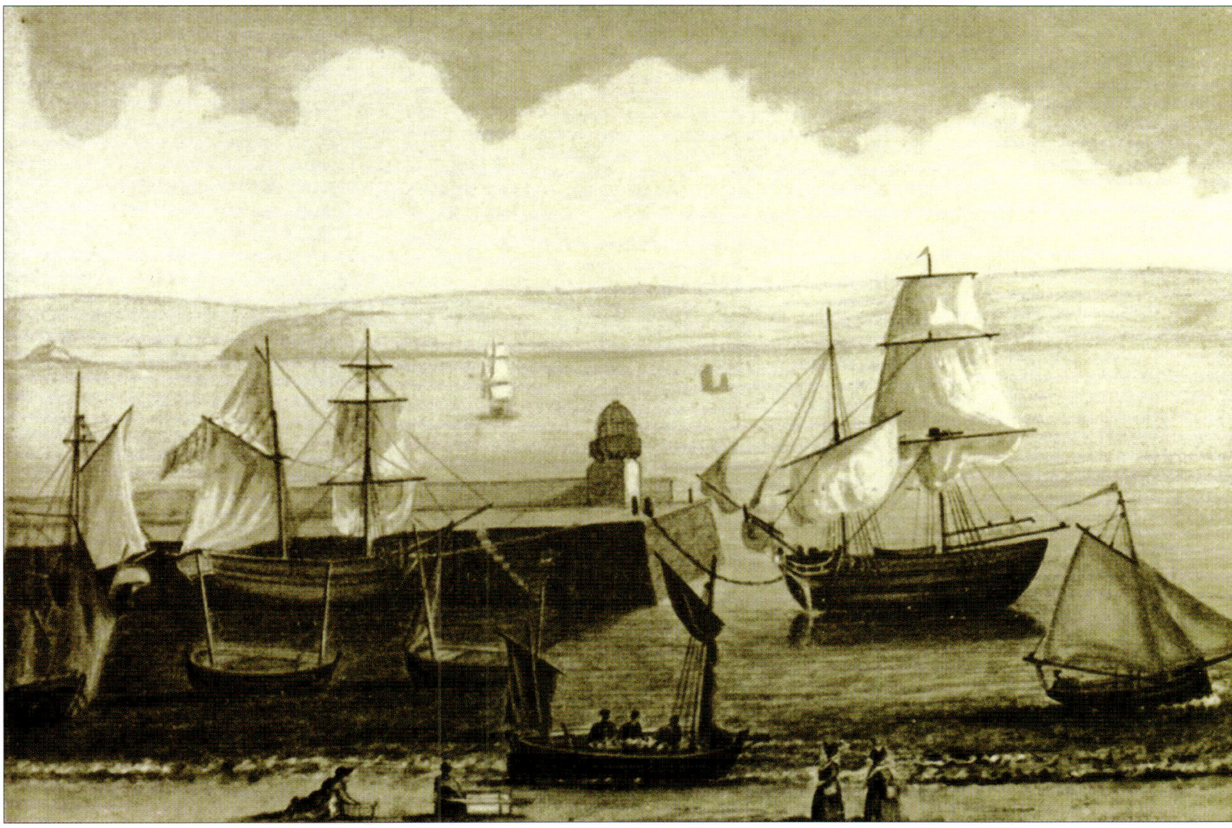

Fig. 0.3 Anon *The Old Harbour at St Ives* (from Cyril Noall's *Beloved St Ives*)

The period 1927 to 1952 has, of course, been covered by me previously in my book *Creating A Splash - The St Ives Society of Artists (1927-1952)*. Together, these books present the truly fascinating story of the early years of Britain's premier art colony.

The last five years, when I have been working full time on this project, have been ridiculously exciting, as each new magical painting or piece of information has come to light. It has also, though, been intensely frustrating, as despite the success of the *Creating A Splash* book and exhibition in 2003-4 and despite the full support of both Penlee House Gallery & Museum, Penzance and, latterly, Tate St Ives, all applications for funding have been rejected. Therefore, all my research expenses, the significant costs of obtaining all the images and the total publication costs have had to be funded from my own pocket. This, of course, is economic madness but I have done it due to my passion for my subject. As a one-man researcher, writer, editor, designer, publisher and marketing manager, I need YOUR help. If you enjoy this book, then please tell others – and perhaps give a few copies as gifts. If you feel like helping with the costs of any of the other volumes in the series, then please make contact. It would be enormously appreciated. I will never make a profit but it would be nice to reduce the loss somewhat! Most importantly, though, enjoy this incredible story.

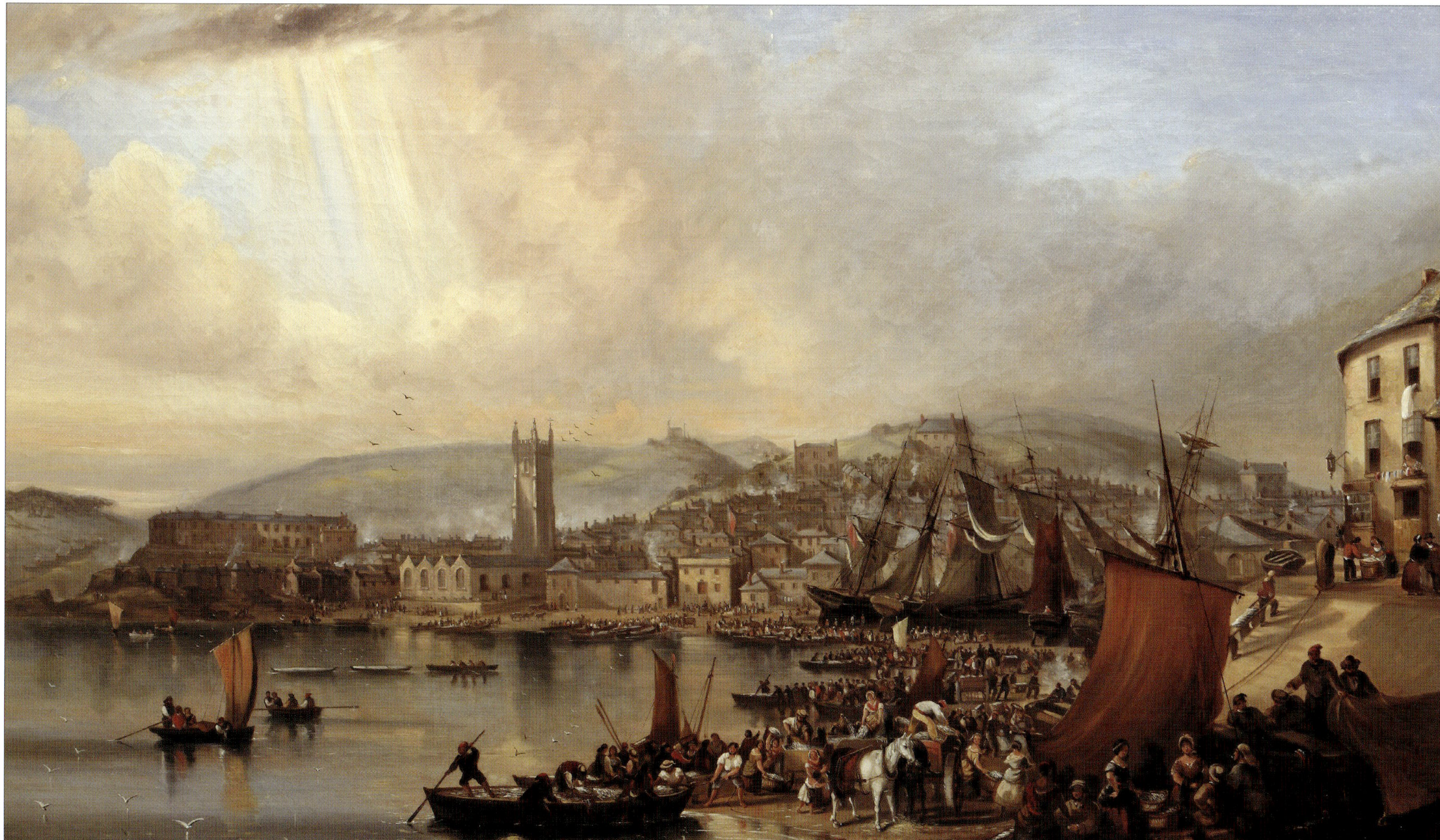

Fig.0.4 N Conata *St Ives* (St Ives Town Collection)

This highly romanticised depiction of St Ives harbour at the time of a huge pilchard catch is nevertheless exceptionally interesting. It gives a very good impression of the intense activity in the town after a shoal of pilchards had been caught in the Bay, as all manner of craft ferry the 'silver jewels' into the harbour, where they would be salted or pressed. To the right of the Parish Church can be seen the long fish cellar, which became the home of the Salvation Army before being burnt down in 1915. To its right is the Lifeboat Inn. To the left of the Church can be seen the houses of The Terrace, built in the 1820s, with those of The Warren beneath, whilst to the far left are the stepped Porthminster Cottages going up Primrose Valley. The structure on the hill to the right of the Church Tower is most likely the engine house of Wheal Trenwith, whilst the big houses at the rear are thought to be Windy Parc, Trewyn and possibly Salubrious House., but there is is clearly a good deal of artistic licence.[1]

1 I am indebted to John McWilliams and Janet Axten for their interpretations of this painting.

INTRODUCTION

The Discovery of Cornwall

Despite the copious amount that has been written on the Cornish art colonies, there has been very little published research on Cornish art prior to the formation of the colonies. Indeed, one is often left with the impression that there was little of note to record before "Birmingham", in the shape of Edwin Harris and Walter Langley, "discovered" Newlyn in 1882 and Whistler "discovered" St Ives in 1884. Only a cursory glance at a few mid-nineteenth century exhibition catalogues reveals that such claims are faintly ridiculous and that the key date in the discovery of Cornwall by artists was 1859, the year that saw the completion of Isambard Kingdom Brunel's railway bridge across the Tamar at Saltash.[2] Prior to that date, Cornwall had remained remote and difficult to reach and, with the ordinary means of travel from Plymouth to Penzance being by a van called a 'kitterine', the journey had taken three days.[3] Accordingly, few artists had made the effort, particularly as the county had failed to shake off its reputation, in some quarters, as a semi-civilised area populated by "the wreckers of the coast and the miners of the hills".[4] To demonstrate the impact of the railway, one needs look no further than the exhibition catalogues of the Bristol Academy for the Promotion of the Fine Arts ("BAPFA"), an institution, founded in 1845, that was the most prestigious venue at which West Country artists could exhibit their work. In the extant catalogues for the years up to 1859, there are, on average, only a couple of Cornish scenes per year. In 1860, however, there are fifteen and, whilst Penzance, Newlyn and Mount's Bay feature prominently, artists have also reached the Lizard, Flushing, Sennen, Porthgwarra and Fowey. As the 1860s progressed, the number of Cornish scenes exhibited increased and the artists spread their net wider and wider. They now had the benefit of John Murray's *A Handbook for Travellers in Devon and Cornwall*, first published in 1851, but updated when the railway link was completed, whilst Robert Hunt's *Popular Romances of the West of England (or the Drolls, Traditions and Superstitions of Old Cornwall)*, reviewed in the *Art Journal* in 1865, aroused further interest. Indeed, the legends of "the land of the giants", with their romantic and poetic associations, were emphasized by Walter Tregellas in articles on the cliffs, moors and valleys of Cornwall as artistic subjects, published in the *Magazine of Art*, in 1878, and in the *Art Journal*, in 1883.[5] Glorious coastline, coupled with romantic associations, was a winning formula - and Marmaduke Langdale's *View of Tintagel* (RA 1865), with its King Arthur connections, was awarded the Turner Gold Medal in 1866 - but such motifs could soon become hackneyed, and artists were prepared to inconvenience themselves and get to the most inaccessible locations, in order to portray attractive subjects, previously unrecorded, in out of the way places. It did not take long, therefore, for most of Cornwall's scenic attractions to be captured in paint and, as the beauty of the Duchy became more widely known, yet further artists came down on sketching trips.

It seems that the majority of these early artist visitors were watercolourists, as the apparatus needed for painting in this medium was so much less cumbersome than for oils. Their subjects were principally topographical scenes, which is unsurprising, given that they were introducing this new, unseen and very beautiful world to the rest of Britain. Depictions of sections of wild coastline, deliberately shown only as the haunt of Nature, were popular. Victorians, however, also liked a narrative element in their paintings and so, in other instances, figures were introduced, showing the locals going about their ordinary lives. As was the Victorians' wont, such scenes were often romanticised or idealised, for the lives of seafarers, being fraught with danger, always provided an excuse for the introduction of sentiment. The many scenes of industry, that must have been witnessed at the tail end of the mining boom, were, of course, largely ignored. Paintings of Cornwall, therefore, had been seen with regularity on gallery walls across the country long before the formation of the art colonies. Indeed, a number of paintings of Cornish scenes had by that time already been acquired by Galleries in as far away places as Australia![6]

St Ives - From "dirty fishing town" to "health resort"

Although St Ives received regular artist visitors from the early 1860s, none showed any inclination to settle in such a remote outpost, particularly as, despite its scenic attractions, it was the centre for a number of industries. The whole area around the town, particularly in the region that is now known as Carbis Bay, was scarred by tin and copper mines, and there were also numerous mining districts in the local Parishes of Lelant and Towednack.[7]

---

2 For instance, in Algernon Graves' list of exhibitors at the British Institution between the years 1806 and 1867, there are remarkably few depictions of Cornwall, let alone West Penwith, prior to 1859. St Michael's Mount and Land's End are featured on a number of occasions - William Daniell (1825), H.W.Burgess (1832), James Fuge (1837), H.Lancaster (1847) and H.J.Johnson (1850), - but I could see no indication of any depiction of St Ives.

3 Robert Hunt, *Popular Romances of the West of England*, 1865 (1923 edition at p.24).

4 ibid.

5 Walter H.Tregellas, *Artists' Haunts: Cornwall - the Cliffs, Magazine of Art*, 1878, pp.8-11 and 141-146 and Walter H.Tregellas, *The moorlands and glens of Cornwall, Art Journal*, 1883, pp.314-316.

6 The National Gallery of Victoria, Melbourne have *St Michael's Mount, Cornwall* by Clarkson Stanfield dated 1830, whilst The Art Gallery of New South Wales, Sydney have Edward Cooke's *On the Coast of Cornwall* of 1875 and Arthur Suker's *Trevose Head* from the mid-1880s.

7 See Plan of Saint Ives, Uny Lelant and Towednack Mining Districts reproduced in C. Noall, *The Book of St Ives*, Buckingham, 1977, at p.97.

In the town itself, the St Ives Consols mine, at the top of The Stennack, was considered, in the 1850s, to be one of the largest tin concerns in the county.[8] Even the cliff scenery nearby at Man's Head and Hor Point was blighted by mine workings and, in 1860, a mine was established on Pednolva Point, opposite the harbour, with a view to mining under the sea. There were also rope-making and shipbuilding industries in the town, whilst the fishing industry, later portrayed as picturesque, resulted in ever-present malignant odours and a good deal of noise in the middle of the night, as the fleet unloaded their catch.

Visiting the town at the very end of the eighteenth century, a young Oxford botanist, Dr W.G.Mathon, commented, "The stench arising from the stores, and from the putrid *rejectamenta* lying about the town, is to strangers almost intolerable" and its reputation as a "dirty fishing town" continued through the nineteenth century.[9] One commercial traveller, who came over to St Ives from Penzance in 1867 to view its ancient properties, concluded, after quickly aborting his visit, that, although he had found "some dwellings which he thought must have been built before Noah's time", they clearly "could never have been cleaned since, from the sickening smells and stunning odours of the very essence of stench which saluted him at every turn as he picked his way through The Digey and leaped the gutters of Chy-an-Chy."[10] Poor drainage and sanitation, when coupled with the odours of the fishing industry, made a vile combination. Furthermore, the fishermen also gutted fish on the harbour beach and this offal was left for scavenging gulls and, unsurprisingly, attracted rats.

In the 1850s, a number of guides to Cornwall began to be published, and they were less than complimentary about the town. Murray's Guide, for instance, having mentioned that the distant vista of the town, with "its old rickety houses ...nestling on the very skirt of the sea", was likely to make the visitor "draw rein", for it formed a very pleasing picture, comparable with Grecian scenery, nevertheless warned that his admiration would be somewhat qualified on a closer inspection, as the town was "tainted with the effluvia" of the pilchard cellars.[11] Some of the open channels in the streets, down which the juices from the pressed pilchards were allowed to flow, can still be seen. Walter White, in 1855, was even blunter, telling his readers not to disenchant themselves by going down into the town at all, for it "appears to be in the process of dilapidation and to have been built without any regard to order".[12] St Ives was, accordingly, a dirty, noisy, stinking town that no artist was prepared to select as his home, whilst the scenic attractions of the town and its environs were significantly impaired.

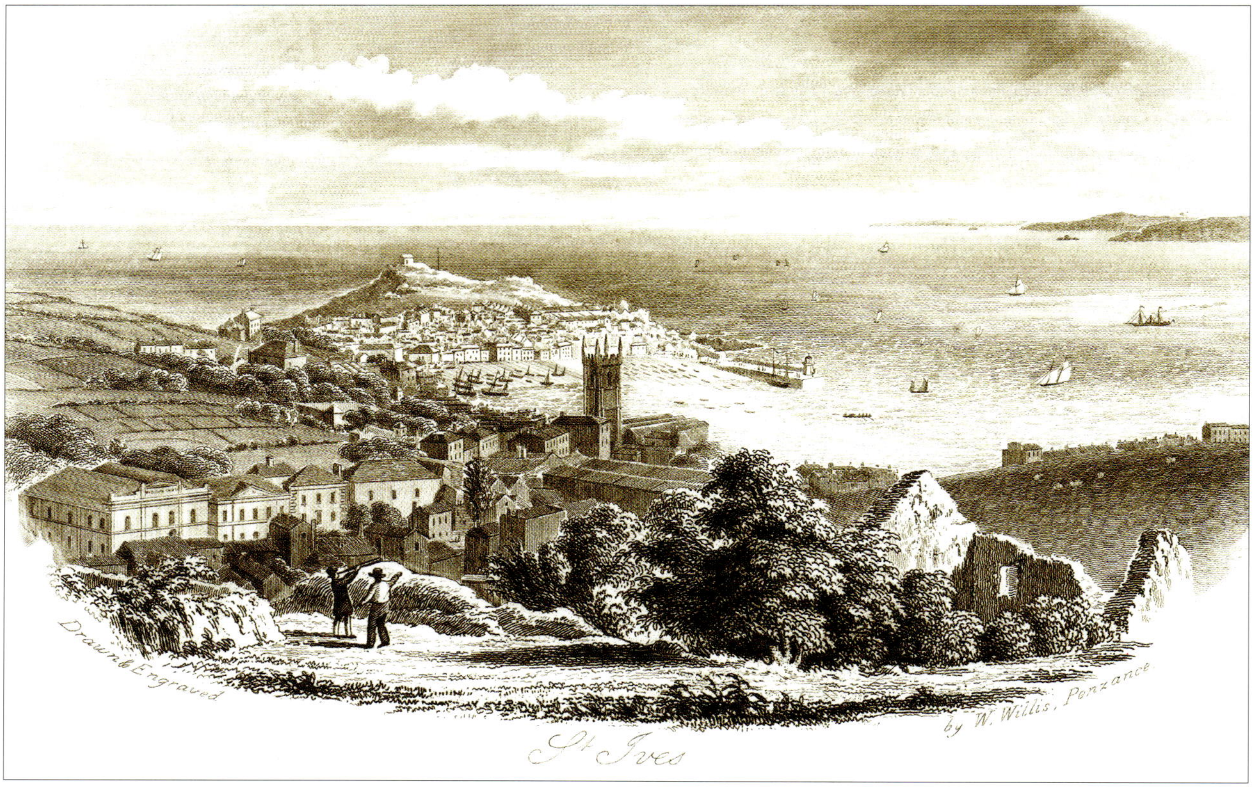

Fig. 0.5 W Willis *St Ives from Park-an-Roper* (c.1844)
An engraving in *The Pictorial World* in 1877 of the same view shows some additional properties off The Stennack and in the Ayr district, but little else has changed, apart from the incompleted wooden pier.

8 Murray's *Handbook for Devon and Cornwall*, 1859 (1971 reprint at p.181). Stennack means 'place of tin'.
9 Ed. R.Pearse Chope, *Early Tours in Devon and Cornwall*, 1967 edition at p.260.
10 An account of this visit was reproduced in *The St Ives Times* on 24/5/1912. The Editor added, "The above picture of the sanitary condition of St Ives in 1867 is not in the least overdrawn, as anyone who can remember the town at that period can testify."
11 Murray's *Handbook for Devon and Cornwall*, 1859 (1971 reprint at p.180).
12 Walter White, *A Londoner's Walk to Land's End*, London, 1855.

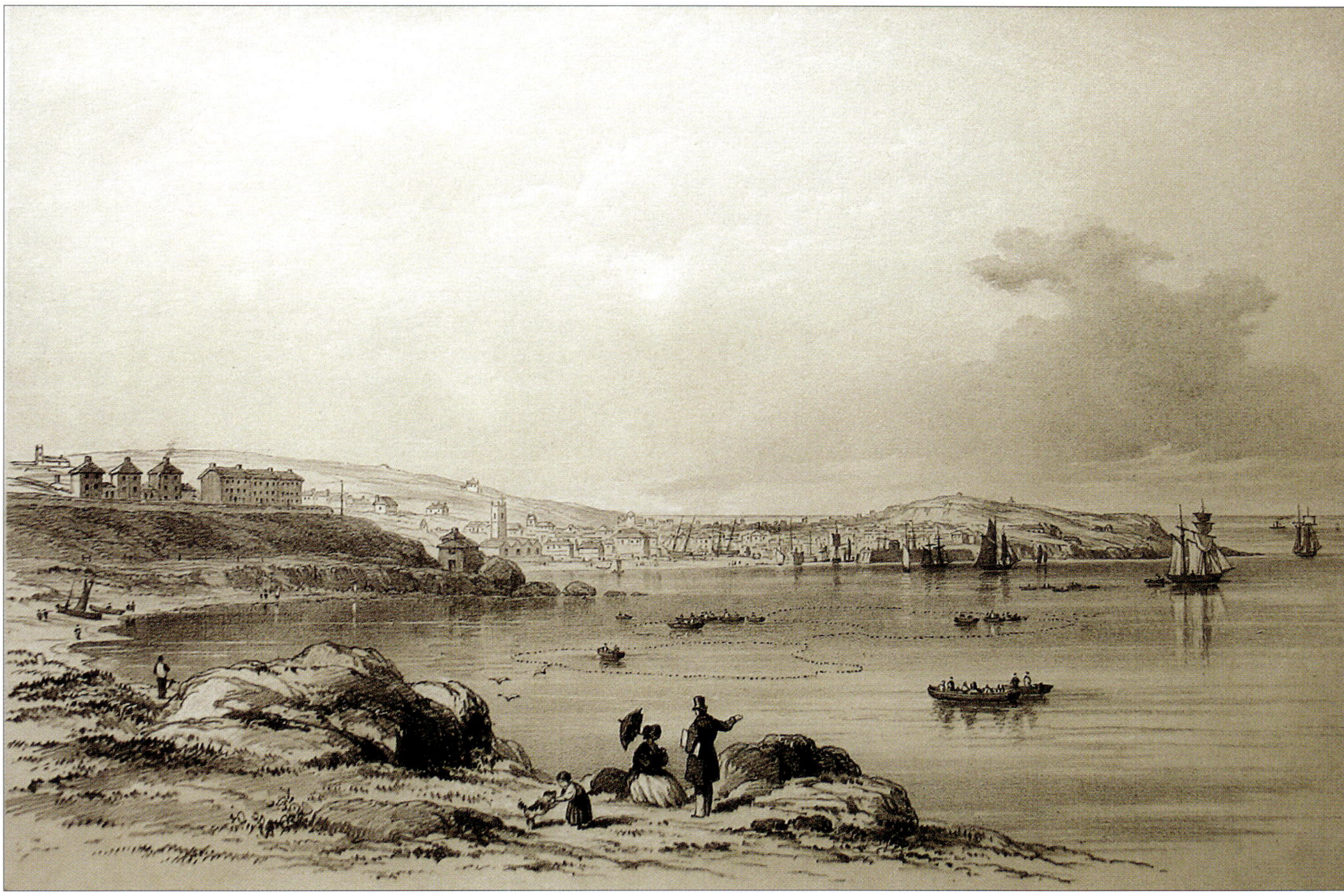

Fig. 0.6 Richard T Pentreath *St Ives, Cornwall* (Private Collection)
Several seine nets enclosing shoals of pilchards can be seen in the Bay.

In the 1870s, however, changes started to occur, prompted no doubt by the collapse in the mining industry, which resulted in many job losses and a significant number of mine closures. The shipbuilding and rope-making industries had also, by then, largely ceased, whilst the fishing catches had become far less dependable. St Ives, accordingly, was in trouble, and it was decided that it needed to re-invent itself as a holiday resort. For this to succeed, though, the Town Council needed not only to clean up the town's image and remedy its defective drainage and water supply, but also to ensure that access to the town was made far easier. Previous efforts in 1844, 1846, 1853 and 1862 to get a rail link to St Ives from the main line had all foundered, and the task was made more difficult in the 1870s, because the railway companies only saw the failed mines and uncertain fisheries.[13] However, they were eventually persuaded that the holiday resort concept might work. Construction of the branch line, accordingly, commenced in 1874 and was completed in May 1877. An illustrated article in the *Pictorial World* in June 1877 proclaimed that St Ives was "one of the most beautiful of our seaside resorts" and "offers equal attractions to the tourist, the artist and the invalid. The views are grand and extensive, comprising hills and vales, coast and sea, cliffs and gorge, sands and beach - the run of country differing entirely in appearance and fertility from east to west. For position and climate, here is all that is desirable to bring this port into popular favour, not only as a watering place, but as a health resort".[14] In truth, there was still much to be done to remove the "dirty fishing town" tag from St Ives and, for some years, the initiatives taken seemed not to have worked. Sir Edward Hain, the shipping magnate and the pre-eminent citizen in the town, later recalled the desperate state to which St Ives had been reduced in the 1880s. He commented, "The railway had been opened for a good many years, but the main purpose for which it seemed to be employed then was to take people out of the place, because they could not get a proper and adequate living in it".[15] This view is confirmed by the Census figures, which saw the population drop from 6965 in 1871, to 6445 in 1881, and, yet further, to 6094 in 1891.[16] St Ives, like many of the other Cornish industrial towns, was dying. That it pulled out of this seemingly terminal decline was, to a significant degree, due to the arrival of the artists and their promotion of its attractions.

---

13 See Cyril Noall, *Yesterday's Town*, Buckingham, 1979 at p.60.
14 *The Pictorial World*, 30/6/1877.
15 Speech at the 1911 Mayoral Banquet, *St Ives Weekly Summary* 10/11/1911.
16 See Janet Axten *Dissertation Migration into and out of St Ives, Cornwall 1871-1901* dated June 2003 - copy held at St Ives Archive Centre.

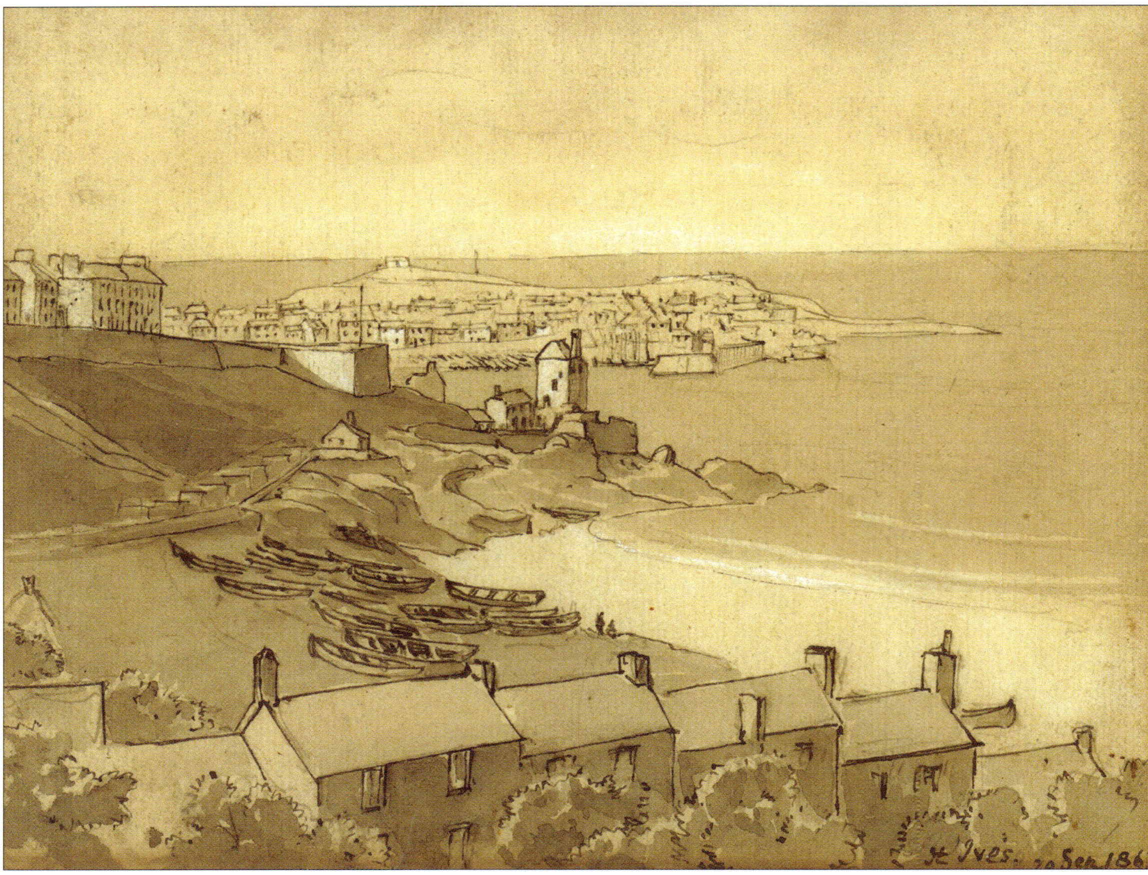

Fig. 0.7 Anon *St Ives (20th September 1863)* (Private Collection)
This shows the original roof of the mine engine house on Pednolva Point.

Rural Art Colonies

The establishment of an artists' colony in St Ives in 1885 was part of a trend that had a major influence on Western art in the late nineteenth century. Clusters of artists gathered together in rural locations all over Europe, particularly in the period 1880-1910. Nina Lubbrens estimates that, by 1900, over eighty rural art colonies were in existence in Europe and, as a number of the artists involved were Americans, over in Europe for study, it is not surprising that the phenomenon was introduced into American art as well.[17]

This move from the urban environment into the country was inspired by a number of factors. Poetry, in the words of Lewis Hind, "pointed the way".[18] Poems extolling the beauty, charm and mystery of the natural world persuaded artists also to open their eyes to its virtues and to seek to capture nature's many moods. Gabriel Weisberg also credits the writings on Naturalism by art critics and novelists, such as Jules-Antoine Castagnary (1830-1888), Émile Zola (1840-1902) and Joris-Karl Huysmans (1848-1907).[19] Zola, in particular, whose novels were immensely popular, she heralds as the "Dean" of literary Naturalism. There was also a new found enthusiasm for open air painting. This was, in part, a reaction against the formulaic practices of studio painting but also reflected a keener interest in the study of light and atmosphere and a desire to capture absolute truth of tone. Furthermore, there was an increasing awareness of the impact of industrialisation, which was arousing in the middle classes a nostalgia for an era of uncomplicated simplicity. Therefore, the artist colonies were invariably established in out of the way locations where modern developments had not yet impinged, and where the artists could capture - or imply that they had captured - vestiges of an unspoilt rural idyll. By actually residing in these places, the artists could witness at first hand these remnants of a dying age, but the hardships of living in such unsophisticated surroundings were made bearable by the company of fellow artists, who could be relied upon to provide, not only assistance on the novel difficulties faced by the open air painter, but also interesting conversation at dinner and often a variety of talents as after-dinner entertainers. It did not take too long, though, for the particular requirements of the artists to be satisfied by some budding local entrepeneur and, where the artists first ventured, they were soon followed by the tourist, seduced by the artists' depictions and accounts of their find. The 'quaint' hideaway was, accordingly, often transformed in a short space of time into a busy vacation centre. St Ives followed this pattern exactly.

17 N. Lubbrens, *Rural Artists' Colonies in Europe 1870-1910*, New Brunswick, 2001 at p.1.
18 C Lewis Hind, *Adventures Among Pictures - In Landscape Land*, London, 1904 at p.26.
19 See Gabriel P Weisberg, *Beyond Impressionism - The Naturalist Impulse in European Art 1860-1905*, London, 1992 at pp.12-23.

~ 1 ~

EARLY VISITORS

1.1 Edward William Cooke and other pre-railway explorers

Sketches of St Ives by both Cornish and foreign fishermen are known from the eighteenth century. The first known published depiction of the town is by Joseph Farington (1747-1821), a student of the landscape artist, Richard Wilson, who visited Cornwall in 1809 to make sketches for his book *Britannica Depicta*. Much has been made of the visit of Joseph William Mallord Turner (1775-1850) in 1811 but, in fact, all he completed was a small pencil sketch in his notebook, showing the panorama from the top of the Stennack, with the mill wheel of Chellew's Mills prominent in the foreground. Cornwall, however, remained relatively inaccessible and, although some prints of vistas of St Ives were produced mid-century by some Cornish artists, such as Richard Pentreath (Fig. 0.6) and W.Willis of Penzance (Fig. 0.5), previous histories of the colony have moved swiftly on to the visit of James Abbott McNeill Whistler (1834-1903) in 1884, implying that few artists of note visited St Ives in the interim period. This is simply incorrect, as numerous distinguished artists, including several Royal Academicians, made it as far as St Ives, even before the completion of the rail link to St Ives itself in 1877. Indeed, the most important image of St Ives from the pre-colony period was exhibited at the Royal Academy as early as 1853. This was a large oil (34" x 50") by the marine artist, Edward William Cooke (1811-1880), who had already been made an ARA in 1851 and who was to become a full Academician in 1863. Cooke is now considered one of the foremost marine painters of his generation and his work commands high prices.[20]

Cooke's father, George, and his uncle, William, were prominent London-based fine art engravers of landscape subjects, their finest achievement being the engraving of Turner's *Picturesque Views of the Southern Coast of England*, issued between 1814 and 1826. Although too young to have been involved to any significant extent, in this series, Edward Cooke always had a high regard for Turner's art and his own desire to explore the south-west of England was probably inspired by Turner's vistas. Unsurprisingly, Cooke trained initially as an engraver, working for his father until he was nearly twenty, and the draughtsmanship required in such a line of work had a marked effect on his subsequent development as a painter. In particular, his paintings always retained a sharpness of outline, which did not always find favour with developing critical taste. He seems to have had an interest in marine subjects from a young age - at the age of sixteen inspiring his father to produce a series of marine and shipping engravings - and artists having an early influence on his painting career included James Stark and Clarkson Stanfield, who were friends of the family and whose work was engraved by his father. Stanfield, in fact, employed Cooke to make studies of ships for him and Cooke's early marine oil paintings show the clear influence of Stanfield, who himself visited the Penwith Peninsula in 1830 and, again, in 1842 with Charles Dickens.[21] Cooke, though, made his reputation, not with paintings of England, but through his depictions of Dutch boats on the waterways of Holland and of sailing vessels on the canals of Venice.

Cooke's first visit to south-west England was in September and October 1848 and he moved from place to place almost on a daily basis.[22] Indeed, the only time that he stayed more than two days in one town was the week that he spent in St Ives from 9th October. Cooke was an avid drawer, having been urged by his father, to draw "everything new and singular", and he made detailed sketch notes wherever he went.[23] A sketch dated 11th October 1848 (Fig. 1.2) depicts the scene on the beach at what Cooke calls Carrick Gladden Cove, now Carbis Bay. Several huts are shown on the beach itself, their wide entrances indicating that they were used as stores for equipment, whilst their roofs appear to be made from upturned seine boats covered with thatching. A 'stretcher' for carrying nets is carefully observed, whilst beach capstans are strategically placed. The following day, he is back on the beach again, this time rather closer to Hawke's Point (see Fig. 1.1), as he depicts a group of men pulling a seine boat out of the water to join several others on the sands. More hovels, with chimneys, are depicted close to the water's edge, whilst on the Point the Huer's Hut can be seen, from where the Bay was scoured for sign of pilchard shoals.

Cooke exhibited at the Royal Academy in 1849 *A Fern Cave - A Scene in Mount's Bay, Cornwall*, a subject that had clearly attracted his botanical interest, but it was not until 1853 that he exhibited *The Pier and Bay of St Ives, Cornwall* (Fig. 1.3), which was sold for the enormous sum of £294 to his patron and neighbour Alderman Sir David

---

20 He was also a man of wide interests, being able to append to his name also the initials FRS, FSA, FLS, FZS and FGS.

21 The National Gallery of Victoria, Melbourne have a painting *St Michael's Mount, Cornwall* by Stanfield dated 1830 and the Victoria and Albert Museum have a drawing by Stanfield from the 1842 visit of Dickens, his biographer Forster, Maclise and himself called *Logan Rock, Cornwall*.

22 He entered Cornwall on 15th September 1848 and his movements thereafter were as follows:- 15. Tamar to Cothele, 16 to Falmouth, 18 Redruth, Hayle, Penzance, 19 Marazion, St Michael's Mount, 20 St Mary's Scilly, 21 Tresco, 22 Peninnis, 23 St Agnes, 25 Old Town Bay, 27 Porthellick, 28 to Penzance, 29 Newlyn, Mousehole, Oct 1 Marazion, 2, St Just, 3 Botallack Mine, 4 Cape Cornwall, 5 Land's End, 7 Penzance, 9 Hayle, St Ives 16 Marazion & Mount, 17 Newlyn, Lamorna and back, 18 Logan Stone, 19 Truro, Exeter.

23 Letter dated 20/10/1828.

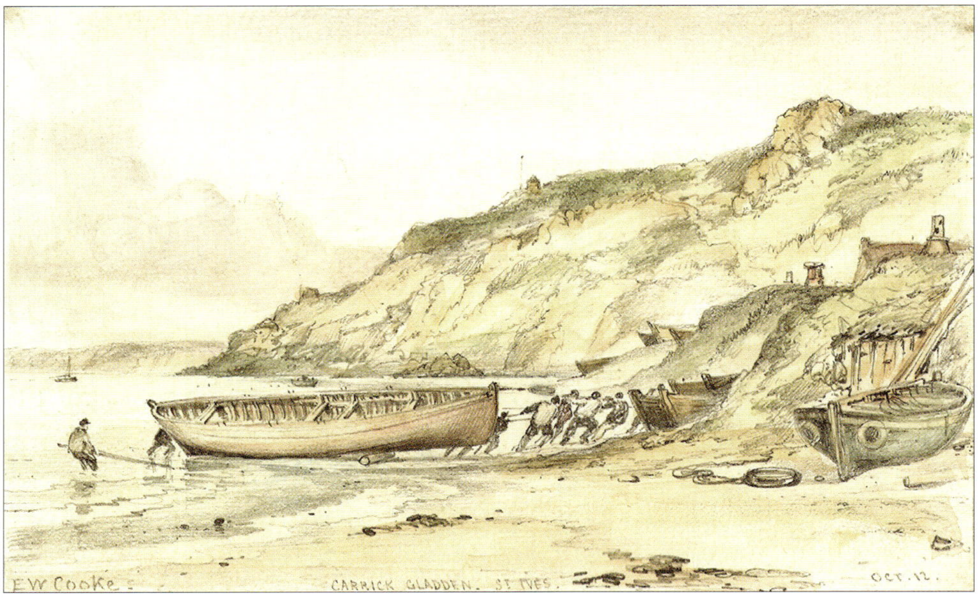

Cooke often worked up sketches from his sketch book in later years as presents and this sketch was given to his friend, Robert Etheridge (1819-1903), a well-known geologist, palaeontologist and Museum Curator.

Fig. 1.1 Edward William Cooke
Carrick Gladden, St Ives
(12th October 1848)
(Private Collection)

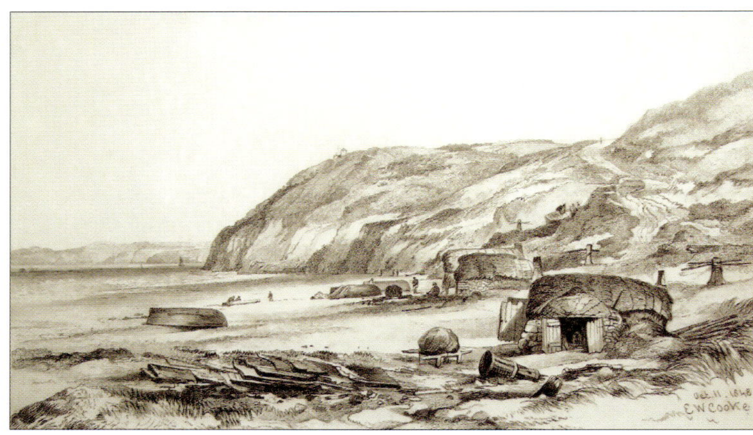

Fig. 1.2 Edward William Cooke
Carrick Gladden Cove, St Ives Bay
(11th October 1848)
(Private Collection)

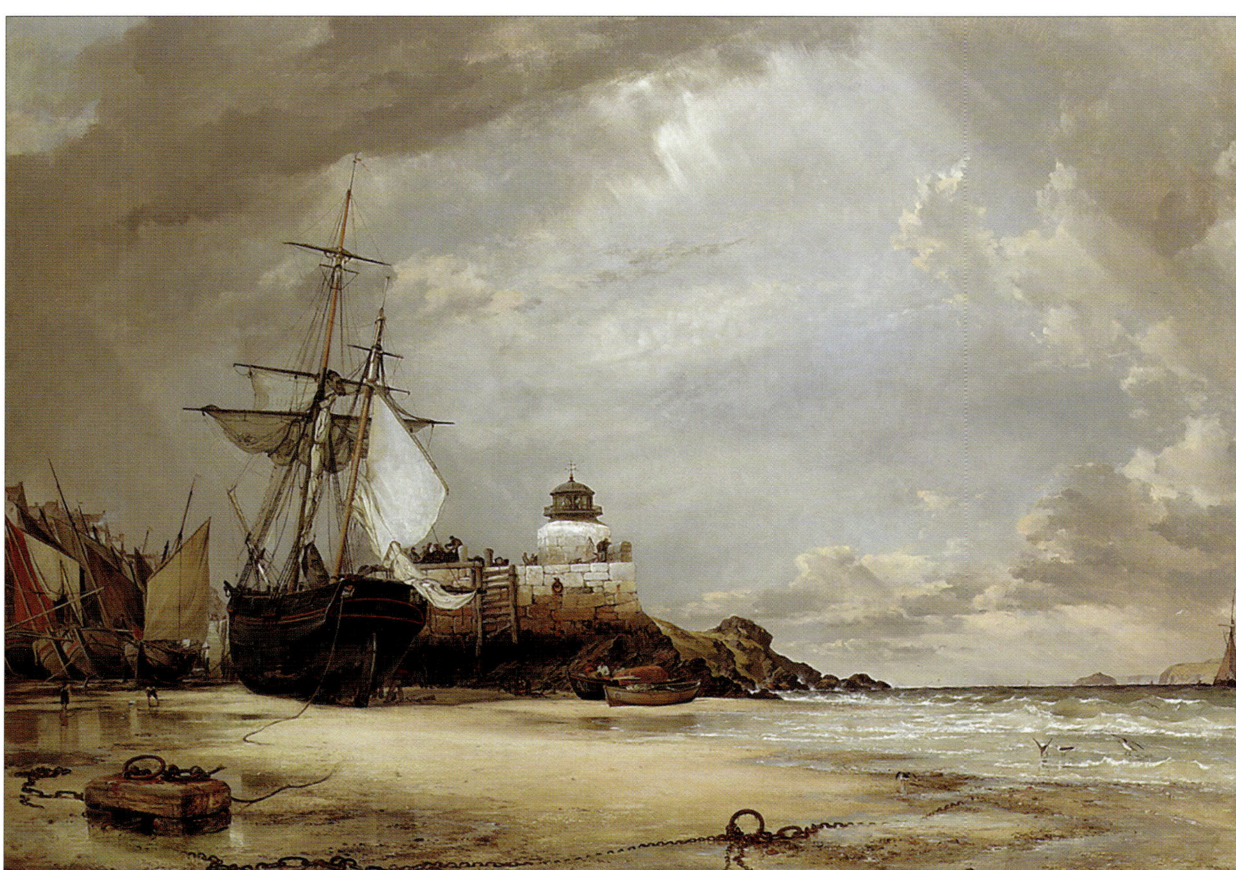

Fig. 1.3 Edward William Cooke *The Pier and Bay of St Ives, Cornwall* (Christies Images)

Salomans, Bt, MP for Greenwich and Lord Mayor of London.[24] This painting, therefore, was not done on the spot but was worked up in his London studio from sketches made during his trip some four years previously. As evidenced by his sketches of Carrick Gladden, the intricate detail that he recorded enabled him to produce an accurate record of the scene, even after such a lapse of time. The painting shows the original extent of the stone pier designed by John Smeaton, built between 1767 and 1770, which ended with the distinctive shaped lighthouse - often known as the pepperpot - which has always been much loved by artists. A seine boat and its follower are beached waiting for the incoming tide, whilst a poleacre brigantine has its mooring rope, known as a junk, attached to an anchored weight located just outside the harbour entrance, which it will use to haul itself out into deeper water, when the tide rises. On the left are some fishing luggers with round apple-shaped bows, a design that was soon to be replaced by something more wedge-shaped.[25] Cooke's paintings were renowned for their sense of atmosphere and the remains of a black cloud on the left of the painting suggest that a squall has just passed over. This is confirmed by the fact that most of the boats in the harbour have left up their colourful sails to dry. Cooke also includes the fine vista out to Godrevy, with rays from the newly emerging sun lighting up the waters of the Bay.[26]

In the same year as Cooke's major St Ives painting was hung at the Royal Academy, James George Philp RI ROI (1816-1885) exhibited *St Ives from Hayle Sands, Cornwall* at the SBA. Philp was a Falmouth-born artist, who was largely self-taught. He worked principally in watercolour and was well-regarded, for he became a member of the Council of the RI. He exhibited many West Cornwall scenes in the period between 1848 and 1854, although based in Camden Town at the time.

1.2 George Wolfe and the Bristol connection

With Bristol at that time being the major city in the south-west of England, it is perhaps not surprising that artists based there should have been some of the first to explore Cornwall. Like Cooke and Philp, Charles Parsons Knight (1829-1897), a leading member of BAPFA, had also been to the Penwith Peninsula before the completion of the rail link to Penzance in 1859, exhibiting *St Michael's Mount* in 1852 and *Coasters off St Ives, Cornwall* in 1854. However, as a result of the improved rail connections, he now returned to Cornwall on an annual basis and exhibited a number of depictions of St Ives during the 1860s and 1870s. Indeed, he continued to come down to the area right up to the time of his death. James Philp, who moved to Bristol briefly during the early 1860s before settling back in Falmouth, also continued to exhibit numerous West Cornwall scenes. On his death in 1885, the very year that the St Ives colony was formed, the local paper recorded that "there is scarcely a strip of Cornish coast that he has not made us familiar with".[27] Another leading member of BAPFA, the watercolourist Samuel Phillips Jackson RWS (1830-1904), was again a frequent visitor to Cornwall in the 1860s and exhibited a painting of St Ives Harbour in 1863. However, the most prolific painter of subjects at St Ives and Hayle from the Bristol group was George Wolfe (1834-1890), who exhibited during the 1860s numerous watercolours of the Penwith peninsula at the Royal Academy, SBA and BAPFA, many of which were priced in the region of £50, an enormous sum for those days. St Ives subjects feature in his exhibits in each of the years 1861, 1862, 1864, 1865 and 1868. Unfortunately, only one of these has been located. It depicts the view across Porthminster Beach to the harbour (Fig. 1.4). The beach was used to store seine boats, when the pilchard season was over, and a selection of these can be seen to the left. The foreground interest is provided by a series of capstans, used for hauling the boats out of the water. One lies broken on the sand, which bears the imprint of hundreds of feet, whilst children play at the water's edge. In the background, the Island, surmounted by the chapel of St Nicholas, then used as a pilot look-out, rises up behind the harbour and the houses of Down-along. A variety of sailing craft can be seen in the harbour and on the harbour beach. There is no sign of the wooden pier, commenced in 1864, or of the mine engine house on Pednolva Point, where mining operations began, with little success, in 1860, and so, unless artistic licence is at play, the work is probably one of his earliest depictions of the town.

A younger member of BAPFA, who was to visit Cornwall repeatedly throughout his career, was Charles Brooke Branwhite (1851-1929), the son of Charles Branwhite ARWS. He exhibited St Ives scenes at BAPFA in both 1875 and 1881.

1.3 James Clarke Hook - the Cornish fisherfolks' "pictorial Homer"

One of the most well-known artists to take advantage of the new railway facility was James Clarke Hook (1819-1907), who visited St Ives for the first time in 1860, the year that he was made a full Academician (ARA 1850). Hook had been taught by Edward Opie (1810-1894), the great-nephew of the Cornish-born Academician, John Opie, and, on this trip, as on many others, he met up with Opie, then living in St Agnes, on his way down. In fact, Hook's son, Allan, who wrote a three volume biography, felt that it was Opie, who first recommended St Ives. Hook was

---

24 When sold at Christies, London on 4/11/1999 (Lot 98), it fetched £52,100.

25 I am indebted to John McWilliams for his interpretation of this picture.

26 Cooke was back in Cornwall in 1871 and a painting of Kynance Cove executed on this visit is owned by the Russell Cotes Art Gallery, Bournemouth. The Art Gallery of New South Wales, Sydney also own his *On the Coast of Cornwall* dating from 1875, which it acquired in 1876. However, he does not appear to have visited St Ives again.

27 Quoted in the catalogue for *The Falmouth School of Artists - A Century of Art in Falmouth 1850-1950*, Falmouth Art Gallery, 1990.

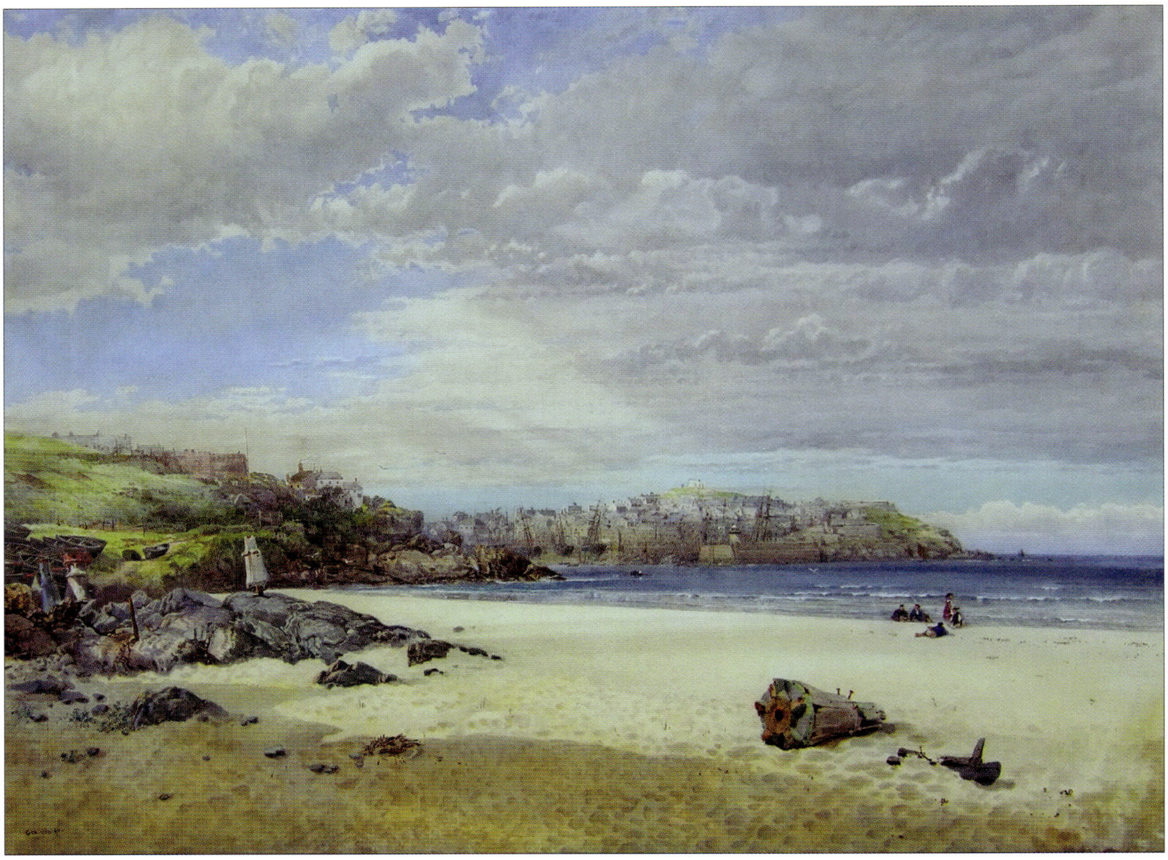

Fig. 1.4 George Wolfe *St Ives from Porthminster Beach* (Private Collection)

immediately impressed by the town's "wonderfully primitive simplicity", by the plethora of subjects and by the fact that "there was everywhere among the fishermen that unmistakable air of being in earnest about work".[28] His first visit to the town proved to be both his longest - from 3rd July to 16th September 1860 - and his most productive, for three of his Royal Academy exhibits of the following year were St Ives scenes.[29] *Leaving Cornwall for the Whitby Fishing* has, sadly, not been traced, for it is, by some distance, the finest of his St Ives works. It depicts a fisherman, Daniel Perkin, saying farewell to his wife and baby on Smeaton's Pier, as his colleagues load the nets and get the boat ready for the journey to Whitby, from where they will fish for herring in the North Sea for several months.[30] It was an anxious time for those left behind and the fisherman's young wife has an array of jerseys, waterproofs and sea-stockings under her arm to ensure that her man keeps warm. Another concerned wife and child are depicted further down the quay. Some young boys lie on the pier edge, taking in all the activity, whilst in the background the houses of The Warren can be seen. The principal interest, however, was in the contrasted features of the fisherman and his red-coated child, whom he holds in his arms, which were considered to be "capital studies of character and beautiful in colour".[31] After the worries of the long absence, one might have imagined that much emotion would have been displayed at the time of the fishermen's safe return in early September, but William Bartlett recorded that the Cornish were not outwardly demonstrative and that, on such reunions, "greetings between the men and their wives consist usually of merely a handshake, anything of a warmer character being reserved till they get home".[32]

This work prompted F.G.Stephens, who published a biography of Hook in 1888, to pass some interesting comments on what he called "the Englishness of the Cornish fisher-folk" - views most probably derived from Hook himself, for he was a great champion of the working man and shared the fisherfolk's ardour for Methodism. "These men are as proud of their uprightness and their honesty as they are incapable of sponging upon their fellow subjects, whether British or Irish. They are sober, brave, and industrious. They have never demanded to be taught their business, never flinched from labour or duty; their boats are their own, not the gifts of other men; their gear is their own, not obtained from the Imperial Exchequer, nor the pockets of the charitable. They have built their own harbours with their own money. Being British, they have never insulted the flag that shelters them." He then went

28 Allan Hook, *Life of James Clarke Hook RA*, privately published.

29 There is a possibility that Edward Opie joined Hook on this visit as his RA exhibit of 1861 was *A fisherman's wife watching the return of the boats, coast of Cornwall*.

30 Stephens indicates that the family that modelled for Hook were called 'Perkins'. However, the name J Perkin can be seen on the stern of the boat, *Wave*, in the painting *Deep Sea Fishing*. John Perkin was a fisherman, born c.1800, whose son, Daniel, married Mary Gregory Wedge, daughter of Thomas Wedge, on 30/1/1858 and they had a daughter, also called Mary, that year and a son, also called Daniel, on 2/7/1860. Daniel, Mary and their daughter, Mary, may, therefore, feature in both *Leaving Cornwall for the Whitby Fishing* and *Compass'd by the inviolate sea*, whilst Daniel (twice) and his father John are likely to be the models for *Deep Sea Fishing*.

31 F.G.Stephens, *The Life and Work of J C Hook RA*, London, 1988 at p.23.

32 William Bartlett, *Summer Time at St Ives, Cornwall*, *Art Journal*, 1897 at p.294.

on to commend them for their enterprise in fishing in the North and Irish seas in the periods of the year when there was little to offer in Cornwall. He concluded, "Such a people Mr Hook is sure to be in love with. He is, in fact, their pictorial Homer."[33]

Hook's second major work, *Compass'd by the inviolate sea* (Fig. 1.6), depicts Daniel and Mary Perkin and their child again, but in a very different setting, for it is a cliff-top scene beyond Clodgy, with a view across St Ives Bay to Godrevy. On this occasion, the young couple lie on the grass admiring their baby, unperturbed that their elder child, modelled by Hook's own son, Bryan, has been exploring on the rocks below and now scrambles back over the edge of the cliff triumphantly bearing a long mass of tawny weed in his arms. Stephens commented, "Nothing could be more delightful than the fresh, soft sunniness of the atmosphere, the delicate yet vigorous colour, and broad wholeness of this thoroughly English picture".[34] The title, however, gave the work extra significance as Tennyson, in dedicating his first book of poems as Poet Laureate to Queen Victoria in 1851, had described her throne as "Broad-based upon the people's will, /And compass'd by the inviolate sea."[35]

Hook's third Royal Academy exhibit of 1861 was *Sea Urchins* (Fig. 1.8), a scene in St Ives harbour, which was described by Stephens as "a couple of idle seaside boys afloat on a huge mooring-block, which in the swift-running tide drags at an enormous iron ring, such as those to which great ships are made fast in harbours. These "urchins" are fishing, or supposed to be fishing, for, with boyish indolence, they do not seem interested in the sport. One fish has been caught and lies on the block, its painting being a testimony to the transcendent skill of the artist and his fine feeling for colour. Before the block, a deep shadow of intensest green is projected into the water, the opaque mass intercepting the sunlight, which, behind the block, illuminates the gently weltering sea, which is grey-green and lighted to its depths. Lines of cork net-floats, a cruising fishing boat, and shores that dip gently to the water, complete the work."[36] This painting is now owned by the Guildhall Art Gallery, London, as is another work that Hook completed on this visit, which he originally entitled *"Another dog!"* but which is now known by the rather more prosaic title of *Deep Sea Fishing* (Fig. 1.7). The painting is a close-up view of the stern of a boat, *Wave*, owned by J.Perkin (probably Daniel's father, John) and prominently marked 'St Ives', from which three fishermen, modelled again by the Perkin family, are line-fishing.[37] The middle fisherman, presumably John Perkin himself, has just caught something on his line, which he has brought to the surface, and the cry 'Another dog!' would have been uttered in frustration as it proved to be another dogfish, an inedible predatory fish that was the scourge of the fishermen and their nets. Hook offered this painting to the Royal Academy as his Diploma work, but it was rejected. A smaller copy is owned by Brighton Art Gallery.

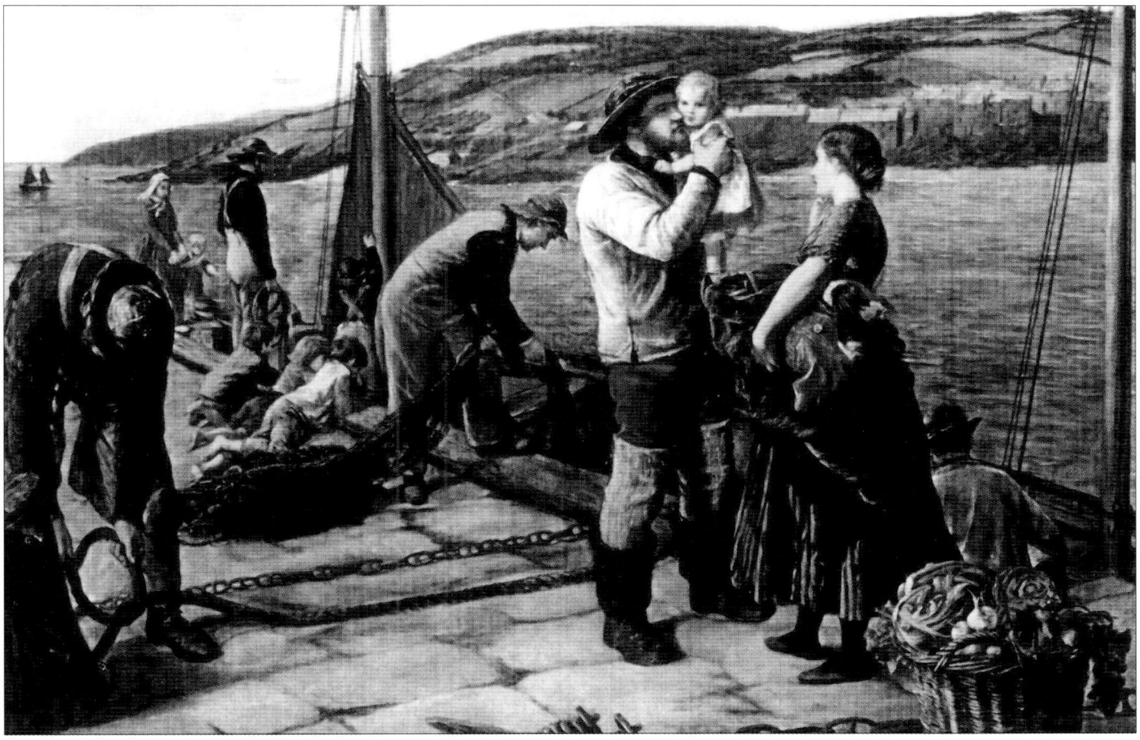

Fig. 1.5 James Clarke Hook *Leaving Cornwall for the Whitby Fishing* (Juliet McMaster)

33 F.G.Stephens, *The Life and Work of J C Hook RA*, London, 1988 at p.23.
34 F G Stephens, *The Life and Work of J C Hook RA*, London, 1988 at p.24.
35 Christiana Payne, *Where the Land Meets the Sea*, Bristol, 2007 at p.80.
36 F G Stephens, *The Life and Work of J C Hook RA*, London, 1988 at p.24. Stephens also tells us that the models for the two boys, were a member of the Painter family - he no doubt means 'Paynter' - , who drowned at sea with his father, and a member of the Bowlings family, who rose to be a skipper. Bowlings is not a known St Ives name. Cowling would be my guess.
37 *Wave* is recorded in 1847 as belonging to John Grenfell Stevens. My thanks to John McWilliams for this information.

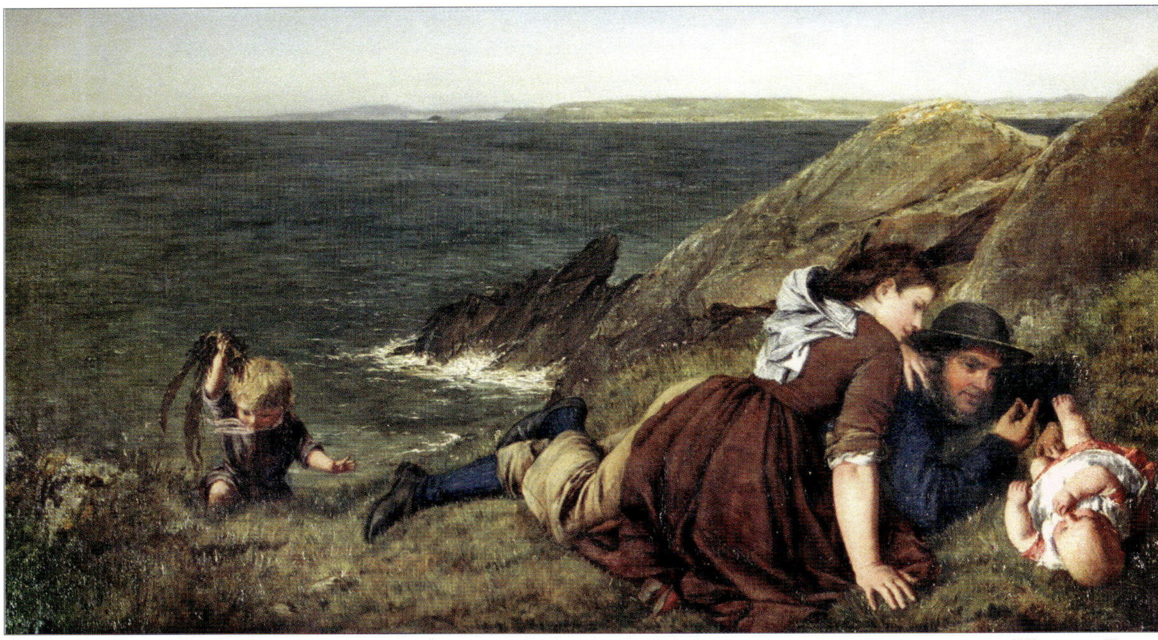

Fig. 1.6 James Clarke Hook *Compass'd by the inviolate sea* (Eleanor Fazan)

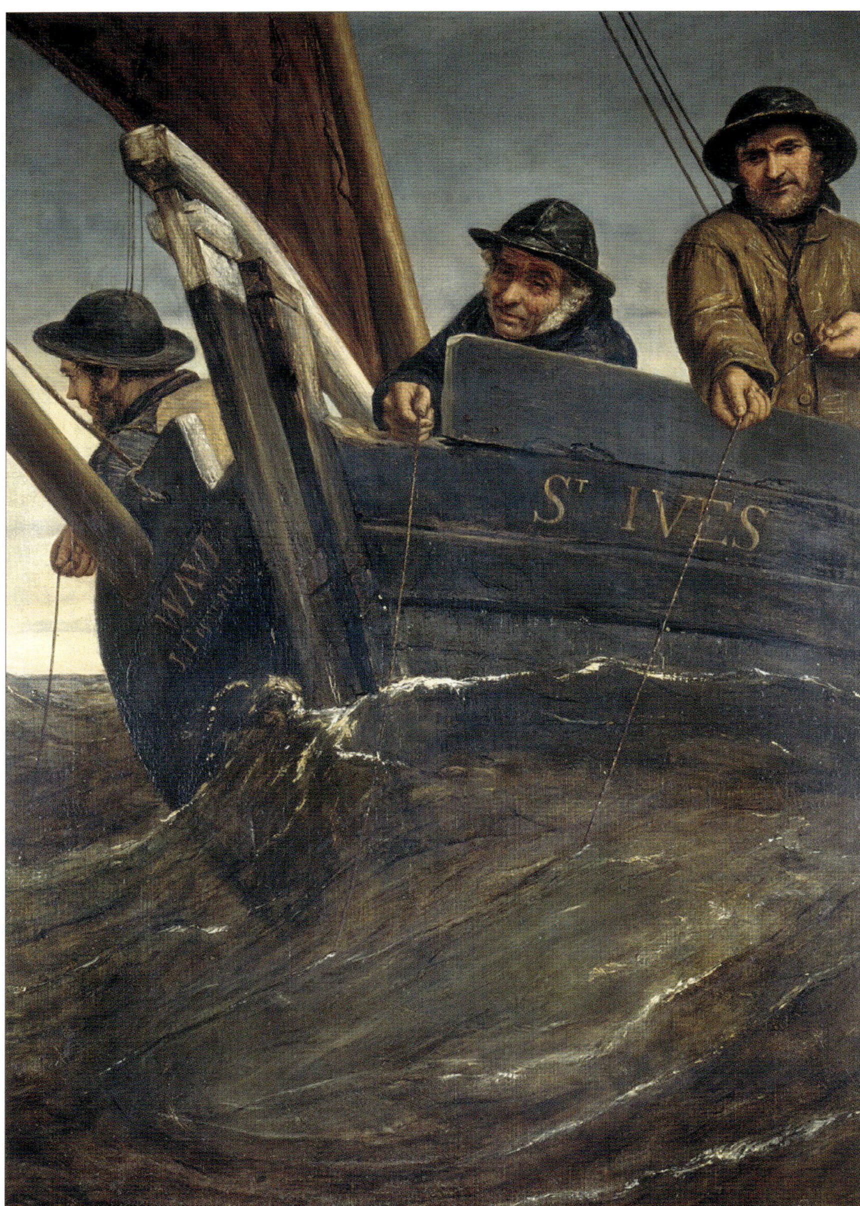

Fig. 1.7 James Clarke Hook *Deep Sea Fishing*
(Guildhall Art Gallery, City of London)

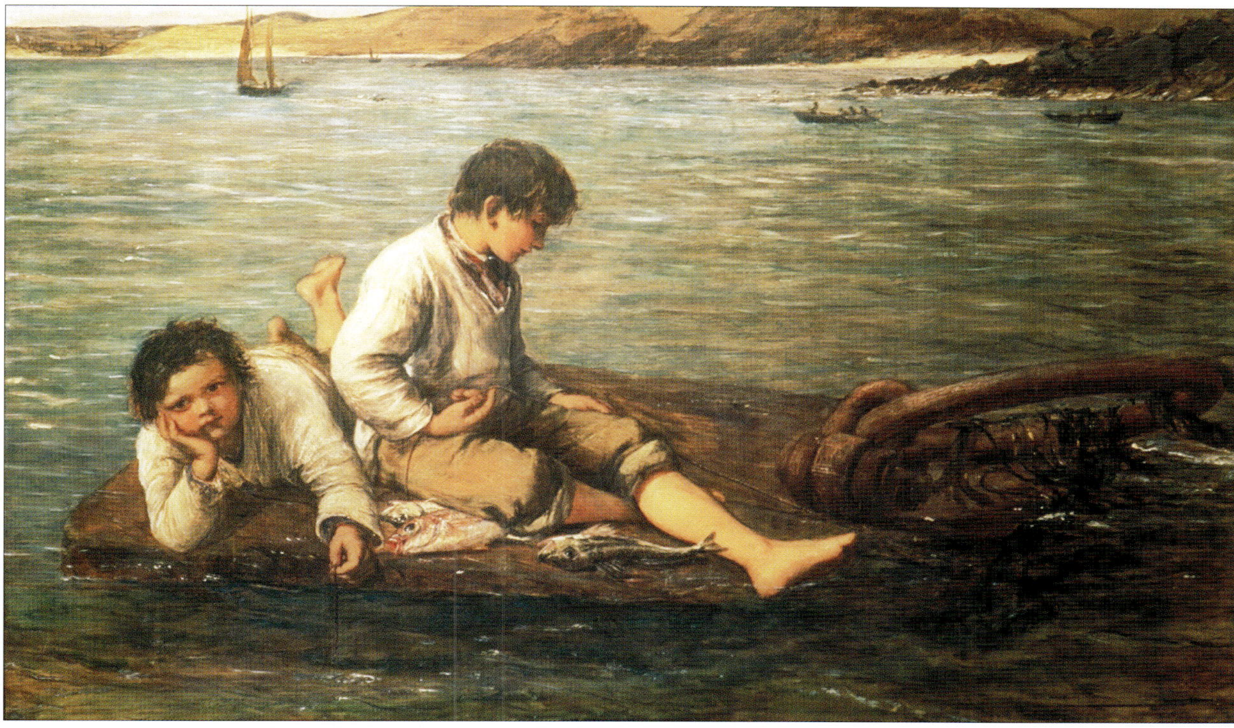

Fig. 1.8 James Clarke Hook *Sea Urchins* (Guildhall Art Gallery, City of London)

Hook had only turned from historical subjects to coastal scenes such as these, featuring sentimentalised rustic figures, in the mid-1850s and he was to improve his depiction of the sea in later years. Indeed, such paintings, which often included children, became so popular at the Royal Academy that they became known as 'Hookscapes'. Hook returned to St Ives in July 1862 and August 1863, for a couple of weeks on each occasion, but his major works in these years featured other parts of Cornwall. Indeed, in 1863, he painted one of his most famous works, *From under the sea* (Manchester Art Gallery), featuring a miner and his family at the Botallack tin mine, where there had been a much publicised accident that April, when nine miners were killed. After painting in Brittany on his summer trips in 1864-5, Hook returned to Cornwall on a number of occasions in the late 1860s, finding subjects at Bedruthan Steps and Coverack. In 1873, he spent some six weeks in Gwithian, near Hayle, before coming on to St Ives for a fortnight, and two Gwithian scenes, *Under the lee of a rock* and *Jetsam and Flotsam*, were amongst his Royal Academy exhibits of 1874.[38] Hook's deep respect for the Cornish fishermen ensured that he made friends with them and the early artist settlers were regaled with stories of 'Squire' Hook. William Bartlett also mentioned that one of the old salts proudly showed him one of his most prized possessions - a telescope given to him by Hook.[39] Although Hook continued to visit and paint in Cornwall, particularly at Sennen Cove, he does not appear to have visited St Ives after the colony formed. However, his work was included in the Cornish Artists' Exhibition at Whitechapel in 1902. The 'Hook' Easel, the travelling easel that Hook invented, was, of course, to be an essential piece of equipment for later *plein air* painters in St Ives.

1.4 John Brett and other visitors of the 1870s

Another early visitor to St Ives was the well-known marine artist, Charles Napier Hemy (ARA 1898, RA 1910). In 1870, some thirteen years before he settled in Falmouth, and whilst he was still using an exhibiting address in Antwerp, where he was studying, he exhibited in Glasgow *Fishing for Gurnets, St Ives*, whilst showing in the same year at the SBA *The Pier Head, St Ives*.[40] In the winter exhibition of the SBA that year, there were two further St Ives scenes - *Evening, St Ives Harbour* and *Dutch Boats Going into St Ives Harbour* - contributed by the Bristol-born marine artist, Edwin Hayes. Hayes, who later had a Cornish subject bought by the Chantrey Trustees, had been visiting Cornwall since 1866 and was back in St Ives in the early years of the colony.

Possibly the first husband and wife team to exhibit scenes of St Ives were Thomas Oliver Hume and his spouse, Edith (née Dunn), who lived initially in London before moving to Petersfield in Hampshire.[41] Their interest in Cornwall clearly stemmed from the fact that Edith had been born in Truro. She was a genre painter, who was

38 The dates of Hook's visits are given in the diary maintained by his wife. See Juliet McMaster, *Woman Behind the Painter- The Diaries of Rosalie, Mrs James Clarke Hook*, Edmonton, Alberta, 2006.

39 See *St Ives as an Art Colony* in *Babcock's Historical Sketch of St Ives and District*, 1896 & W H Bartlett, *Summer Time at St Ives, Cornwall*, *Art Journal*, 25/9/1897.

40 As one of the leading Cornish artists, Hemy later paid a number of visits to St Ives, staying in the town with his family and being signed in as a guest at the Arts Club. His brother, Thomas, also settled in the town briefly in 1890.

41 Despite presumably marrying before the birth of her son in 1858, Edith Hume exhibited as Edith Dunn, her maiden name, between 1862 and 1867, and only as Mrs Thomas O Hume from 1870. Thomas first exhibited at the RA in 1871.

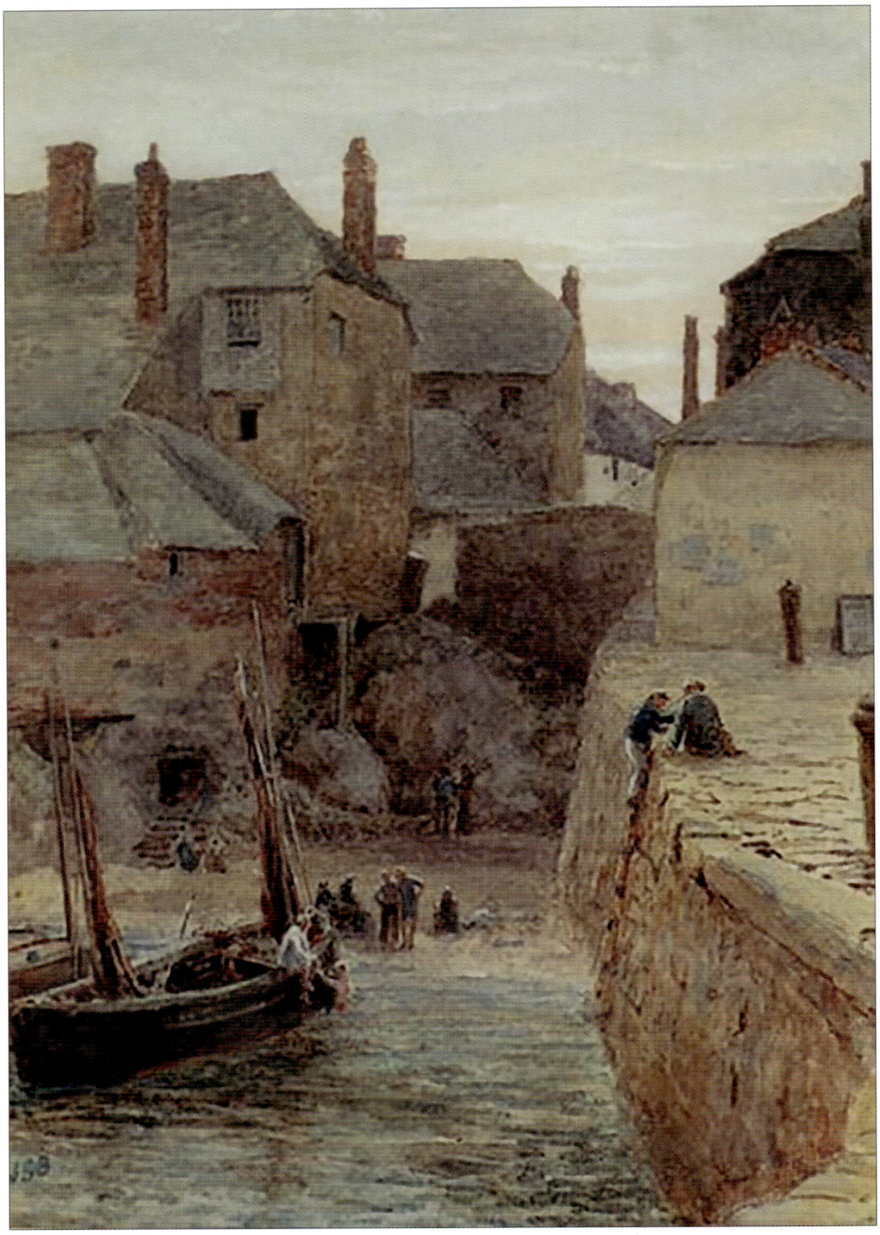

Fig. 1.9 James George Bingley *St Ives, Cornwall* (Private Collection)
This view of the old cottages at the base of Smeaton's Pier probably dates from 1875 as Bingley, a Surrey-based watercolourist, exhibited that year a painting of Newlyn at the Royal Academy and a work called *Mending Nets in a West Cornwall Fishing Village* at Bristol.

very fond of depicting fisherfolk, often in a rather sentimentalised manner, and she showed *St Ives Sandwoman* at the 1872 Winter Exhibition of the SBA, whereas Thomas, a landscape painter, who had been born in Rothbury, Northumberland, contributed moorland scenes near Hayle and St Ives the following winter.[42] They probably also accompanied their son, John Henry Hume (1858-1881), when he produced his 1878 Royal Academy exhibit *A Peep at St Ives*, and must have been devastated by his early death in 1881.[43] Royal Academy exhibits by Thomas of Clodgy Moor and St Ives Bay from the 1880s indicate several other return visits. In fact, quite a number of Edith's fishing subjects from the 1870s and 1880s might also be St Ives scenes and she may have accompanied Richard Harry Carter on his visit to St Ives in the early 1880s, as he had married her sister, Ellen, a Professor of Music.[44] The sketch in *Academy Notes* of her 1885 Royal Academy exhibit, *Preparing the Tackle* (Fig. 1.20), certainly places this scene in St Ives and she clearly had a keen affection for the town, as both her sister and herself were moved to make a contribution to the Flood Relief Fund in 1894.[45]

42 As Thomas exhibited St Ives subjects in 1873, Edith's painting, *The Knitting Match*, which she showed at the SBA in 1873 might also be a St Ives scene.
43 The *Dictionary of British Artists 1880- 1940* has J Henry Hume as Thomas' brother but the 1881 Census records that he was his son. They were all living together in Harting, Sussex.
44 His later exhibits include *Clodgy Moor, near Land's End* (RA 1881), *On the Cornish Coast* (RA 1884), *St Ives Bay* (RA 1888) and *A Cornish Moorland* (RBA 1890). Her later exhibits include *Fishing on the Old Pier Head* (RA 1874), *Packing Fish* (RA 1879), *The Departure of the Herring Boats* (RA 1883), *Mending Nets* (RA 1884) and *Preparing the Tackle* (RA 1885).
45 *St Ives Weekly Summary*, 13/12/1894.

A highly regarded marine painter, who paid a number of visits to Cornwall during the 1870s and 1880s, was John Brett (1831-1902). The son of an army veterinary surgeon, Brett had lessons initially from his father, who was a keen amateur artist, and then attended at the Royal Academy Schools from 1853. An admiration for the writings of John Ruskin, coupled with an interest in geology, led him in the late 1850s to begin to produce exceptionally detailed landscapes, following Ruskin's advice to young artists in *Modern Painters* that they should "go to Nature in all singleness of heart....rejecting nothing, selecting nothing, and scorning nothing". During this period, Brett won high acclaim and his works are now considered some of the prime examples of the Pre-Raphaelite landscape style but, in the mid-1860s, he fell out with Ruskin, who had come round to the view that too literal a transcription of landscape could not communicate emotion.

By 1870, when Brett first visited Cornwall, his life, which had been characterised by frequent travels and adulterous affairs, had become more regular. He settled down with Mary Ann Howcroft, who bore him seven children, and they began to spend their summers on painting campaigns in coastal locations, frequently in Cornwall, whilst their winters were spent in London, where Brett worked up his sketches in his studio into major exhibition pieces. On their second trip to the county in 1872, they spent much of the month of September based in St Ives, staying at 3 Bowling Green Terrace, and Brett did some fifteen sketches of the town and the Bay in various media, a number of which were exhibited in the 2006 Exhibition, *John Brett - A Pre-Raphaelite in Cornwall*. At this time, he was beginning to sketch in oils, as well as in watercolour, and had recently devised a 7" x 14" board, which he found to be the optimum size for sketching in this medium. There are many studies of boats and fishermen at work. One completed oil sketch shows Mary and their first child, Michael, then aged one, sitting, fashionably attired, on Porthminster Beach, whilst a ketch, a lugger and a two-masted topsail schooner sail across the waters of the Bay. Two sketches feature the distinctive pepperpot lighthouse at the end of Smeaton's Pier, as fishermen work on their boats in the harbour (see Fig. 1.12). Of particular interest is the unfinished oil sketch, *Net Day at St Ives* (Fig. 1.10), showing a variety of boats beached in the harbour, with the harbour sands reaching right up to the doors of the houses on The Wharf. Some of these sketches he later worked up into larger finished pictures in his studio and he exhibited *At St Ives* at the Spring Exhibition of the RBSA in 1874 and *St Ives Bay* (Fig. 1.11) at the Royal Academy in 1881. However, the latter magnificent work, which depicts a variety of vessels off Godrevy, is dated 1878. Having been brought for £300 from the Academy show in 1881, it was donated to Kelvingrove Museum and Art Gallery, Glasgow in 1928.

Brett continued to return to Cornwall with regularity and, during the 1870s and early 1880s, was highly successful, producing some stunning large paintings of interesting atmospheric effects witnessed on the Cornish coast. However, by the time that the marine section of the St Ives colony was beginning to come to the fore in the 1890s, his work had fallen out of favour. The early St Ives settlers considered Brett's work soul-less and to be admired, if at all, merely for the patience with which it had been executed. W.H.Hudson also records that Brett's outspoken atheism and brusque manners greatly offended the Cornish fisherfolk, who were finally convinced that he was a little queer in the head when they saw him apply paint, not with a brush, but with a palette knife.[46] Nevertheless, Brett was asked to exhibit with the Cornish artists at Whitechapel in 1902, the year of his death.

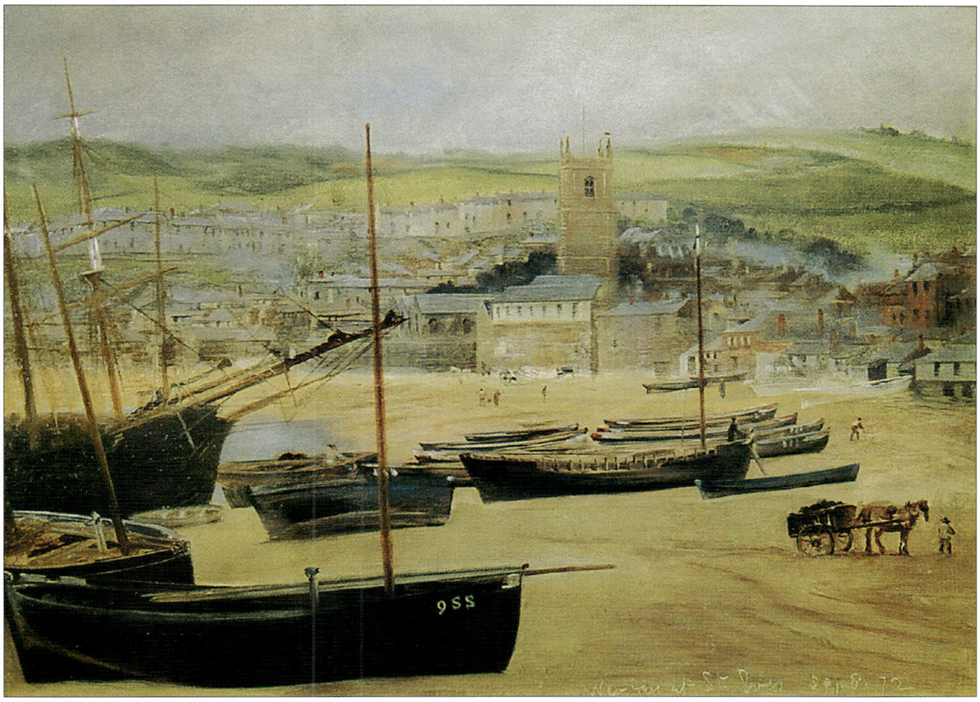

Fig. 1.10 John Brett *Net Day at St Ives* (1872) (Private Collection)

46 W.H.Hudson, *The Land's End*, London, 1908, at p.170.

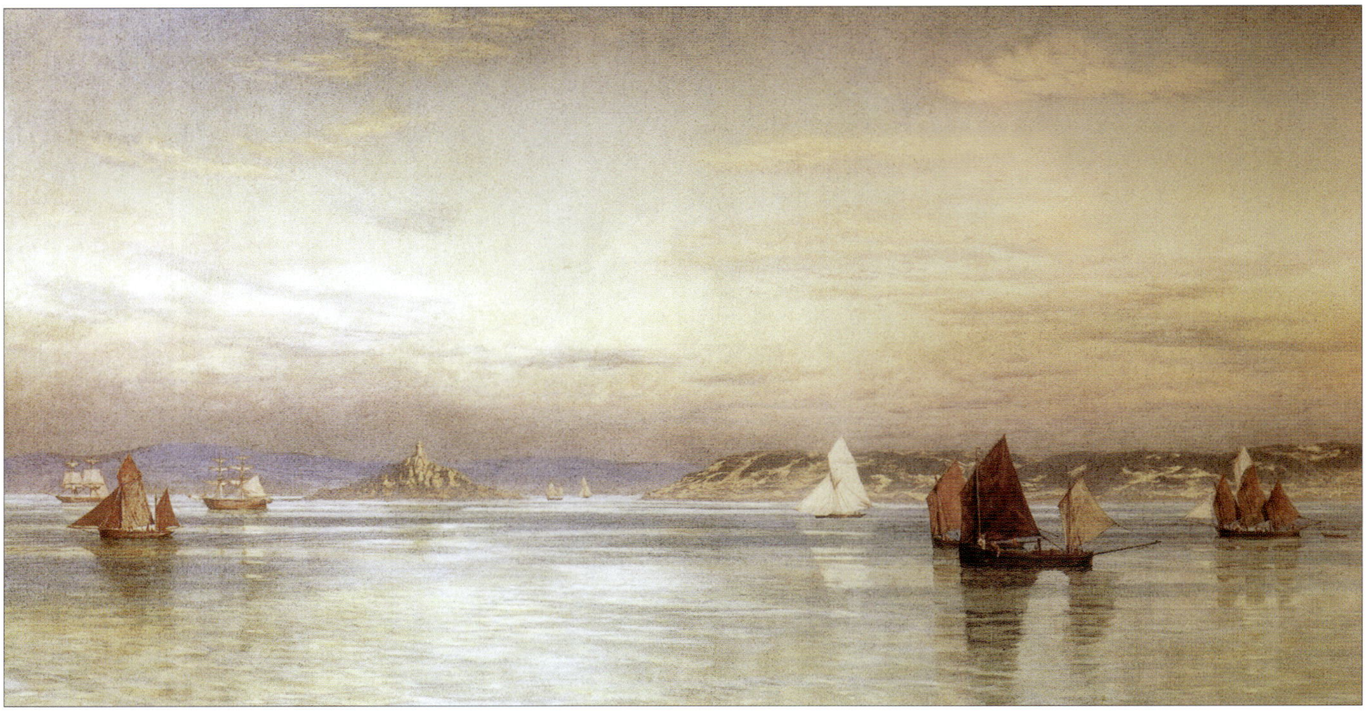

Fig. 1.11 John Brett *St Ives Bay* (Kelvingrove Art Gallery and Museum, Glasgow)

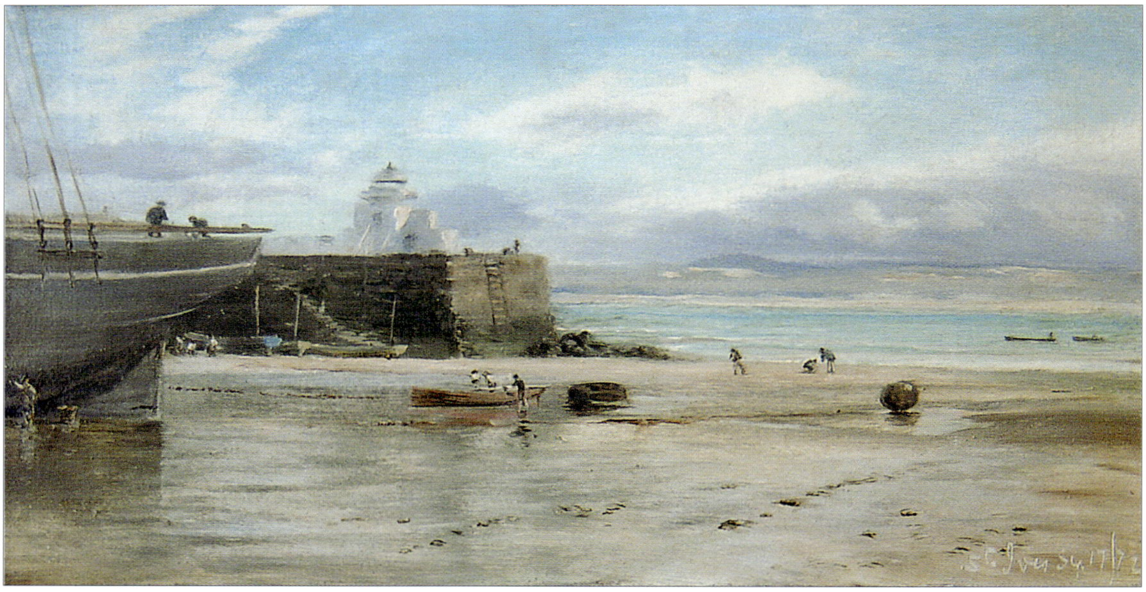

Fig. 1.12 John Brett *St Ives, Sep 1872* (Private Collection)

TABLE A - SOME DEPICTIONS OF ST IVES EXECUTED PRIOR TO 1884

1848	Edward William Cooke	London	sketches	Sketchbook/Diary
1853	Edward William Cooke	London	The Pier and Bay of St Ives, Cornwall	RA
	James G Philp	London	St Ives from Hayle Sands, Cornwall	SBA
1854	Charles P Knight	Bristol	Coasters off St Ives, Cornwall	BAPFA
1857	M W Williams	Topsham	A Scene on the North Coast of Cornwall from Hayle	BAPFA
1861	George Wolfe	Bristol	St Ives Pier and Harbour, Cornwall	SBA
			Various Hayle scenes	SBA/BAPFA/Liverpool
1862	Charles P Knight	Bristol	Hayle Harbour, St Ives Bay	BAPFA
	George Wolfe	Bristol	Crossing the Sands, St Ives Bay	BAPFA
1863	Samuel P Jackson	Bristol	St Ives Pier and Harbour	BAPFA
1864	George Wolfe	Bristol	A Brig in St Ives Harbour, Cornwall	RA (also BAPFA 1865)
1868	George Wolfe	Bristol	St Ives Pier and Harbour, Cornwall	SBA
1870	C Napier Hemy	Antwerp	Fishing for Gurnets, St Ives	Glasgow
			The Pier Head, St Ives	SBA
	Edwin Hayes	Bristol	Evening, St Ives Harbour	SBA (W)
			Dutch Boats Going into St Ives Harbour	SBA (W)
1872	Edith Hume	London	A St Ives Sandswoman	SBA (W)
	John Brett	London	St Ives Sep 3 72	2006 Brett Exhibition
			St Ives Sep 3 72	Christies sale 21/2/1989
			St Ives Sep 6 72	2006 Brett Exhibition
			Net Day at St Ives Sep 8 72	2006 Brett Exhibition
			St Ives Sep 12 72	2006 Brett Exhibition
			St Ives Sep 17 72	2006 Brett Exhibition
1873	Thomas Hume	London	Near St Ives, Cornwall	SBA (W)
			Moorland, near Hayle, Cornwall	SBA (W)
1874	John Brett	London	At St Ives	RBSA (S)
	Arthur Severn	London	At St Ives	RBSA (A)
1875	C Brooke Branwhite	Bristol	On the Cornish Coast near St Ives	BAPFA
1876	Frederick Mercer	Birmingham	St Ives from Tregenna	Dated Work
1878	J Henry Hume	Petersfield, Hants	A Peep at St Ives, Cornwall	RA
	William Trost Richards	Philadelphia	Porthmeor Beach and the Island	Dated Work
	Charles P Knight	Bristol	St Ives Bay	BAPFA (Loan exhibition)
1879	Charles R Aston	London	Saint Ives, Cornwall	RBSA (S)
	J Henry Hume	Petersfield, Hants	Clodgy Point, Cornwall	BAPFA
1880	William Trost Richards	Philadelphia	Fishing Boats at St Ives, Cornwall	Estimated Date
1881	William John Whittemore	New York	The Wharf, St Ives	Dated Work
	John Brett	London	St Ives Bay	RA
	Henry Moore	London	Sunset at St Ives	RBSA (S)
	W H Dixon		Target Point, St Ives	RBSA (S)
	Nora Taylor	London	Rosemergie Forge, nr St Ives	SBA (W)
	C Brooke Branwhite	Bristol	Moonlight near St Ives, Cornwall	BAPFA
1882	Edwin Ellis	London	St Ives, Cornwall	All SBA (W)
			Drawing A Seine, St Ives	
			St Ives Pier (also BAPFA 1883)	
			Mending Nets St Ives (also BAPFA 1883)	
			(Also Running for Shelter, Mackerel Boats, Cornwall & Pilchard Fishers)	
	George Henry Boughton	London	St Ives Bay, Cornwall	RA
	Edward Wilkins Waite	Blackheath	A Street in Old St Ives	SBA (W)
	James G Philp	Falmouth	St Ives Bay - Too Rough for Fishing	BAPFA
1883	Agnes Gardner King	London	Bunker's Hill, St Ives	SBA (W)
			Dick's Hill, St Ives	SBA (W)
	Hugh Carter	London	Baiting Hooks, St Ives	Liverpool (A)
			Interior of a Net Loft, St Ives	Liverpool (A)
	Richard Harry Carter	Truro	Dead Low Water, St Ives	Liverpool (A)
	Walter Sickert	London	On the Sands, St Ives	Tate Gallery Exhibition
	Miss Nora Davison	London	A Fishing Fleet, St Ives, Cornwall	BAPFA
	Mrs Val Bromley	London	A Street in St Ives	SWA

Alberto Ludovici Jnr is also known to have painted in St Ives this year. Both he and Sickert describe other artists at work

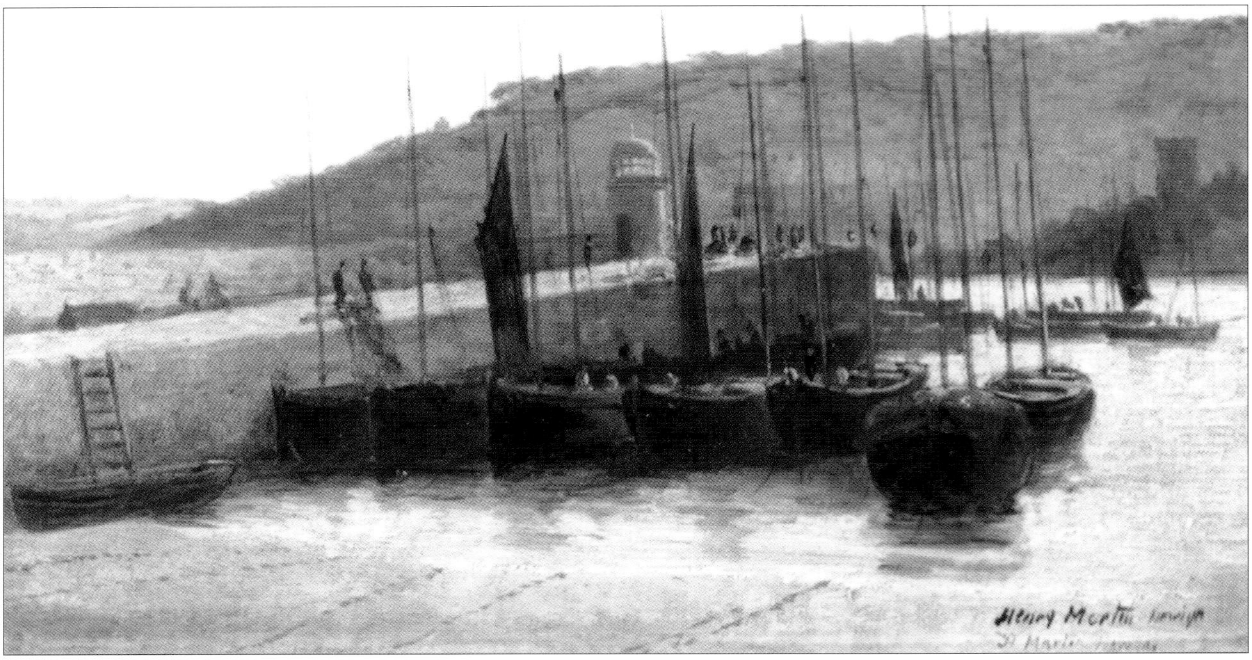

Fig. 1.13 Henry Martin *St Ives Harbour* (David Lays Auctions, Penzance Auction House)

1.5 Depictions of the ill-fated wooden pier

From as early as 1816, various attempts had been made to provide safer anchorage in the harbour, with no success, and, in 1864, work was commenced on a lengthy wooden pier, branching off almost at right-angles on the seaward side of Smeaton's Pier. However, partly due to the death of the contractor, this was never finished. In any event, it soon proved unable to withstand strong gales and began to break up in the late 1870s. By the time the art colony was formed, it had been reduced to a few broken piles. In the years 1888-90, an extension to the stone pier itself provided a solution and these works prove invaluable for dating paintings.

Thomas Hart (1830-1916) was a Cornish-born watercolourist, who spent his entire career living either in Falmouth or the Lizard, and, in the 1870s, he painted a fine panorama of St Ives from Porthminster Point. This view, which was shortly to be severely affected by the advent of the railway, takes in the seine boats pulled up on Porthminster Beach, the old mine building on Pednolva Point, the great sweep of the harbour beach and boats sheltering behind both the stone and wooden piers, whilst the old Long Rock Battery can be seen on The Island. Hart, not surprisingly, made a number of return visits to St Ives.[47] Another locally based artist, who made trips across to St Ives to paint in the late 1870s and early 1880s was Henry Martin, who first exhibited at the Royal Academy in 1874 when living at Paul, near Penzance and then, the following year, moved to Newlyn. He is best known for his coastal and harbour scenes around Mount's Bay but several depictions of St Ives have passed through the auction rooms.[48] However, he chose to leave Newlyn in the early 1880s, just as other artists started to settle there.

In the autumn of 1876, the Birmingham artist, Frederick Mercer (b.1851), made a tour of West Cornwall, painting in Newlyn in September before coming on to St Ives in October. In that month, he completed a watercolour, showing a view of St Ives from Tregenna, a vantage point not dissimilar to that adopted by Turner. This too shows the old wooden pier, probably at its greatest extent and seemingly in good order. The mill-wheel shown in the middle of the picture is that of 'Chellew's Mills', near Trenwith Terrace, one of three mills which served the town at that time.[49] It seems likely that Mercer was visiting a relation, John Mercer, who was staying at Trenwith Terrace, whilst working on the completion of the branch line from St Erth to St Ives, which was opened in 1877. Matthews records that the coming of the railway had a major impact, as, before this, "St Ives was hardly ever visited by tourists, and had but little communication with the outer world."[50] Artists, however, may have been rather ambivalent about the easier travel arrangements, as they did not like tourists impacting on their quaint hideaways. Nevertheless, there were only two through trains to London per day - the journey taking over twelve hours - and it took some years before tourism had a marked impact.[51]

---

47 A painting of St Ives dated 1886 was sold at Christies, South Kensington on 5/6/2003.
48 See David Lay auction, 3/10/1991 Lot 159, for example.
49 The wheel was replaced by a gas engine in the early years of the twentieth century by the then miller, James Nicholls.
50 John Hobson Matthews, *Guide to St Ives*, 1884.
51 The first through train left St Ives at 9.55 a.m., arriving at Paddington at 10.20 p.m., whilst the mail train left at 3.40 p.m. and arrived in London at 4.35 a.m. the following morning.. From Paddington, trains left at 5.30 a.m., arriving in St Ives at 7.15 p.m. that evening or at 11.45 p.m., arriving the following morning at 10.30 a.m. There were only five trains in all per day. See *Things Seen and Heard*, *St Ives Times* 25/2/1921.

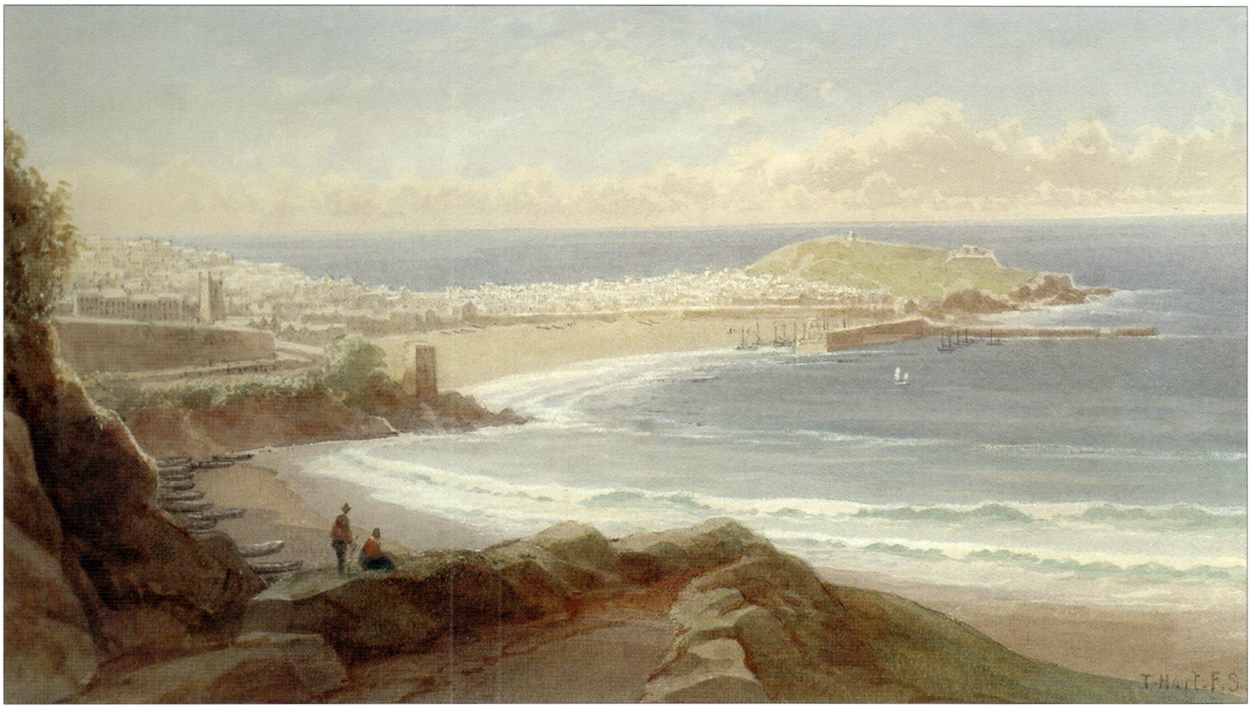

Fig. 1.14 Thomas Hart *St Ives from Porthminster Point* (Private Collection)

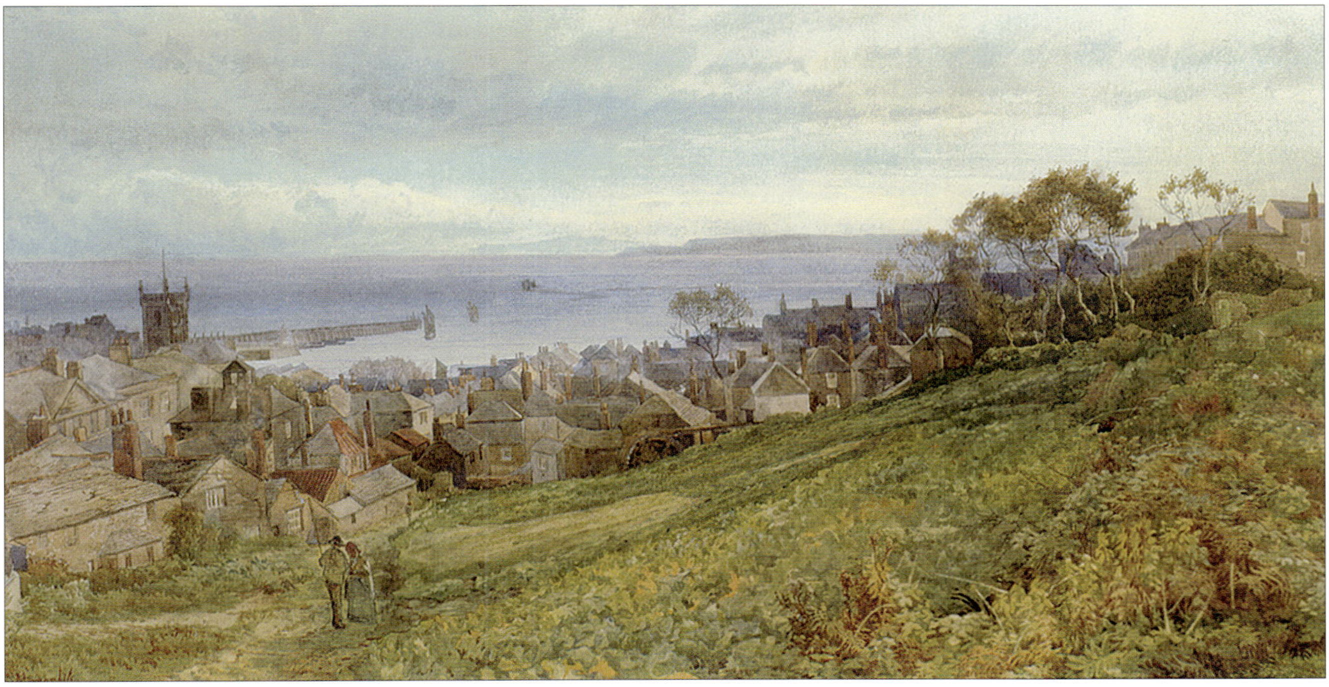

Fig. 1.15 Frederick Mercer *St Ives from Tregenna* (John Collins Fine Art, Bideford)

1.6 William Trost Richards - an early American visitor

The earliest foreign artist visitor that I have uncovered was the 'American Pre-Raphaelite' marine painter, William Trost Richards (1833-1905), who first painted in St Ives in 1878. Richards has earned the tag 'Pre-Raphaelite', in much the same manner as John Brett, for his detailed and meticulous depictions of coastal scenery and sea, and his work commands significant prices in America. Richards was born and brought up in Philadelphia and, by 1850, was studying painting there as "a sort of honorary pupil" to the German landscape painter, Paul Weber, as well as working as a designer of ornamental metal work. In 1855, he paid his first visit to Europe, spending the winter in Italy and the spring of 1856 in Dusseldorf. On his return to America, he began to gain a significant reputation as a landscape painter and, from the mid-1860s, enjoyed the patronage of the wealthy cast-iron wheel manufacturer, George Whitney. However, by the late 1870s, the taste of American collectors for the descriptive realism of mid-century landscapes had reduced significantly and a more painterly, subjective approach was demanded. This change of taste affected Richards badly and he felt the need to expand his repertoire, turning to marine painting.

The idea of a trip to paint England's coastline in 1878 seems, however, to have come from *Harper's Magazine*, who specifically wanted an illustrated article on the Cornish coast.[52] This confirms that the glories of the coastline of Cornwall were already known in America; indeed, that magazine had published, as early as 1851, an article on the Cornish pilchard fishery by Wilkie Collins. Richards, however, could summon up little enthusiasm for the idea, feeling that "the trouble and toil of going will be very great".[53] Eventually, when *Scribner's Magazine* also expressed an interest in articles on the English coast, he decided to make the trip but only "from a sheer sense of duty".[54] Whitney agreed to help with the finances of the venture but nevertheless Richards sailed for Liverpool on 1st August 1878, with "a fainting heart" and "all my available capital".[55] Due to Whitney's patronage, Richards made an effort during his visit to write to him every other Sunday, recounting his experiences, and these letters, in themselves, make fascinating reading. However, he often included what he called a "coupon" - a superb miniature watercolour (c.3.5" x 5.5") of a scene that he had witnessed. These not only gave Whitney a visual record of the sights that his generosity had allowed Richards to visit, but also proved useful marketing tools, for Whitney was often able to persuade acquaintances and fellow collectors to commission off Richards larger versions of these scenes.[56]

On his arrival in Liverpool, Richards headed with his family straight down to Cornwall, but he complained to Whitney that rail travel in England was not very comfortable, being rather "shaky", albeit the officials were very helpful.[57] They stayed initially in Penzance before moving to Marazion, and he was very impressed with the local landscape, which was much more varied than he had imagined. He told Whitney, "I have been busy surveying the coast and think I ought to be here a lifetime to do any justice to it....Some of the strangeness is wearing off, but I find these cliffs very different from anything I have ever seen before."[58] He was particularly taken with Land's End, which he described as "the realisation of all that Conanicut hints at".[59] It became the yardstick by which all other cliff vistas were judged. However, it was not just the cliff scenery that enthused him. "The days are not long enough for sketches of all the picturesque old churches, romantic coves, and tremendous rocks... It is impossible to concentrate the mind upon a single subject when all is so strange and so exciting."[60]

Richards and his family moved to St Ives on 18th September and stayed there for a week. Interestingly, he told Whitney, "It is one of the least frequented towns of this district, partly because of a bad reputation as a dirty fishing town, and partly because it has been a little out of the main line of travel".[61] This comment, made so shortly after the article in *The Pictorial World* the previous year promoting the town as a "health resort", demonstrates that the "dirty" label could not be erased quickly and, indeed, much of the work needed to remedy the water supply and drainage problems was not done until the 1880s. As has been seen, though, the added difficulty of getting to the town had, by the time of Richards' visit, been overcome by the completion of the branch line from St Erth. Richards also mentioned that the Great Western Railway had just "hired a real castle on a hill above the town and turned it into a first rate hotel, where the Duke of Newcastle and other swells have been lodging".[62] Clearly, therefore, the opening of the Tregenna Castle Hotel had a marked impact on the type of

---

52 Letter from W.T.Richards to G.Whitney dated 19/3/1878 - Archives of American Art, Smithsonian Institution, W.T.Richards Papers, Reel 2296.
53 Letter from W.T.Richards to G.Whitney dated 9/6/1878 - Archives of American Art, W.T.Richards Papers, Reel 2296.
54 ibid.
55 Letter from W.T.Richards to G.Whitney dated 1/7/1878 - Archives of American Art, W.T.Richards Papers, Reel 2296.
56 See Linda Ferber, *Tokens of A Friendship: Miniature Watercolors by William T Richards*, New York, 1982. The following coupons of Cornish scenes are in the Richard and Gloria Manney Collection at the Metropolitan Museum of Art, New York. Richards gave each a number and the dates recorded are when they were received by Whitney. *Kynance Cove* (61 - 21/10/1878). *The Cornish Lions* (62 - 13/11/1878), *Newlyn* (67 - 12/12/1878), *Trebarwith Strand* (69 - 27/12/1878), *A Stamping Mill, Coast of Cornwall* (77 - 27/3/1879), *The Eagle's Nest, nr St Ives* (84 - 19/5/1879), *Mount's Bay, Cornwall* (85 - 24/5/1879), *Mill Bay, Land's End* (113 - 24/2/1880).
57 They went via Wrexham, Hereford, Tintern, Bristol and Exeter.
58 Letter from W.T.Richards to G.Whitney dated 1/9/1878 - Archives of American Art, W.T.Richards Papers, Reel 2296.
59 Letter from W.T.Richards to G.Whitney dated 17/9/1878 - Archives of American Art, W.T.Richards Papers, Reel 2296.
60 ibid.
61 Letter from W.T.Richards to G.Whitney dated 29/9/1878 - Archives of American Art, W.T.Richards Papers, Reel 2296.
62 ibid.

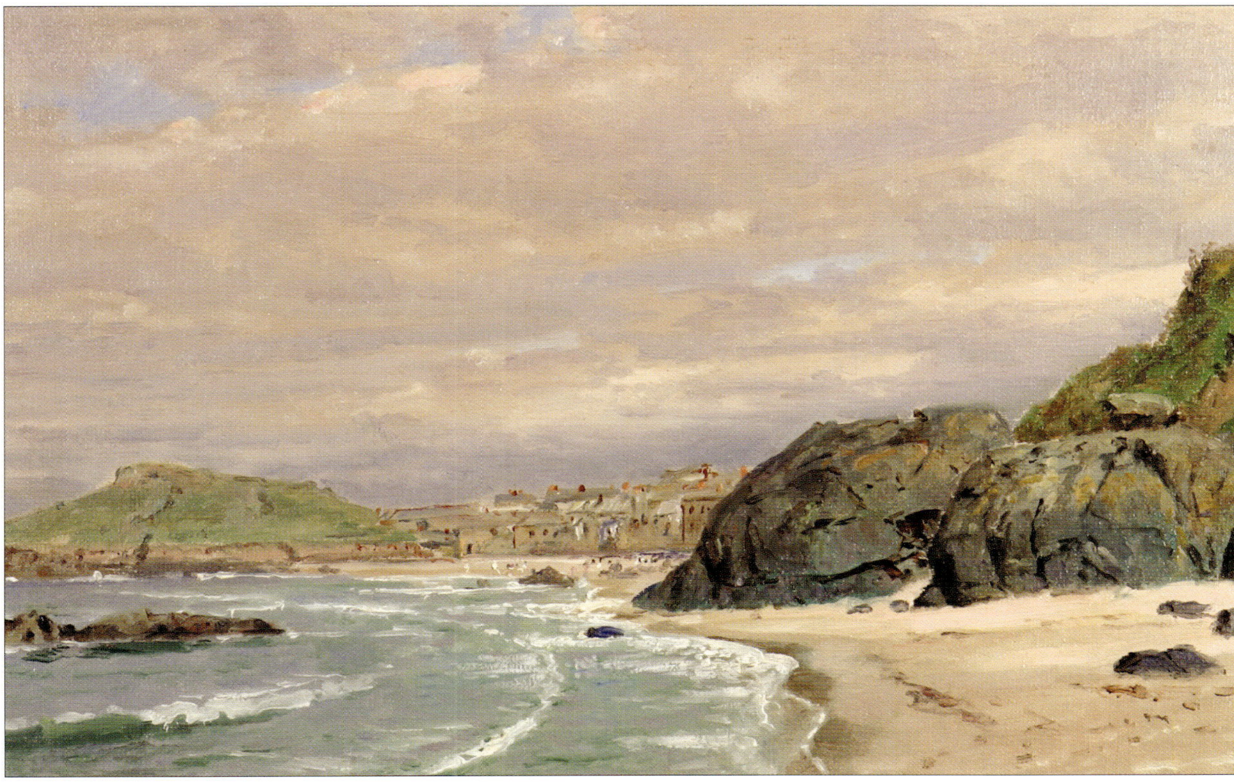

Fig. 1.16 William Trost Richards *Porthmeor Beach, St Ives* (dated 1878) (William Vareika Fine Art)

visitor that came to St Ives. Richards, however, did not stay there but found "modest lodgings whose windows overlook the town, the bay and the wide beach." He described St Ives as "a very primitive fishing town, full of old picturesque houses and fishing boats", with "enough subjects for figure pictures to last a first-rate painter a lifetime."[63] Richards, though, was not a figure painter but he did a small oil of the view looking across Porthmeor Beach towards the Island.[64] It is an unusual composition, for he cuts off the end of the Island, preferring to concentrate on the rocky promontory of Carrick Du in the foreground and the gentle curve of the breaking waves. At the back of the beach can be glimpsed the net lofts, that were soon to be converted into studios. He was also very taken with the Lelant Towans. "One of the most interesting points of Cornish scenery is the long beach and the sand hills or Towans, as they are called, around the bay of St Ives. They are 200 or 300 ft high, covered with grass and inhabited by millions of rabbits! The Church of Lelant is built in among these sand hills, and you can imagine I found a beautiful picture in this lonely church and the wind-swept sand!"[65] Richards fitted in a quick trip to Tintagel, where he witnessed a beautiful sunset, and Trebarwith Sands, where he admired the surf, before moving on to Kynance Cove, a setting that was to prove a never-ending source of inspiration. Their stay there, in the only accommodation available, which was little better than a log-cabin, he described as "our happiest experience of the Cornish Coast".[66]

In mid-October, Richards left Cornwall for London, where he intended to spend the winter, producing exhibition pictures from his sketches.[67] He took a property in Bayswater but found the smog, which he likened to a "dirty yellow blanket", very trying, some days having to paint by gaslight all day. Whilst in London, he made special efforts to look at, and learn from, the work of the English watercolourists, for whom he developed a great respect.[68] Turner's vignettes were particularly influential. He told a fellow American artist, "While they are not like nature and do not pretend to be real, they are so exquisite in gradation, so refined and thoughtful that you almost believe them to be better than nature".[69] This intense study resulted in him working in watercolour much more than previously and, although initially dubious, he became a champion of the rougher paper used for watercolour work in this country. To his surprise, his watercolours, in what he termed his "Grand Style", began to develop quite a following.

63 ibid.
64 He also told Whitney, with amusement, that he was painting some houses in the town one day, when a fisherman approached him and said, "one fellow made a thousand pounds by a picture of those houses, but for my part, I can't see anything much in them." Letter dated 1/8/1879.
65 ibid.
66 ibid.
67 His time in London coincided with the Whistler-Ruskin libel trial and he sent Whitney cuttings about this, observing, "The whole thing is too silly to move me to serious comment." Letter dated 7/1/1879.
68 Letter from W.T.Richards to G.Whitney dated 13/2/1879 - Archives of American Art, W.T.Richards Papers, Reel 2296.
69 Letter from W.T.Richards to W.H.Willcox dated 4/9/1879 - Archives of American Art, W.T.Richards Papers, Reel 2296.

His entry into London artistic circles was greatly helped by making the re-acquaintance of George Henry Boughton (1833-1905), an artist who, although born in Norwich, had been brought up in America, becoming a member of the National Academy of Design in 1871. He had, however, been based in London from 1861 and, during Richard's trip, was made an ARA. Richards was most impressed by his work, calling him "one of the few real painters of our time", and by the size and the tasteful decoration of his new house on Campden Hill, upon which he was said to have spent £20,000. The two became firm friends and, whilst Boughton's connections proved most useful to Richards, the latter's enthusiastic accounts of his time in Cornwall led Boughton himself to pay a visit in 1881, which resulted in his painting *St Ives Bay* being shown at the Royal Academy in 1882.[70] This - or possibly another work - was described by the *Magazine of Art* as being of "trees and cottages and wrestling boys in St Ives".[71]

Richards was always prone to self-doubt - not helped by the added responsibilty resulting from the birth of another daughter in January 1879 - and he was not at all certain that he would be able to make a mark in London. Accordingly, he was greatly heartened by the sale of two big watercolours at Manchester and his two works at the Dudley Gallery and, most of all, by the fact that both of his Cornish oils at the Royal Academy were sold within the first week of the exhibition. He later learnt that James Clarke Hook, who was on the selection panel that year, had been largely responsible not only for getting his work accepted but also hung well and that he had specifically recommended a collector to buy his painting of Trebarwith Strand, commenting on the beauty of the painting of the water. This was doubly gratifying to Richards, as he had previously picked out Hook's works as being the finest sea paintings in the exhibition.[72] These successes persuaded him to stay another year "and make real efforts to fire things - then I could come home, with the likelihood that year after year I can send to all these exhibitions and so widen my market."[73] He also soon found himself inundated with requests for his work from London dealers, such as Tooth's and McLean's, and from public Art Galleries, such as Brighton and Manchester. He told Whitney, "You see I am going into a sort of wholesale business!"[74]

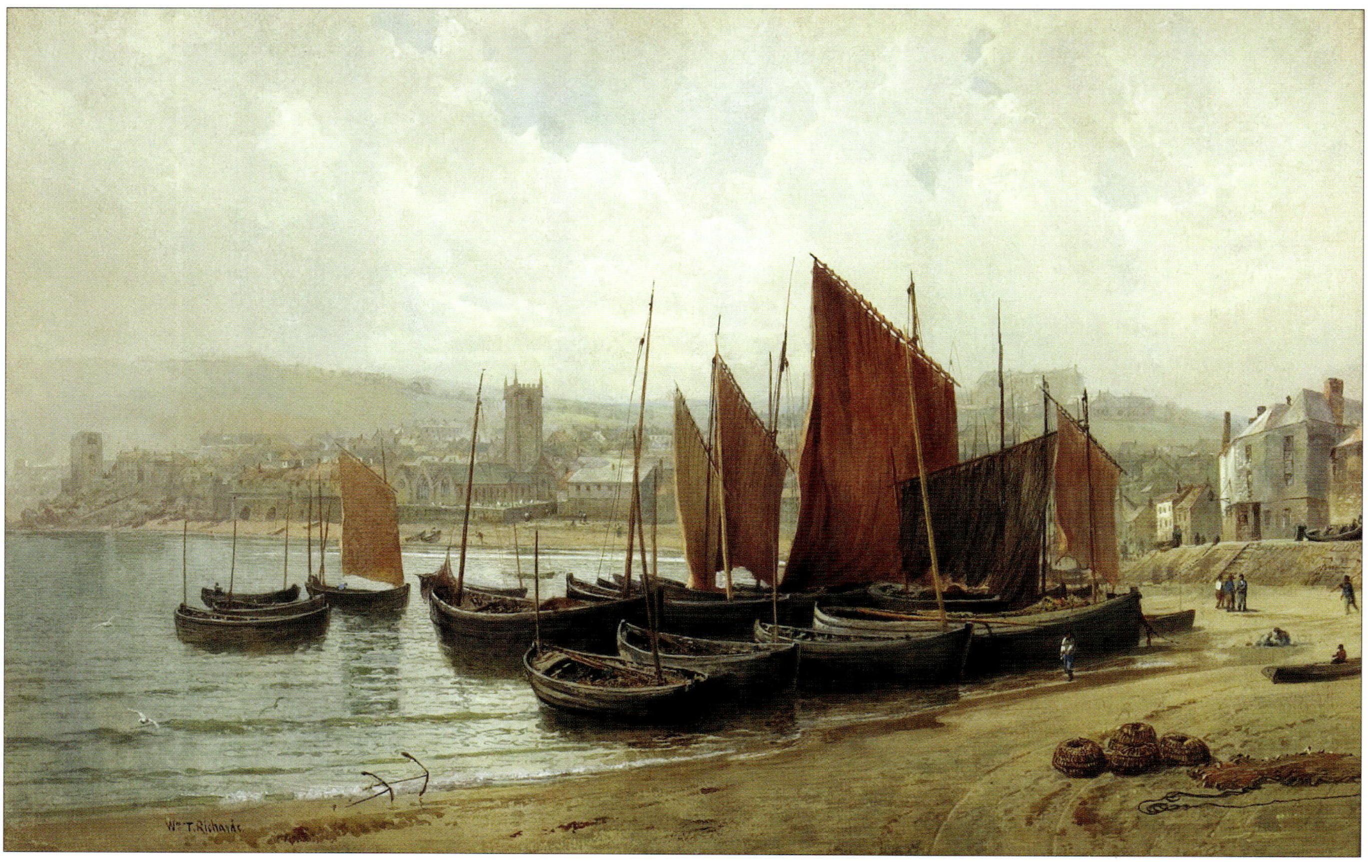

Fig. 1.17 William Trost Richards *Fishing Boats at St Ives, Cornwall* (William Vareika Fine Art)

70 Richards and Boughton were born and died in the same years and their executors arranged for the contents of their studios to be sold in the same auction in 1906.
71 *Magazine of Art*, 1882, Art Notes.
72 Letter from W.T.Richards to G.Whitney dated 16/4/1880 - Archives of American Art, W.T.Richards Papers, Reel 2296.
73 Letter from W.T.Richards to G.Whitney dated 14/3/1879 - Archives of American Art, W.T.Richards Papers, Reel 2296.
74 Letter from W.T.Richards to G.Whitney dated 14/7/1879 - Archives of American Art, W.T.Richards Papers, Reel 2296.

In the summer of 1879, Richards decided to base himself at Wyke Regis, near Weymouth, but although he marvelled at the surf and fearsome undertow at Chesil Beach and admired the scenery at Lulworth Cove, he considered the coastline not nearly as interesting as that of Cornwall and the people "not of so fine a character as the Cornish"[75]. Atrocious weather also kept him indoors for extended periods and he seems to have spent his time producing further paintings from his Cornish sketches. In early September, he got away on his own for another visit to Cornwall, the aim of which was to "reinforce my former studies".[76] He spent a good portion of the time in the Land's End region, working from dawn to dusk, and it is not clear whether he revisited St Ives. Clearly, a coupon of Eagle's Nest that he sent to Whitney in May 1879 was based on his earlier visit but a painting *Towards St Ives*, said to date from 1879, was included in an exhibition of Richards' work in 1976.[77]

Richards spent the winter of 1879-80 back in London and, again, he seems to have used his Cornish, rather than his Dorset sketches, for his major works. Tragedy struck in March, when his young baby died of measles, but he continued to enjoy great success and sold his Royal Academy exhibit. The summer of 1880, during which the weather was glorious, was largely spent on the Isle of Wight but, in August, he took his brother-in-law, Charley Marlack, on a whistle-stop tour of England, which included some of his favourite places in Cornwall. St Ives was one of the places that he revisited and a large, impressive watercolour, *Fishing Boats at St Ives, Cornwall*, is thought to date from this visit.[78] It depicts the view, on a mizzly day, from the beach by Smeaton's Pier across the harbour to the Parish Church and the mine building on Pednolva Point. Mackerel and pilchard boats are pulled up on the sands, several with their sails left up to dry. As the clouds begin to clear, an ethereal light appears on the waters of the harbour. It ranks as one of the finest watercolours ever painted in St Ives and works much more effectively than an oil version of the same scene that Richards did in 1883.

Richards returned to America in October 1880, having achieved far more than he had dared dream, for his trip had reinvigorated his art and his reputation. His detailed study, at first hand, of the work of the greatest English watercolourists had improved his own watercolour style and his works in this medium became as highly rated as his oils, where critics also noticed a transformation in his palette. Furthermore, there are distinct similarities in approach in the subsequent work of Richards to that of John Brett, suggesting that Brett may have been a prime influence. Certainly, Brett's *Britannia's Realm*, which Richards saw at the Royal Academy in 1880, impressed him immensely, for he told Whitney, "This has never in its way been equalled, will perhaps never be rivalled by anyone". However, that is the only time that Brett's work is mentioned in his correspondence and he was equally impressed with the very different work of Henry Moore and James Hook. Richards also learnt during his visit how the English market operated and, having broken into that market, he was able to send work to the Royal Academy and other English shows for the rest of his life. However, more than anything he found himself a subject - the Cornish coast - that enthralled him and sold well.[79] He was to pay four more visits to England and explore other coastal regions, but his love for the Cornish coast never dimmed. Indeed, in 1905, perhaps prescient of his impending death, he returned to Cornwall to revisit all those areas that had proved unending sources of inspiration - Tintagel, Trebarwith Strand, Sennen and Land's End, Mullion and Kynance Coves and St Ives. He told his brother-in-law, who had made much the same trip with him twenty-five years previously, "In St Ives, I propose to stay a couple of weeks for there is, as you know, a good beach there without distracting cliffs. I want especially to study the sea and know of no place here where it can be done more conveniently than at St Ives."[80]

Although, by the time of his death, his meticulously detailed renderings of coastal scenery had fallen out of favour with the critics, it is a complete mystery why such a high profile artist, who was not only one of the earliest foreign visitors to Cornwall but also one of the most regular, should have been ignored completely to date in this country. The wealth of his depictions of the British coast, particularly of Cornwall, many of which are in American public collections, when combined with his first hand accounts of his impressions of English scenery, customs and the London art market, would make a fascinating and informative project.

75 Letter from W.T.Richards to G.Whitney dated 15/6/1879 - Archives of American Art, W.T.Richards Papers, Reel 2296.
76 Letter from W.T.Richards to G.Whitney dated 1/7/1879 - Archives of American Art, W.T.Richards Papers, Reel 2296.
77 Art Association of Newport, *William Trost Richards 1833-1905*, February 1976, No.60.
78 Richards' letter to Whitney of 2/9/1880 recording this tour does not detail where they went in Cornwall but his letter to Marlack on 27/7/1905 reminisces about the places that they had visited "so long ago" and makes clear that they had been to St Ives together.
79 Whitney himself bought one of Richard's major works, a 60" x 40" oil of Land's End dated 1880.
80 Letter from W.T.Richards to C.Marlack dated 27/7/1905 - Archives of American Art, W.T.Richards Papers, Reel 2296.

1.7 Edwin Ellis and other visitors of the early 1880s

A painting of figures on the Wharf in St Ives dated 1881 indicates an early visit by another American artist, William John Whittemore (1860-1955), and, like Richards, he appears to have made a number of return trips to Cornwall. Having commenced his art studies in New York, Whittemore enrolled at the Julian School in Paris and his first visit in 1881 was undertaken whilst he was based in France. He returned on several occasions during the 1890s and Cornish scenes feature at American exhibitions in the years 1892-6.

A London-based artist, who made a number of trips down to Cornwall in the late 1870s and early 1880s was the watercolourist, Charles Aston, and he exhibited a depiction of St Ives at the 1879 Spring show at the RBSA, which, at that juncture, was devoted solely to watercolours. In the 1881 Spring exhibition, there were two further watercolours of St Ives - *Target Point, St Ives* by W.H.Dixon and *Sunset near St Ives* by the future Academician, Henry Moore (1831-1893). Moore was quite a regular visitor to Cornwall. His 1866 Royal Academy exhibit, *The Pilot Cutter*, was a Cornish sunset scene and paintings of the Penzance area, dated in 1872 and 1877, have passed through the salerooms in the last decade. In the early 1880s, however, he made a number of voyages along the Cornish coast on the yacht, *Dawn*, owned by his friend, George Burnett, an amateur artist. Sketches done during the cruise in the summer of 1883 led to *Summer in Cornwall* (Birmingham Art Gallery) and his Chantrey work *Catspaws off the Land* (RA 1885). Moore acknowledged that these cruises, which had started in 1873 and during which he worked incessantly, were the making of him, for they inspired him to turn away from his previous rather grey, sober depictions of seashore incidents and to concentrate exclusively on pure seascapes - salt-tanged depictions of the mid-Ocean deep, often painted in vivid blues, which were to win him acclaim both in France and Britain. Indeed, he was the artist that later St Ives marine painters, Louis Grier and Julius Olsson, listed as an important influence. Frustratingly, I have found no precise record of the dates of Moore's visits to St Ives, but Harry Robinson indicated that he was known well by the St Ives fishermen, which suggests that he is also likely to have sailed with them on occasion to sketch the waters of the Bay.[81]

The most impressive series of paintings of St Ives exhibited before the birth of the colony was by the Nottingham-born marine artist, Edwin Ellis (1841-1895), at the SBA Winter Exhibition in 1882. Largely self-taught but a member of the SBA since 1875, his set of eight paintings, which were priced between £40 and £150, were probably all, with one exception, St Ives subjects and would have given a fascinating insight into the local fishing industry. Titles include *Drawing A Seine: St Ives*, *Pilchard Fishers*, *Mackerel Boats, Cornwall*, *St Ives Pier*, *Mending Nets* and *Running for Shelter*. At this juncture, Ellis' work was often being singled out for its strength and vigour and the *Magazine of Art* felt that his contributions to this exhibition stood well out from those of his fellows.[82] Furthermore, another depiction of St Ives was in the same show. This painting, entitled *A Street in Old St Ives*, was contributed by the Blackheath-based artist, Edward Wilkins Waite (1854-1924), and depicted a scene in The Warren. Two fisherfolk have put down their loads - his a lobster pot, hers two stone jars - as they stop for a chat. The impact of this group of paintings should not be underestimated. In my view, they will have led to far more visitors to St Ives than the more famous later works of Whistler.

1883 seems to have seen both Hugh Carter (1837-1903) and Richard Harry Carter (1839-1911) in St Ives, for both exhibited St Ives subjects at the Liverpool Autumn Exhibition that year. Richard Carter showed *Dead Low Water, St Ives* (£42), whilst Hugh Carter showed *Baiting Hooks, St Ives* (£57-15-0) and *Interior of a Net Loft, St Ives* (£26-5-0). Hugh's painting *Cornish Seine Boat at Anchor - Waiting for the Signal*, which he exhibited as part of the ROI's contribution to the 1884 Liverpool show, may have been executed on the same visit. The presence of Hugh and Richard Carter in St Ives together might suggest that they were related, but this is unlikely as Hugh was born in Birmingham and was at that time London based, whilst Richard Carter, whose father was in the Navy, was born and based in Truro.

Richard Carter started painting only as a sideline, for his principal career initially was as a buyer of tin for Messrs Vivian, and the first Census in which he recorded his sole profession as 'artist' was in 1891.[83] However, he had a passion for both Art and Nature that lifted his work way beyond that of a mere amateur, and he exhibited at the Royal Academy and other London societies and has impressive works in the collections of Cornish Museums. His most significant painting of St Ives is *The Return of the Missing Boat, St Ives*, a huge watercolour, which depicts an anxious fishwife and child by a gale-swept Smeaton's Pier, hoping that the sail spotted on the horizon is, in fact, the boat containing their loved one that had failed to return with the rest of the fleet. This was one of his most highly regarded works and photogravures of it were published. He also exhibited, at the Penzance School of Art exhibition in January 1884, a similar scene, *A Wild Shore near St Ives Head*. This depicted anxious women sheltering under a dark cliff, as they tried to catch sight of boats from the fleet caught in a violent storm. This exhibition was the seventh held by the School and the most impressive to date, as it contained some

---

81 See *St Ives as an Art Colony* in *Babcock's Historical Sketch of St Ives and District*, 1896.

82 *Magazine of Art*, 1882, Review of SBA exhibition. Ellis also exhibited two watercolours, *Sandhills* and *Taking Fish to Market*, both possibly St Ives scenes, at the exhibition of watercolours at Agnews, Old Bond Street, in 1882 with the latter being rated by the *Magazine of Art* as "the best and strongest bit of watercolour work in the exhibition."

83 See his obituary in *St Ives Weekly Summary*, 17/2/1911. In 1871, he called himself 'Artist/Accountant' and, in 1881, 'Artist/Banker'.

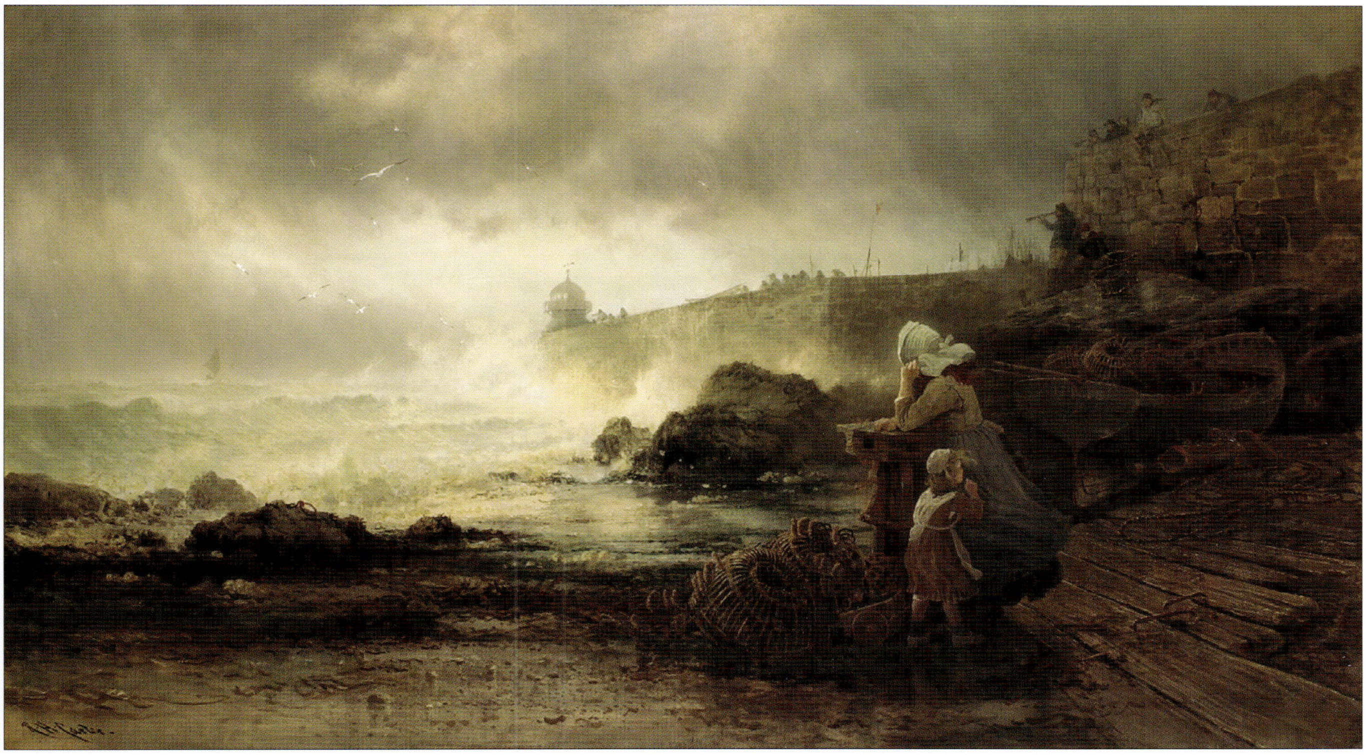

Fig. 1.18 Richard Harry Carter *The Return of the Missing Boat, St Ives* (Private Collection)
(image courtesy of Godolphin Fine Art, Chagford)

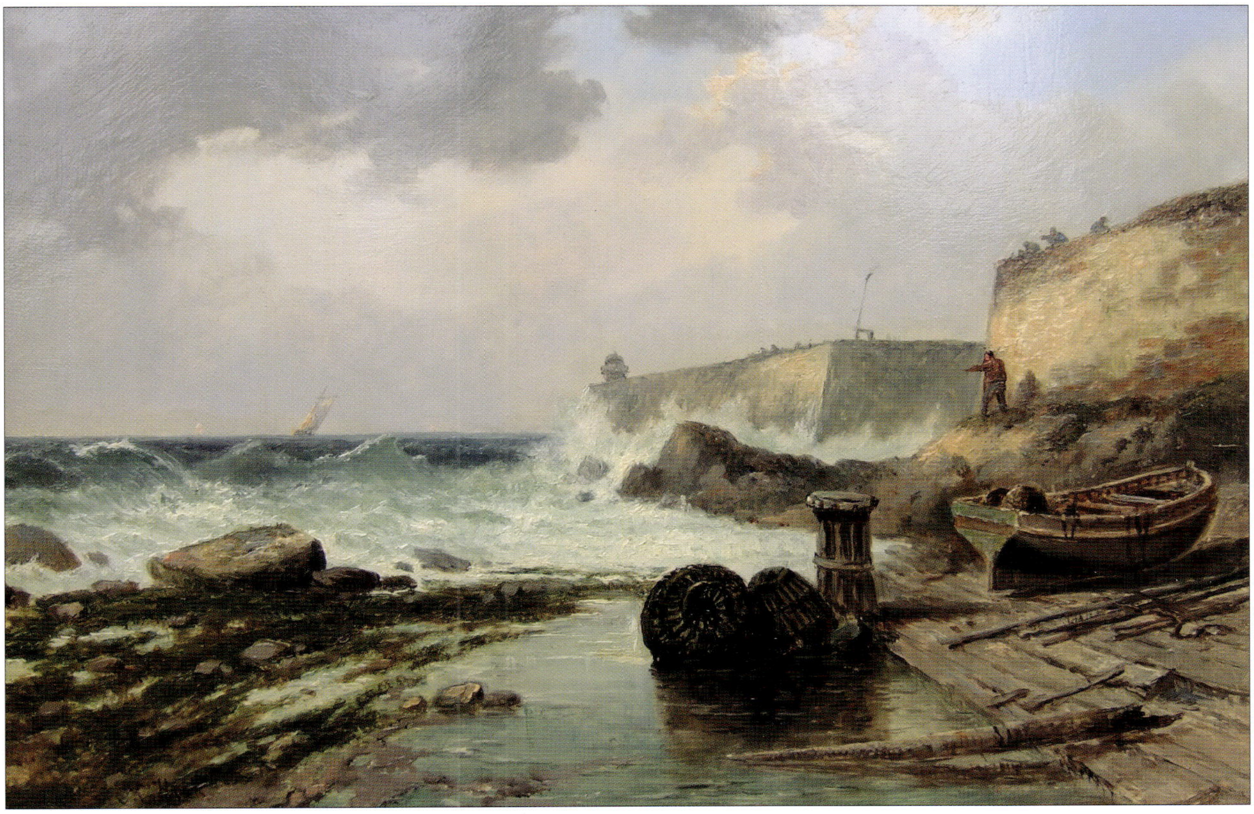

Fig. 1.19 James Clarke Hook *Smeaton's Pier, St Ives - The Return of the Fishing Fleet* (Private Collection)

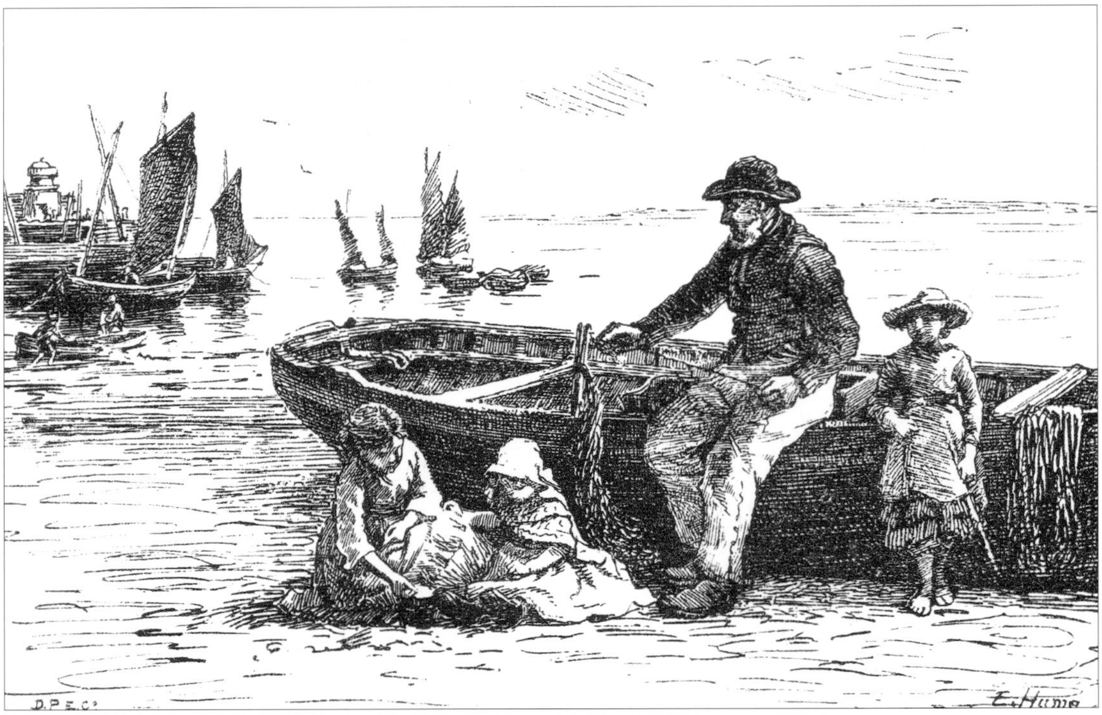

Fig. 1.20 Edith Hume *Preparing the Tackle* (sketch from *Academy Notes* 1885)

ninety works by Richard Pentreath (see Fig. 0.6), as well as a number of paintings by the early Newlyn settlers. In addition to two depictions of St Ives by Carter, a work, *Seine Fishing, St Ives*, was also contributed by the Penzance watercolourist, James Clarkson Uren. During the exhibition, Richard Carter gave a lecture on art, in which he warned about the "great danger of letting slip the poetry of Art, for the more photographic reproduction of objects and detail", particularly in an era, when the stock-in-trade motifs of a former generation of landscape artists were fast being swept away, leaving only ugliness. This was a clear criticism of the Pre-Raphaelite landscape style, and he believed that, although artists needed to go to Nature for inspiration and facts, "Nature is not everything to the landscape painter. Nature is the raw material; the artist is at once the loom which turns out the fine fabric, and the operator, who guides the loom. Clouds, shadows and sunshine, flashes of sunlight come and go, as the painter sits before his subject, and he turns out the fine fabric as he is impressed."[84]

Another London artist, who was in St Ives in the summer of 1883, most probably due to Ellis' display of paintings at the SBA, was fellow member Alberto Ludovici Jnr. Boasting Venetian noble ancestry and having a father who was Treasurer of the SBA, he had studied in Paris a decade before the artists who first settled in St Ives. Bastien-Lepage, therefore, who was to prove an inspiration to many of the early Cornish settlers, had not been a cult figure at that time but one of his fellow *nouveaux* at the École des Beaux Arts and Ludovici recalled how, during the obligatory nude song and dance routine, Lepage had had stools hurled at his legs whenever he stopped![85] In St Ives, Ludovici was applying his *plein air* principles by working on the beach surrounded by a group of fishermen and children, when he was approached by another artist, who complimented him on his courage in coping with such a crowd, intimating that he himself could never do so. This surprised Ludovici as the artist had had a painting of St Ives "fishermen and fish wives with boats and fish on the sands", hung on the line at that year's Royal Academy. However, he was truly astonished to be told that this work had been painted in the grounds of Tregenna Castle Hotel, about a mile away, the artist viewing the scene through opera glasses![86]

It was on the beach as well that Ludovici met Walter Sickert, who was staying in the town with his family. Whilst sketching on the beach, Sickert was much amused by the travails of an avid *plein airist*, who had to enlist the services of four fishermen to hold down his easel and canvas with ropes, while he worked away in a howling gale.[87] Indeed, he enjoyed his time in St Ives that summer so much that he recommended the place to his master, Whistler. I shall return to Whistler's visit, however, after a review of the experiences that the early settlers of the St Ives colony had shared previously in France, as the significance or otherwise of Whistler's visit can only be appraised in the light of these. It can be seen already, however, that St Ives was certainly not unknown at the time of Whistler's visit and that other distinguished artists had painted its attractions previously. Whistler was just another in a long line of artist visitors.

84 *Cornish Telegraph*, 24/1/1884.
85 A Ludovici Jnr, *An Artist's Life in London and Paris*, London, 1926 at p.23.
86 A Ludovici Jnr, *An Artist's Life in London and Paris*, London, 1926 at p.73-4.
87 From a lecture at Thanet School of Art, 9/11/1934 - A G Robins, *Walter Sickert; The Complete Writings on Art*, 2000 at p.646.

~ 2 ~

SHARED EXPERIENCES OF THE EARLY SETTLERS IN FRANCE

2.1 Common Bond

It is perhaps not too surprising that the training of the artists connected with the Newlyn art colony was remarkably similar, in that most members of the colony were male and British and, as was the fashion at that time, they had followed up their training in England with spells at ateliers in Paris and/or Antwerp. The great variety of nationalities amongst the artists that first settled in St Ives clearly made such uniformity impossible but, nevertheless, most of them had something in common - their experiences in the ateliers and art colonies of France. Whatever they had learnt at art school in their own respective countries, their attitude towards their own art and to the art world as a whole was moulded by the teachings of the masters under whom they studied in Paris, by the cults that dominated the Parisian art world at the time and by the company that they kept in the thriving art colonies in France, particularly those in Brittany. It was a period when there was a reaction against studio work, and nature's truths were sought by painting in the open air. This posed new problems, which led to experimentation with novel methods and techniques, and different colour values and levels of finish. For artists who had merely studied in indoor schools, a whole raft of new challenges awaited. However, the artists felt a sense of real excitement that they were at the forefront of an important development in art history.

Unfortunately, the British artists, who became early settlers in St Ives, have not left much written material describing their experiences in France, but many were in Paris and Brittany at much the same time as their Newlyn counterparts, and the descriptions of their French sojourns by Stanhope Forbes, Thomas Gotch, Norman Garstin and others have been reproduced many times. Happily, though, the American artists, who contributed so significantly to the reputation of the St Ives colony in its early years, have left more extensive records. Edward Simmons (1852-1931), from Concord, Massachusetts, played a significant role in the development of the art colonies in both Concarneau (1881-5) and St Ives (1886-1891), and his autobiography, written in 1922, contains much of interest, albeit it is frustratingly selective in the events and personnel recorded. The voluminous correspondence from New Yorker, Howard Russell Butler (1856-1934), to his family, during his time in Europe (1885-7), is invaluable, as is his unpublished autobiography. Butler, who had started out in a legal career, only decided to take up painting seriously in 1884, and only had a short time studying under Frederick Church in Mexico, before arriving in Paris in early 1885. The extent of his early success never truly convinced him that he had made up for all the time that he had lost by failing to embrace a career in art earlier. Another useful source is an article by Arthur Hoeber (1854-1915), born in Nutley, New Jersey, on his first summer in Pont-Aven in 1883. Hoeber became a good friend of Simmons and Butler, whilst in France, and spent a summer in St Ives in 1893. Another American, who was a key figure in the art colonies of Pont-Aven and Concarneau during this period, and who achieved notable success at the Paris Salon, was Alexander Harrison (1853-1930). His work clearly influenced the marine paintings of Simmons and Butler, with whom he worked in Concarneau, and he too later visited St Ives. From these and other sources, it is possible to reconstruct the experiences enjoyed by both British and foreign artists in France prior to their arrival in St Ives.

2.2 Paris Ateliers

Paris was, at this juncture, considered to be not only the art centre of the world, but also the art school and the art market of the world. Accordingly, students of all nationalities flocked there to enrol in one of the many ateliers. In 1885, Howard Butler calculated that there were at least one hundred American students in the city. The system resulted in the teachers assuming a manner of extraordinary authority and importance. "The students, gay, light-hearted, and full of fun at other times", commented Adrian Stokes, "were reduced to a state of silent awe when their masters were present." He added, "Each student, when choosing a school, looked for the master with whom he felt most in sympathy; but, really, I believe, the teaching of all of them had become a matter of tradition and was very much alike."[88] Charles Adrian Scott Stokes (1854-1935) was born in Southport but his father, who was an Inspector of Schools, moved on a regular basis and, by 1861, Adrian and his six siblings were living in Liverpool. After a brief stint with a Liverpool cotton broker, he studied at the Royal Academy Schools from 1872-5, but then spent the next decade training further in Paris and working in a variety of European art colonies. His experiences, particularly in Barbizon and Brittany, were to have a profound influence on the style of painting adopted by many of the early St Ives artists.

Most students arriving in Paris, who had trained elsewhere previously, were spared drawing from the antique and could join the life class immediately. However, those who had been brought up on the cross-hatching method of drawing, using a stump, which found favour, for instance, at South Kensington, had to adapt to the swift

88 Adrian Stokes, *Landscape Painting*, London, 1925, p.25.

TABLE B - SHARED EXPERIENCES OF THE EARLY ST IVES SETTLERS

ARTIST	HOME COUNTRY TRAINING	EUROPEAN TRAINING	ART COLONIES
Elizabeth Armstrong	Art Students League 1877-80	Munich 1882	Pont-Aven 1883 Zandvoort 1884 Newlyn from 1885 St Ives from 1886
Howard Russell Butler	Art Students League 1884	Paris - Dagnan Bouveret, Roll and Gervex 1885-7	Concarneau 1885 Grez 1886 St Ives from 1886
Emma Lowstadt / Chadwick		Paris - Colarossi's 1881-2	Grez 1882-6 Concarneau 1883-4 St Ives from 1886
Frank Chadwick		Paris - Julian's 1870-1881	Grez 1882-6 Concarneau 1883-4 St Ives from 1886
Alfred Conquest			Pont-Aven/Concarneau 1880-4, St Ives from 1884
Alfred East	Glasgow	Paris - Beaux Arts & Julian's - c.1881-2	Barbizon 1882 St Ives from 1887
Stanhope Forbes	Lambeth	Paris - Bonnat 1880	Cancale 1881, Quimperle 1882-3, Newlyn from 1884, St Ives from 1886
E Wyly Grier	Slade - 1879-81	Rome - 1881-2 Paris - Julian's 1882-4	St Ives from 1887
Melicent Grose			Pont-Aven 1879-1884 St Ives from 1885
Marianne Preindlsberger (later Stokes)		Munich 1874-1880 Paris - Colarossi's 1880-2	Concarneau 1881 Pont-Aven 1883-4 Skagen 1886 St Ives from 1887
Henry Harewood Robinson		Paris - Julian's 1882-3	Concarneau 1884 St Ives from 1885
Helene Schjerfbeck		Paris - Colarossi's 1881-3	Concarneau 1881 Pont-Aven 1883-4 St Ives from 1887
Edward Simmons		Paris - Julian's 1878-80	Concarneau 1880-5 St Ives from 1886
Adrian Stokes	RA Schools - 1872-5		Pont-Aven 1876 Fontainebleau Concarneau 1881 Normandy 1882 Pont-Aven 1883-6 Skagen 1886 St Ives from 1887
Émile Vernier			Concarneau 1881-5 Pont-Aven 1883 St Ives from 1884
Dorothy Webb (later Robinson)		Paris - Julian's 1882	Concarneau 1883-4 St Ives from 1885
Maria Wiik		Paris - Julian's 1875-1880 - Colarossi's 1881-1883	Pont-Aven 1883-4 St Ives from 1888

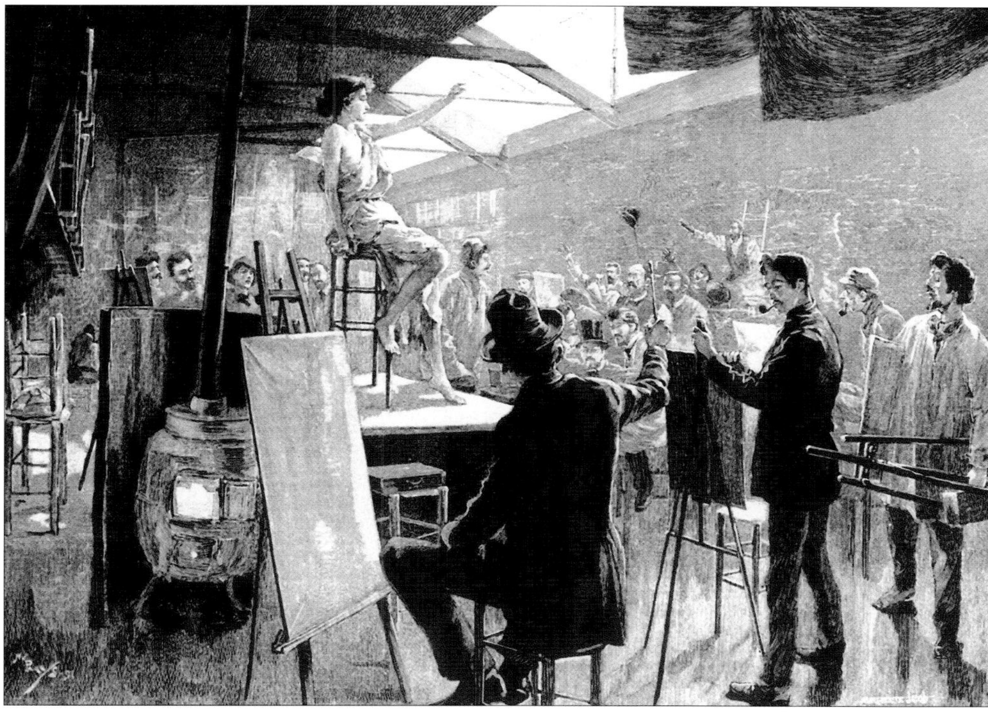

Fig. 2.1 The Julian School - *Posing the Model* (*Black and White*)
Drawn by A. Parys : Engraved by Marguerite Jacob

point to point freehand drawing required in the ateliers. The concentration on drawing the nude figure was also novel for English students. Stanhope Forbes, who had a brief flirtation with St Ives before settling permanently in Newlyn, moaned to his mother, "These beastly nude figures puzzle me so but of course it is the great way to learn thoroughly. French students work for years at nothing else and the result is that the French School is far ahead of ours as far as training goes."[89] Nevertheless, the teachers were all fervent traditionalists and modern movements, such as Impressionism, were still given short shrift.

A student could not 'book' himself a place in one of the ateliers and, accordingly, would have to go round the various recommended ateliers with his drawings, hoping that these would win the approval of one of the masters. Sometimes, a student could get rejected merely because there were too many artists of his nationality in that particular atelier at that time. Ateliers had different customs and these could be quite daunting for an applicant. At the Julian School, for instance, Simmons confirms that newcomers got a rough reception. "If anyone came into the room, other than Julian or an *ancien* (old student), there were hurled at him paint tubes, stools, cigar butts, oaths and comments upon his appearance and clothing. This was a tradition of the school and had to be lived up to."[90] Even when accepted, *nouveaux* were invariably put upon. Their *bienvenue* (or footing-money) was used to provide drinks all round at a café and they were normally forced to perform some humiliating act, such as duelling with paint-laden brushes whilst naked.[91] They could be also be given particular tasks, such as cleaning all the other students' brushes at lunchtime. Stanhope Forbes mentioned a Spanish *nouveau*, who refused to act as stoker of the stove, and, accordingly, was systematically victimised before being dowsed with a bucket of cold water.[92]

At some ateliers, the very keen students could attend three sessions a day - from 8a.m. to midday, from 1p.m. to 5p.m. and from 7p.m. to 10 p.m, but few were able to keep up such a concentrated commitment for long, for the ateliers were crowded, noisy and smoky, and newcomers found the routine exhausting at first, particularly those, such as the British, who had been used to absolute silence previously. Most attended the morning sessions and, during the afternoons, made their own arrangements. Many would go to the Louvre, in order to copy one of the masterpieces there or to do some other painting that might bring in a few francs to help with their living expenses. Some of the better off students, like Forbes, who had their own studio, would hire their own models for afternoon

---

89 Letter from Forbes to his mother, May 1880, Tate Gallery Archives 9015.2.1.68.

90 E E Simmons, *From Seven to Seventy*, London, 1922, p.119. Howard Butler had a similar experience when he applied to join Atelier Humbert-Gervex. As he descended the long staircase to talk to the Master, the students all stopped work and began stamping their feet in time, shouting "Chapeau". Not getting the slightest hint of encouragement from either Master or pupils, Butler was about to walk out, feeling embarrassed and dejected, when he was spotted by a friend. In the ensuing break, he was elected unanimously to the Société de la Palette, a prerequisite before he could be enrolled in the Atelier. On turning up for study for the first time, he was "put through the usual hasing" and had to perform some unusual stunt for everyone's amusement. (H.R.Butler, Unpublished Autobiography, p.169-71, Archives of American Art, Smithsonian Institution, Washington DC, Howard Russell Butler papers, Reel 93.)

91 See Shirley Fox, *An Art Student's Reminiscences of Paris in the Eighties*, London, 1909 at p.116-9.

92 Letter from Forbes to his mother dated 30/4/1880, Tate Gallery Archives, 9015.2.1.64.

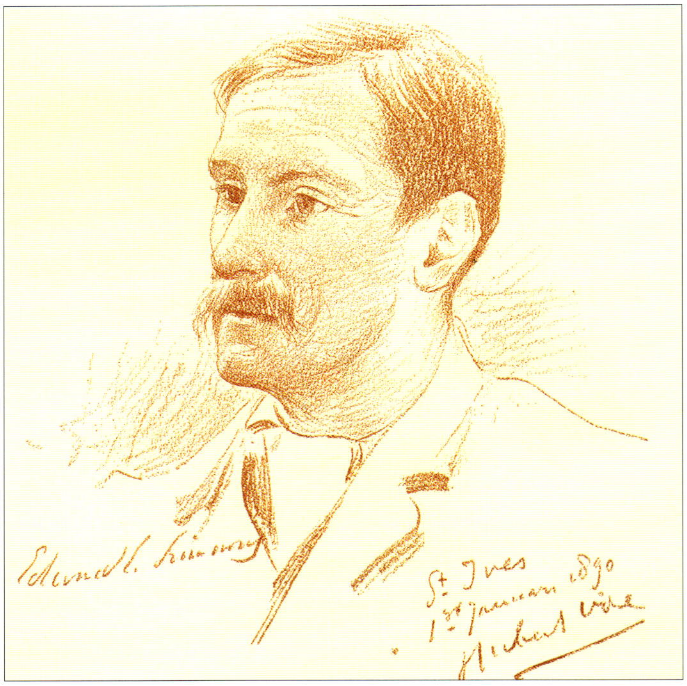

Fig. 2.2 Hubert Vos *Edward Simmons*
Drawn at the Stokeses' New Year's Day party 1890

sessions. In addition, the atelier might run competitions amongst the students. The Julian School, for instance, ran five *Concours* a year, commencing in October and taking place in the last week of that and succeeding months. All were figure studies of some type. A strong work ethic seems to have existed amongst those keen to succeed and Forbes admitted, "I get just twice if not more the number of hours work done here that I used to do in England...One thing I feel more and more that very few of us in England work hard enough or stick long enough at the training."[93]

On Monday mornings, there was a Model Market at the Place Pigalle, which was thronged by all types of men, women and children anxious to get an engagement for the week. The models, however, earned their wage for, at most ateliers, they posed for eight hours a day, having just an hour's rest at lunchtime and a ten minute breather every hour. The model for the week was often chosen by the head student or *massier,* and the older students might have a hand in selecting the pose to be adopted. All students tended to arrive early that day to ensure a good position for the week. In some ateliers, such as the Julian School, this was determined on a first come, first served basis, whereas in others, it was done by lot. As a rule, the ateliers were visited by different professors twice a week but, with so many students, there was only time to pass comment to a few and their criticisms could often be quite severe. The experience of Edward Simmons gives an insight into how they operated. Simmons, on arriving at the Julian School, confidently pitched right in with paint, but was reduced to tears when told by Boulanger that he "might as well go home and make shoes" if he did that. However, he offered no constructive comment. Only when Simmons confronted him later, did he tell him to study the outline drawings of Gérôme and to draw the model in that manner. For months thereafter, Boulanger completely ignored him, giving him no idea as to his progress, until he suddenly stopped one day behind Simmons' easel and announced to the class "None of you could do a drawing like this, and I doubt if any of you could copy it." The effect on Simmons was instant. "I switched from being a loafer and *chiquer* from that moment, and realized that only by eight hours' daily work and hard digging could I become a painter." [94] Stanhope Forbes, who studied at Bonnat's atelier, indicates that Bonnat only ever came to review their work once a week but, particularly when he was on jury service at the Salon, several weeks could pass by without a visit. However, he tells his mother, "I don't think you need be alarmed about the rarity of his visits. He says a great deal in a short time and it is the right thing always."[95]

The Julian School, which Simmons attended from 1878-81, proved particularly popular with artists who later came to St Ives, as it was much easier for foreign artists to enrol there than at the École des Beaux Arts. It was located at 48 rue de Faubourg, St Denis. In addition to Simmons, in the years 1881-3, Noble Barlow, Alfred East, Wyly Grier, Harry Robinson, Dorothy Webb, Middleton Jameson and William Titcomb all studied there, but to what extent any of them overlapped is not known. Later students there who came on to St Ives include the Australian Emanuel Phillips Fox, the Dutchman Sigisbert Bosch Reitz, Terrick Williams, Harry Bishop, George Roller, Walter Jevons, Harry Browne, Allan Deacon, who was looking after a young William Nicholson, and the American Elmer Schofield. The School was run by Rodolphe Julian, whom Simmons describes as follows:-

93 Letter to his mother, 17/5/1880, Tate Gallery Archives 9015.2.1.67.
94 E E Simmons, *From Seven to Seventy*, London, 1922, p.124-5.
95 Letter from Forbes to his mother dated 17/5/1880, Tate Gallery Archive 9015.2.1.67.

"He was a Hercules and quite a romantic figure about whom there were many stories. They say he was the Masked Man who used to wrestle on the stage and at county fairs. This hulking fellow had been rather a good painter and had become a most successful business man. Born an Italian peasant, he had spent the early years of his life as a goatherd. To me he always looked like a great big orangutan".[96]

One of the greatest attractions of his School was that he had persuaded four eminent jurors of the Salon to be visiting professors. Adolphe Bouguereau and Robert Fleury corrected and criticised the work in one studio and Jules Lefebvre and Gustave Boulanger supervised the students in the other. Julian was styled by George Moore as the "Warwick of the Salon Juries" and his students hoped that, if one of these eminent artists awarded them a prize in the monthly competition, then they had a great chance of exhibiting in the annual exhibition at the Salon.[97]

The atelier was, however, dreadfully overcrowded. Even if you were lucky enough to get a position in the front row, you were so hemmed in by neighbouring easels that you were hard pushed to lift an arm. Palette scrapings made a frieze up to the height of an outstretched arm and these gave off a rank odour as the room heated up. Everybody smoked incessantly. Simmons considered it the dingiest place imaginable. "The room was dirty and dark, despite the skylight above; at one end, a platform, and near it a soiled bit of drapery behind which the women models stripped. On a hot July day, what with paints, dirty Frenchmen, stuffy air, nude models, and the place below (a public toilet), this room stank worse than anything I can think of. Not much calculation for comfort, but possibly an enormous inspiration for genius." [98]

Another atelier, which seemed to attract a number of Scandinavian artists, and which welcomed female students, was the Academie Colarossi, which was at 10 rue de la Grande Chaumière. The principal teacher there was Gustave Courtois, although other artists who taught at the atelier from time to time were Raphael Collin and Jean-Charles Cazin. The atelier's working hours were 8a.m. to noon and 1p.m.-5p.m., with different models for each session. It was whilst studying here in the years 1881-3 that a number of the foreign female artists, who made a big impression in the early years of the St Ives colony, first met. The Finns, Helene Schjerfbeck and Maria Wiik, and the Austrian, Marianne Preindlsberger, in particular, became firm friends.

Maria Wiik (1853-1928) was rather older than the other girls. Having been brought up and educated in Helsingfors, she studied at the Adolf von Becker Private Academy there in 1873 before coming to Paris for the first time in 1875. Although frequently returning to Finland, she studied on and off at the Julian School until 1880, spending a summer

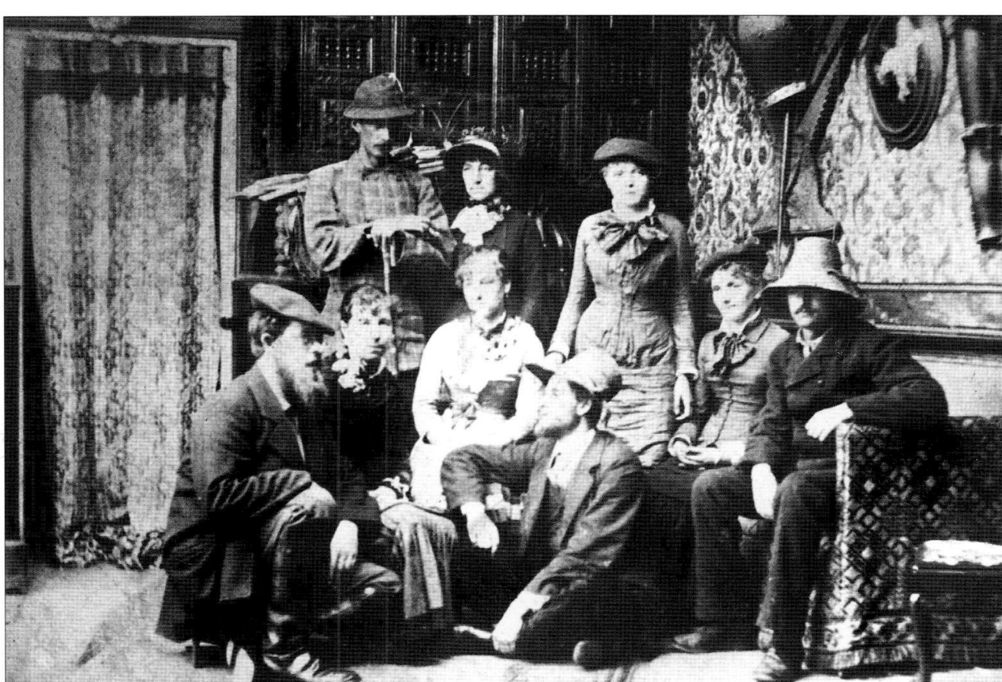

Fig. 2.3 Artists at Colarossi's (National Board of Antiquities, Finland)
Helene Schjerfbeck is in the centre, with a beret. On her left is Marianne Preindlsberger and Per Ekstrom. To her right, is believed to be the Finnish artists Amélie Lundahl and Aukusti Uotila. At the front, on the left, is August Hagborg. The other two women have not been formally identified but might include Emma Lowstadt or Maria Wiik.

96 E E Simmons, *From Seven to Seventy*, London, 1922, p.119.
97 Julian did not take kindly to Alexander Harrison luring some of his top students away and threatened to arrange for them never to be hung at the Salon again - a threat he proved unable to carry through. Nevertheless, the School proved so successful that Julian had to enlarge his original scheme and eventually set up seven immense ateliers distributed all over Paris, catering for some four hundred students.
98 E E Simmons, *From Seven to Seventy*, London, 1922, p.118.

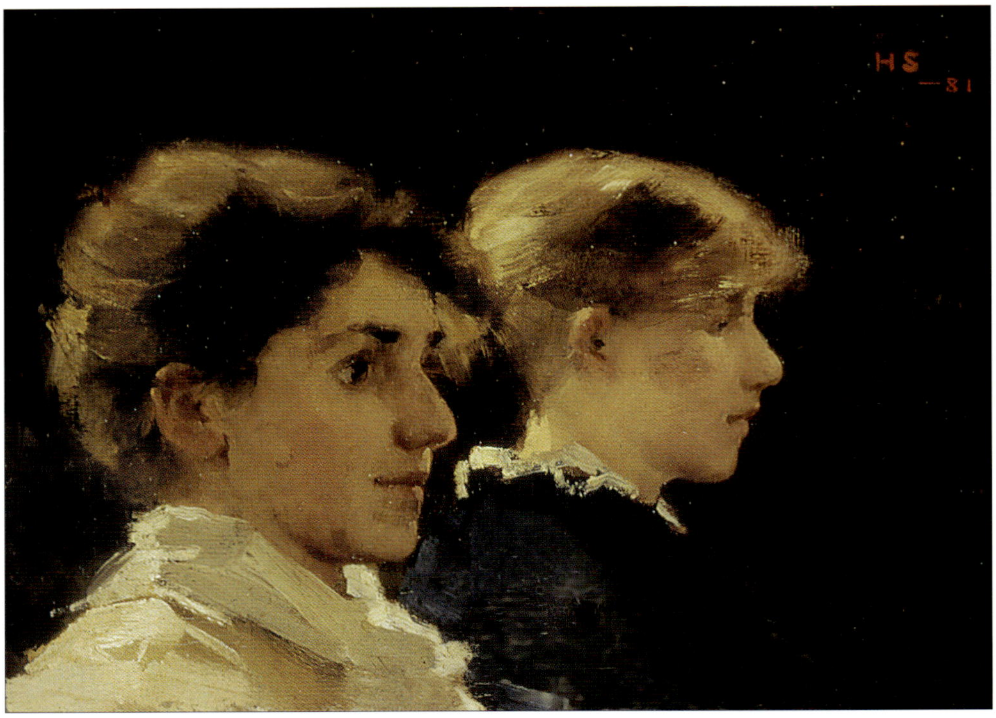

Fig.2.4 Helene Schjerfbeck *Two Heads - Studies from the Colarossi Academy, Paris* (featuring Marianne Preindlsberger and Maria Wiik) (Finnish National Gallery, Helsinki) (photo: Central Art Archives/Hannu Aaltonen)

in Normandy in 1879. She then moved to Colarossi's in 1881, where she became friends with Helene Schjerfbeck. Born in Helsinki, Schjerfbeck (1862-1946) had an accident when aged four that injured her hip and made her lame for the rest of her life. Her childhood years were overshadowed by illness and, to help her pass the time, her father gave her a pencil and paper. Her artistic promise was soon recognised and, when only eleven, she started at the Finnish Art Society's drawing school before continuing her studies at the Adolf von Becker Private Academy in Helsingfors until she was eighteen. With the aid of a travel grant from the Imperial Senate, she set off for Paris in September 1880 and painted initially at the Cluny Museum and then at Trélat's until moving to Colarossi's in January 1881.

Marianne Preindlsberger (1855-1927) was born in Graz, Austria. Her father was a businessman. In 1874, she moved to Munich, where she studied art, principally under Professor W. Lindenschmidt and won a prize with her first painting.[99] However, writing later to Jessie Titcomb, she did not recommend Munich. It might be cheaper than Paris but it was much less good, as well as being cold and unhealthy. It was also impossible in her day for ladies to work from the nude at an art school, and Munich models were very common.[100] For Marianne, her time in Paris was infinitely more rewarding. In an interview in 1891, she commented, "My ambition was to go to Paris and see the Salon. This I did in 1882 and, what is more, on the strength of my own earnings! In Paris, it seemed as if scales fell from my eyes, and I soon understood that Paris is the place, and the only place, to which one must go to see the ABC of art."[101] In fact, Marianne probably first went to Paris in 1880, where she attended both Academie Trélat and Colarossi's, where she was awarded a silver medal in 1882.

Schjerfbeck's portrait of Marianne and Maria, entitled *Two Heads - Studies from the Colarossi Academy, Paris* (Fig. 2.4), was exhibited at the Finnish Art Society exhibition in Helsinki in 1881 and the three friends often visited the Breton art colonies together in the years 1881-5. Another long-term St Ives visitor, the Swede, Emma Lowstadt, who was born in Stockholm, was also a member of their class. Like a number of other Scandinavians, she settled in Grez, where she married the American, Frank Chadwick. Noble Barlow was one of the few male artists later resident in St Ives, who was at this atelier at this juncture, whilst Howard Butler also studied there initially on his arrival in 1885. The Canadians, Mary Bell, May Houghton and Harriet Ford - all subsequent St Ives visitors - were there later in the decade.

2.3 Accommodation and Social Life

Most students were poor and had to live in cheap lodgings. Simmons' apartment in Montmartre was six flights up, with a trap door for a window, and was furnished with two iron cots and very little else. There was no heating

99 In the 1770s, a poor drawing master left his savings, amounting to only a few gulden, to accumulate and be offered as a prize at the end of 100 years to the most promising Styrian art student. The prize was won by Marianne with her first painting, *Muttergluck - Magazine of Art* 1895 at p.18.

100 Letter from Marianne Stokes to Jessie Titcomb dated 20/9/1895.(Titcomb family archive)

101 Article in *Lady's Pictorial*, reprinted in *St Ives Weekly Summary*, 4/4/1891.

and so it was unspeakably cold in winter. As students could not afford to keep up rooms during their painting trips to the country, there were constant moves. A bit of studio space was a luxury that from time to time might be enjoyed.[102] Stanhope Forbes seems to have been particularly lucky to find a "fine large place" with "capital light" at 18 Rue Veron, which he shared with Arthur Hacker. He tells his mother, "The furnishing is going on by degrees. We get something every day and our precious objects now comprise a stove, stools, forms, a filter, a lamp, a tub and curtains of brown paper", an initiative he referred to as "a dodge".[103] The walls were covered with their life drawings from the atelier, but these had to be turned to face the wall when respectable French matrons and their children came to sit for them! Lack of funds often meant that cultural attractions, such as the theatre, were out but, as Simmons commented, "it did not take much to start a party in those days".[104] If his own reminiscences are anything to go by, it did not take much to start a brawl, either! Meals were taken in dingy, smoky cafés and Butler, who teamed up at mealtimes with fellow Americans Arthur Hoeber and Herbert Denman, was quite shocked to find that the beef he thought he had been consuming was, in fact, horsemeat.[105]

2.4 The Paris Salon Exhibitions

For all artists working in France in the early 1880s, the annual exhibition at the Salons de la Société des Artistes Francais in Paris was the highlight of the artistic calendar. Simmons records that the students would congregate at the Palais de l'Industrie and watch the four or five thousand pictures arrive for selection. Most would generate ribald comments, it being "everybody's business to be funny", but occasionally there was a hushed reverence as a work by one of their masters arrived. For advanced students, selection of a work for the exhibition was the ultimate goal and a number of the early settlers in St Ives had works hung at the Salon during their student days. Edward Simmons was the first to make a name for himself, winning a Mention Honorable in 1882, and being hung most years thereafter. Of the British contingent, Alfred Conquest had Pont-Aven scenes accepted in both 1882 and 1883, Dorothy Webb had four Breton works hung in the years 1883-5, and Adrian Stokes was successful in 1883 and 1884. His fiancée, Marianne Preindlsberger, won a Mention Honorable in 1884 for *Condamné at Mort* (the painting now owned by the Walker Art Gallery, Liverpool and called *A Parting*) whilst her friend, Helene Schjerfbeck, was hung in both 1883 and 1884. Eardley Blomefield had a work accepted in 1885 and both Charles Greville Morris and Frank Emanuel were hung in 1886, the year that Howard Butler won a Mention Honorable at the first attempt. However, whether or not one was hung, it was the place to go to review the latest productions of the masters of the day and to determine new trends, new ideas and new subjects.

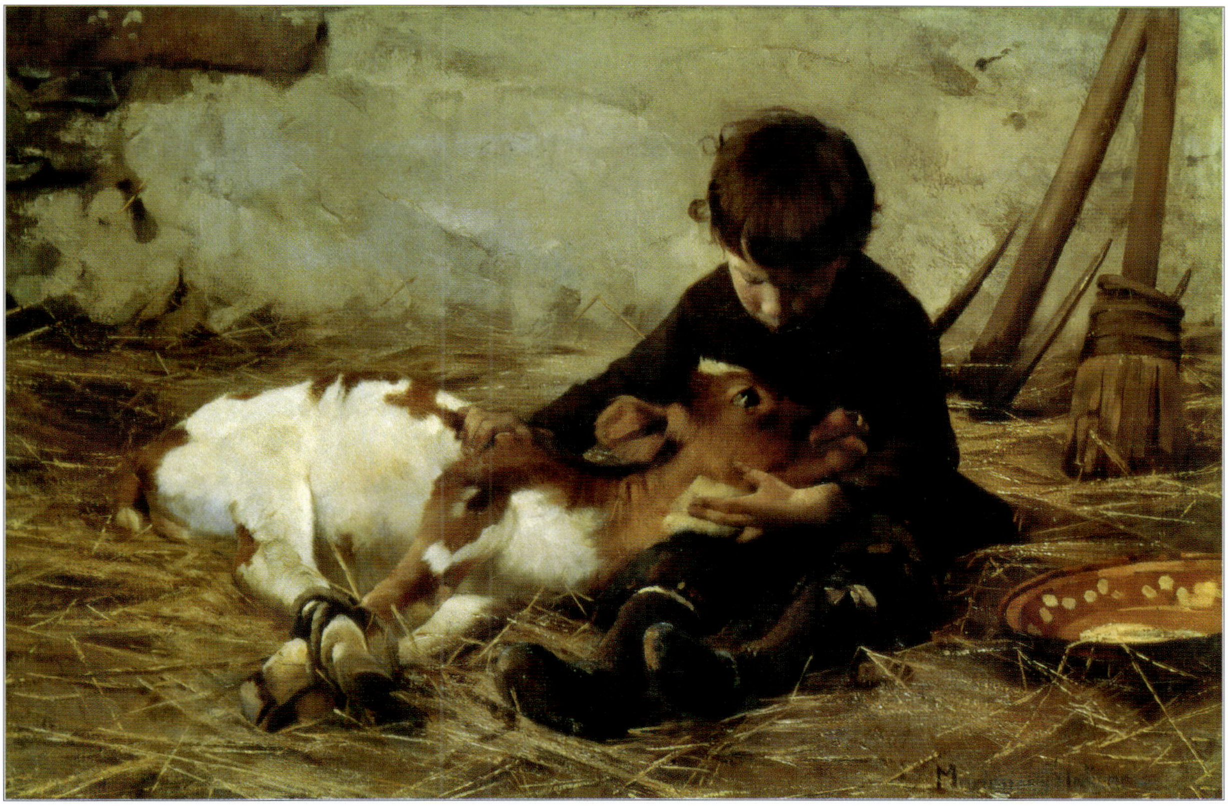

Fig 2.5 Marianne Stokes *A Parting* (The Walker Art Gallery, National Museums, Liverpool)

102 For example, in early 1883, Schjerfbeck and Wiik shared one on rue Vaugirard, whilst Butler was using one on rue Descambes, with views of the fortifications, on his return from Concarneau in 1885 and one on Avenue de Villiers, shortly before leaving for St Ives in 1886.
103 Letter from Forbes to his mother, March 1880, Tate Gallery Archives, 9015.2.1.61.
104 E E Simmons, *From Seven to Seventy*, London, 1922, p.121.
105 H.R.Butler, Unpublished Autobiography, p.135, Archives of American Art, Smithsonian Institution, Washington DC, Howard Russell Butler papers, Reel 93.

2.5 Barbizon

The period during which most of the early settlers in St Ives worked in France was the heyday of *plein air* painting. Artists had been sketching out of doors for many years, but most still tended to execute their major pictures in the studio. It was now felt, however, that studio representations could not hope to capture true colour, light and atmosphere and were in danger of becoming formulaic. To master truth in Nature, an artist had to execute not only his sketches, but also his major exhibition pieces, on the spot. The landscape artists at Barbizon had led the way, trying to imbue their paintings with a vital sense of light and air. Lewis Hind succinctly described their legacy, "They gave to the world a new vision of nature, new because they loved light, atmosphere, tone and ignored Roman ruins and classical compositions."[106] It is not surprising, therefore, that a number of British students felt compelled to visit the colony at Barbizon, even though few of the artists that had made its name were still there. Those that were keen to practice landscape painting found the experience particularly useful, as this subject was not formally taught at English art schools or, for that matter, in the Parisian ateliers. Practice in the open air alongside other devotees was, accordingly, crucial to development.

Edward Simmons, who spent summers at Carrière St. Denis, Grez, Montreuil and Stuttgart, also spent a summer at Barbizon, where he met Middleton Jameson, who visited St Ives quite regularly during the 1890s. Jameson, a Scot, was the brother of the famous Dr Lanner Jameson, a friend and business associate of Cecil Rhodes in South Africa, and was greatly indebted to his sibling for supporting his career. However, it was Alfred East, who worked there in 1882, and Adrian Stokes, who visited with his American friend, William Picknell, who were most deeply influenced by their time there. Indeed, the advice given to Picknell by Charles Daubigny on the treatment of tonal and colour values became the cornerstone of Stokes' own work and, through him, of the whole landscape section in St Ives in the early years of the colony.

2.6 The Cult of Bastien-Lepage

Norman Garstin, the art critic amongst the Newlyn artists, when recalling Paris in the early 1880s, confirmed the overriding interest at that time in out of doors work, "The *plein airists* were then in the ascendant. Millet and Manet with their palettes of revolt, and Lepage with less of a revolt, but with a very clear open air eye. The direct inspiration of nature was the creed of the day, and a feeling of reaction from academic traditions, and studio work, as opposed to work on the spot, activated most of the students".[107] Impressionism, however, was still derided in many quarters, and it was the work of Bastien-Lepage that inspired the majority of the students. Accounts of life in Paris in the early 1880s, whether written by English, Scottish, Scandinavian or American students, are full of references to Bastien-Lepage. To a degree that later art historians find difficult to understand, he inspired hero-worship.

For some years after the initiatives of the Barbizon School, figure painters still found it easier to pose their models in the studio, because the ever-changing lighting conditions outside presented a real problem for a large-scale figure painting which could not be painted swiftly. However, Bastien-Lepage keenly advocated *plein air* painting for figure painters as well, pointing out that truth of tone could not possibly be obtained if one placed a figure painted in the light of the studio into a landscape setting painted out of doors. Nevertheless, the difficulties in painting an exhibition-sized canvas containing figures out of doors proved immense, and artists found that it was preferable to paint on grey days, when moving shadows from the sun were less of a problem.

The influence of Bastien-Lepage on the Newlyn School artists, not only with regard to *plein air* work but also due to his refusal to beautify or idealise his peasant subjects, has been well-documented, but it should be noted that he had an equally important influence on a number of the artists, who later settled in St Ives. Indeed, some record personal meetings with him. His brief presence in the art colonies of Pont-Aven and Concarneau in the last couple of years of his life, tragically cut short by tuberculosis, added much kudos (and many visitors) to those colonies. The Americans, Edward Simmons and Alexander Harrison, were big admirers of his work - Harrison even pleaded with him to be allowed to style himself as his *élève*. Simmons, who called him "one of the most lovable men I ever met, bright, smiling, but with a certain undercurrent of sadness", recalled in his autobiography a typical after dinner exchange during Lepage's time in Concarneau.

> "One day I caught him painting a sketch of the little stone church on the shore at the edge of the town, something we had all tried. He was drawing and painting, with meticulous care, every slate on the roof, each with its little lichen. I brought the subject up, after dinner, when we were sitting on the sidewalk after our coffee.
>
> "M.Bastien" I said (no one ever called him Lepage) "we have all been taught by Lefebvre, Boulanger, Cabanal and Duran to *ébaucher* our subject broadly and put in only the details that are absolutely necessary. I saw you today painting every slate on the roof for its own sake. How about it?"

---

106 Lewis Hind, *Landscape Painting* Volume II, London, 1924, p.51.
107 Norman Garstin, Introduction to Whitechapel Art Gallery Exhibition, Spring 1902.

He laughed. "I have tried all these different methods, but none of them got me what I saw; so now I do everything as truthfully as I am able, then take my picture to Paris, where, in my studio, away from nature, I can consider it broadly and remove all the unnecessary detail."

"Yes" said Harrison, "but when we younger men see your picture in the Salon we do not think you have done what you say you do."

He threw his hands in the air. "Helas! Helas! Sacre Nom de Dieu! Vous avez raison. I am so much in love with it when I see it in my studio that I cannot bear to touch it."[108]

This variation in the level of finish in Lepage's work has tended to make classification of his style difficult, but Howard Butler makes an interesting point. Butler arrived in France shortly after Lepage's death in the winter of 1884 but just in time to see the Memorial Exhibition of his works. He recorded in his diary, "Lepage has been a revelation to me. I shall always be thankful that I came when I did for had I come a week later (when all his works were scattered) I should never have understood him. Some parts of his pictures are carried very far, others barely suggested with large washes of color. The result is that you see at once what the artist wished you to see."[109] Butler, in fact, managed to buy from the sale of his works an oil study of the figure of the dead Christ made for *Mise en Tombeau* - the original of which was bought by Butler's master, Dagnan-Bouveret - and he kept this in his studio for the rest of his life.

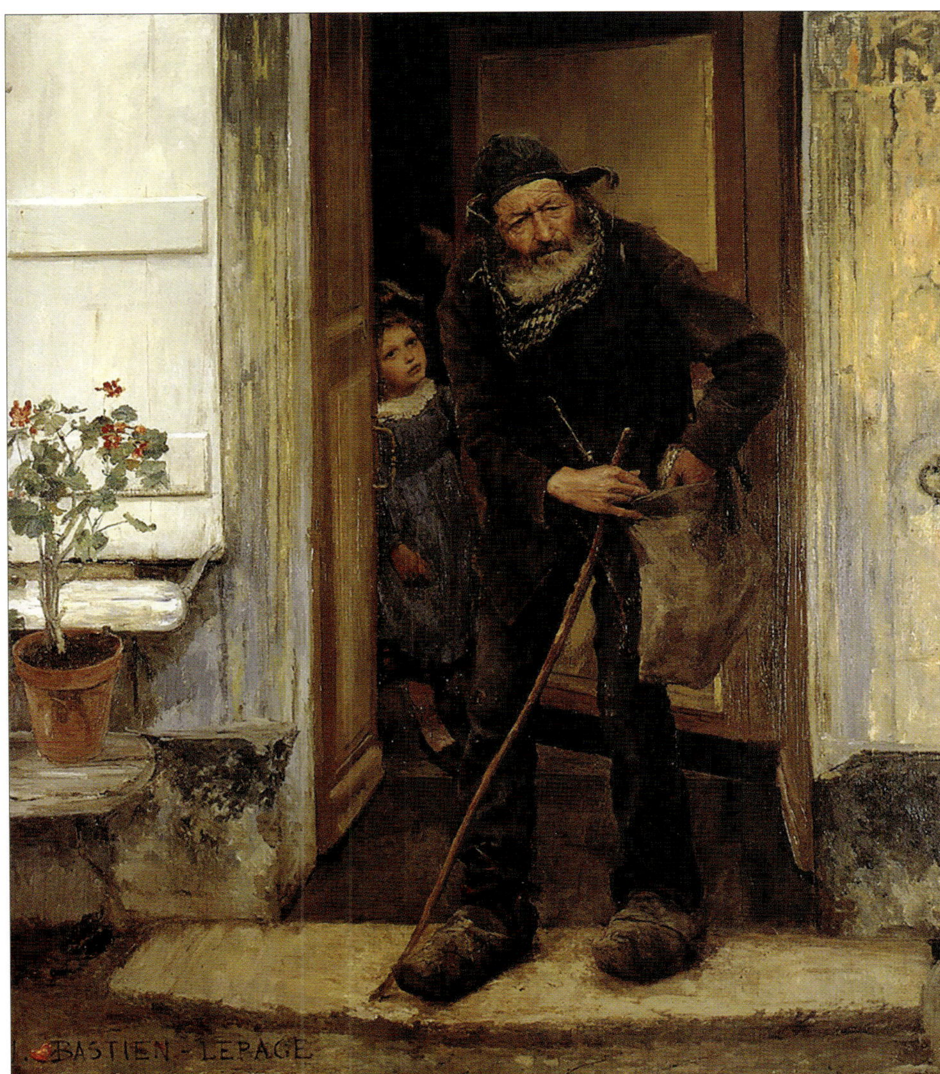

Fig. 2.6 Bastien-Lepage *A Mendicant* (Ole Haupt, Ny Carlsberg Glyptotek, Copenhagen)

John Forbes-Robertson, who considered this work to be the picture of the year in his review of the Paris Salon exhibition of 1881, commented, "Anything with a more open air and naturalistic effect I never saw projected on canvas, and it makes everything around it look conventional and artificial".[110]

108 E E Simmons, *From Seven to Seventy*, London, 1922, p.145-7.
109 Diary Entry for 17/5/1885 - H.R.Butler, Unpublished Autobiography, p.134-5, Archives of American Art, Smithsonian Institution, Washington DC, Howard Russell Butler papers, Reel 93.
110 *Magazine of Art*, 1881 at p.383-4.

2.7 Pont-Aven and Concarneau

Once the Salon exhibition had finished, Paris became deserted. Howard Butler wrote in 1885, "The Salon is over. The medals have been given. A new art fiscal year has begun. Paris has no longer any attraction to the artist. In a week's time, they will nearly all be gone. ...It is under the inspiration of one Salon that the subjects for the next are chosen. Many of the artists go with the intention of spending a whole year ('till the opening of the next Salon) in painting a single picture, all working for the *medaille d'honneur*."[111] For the vast majority of the artists who later chose St Ives as their source of inspiration, the Breton towns of Pont-Aven and Concarneau had been the initial attraction.

Pont-Aven, in Finistère, had attracted artists from the mid-1860s. It was isolated, picturesque and had an attractive river running through it and, importantly, it offered cheap living. It had been initially almost exclusively an American preserve, but Adrian Stokes worked there for the first time in 1876, during which time he struck up a close friendship with the American landscape painter, William Picknell, and an article in the *Magazine of Art* by Henry Blackburn in 1879 brought its attractions to the attention of more British artists. The Hotel des Voyageurs, run by the understanding Mlle Julia Guillou, and the cheaper Pension Gloanec, described by Blackburn as "the true Bohemian home in Pont-Aven", soon acquired legendary status. Several photographs taken in 1880-1881 of groups of artists in front of the Pension Gloanec feature, in a distinctive wide-brimmed, round-topped hat, the Essex-based Englishman, Alfred Conquest, who first visited St Ives in 1884. Between 1880 and 1884, however, Conquest's exhibits at the SBA were all Pont-Aven or Concarneau scenes, suggesting that he was a regular visitor, if not a permanent settler. He was also successful at the Paris Salon in 1882 with *December in Brittany* and, in 1883, with *The Banks of the Aven, Finistère* and his work, albeit neglected now, was then highly regarded, being considered "masterly in execution and sincere in observation of nature".[112]

Another English artist, whom Conquest will have known throughout his time in Brittany, was Melicent Grose, a landscape and figure painter, who exhibited for over forty years and had more than 180 works hung at the SWA.[113] Intriguingly, she may have been born in Truro, whilst her mother may have come from Newlyn, and so she may well have been able to confirm to her colleagues the attractions of the Duchy.[114] She, in fact, probably arrived in Pont-Aven before Conquest, because she exhibited several scenes from Pont-Aven at the 1879 Winter show of

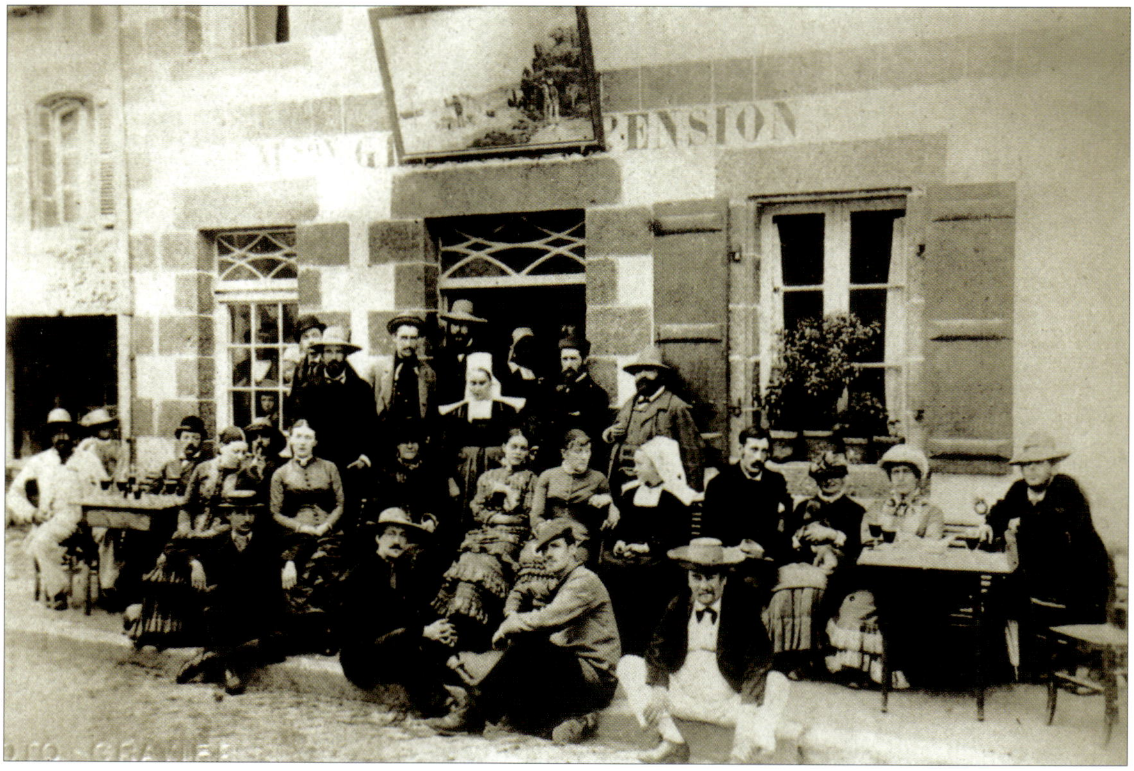

Fig. 2.7 Artists outside Pension Gloanec, Pont-Aven
Alfred Conquest is sitting on the pavement with his hands round his left knee. It is possible that Helene Schjerfbeck and Marianne Preindlsberger are sitting behind him.

111 Letter from H.R.Butler dated 3/7/1885, Archives of American Art, Smithsonian Institution, Washington DC, Howard Russell Butler papers, Reel 1189.
112 See, for example, *Magazine of Art*, 1886, Art in November, Nineteenth Century Society.
113 Despite this, the appearance of her works at auction is rare.
114 The only possibly relevant Melicent Grose that I can find on www.ancestry.com was born in Truro in 1844 and had a mother also called Melicent, who was born in Newlyn in 1807.

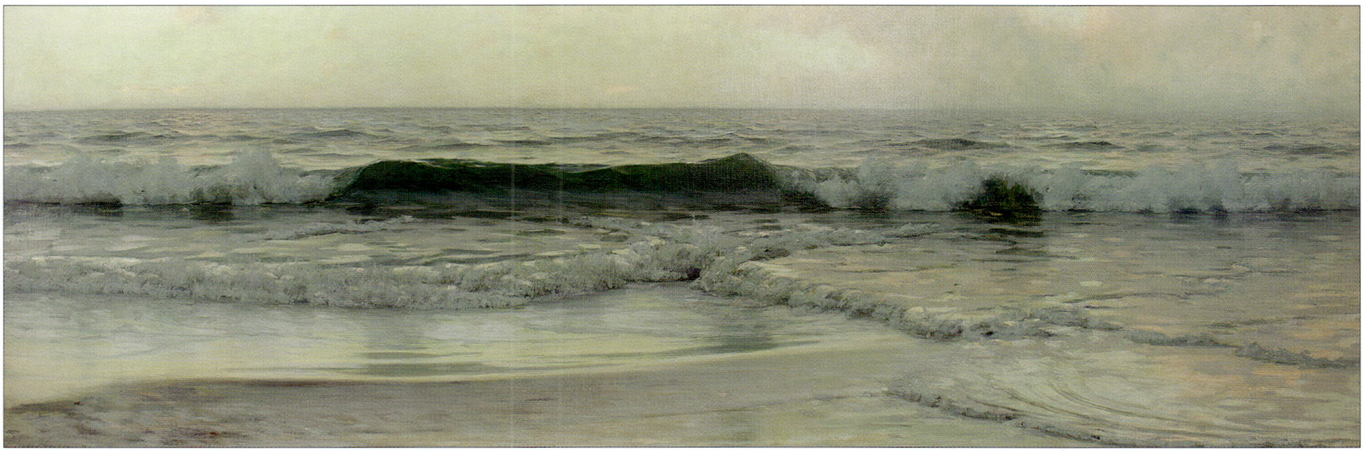

Fig. 2.8 Alexander Harrison *The Wave* (Pennsylvania Academy of the Fine Arts, Philadelphia. Joseph E. Temple Fund)

the SBA, including a depiction of another place to stay in the village, the Hotel du Lion d'Or. She continued to send watercolours of Pont-Aven scenes - such as *"A Watched Pot Never Boils"* and *Embroidering the Wedding Skirt* - on a regular basis to the SBA until 1885, by which time she too had visited St Ives.

Another long-term resident during this period was the Australian-born Mortimer Menpes, one of Whistler's future St Ives companions, who arrived in Pont-Aven with his young wife in 1880, intending to stay three months. They ended up staying three years. The experience, he considered, was a great education, for in such surroundings an artist came into contact with modern movements. Amidst the gathering of geniuses and mere daubers, there were champions of an astonishing variety of different methods of painting - Stripists, Dottists, Spottists, Primitives, members of the Bitumen School and artists who contended that true art could not be produced unless one was physically unhealthy or drunk. Accordingly, Menpes was "free to work at whatever he liked, yet with unlimited chances of widening, by daily argument, his knowledge of technical problems."[115]

In 1882, Menpes, Conquest and Grose will have met the Birmingham artist, Edwin Harris, and the Canadian, Elizabeth Armstrong, who spent some months in Pont-Aven with her mother that year. Both later settled in Newlyn, Armstrong as the wife of Stanhope Forbes, but not before she had spent much of the summers of 1886 and 1887 in St Ives. Armstrong had first come over to England in 1873, when she had undertaken some training at South Kensington, but her most significant period of study had been under William Merritt Chase at the Art Students' League in New York between 1878 and 1881. She was then advised by Chase to study further in Munich, rather than Paris, but this had proved an unrewarding experience, as she found that there was hostility towards 'American' students and restricted opportunities for women. Whilst in Pont-Aven, Armstrong received some lessons in etching from Menpes, which ultimately led to her involvement in Whistler's circle, and she recalled with fondness the long evenings spent discussing art with like-minded souls in the restaurants of the town. Without the support, assistance and praise of her fellow painters, she admitted that she might well have succumbed to "hopeless depression", for "the poor fledgling of the atelier finds himself for the first time face to face with all the problems of choice and arrangement of subject, complicated with all the material difficulties of changing effects, recalcitrant models and of the technique of the material in which he works."[116]

In 1883, there came together, in Pont-Aven, many of the artists who were to form the early group of St Ives settlers. The American, Arthur Hoeber, whose social accomplishments are mentioned as much as his artistic ones, recalled his first summer at Pont-Aven that year.

> "It was an interesting colony we had that year at Pont-Aven. There were nearly a hundred painters - American, English, French, and scattered nationalities, - some already famous, others since arrived at distinction. The brothers Harrison, Alexander and Birge, Walter Gay, Eugene Vail, Frank Penfold, and a host of lesser lights; the Englishmen Stanhope Forbes, Adrian Stokes, Frank Bramley, Mortimer Menpes, and poor Paul Peel, the Canadian, carried off at the threshold of fame and success some years later; among the Frenchmen, Émile Vernier, the landscapist Pelouze, and finally the great Bastien-Lepage, with his inseparable comrade, Charles Bode, the wood-engraver. All were men of sterling ability, interesting, companionable and serious workers. Out of doors, around the small tables after *dejeuner* and over our coffee, what pleasant stories and reminiscences, what sociability and good fellowship!"[117]

---

115 Dorothy Menpes, *Brittany*, London, 1905 at p. 138. The whole chapter on Pont-Aven is well worth reading. Menpes' wife confided in her daughter that the artists were all strange rough and weird - "More like wild beasts they looked than human beings".
116 Judith Cooke, Melissa Hardie and Christiana Payne, *Singing from the Walls : The Life and Art of Elizabeth Forbes*, Bristol, 2000 at p.47.
117 Arthur Hoeber, *A Summer in Brittany*, *The Monthly Illustrator*, vol IV, no 2, 1895, pp. 74-80.

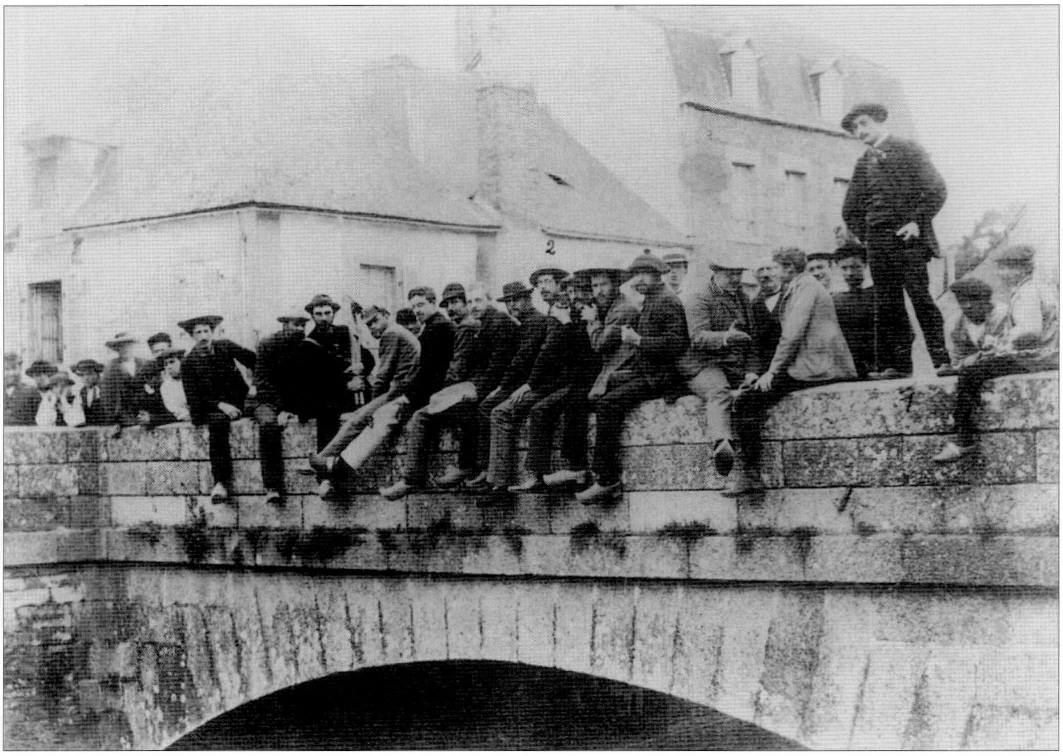

Fig. 2.9 Artists on the Bridge at Pont-Aven 1886
Adrian Stokes is the portly figure with his back to the artist in the tam o'shanter. Other English artists known to be in the town that year are Archibald Hartrick and Greville Morris - possibly the artist standing on the bridge.

The presence of Émile-Louis Vernier, who was to play a key role in the establishment of the art colony in St Ives, is of great interest. Vernier was also in Concarneau that year, as the Musée Quimper own a Concarneau scene dated 1883. However, it seems unlikely that Vernier had already visited St Ives at this point. Nevertheless, from this group, Vernier, Menpes and Alfred Conquest all visited St Ives in 1884, the only common factor between them being their prior presence in Pont-Aven.

The inclusion of Stanhope Forbes in Hoeber's list might appear surprising, given that he only spent a weekend in Pont-Aven in October 1883, but his letters reveal that Hoeber, together with the Bridgwater-born artist, Tom Trythall Rowe, took rooms for several months that autumn at the old Post Office in Quimperlé, where Forbes was based that year, and that he joined them on a number of occasions in the evenings, particularly as they had hired a piano from Lorient, enabling them to put on some musical soirées. In fact, it was Rowe, whose parents were both Cornish and who later exhibited with the St Ives artists at Nottingham, who prompted Forbes' visit to Pont-Aven, where they stayed at the Pension Gloanec on the grounds of economy. Amongst the many artistic acquaintances they met, Forbes singles out in a letter to his mother, Adrian Stokes, who had "just arrived to stay the winter", for they had both met him, most probably in Brittany, the previous year as well.[118]

Female artists are noticeably absent from Hoeber's account but, in addition to Melicent Grose, there were in Pont-Aven that summer the Finn, Helene Schjerfbeck, and the Austrian, Marianne Preindlsberger, who had come down from Paris in July, and they were later joined by their Finnish friend, Maria Wiik. It was during this visit that Marianne's relationship with Adrian Stokes blossomed and they were married the following year. This did not impede her painting, though, as she won an Honourable Mention at the Salon that year. Helene Schjerfbeck also formed an attachment with an English artist during this visit, but he broke off their engagement in 1885, much to her distress. Whilst there, though, she experienced the thrill of Alexander Harrison bringing Bastien-Lepage to her studio to see her work, and her *Funeral in Brittany* was also hung at the Salon in 1884.

The majority of artists who later came to St Ives, therefore, experienced Pont-Aven before the arrival of Gauguin and the other artists now associated with the Pont-Aven School, but a photo taken in 1886 (Fig. 2.9) shows Adrian Stokes sitting on the bridge in the town along with Gauguin, Laval, du Puigaudeau and others. The photo might also feature Greville Morris, from a Salford cotton spinning family, who is known to have lived in the town that year as well. Indeed, it seems that a friendship between Morris and Stokes developed at this time, which was to have important consequences for St Ives art.

---

118 Letter from Forbes to his mother dated 22/10/1883, Tate Gallery Archive, 9015.2.1.175. Forbes' letters also mention his future Newlyn colleague, Blandford Fletcher, who moved between Pont-Aven and Quimperlé that summer.

The huge numbers of artists in Pont-Aven put many painters off and, as the popularity of the colony increased and new motifs became hard to find, artists began to search in the locality for other places to settle. The port of Concarneau proved ideal. Birge Harrison, one of the first artists to switch allegiance, described the town, which his brother dubbed 'Sardineopolis', due to its concentration on the sardine fishing industry.

> "Concarneau is an offshoot of Pont-Aven, but an offshoot that has grown into a formidable rival. It lies about eight miles to the west, in the curve of a great bay. The land slopes gradually away from the shore, the town rising with it, until the streets finally lose themselves in winding *chemins creux*, lined with the pollard oaks which give such a distinctive character to all the Breton landscapes. There is a deep inner harbor, whose mouth is protected by a very ancient citadel still connected with the land by an old drawbridge. Opposite this is the public *place*, beyond which stretches the more modern but still ancient town, with its great rambling usines, or sardine packing establishments. The shore in front of and beyond the town is a mass of magnificent rocks, richly and deeply colored, carpeted with moss and lichens, and broken with quiet reaches of sand."[119]

In weeks when sardine catches were good, the smell all over the town was overpowering, but the catches had dropped off and one enterprising local had converted his sardine factory into studios, prompting Harrison to comment that "many a well-known picture has gone out into the world from this place redolent with the odor of sardines". Early visitors to Concarneau included Helene Schjerfbeck and Marianne Preindlsberger, who painted there between July and September 1881. Helene's *Boy Feeding his Little Sister*, executed on that trip, was, in fact, bought that year by the Imperial Senate in Finland and donated to the Finnish Art Society. However, one of the first foreign artists to settle in Concarneau was Edward Simmons, who was based there between 1881 and 1885, and it was the publication of the novel, *Guenn*, by the American Blanche Willis Howard in 1883, in which the character of the hero, Everett Hamor, was clearly based on Simmons, that made Concarneau an essential stop for American artists. Howard had shared Simmons' Concarneau studio and the novel was accepted by all as an excellent description of the town and its artistic community, and a sympathetic account of the quirks of the locals. In his autobiography, Simmons commented, "The British artists passed by Concarneau and went on to Pont-Aven, where there were ready made landscapes for watercolorists. Truth to tell, they were frightened by the bigness of the coast and left it to the French and the Americans, who formed a very happy crowd, all living at the Hotel des Voyageurs. There was Thaddeus Jones, who has since painted a portrait of the Pope, Alexander Harrison, the famous marine painter; Frank Chadwick; Howard Russell Butler; M Briton; Émile Renouf; Paul Dubois, the sculptor and Bastien-Lepage. Bastien was the first in importance in the Concarneau older set, being almost the father of the Realist movement."[120]

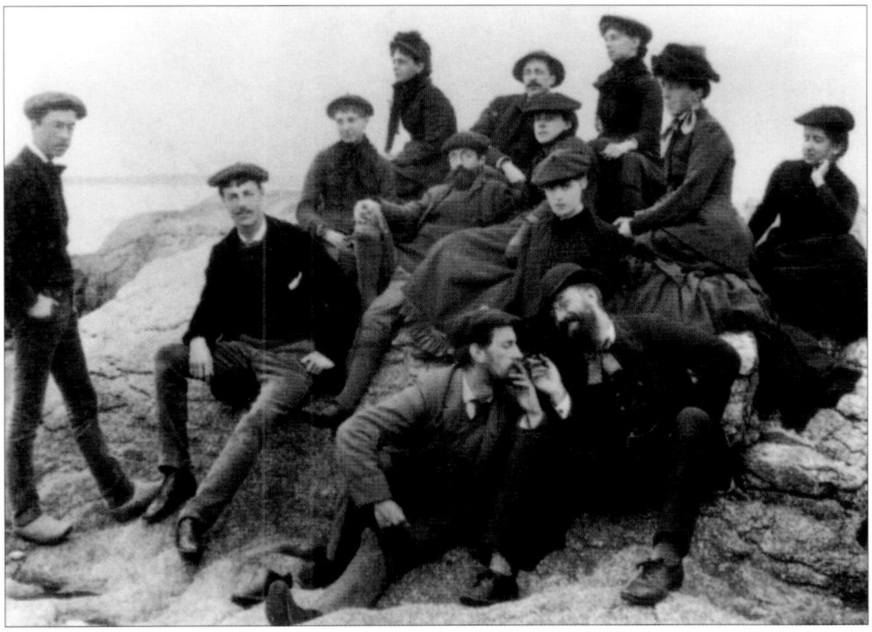

Fig. 2.10 Edward Simmons and Arthur Hoeber at the front of a group of artists on the rocks at Concarneau in 1884 that also includes Vesta Simmons (probably behind Simmons/Hoeber), Harry Robinson (with beard and glasses in centre) and Dorothy Webb (probably second from right)[121] (Faith Andrews Bedford)

119 L Birge Harrison, *Quaint Artistic Haunts in Brittany; Pont-Aven and Concarneau*, *Outing*, vol XXIV, April 1894.

120 E E Simmons, *From Seven to Seventy*, London, 1922, p.145.

121 The full listing given, which is not easy to work out, is "Left to right: Joseph Smith, Frank Benson, Edward Simmons, Arthur Hoeber. Centre: Harry Robinson, Miss Clemons, Vesta Simmons. Top: Ellen Pierson, her mother, Prevost Grayson, Katie Pierson, Dorothy Webb and Mary Trotter." Beacon Hill Art, *American Painters on the French Scene 1874-1914*, New York 1996 at p.36.

Special Feature A

Guenn - A Wave on the Breton Coast by Blanche Willis Howard (London and New York, 1883)

This novel records the inter-reaction between artists and fisherfolk in a Breton fishing village and art colony called Plouvenec - clearly Concarneau. The principal character is a newly arrived artist, Everett Hamor, who is focused solely on his art and the production of his next Salon painting. He spies a particularly good looking fishergirl of great spirit, Guenn, who takes some persuading to sit for him, but, when she finally consents, she falls in love with him. Hamor, who is charming to everyone, does not notice and, when he is called away unexpectedly because the painting featuring Guenn has been a success at the Salon and is attracting some keen interest from a well-known collector, he leaves without saying goodbye to Guenn. Heartbroken, she drowns herself.

Immediately the book was published, it was recognised that the character of Hamor was based on that of Edward Simmons. Like Simmons, Hamor had had a New England childhood; he had been reared exclusively by women and, when he had first gone to College, had been somewhat delicate physically and unusually ignorant of life. His strong but sleeping artistic tendency was half crushed by the weight of family tradition. He determined to toughen up and, like Simmons had done, went out West and roughed it with hunters and guides, studied human nature and found he had a gift for teaching. There, the vastness of Nature persuaded him to pursue a career in art and, in no time, he had set sail for France. One feels from the surprising detail and psychological musings that feature in this section, none of which is of great relevance to the rest of the story, that Howard had been privy to an intimate dissection of his early life by the loquacious Simmons.

Once in Paris, the stimulus of a great atelier, the companionship of eager, ambitious men, the brief, weighty word of criticism from masters and hard work had led Hamor to be singled out as "a strong draughtsman" and an artist whom the experts agreed had "something in him". Now, assessed Howard, as Hamor arrived in Concarneau, his "dominant mental quality was unbounded faith in his own future". He had "the conviction of coming greatness". "He had been heard to make the savage assertion that to reach his goal he would not hesitate to walk over the bodies of babes and virgins". However, despite two successes at the Salon, one of which had gained a mention honorable, "the world at large was unaware of the existence of our American Raphael" and, after a summer in the lovely Fontainebleau Woods, Hamor had decided to "retire to a remote Breton fishing-village, for a season of inexpensive living, improvement in color, outdoor work and inward growth". This all fits with Simmons' own career.

Howard was no less brutal in her assessment of some of Hamor's other characteristics. He might be punctiliously courteous to the lower classes, but this was normally to ensure he could observe some interesting trait that had attracted his artistic eye. In the company of his peers, however, he "was an extremely poor listener, and an inveterate and oblivious interrupter, caring, in general, little for what other people had to say". "He would often chatter volubly, in a sunny, irrelevant, expansive fashion, about topics as indifferent to himself as to his hearers, unconscious that the mental wires were down between him and his surroundings, and regardless of the general devastation." However, if full of scatter-brained theories, he was "a man of principle in matters which he regarded as the real conduct of life". Simmons' loquacity is constantly referred to by his colleagues and drove Stanhope Forbes mad.[122]

Physically, Hamor was described as an attractive man, with a long, lank figure and exceedingly well trained in all kinds of bodily exercise. He had an "easy fashion of wearing his clothes, evidently regarding them as of the least possible importance". A secretive obstinate mouth, changeable eyes, too near together, beneath a narrow and solemn ministerial forehead were offset by a smile that was sunny, kind, and free. Howard concludes "Hamor was then enigmatical, elusive, and not what women call a satisfactory person".

Despite this character assessment, Hamor in fact behaves almost impeccably throughout the novel. At no time does he flirt with Guenn or lead her on, and his inability to say goodbye to her is not his fault. References to Simmons by Butler and Louis Grier, amongst others, speak of him as being the hero of the novel and, if one ignores Chapter 2, which contains these hefty swipes at his character, so he is. Interestingly, Simmons himself barely mentions the novel in his autobiography, although he admits that Howard wrote it in his studio. Perhaps they had a relationship that went awry.

---

122 In a letter to Elizabeth Armstrong in late September 1886, Forbes comments, "Simmons is very much distressed. A mad parson has turned up who talks him out of the field. Mrs Simmons tells us he lost so much time the evening they spent together that he has been hard at it ever since trying to make up." Tate Gallery Archives 9015.2.2.6.

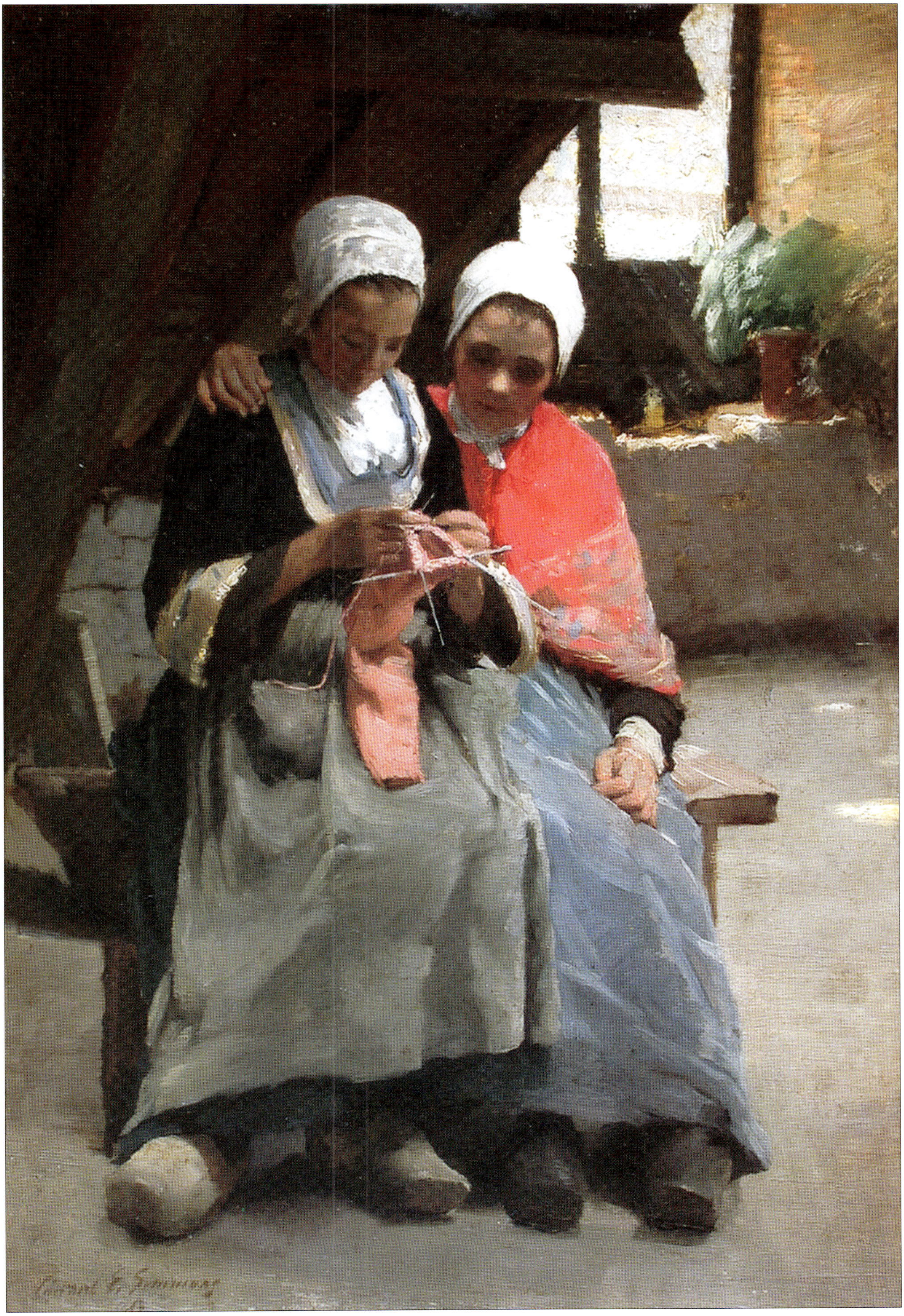

Fig. 2.11 Edward Simmons *Jeanne* (courtesy Fausto Manara)
This features Jeanne Ronan knitting with Louise Nevis, the inspiration for Guenn, in Simmons' Concarneau studio. Hamor is painting Jeanne knitting in his studio when Guenn finally gives in and agrees to become his model.

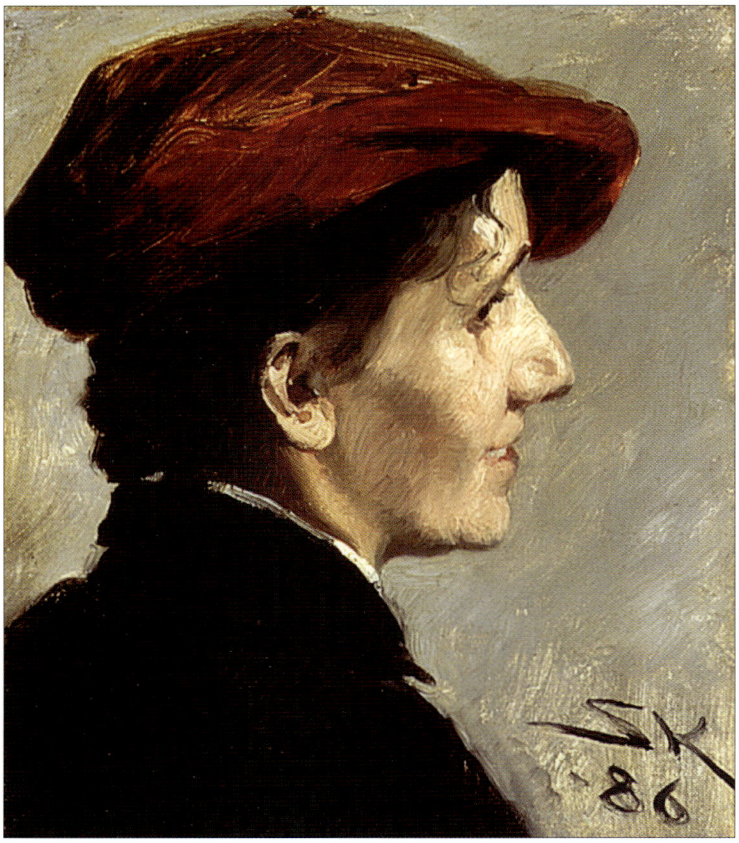

Fig. 2.12 Peder Severin Kroyer *Adrian Stokes* (Skagen Museum)

Not all British artists, however, avoided Concarneau and, in fact, in *Guenn*, Hamor, the character based on Simmons, shares his studio with a long-legged, brown-bearded Scot, called Douglas, and a "strong" English landscape painter, called Staunton, whom Hamor had known from his Paris days and for whom he had a profound respect. Wilfred Meynell, in an article in the *Art Journal* in 1900, confirms that the character of Staunton was based on Adrian Stokes, thus confirming that Stokes and Simmons not only knew each other before meeting in St Ives but had shared a studio.[123] In the novel, Staunton falls for a Danish lady artist working in Pont-Aven and this therefore records the romance of Stokes and his Austrian, rather than Danish, girlfriend and future wife, Marianne Preindlsberger. Echoing Simmons' own views, the artists of Pont-Aven are generally dismissed in the novel as lightweight painters, often watercolourists, requiring ready-made motifs. The women artists there in particular were singled out for opprobrium - "the broader the hat, the narrower the talent, the more expansive the frills, the more limited the diligence."[124] The character based on Marianne was, however, applauded as "a faithful, hard-working artist, wearing a small hat and no lace frills".[125]

Adrian and Marianne Stokes were invited to spend the summer of 1886 at the Danish art colony of Skagen by Kroyer, whom they had met in Pont-Aven. He completed their portraits during their stay, whilst Adrian Stokes painted Helga, the daughter of Danish artist, Michael Ancher. Several works by both Adrian and Marianne done during their time there are owned by the Skagen Museum, whilst Adrian's principal work, *Among the Sandhills, Jutland* was bought by Christchurch Art Gallery, New Zealand. A watercolour, *By the Cattegat*, is owned by Gallery Oldham.

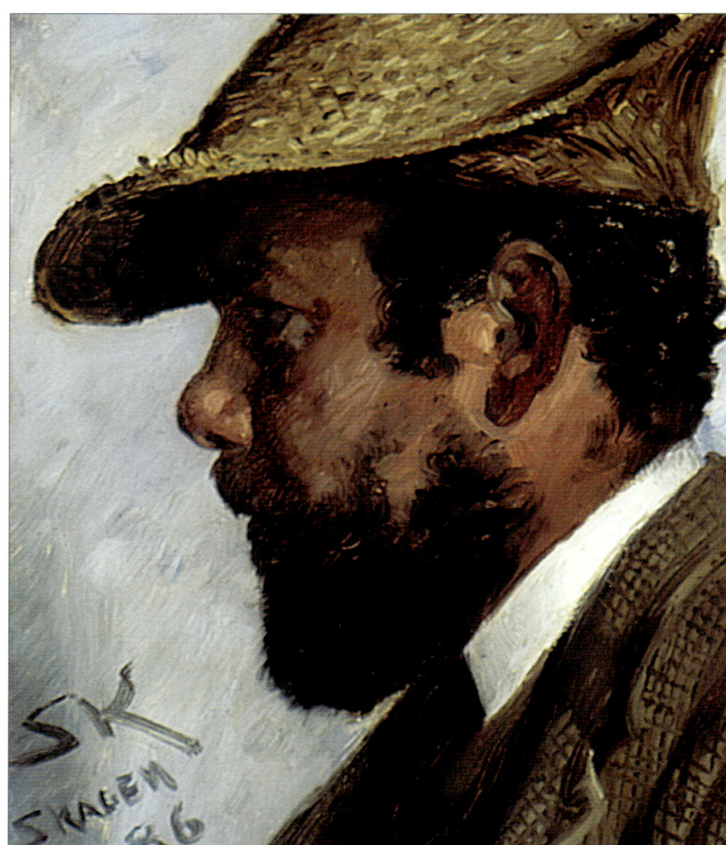

Fig. 2.13 Peder Severin Kroyer *Adrian Stokes* (Skagen Museum)

---

123 W Meynell, *Mr and Mrs Adrian Stokes*, *Art Journal*, July 1900, pp. 193-8. The Scot might be Middleton Jameson.
124 B W Howard, *Guenn,* London and New York, 1883, at p.294.
125 ibid.

Henry Harewood Robinson (1850-1904) and his future wife, Maria Dorothea Webb (c.1850-1920), the first settlers in St Ives, were two other British artists, who settled in Concarneau. Harry Robinson was born in Almondbury in Yorkshire and was the eldest child of a wool merchant, who later turned to farming. He is understood to have trained as a barrister before turning to art. Webb, on the other hand, was an Irish girl, who was born in Northern Ireland, but who had been working in Dublin before she enrolled at the Julian School in 1882, which is where she is likely to have met Robinson. She is often referred to as Maria Webb, but she signed herself Dorothy in her letters and, accordingly, I refer to her throughout this book as Dorothy. Robinson and Webb clearly knew Simmons, for a photograph from 1884 shows Simmons and his wife, Vesta, along with Arthur Hoeber and others, standing with them on the rocks at Concarneau (Fig. 2.10). Webb, in fact, used the Hotel des Voyageurs in Concarneau as an exhibiting address for her SBA exhibits in the winter show of 1883, and they both exhibited a number of Breton scenes in the next few years, with Dorothy being successful repeatedly at the Paris Salon. Her painting *The Net Menders* (Paris 1884, Liverpool 1884, Dublin 1886 and RA 1888), showing an old woman with her grand-daughter in an interior, now hangs in the Merrion Hotel in Dublin and is highly regarded for its depiction of the face and hands of the old crone and of the broken net draped over her green skirt. It seems that during her time in Brittany, Dorothy Webb made friends with the Finn, Maria Wiik, as she presented her with a signed photograph of a painting. A view of Concarneau, in an elongated horizontal format, by Harry Robinson, possibly his 1884 Royal Academy exhibit *Entrance to the Port, Concarneau*, was included in the exhibition *British Painters in Brittany* held at the Musée de Pont-Aven in 2004.

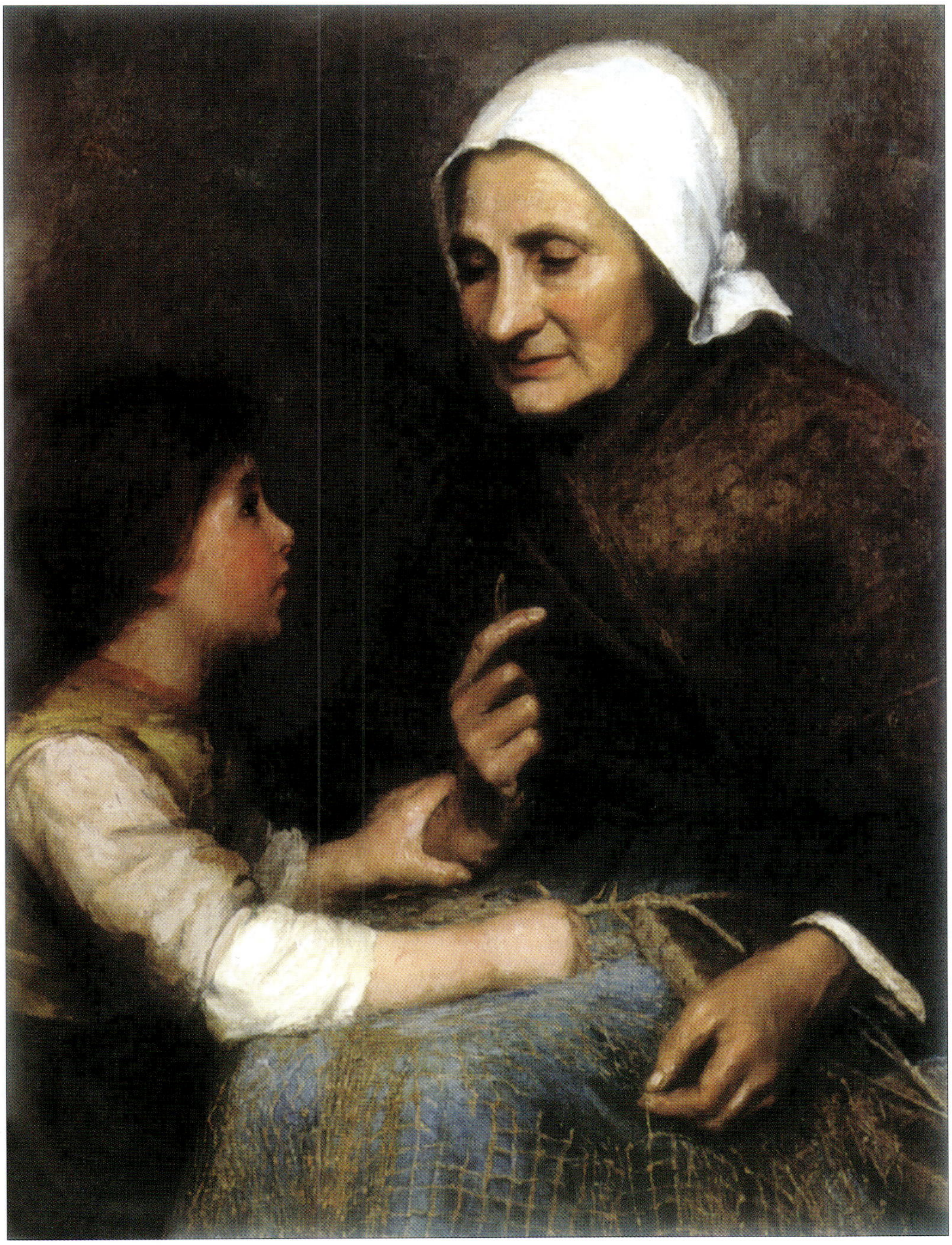

Fig. 2.14 Dorothy Webb *The Net Menders* (Hotel Merrion, Dublin)

Two of the Americans Simmons listed - Frank Chadwick and Howard Butler - were to accompany him to St Ives in 1886, but they were not all in Concarneau at the same time. Chadwick, like Simmons, was from Boston and they will have known each other from their youth, as their times at Harvard overlapped. A man of considerable means, Chadwick had been in Europe for some years, but was felt to lack the talent, if not the application, to be an artist of the first rank. A fine portrait of him by John Singer Sargent executed in the spring of 1880 in Haarlem, when they were part of a group of students who had gone there to study the work of Frans Hals, shows a handsome, blue-eyed and ginger haired man, with an impressive moustache. In 1882, he married the Swedish artist, Emma Lowstadt, and they became based primarily in Grez. However, they spent some time in Concarneau in 1883-4, as Emma exhibited what was hailed as "a great Brittany coast picture" in New York in 1884. This was probably *Off to Sea* (Fig. 2.7), a huge painting measuring 115" x 83.75", which sold for $41,400 at Sotheby's, New York, in November 1998. It is indeed an impressive work. A burly, bearded Breton sailor, sitting astride the bows of his boat, holds his young child aloft, as he bids farewell to his wife, who stands barefoot on the rocks at the water's edge. An elder child is in the boat with his father and will be going off to sea as well.

Butler was in Concarneau the following year. Newly arrived in France, he decided to spend the summer of 1885 in that Breton colony as it included such "strong men" as Edward Simmons, Alexander Harrison, Clifford Grayson, 'Shorty' Lasar, Herbert Denman and Arthur Hoeber. He considered Simmons a "pleasant and talented fellow" but "not over-humble and of an argumentative disposition".[126] Denman and Hoeber he already knew well from Paris and he and Denman found some excellent rooms just outside Concarneau with a Monsieur Gaso, who allowed them to use his photographic atelier as a studio. He commented, "Through July and August I was hard at work in company with Alexander Harrison and Herbert Denman, trying hard to keep my color pure and introducing figures into my landscapes."[127] Harrison, in particular, who had won an Honorable Mention at the Paris Salon that year with

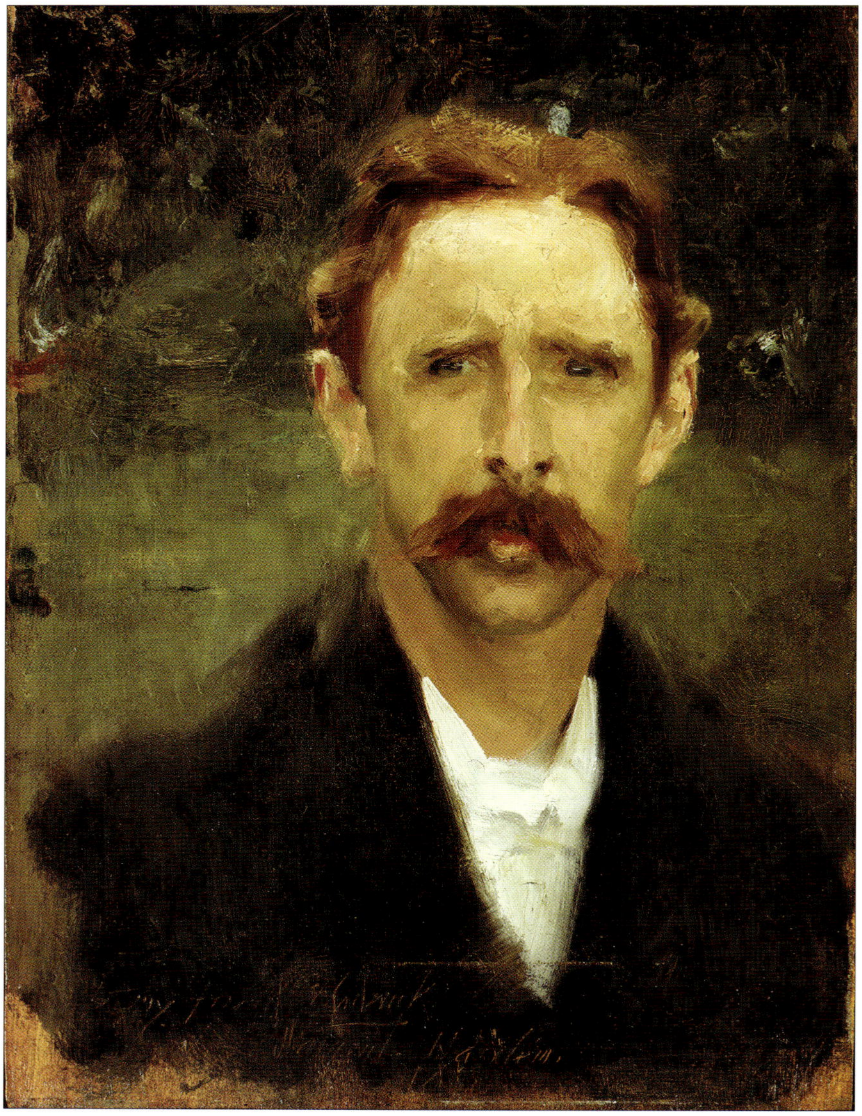

Fig. 2.15 John Singer Sargent
Francis Brooks Chadwick
(Christies Images)
(dated Haarlem 1880
and inscribed
to my friend Chadwick)

126 Letter from H.R.Butler to his father dated 31/8/1885, Archives of American Art, Smithsonian Institution, Washington DC, Howard Russell Butler papers, Reel 1189.

127 H.R.Butler, Unpublished Autobiography, p.143, Archives of American Art, Smithsonian Institution, Washington DC, Howard Russell Butler papers, Reel 93.

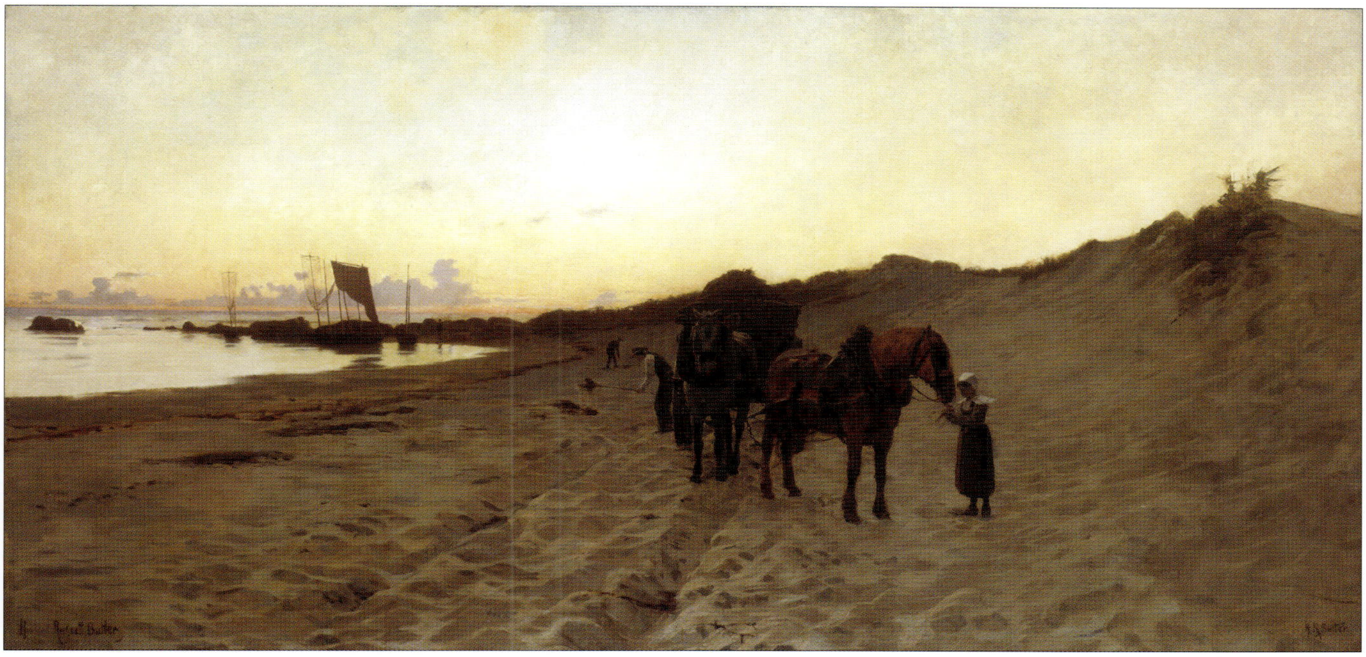

Fig. 2.16 Howard Butler *The Seaweed Gatherers* (Smithsonian American Art Museum, Gift of Howard Russell Butler, Jr.)

his seminal work *The Wave* (Fig. 2.8), a painting that had much impressed Butler when he had seen it at the Salon shortly after his arrival, was a major influence. However, clearly all artists were willing to proffer advice, for Butler commented, "I notice a curiously sensible etiquette among the artists here. One will call on another in the most friendly way and pitch into his work with a vengeance but it is all in the hope that the discovery of some fault may serve to help him."[128]

From the sketches that he did this summer, Butler produced a huge canvas, *The Seaweed Gatherers* (*Le Recolte des Varechs*), which won a Mention Honorable at the Salon in 1886. A little surprised at winning such an accolade so soon, Butler was nevertheless thrilled to be associated with what had been dubbed the "Concarneau School". "Of our party of last summer at Concarneau, Simmons and Groupon have carried off two of the four prizes given in America this year, Harrison has already taken a similar prize last year and an Honourable Mention and Denman and I have received Honourable Mentions. Hoeber must brace up."[129]

Hoeber's artistic career never really took off and he later turned more successfully to art criticism.[130] His account of his first summer in Pont-Aven, although written more than a decade later, captures very well the great attractions that the Breton colonies had for painters.

> "As the summer slipped away and the days became shorter, the sunlight of August and September faded into the gray of autumn, that Brittany gray, the like of which is seen nowhere else in the world - a soft, pearly luminous color, giving qualities of opalescent light to the landscape and enveloping everything in a tender tone of sentiment and poetry, a joy to look at and an inspiration to the painter. Then the artists began to evolve their Salon pictures, and in flannel blouses and straw-lined sabots, for the roads became muddy and damp, and the ordinary shoe of civilisation became of no avail, they could be seen at big canvases, utilizing all the daylight and plodding away. Easels were set up in the fields, on the roadway, and in cottage and garden, while old and young men, women and children were pressed into service as models. So usual a sight was the painter at work, that his arch enemy, the small boy, no longer thought to stop and watch him. ...Studios were improvised by those who could afford no such formal luxury, and garrets and lofts did duty for painting rooms after the rainy weather set in.

---

128 H.R.Butler, Unpublished Autobiography, p.147, Archives of American Art, Smithsonian Institution, Washington DC, Howard Russell Butler papers, Reel 93.

129 Letter from H.R.Butler to his sister, Harriet, dated 6/6/1886, Archives of American Art, Smithsonian Institution, Washington DC, Howard Russell Butler papers, Reel 1189.

130 In November 1885, in response to a letter from his sister, Mary, enquiring about Hoeber's latest work, Butler wrote, "Hoeber is a man to whom I am greatly indebted for many favours and much generous treatment since I have been here. I do not like his work. His pictures are to me *aggregations* rather than compositions and he does not draw well. For color, atmosphere and general value, he is not so bad and these are the only points in which *Pain Quotidien* could be said to excel. But it lacks art - it does not appeal to one in the least." Letter from H.R.Butler to Mary Butler dated 22/11/1885, Archives of American Art, Smithsonian Institution, Washington DC, Howard Russell Butler papers, Reel 1189. On a short return visit to the USA in 1886, Hoeber met and made a poor impression upon Butler's parents. Butler, feeling the need to defend his choice of acquaintance, reiterated Hoeber's qualities as a good friend and enjoyable companion but went on, "You must not look at him as a representative of the class to which I would belong either as an artist or a man...*Entre-nous*, I have very little faith in Hoeber's art prospects, and he is not a representative of the serious student class." Quoted in M Jacobs, *The Good and Simple Life*, Oxford, 1985, p.74.

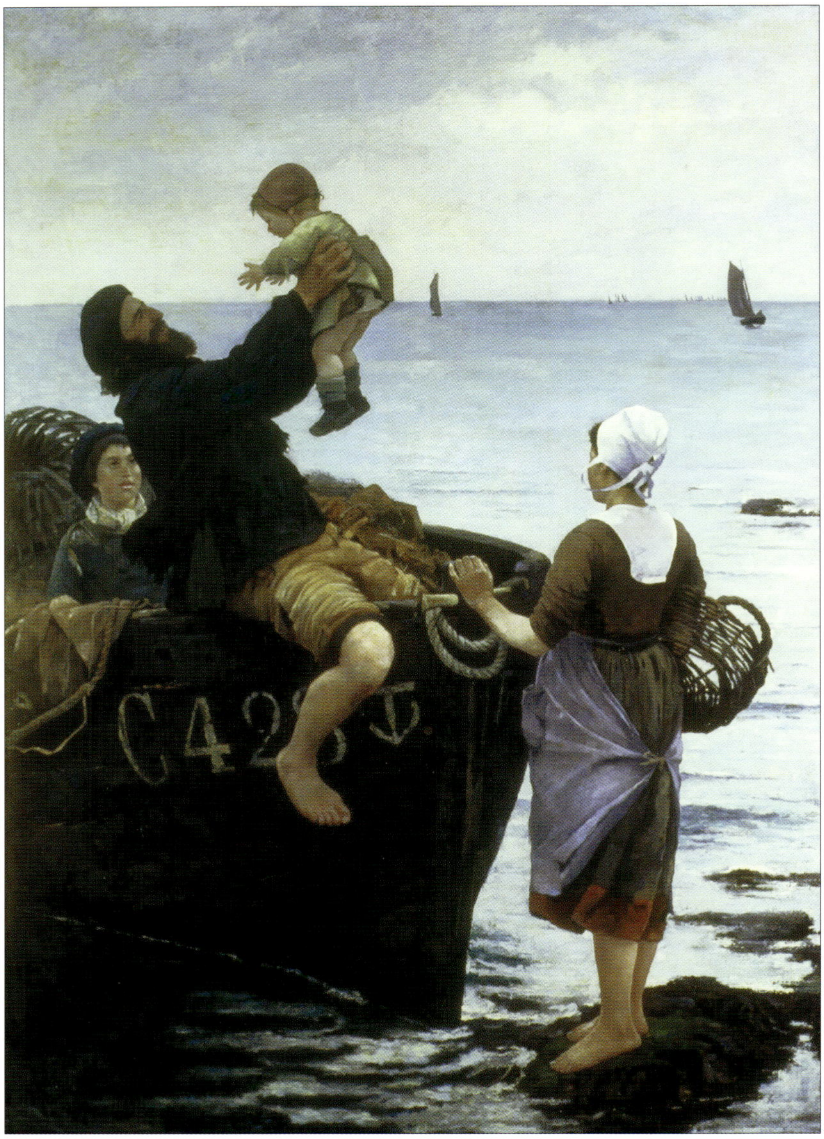

Fig. 2.17 Emma Chadwick *Off to Sea* (Private Collection) (Photo Sotheby's, New York)

> When the night came, the men gathered in the dining room of the hotel, and after the evening meal was disposed of, settled down to quiet talk and exchange of ideas. The walls of the room were covered with panels, painted by the artists who from time to time had sojourned there, many of them characteristic bits; fresh impressions that stood out in bold relief, challenging admiration and interest.....It was a delightful crowd of intellectual men, all animated by the same impulses, serious students of nature, and careless of all the little things of life, but true to their art."[131]

Artists liked the grey Breton days not only for the quality of the light, but also because the presence of the sun meant that the effects they were trying to capture on large canvases were constantly changing. This love of grey days was also an attribute noted about the Newlyn School artists at the outset. However, Howard Butler became frustrated that his brother brushes only seemed to be inspired to paint when the weather was gloomy, and determined to show them "what can be done in sunlight". As a result, sunny spells became known as "Butler weather"![132] Looking back on his Concarneau work the following year, Butler had already become dissatisfied with it. "The scenes there are too grey and colorless for me", he confided in his mother, and one of the first attributes he noted on his arrival in St Ives was that the colour was "exceedingly rich". Nevertheless, for most artists, the Breton colonies provided an attractive place to put into practice the lessons they had learnt in the ateliers in Paris and offered a perfect combination of circumstances -- a special light, a wealth of subjects, willing models, cheap living and agreeable like-minded company. What is more, mastering, alongside others, the unique difficulties of *plein air* painting and exchanging ideas about art and art techniques in relaxed evening sessions may well have played an even more important role in an artist's development than long hours spent before the model in a crowded, noisy, stinking atelier. It was just this same combination of circumstances that the first settlers in St Ives hoped to find.

---

131 Arthur Hoeber, *A Summer in Brittany*, *The Monthly Illustrator*, vol IV, no 2, 1895, pp.74-80.
132 Letters from H.R.Butler to his sister, Mary dated 19/7/1885 and to his sister Hattie dated 2/8/1885, Archives of American Art, Smithsonian Institution, Washington DC, Howard Russell Butler papers, Reel 1189.

~3~

WHISTLER VERSUS VERNIER

3.1 Whistler's Visit and the Dowdeswell Exhibition of 1884

The visit of James McNeill Whistler (1834-1903) and his two pupils, Mortimer Menpes (1860-1938) and Walter Sickert (1860-1942), in December 1883 and January 1884 is normally portrayed as an event of immense significance in the history of St Ives art. This is not only because Whistler is now considered one of the most important and innovative artists of the late nineteenth century, but also because the visit is much better documented than any other. Furthermore, its proximity to the establishment of the colony in 1885 has led it to be given an importance in this regard that a closer analysis suggests that it does not warrant.

Whistler, who had been made bankrupt in 1879 following his libel action against John Ruskin, was, at this juncture, trying to re-establish his reputation. It was a time when, as Menpes admitted, "scarcely a single critic of a single London paper failed to rail and jeer at him and his work".[133] The Fine Art Society, with whom he had exhibited his Venice etchings and pastels of 1880-3, was no longer interested in his work, and he had turned, therefore, to that Society's former employee, Walter Dowdeswell, whose family had set up on their own in 1878. Given the expense of staying in St Ives with his two pupils, the trip was probably funded by Dowdeswell, who had agreed to put on a spring show in 1884. The choice of St Ives was undoubtedly due to Sickert. Menpes has indicated that Sickert had visited St Ives during his brief acting career (1877-1880), but Matthew Sturgis, in his recent comprehensive biography of Sickert, doubts this.[134] However, Sickert and his family did visit St Ives in the late summer of 1883 and met a number of artists, including Alberto Ludovici (Junior), who later arranged for Whistler to be elected to the SBA.[135] According to Menpes, who joined him in December to prepare the way for the arrival of the Master, Sickert had assumed a "jersey and top boots and had completely won over the fishermen, fascinating them with his kindly bonhomie".[136] With the gifts of fish that he received from the fishermen, almost on a daily basis, he then ingratiated himself with the elderly landlady with whom they stayed at 14 Barnoon Terrace, much to the subsequent annoyance of Whistler, who considered these arrangements undermined his position as the Master.[137]

Whistler duly arrived shortly after Christmas. Menpes commented, "Whistler himself loved St Ives. The boats, the sea, the fishermen - all fascinated him. He did not like the country for itself alone: pictorially, trees and farms and pasture lands had no attraction for him. But St Ives he revelled in, and he did much fine work there".[138] Whistler's own letters reveal that he was originally only intending to stay in St Ives for a week or so but he became so enthused by the ocean - "the sea to me, is, and always was, most fascinating"[139] - that he stayed some five weeks. Nevertheless, he soon grew weary of the countryside. He tells his sister-in-law, "For dulness, this place is simply amazing! - nothing but Nature about - and Nature is but a poor creature after all". He also missed the London night life and found the company unstimulating "and artistically often offensive".[140]

Sickert, who had decided to throw in his studies at the Slade under Legros in favour of becoming Whistler's pupil, and the Australian-born Menpes, who had just come back from three years in Brittany, assisted Whistler by preparing his panels, mixing his paints and cleaning his brushes and pochade box. Up at the first light of day, Whistler would rouse his pupils at 6 o'clock and then pace impatiently along the corridor of their lodgings "screaming reproaches, instructions, taunts and commands, all in a breath, at the somnolent followers". However, they also found time to do some work of their own. Menpes tended to accompany Whistler, painting the same subjects as him, but was later dismissive of his efforts and none are known to have survived. Sickert, on the other hand, preferred the company of the fishermen and, according to Menpes, could produce as many as five or six works a day. The few of these that have survived, such as *Clodgy Point* (Hunterian Art Gallery, Glasgow), indicate that, in stark contrast to the sunny, breezy pictures that he had done before Whistler's arrival, he now felt obliged to work in the low-toned style of 'The Master'.[141]

---

133 Mortimer Menpes, *Reminiscences of Whistler*, *The Studio*, 1903, Vol 29, at p.245.

134 M Sturgis, *Walter Sickert - A Life*, London, 2005 at p.114.

135 A Ludovici Jnr, *An Artist's Life in London and Paris*, London, 1926 at p.74.

136 Mortimer Menpes, *Whistler as I Knew Him*, London, 1904, p.139.

137 Menpes records that Whistler was so annoyed with Sickert's hold over the landlady that, on seeing fishermen carrying a huge ray, the size of a dining room table, through the town, Whistler on impulse bought it for half-a-crown. However, after a cursory inspection, he left it to rot on the pavement. *Reminiscences of Whistler*, *The Studio*, 1903, Vol 29 at p.254.

138 Mortimer Menpes, *Whistler as I Knew Him*, London, 1904, p.135.

139 Letter to Ernest George Brown dated 20/1/1884, Glasgow University Library, MS Whistler LB 9/16.

140 Letter to Helen Whistler dated January 1884, Library of Congress, Manuscript Division, Pennell-Whistler Collection, PWC 3/26/1.

141 A drawing of an itinerant field worker, in tam-o'-shanter and 'yorks', inscribed 'Tregurtha' - an area of farm land near St Hilary - is illustrated and discussed by Denys Wilcox in *'A new drawing from Sickert's stay in St Ives 1883-4'*, Burlington Magazine, Vol 138 No 1114, Jan 1996 at p.30.

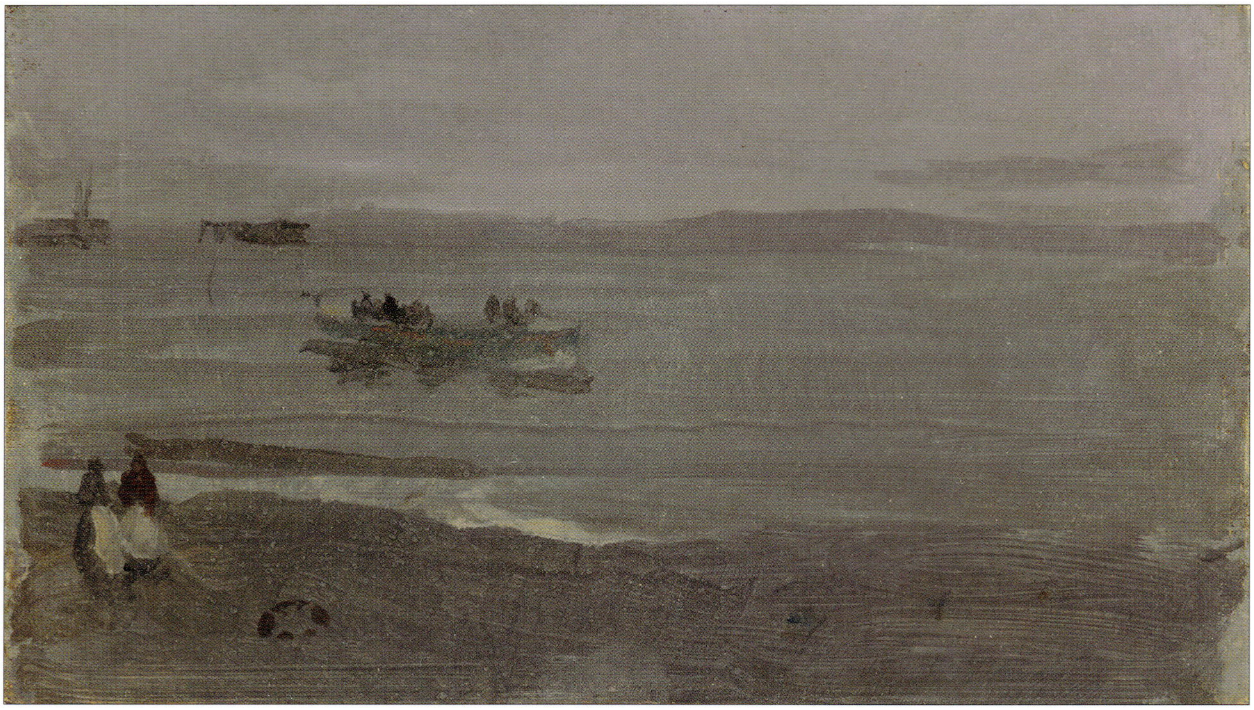

Fig. 3.1 J.M.Whistler *Grey and Silver Mist - Life Boat*
(Freer Gallery of Art, Smithsonian Institution, Washington, D.C., Gift of Charles Lang Freer, F1914.1a-c)

Still with limited resources, Whistler painted mostly in oils on small panels, primed in grey, but he also executed a number of watercolours, a medium that he had rarely used before 1881. He did not paint any of the classic vistas of St Ives or any of the usual scenes witnessed in a fishing port, preferring instead to concentrate on little incidents or effects that would have passed most other artists by. Art, he considered, should be concerned with formal beauty and he decried literary or anecdotal elements in a work. His subjects were principally views of sea and sky seen from the beach, but he also continued his series of close-up depictions of shop-windows, which, with their emphasis on tonal values and geometric design, are considered some of his most innovative work of the period. Most of Whistler's St Ives paintings are small - roughly 5" x 9", with some as tiny as 3.5" x 5.75" - , and his letters constantly emphasize the small scale upon which he is working. He refers to his oils as "little beauties", "little things" and "little games". In fact, he uses the term, "game", more than once. For instance, he tells the American sculptor, Waldo Story, he has been doing "delightful things - and have a wonderful game to play soon".[142] The small size and lack of finish of his Venetian etchings and pastels had been one of most remarked upon aspects of his Fine Art Society shows. If such comments were forthcoming in relation to works in those media, where large-sized works were uncommon, Whistler was already anticipating the furore that would be caused by his small works in oil, a medium in which it was generally accepted that size denoted significance. Indeed, Menpes indicates that the other artists in St Ives at the time found Whistler "a continual source of wonder". " "The man must be idling." they said. "How can one work in earnest sitting on a borrowed chair and with nothing but a small pochade box and a grey-tinted panel? Real hard work necessitates a great canvas and easel, large brushes, and at least a sketching umbrella." "[143]

Sickert, who later fell out with Whistler and who was particularly severe in his criticism of some of Whistler's larger works, nevertheless commented after his death, "I imagine that, with time, it will be seen that Whistler expressed the essence of his talent in his little panels - *pochadas*, it is true, in measurement, but masterpieces of classic painting in importance. ....The relation and keeping of the tone is marvellous in its severe restriction. It is this that is strong painting. No sign of effort, with immense result. He will give you in a space nine inches by four an angry sea, piled up, and running in, as no painter ever did before. The extraordinary beauty and truth of the relative colours, and the exquisite precision of the spaces, have compelled infinity and movement into an architectural formula of eternal beauty. Never was instrument better understood and exploited than Whistler has understood and exploited oil-paint in these panels. He has solved in them a problem that has hitherto been insoluble; to give a result of deliberateness to a work done in a few hours from nature."[144]

About a dozen of the paintings executed by Whistler whilst in St Ives were included in an exhibition of sixty-seven works held at Dowdeswell's in May that year, entitled *"Notes" - "Harmonies" - "Nocturnes"*. Whistler's concern

142 He also boasts to his sister-in-law, "I have such inspirations too! in the way of 'games' for other shows - indeed I am sometimes quite bewildered with my own sparkling invention". Letter to Helen Whistler dated January 1884, Library of Congress, Manuscript Division, Pennell-Whistler Collection, PWC 3/26/1.
143 Mortimer Menpes, *Whistler as I Knew Him*, London, 1904, p.138-9.
144 W. Sickert. *The New 'Life of Whistler'*, *The Fortnightly Review*, December, 1908.

with every minute aspect of an exhibition was both novel and legendary, and the difference in presentation between a Whistler exhibition and any other show of the period was dramatic.. The design of the frames, how the works were cut to fit the frames, the arrangement of the pictures to form a decorative design, the colouring of the walls, the format of the catalogue, and the lettering of the invitations were all matters to which he attended personally. The Private View invitation referred to the 1884 exhibition as an *Arrangement in Flesh Colour and Grey* and the gallery was especially redecorated in these colours. The fireplace was hung with a dove coloured drape, with a flesh coloured chord, and white and grey chairs were introduced. Whistler even demanded that the uniform of the doorman should be grey with flesh-colour facings, so that the colour scheme could overflow a little into Bond Street! He also dropped hints to his lady friends in fashionable circles as to the appropriate colour - *coquelicot* or poppy red - for the ladies to wear. For this show, he designed an unusually wide frame - 5.56" for the 9" x 5" works and 4.375" for the 5" x 3.75" works. The moulding was therefore larger than one dimension of the painting. The same frame was used for works in all media, thus challenging the implicit assumption that oils were more important than watercolours. Although the colour of the gilding was varied to complement the colour harmonies of individual paintings, the use of the same style of frame throughout added a new dimension to the visual impact of the show. Most importantly, works were given their own space, rather than hung in rows with frames touching. The exhibition was, accordingly, not merely about the paintings but was an artwork in itself and the fashionable set in London was invited to participate in the piece. In fact, Kenneth Myers' recent book on this exhibition calls it "the most ideologically purposeful exhibition that Whistler ever mounted" and highlights its considerable significance in the history of art presentation.[145]

TABLE C - JAMES WHISTLER - ST IVES PAINTINGS INCLUDED IN THE 1884 DOWDESWELL EXHIBITION

The Pier - A Grey Note	No.1	Fine Arts Museum of San Francisco
The Angry Sea	No.2	Freer Gallery, Washington D.C.
Grey Mist at Sea (w/c)	No.22	Birmingham Art Gallery
Violet and Silver - The Great Sea	No.33	Freer Gallery, Washington D.C.
The Sea and Sand (probably Sea and Storm - Grey and Green)	No.36	Freer Gallery, Washington D.C.
Cliffs and Breakers (probably The Green Headland)	No.37A	Hunterian Museum, Glasgow
Grey Note - Village Street (probably Little Shop - Grey Note)	No.41	Hunterian Museum, Glasgow
Low Tide (probably Sands, Blue Note)	No.45	Freer Gallery, Washington D.C.
Note in Blue and Opal - The Sun Cloud	No.52	Freer Gallery, Washington D.C.
Grey and Silver Mist - Life Boat	No.54	Freer Gallery, Washington D.C.
Sunrise - Gold and Grey (w/c)	No.55	National Gallery of Ireland
Blue and Grey - Unloading	No.56	Freer Gallery, Washington D.C.

This Table is drawn from Kenneth Myer's excellent book on the exhibition and records his views of which works were executed during Whistler's St Ives visit and what the original titles for certain works should be. The only work listed that is not a St Ives scene but may possibly be a Cornish scene is *Note in Blue and Opal - The Sun Cloud*, an inland depiction of a run of cottages.

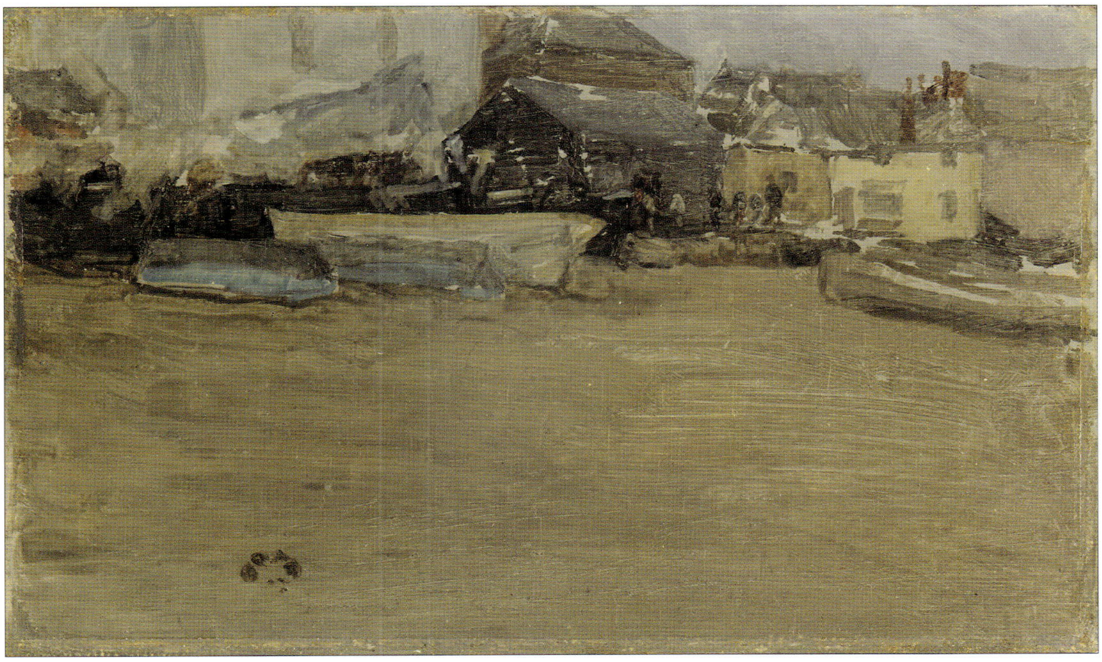

Fig. 3.2 J.M.Whistler *Low Tide* (or *Sands, Blue Note*)
(Freer Gallery of Art, Smithsonian Institution, Washington, D.C., Gift of Charles Lang Freer, F1902.156a-b)

145 Kenneth John Myers, *Mr Whistler's Gallery : Pictures at an 1884 Exhibition*, London 2003 at p.13.

There were, accordingly, many novel features about Whistler's work in St Ives and about the exhibition in which they featured. In his "little game", he challenged a number of long-held assumptions about the importance of size, medium and finish and he championed works principally concerned with tonal effects. His treatment of an exhibition as an art installation in its own right was also revolutionary and one of his most important legacies. These were ideas that were far in advance of their time and it is for this reason that Whistler's stock is held so high by art historians of the modern movement. These facets of his work, however, were not appreciated by many outside his immediate circle at the time and their significance has only become recognised over the years as an important branch of art developed along the lines that he had championed.

Although the Press was by no means friendly, Whistler realised that he could exploit his notoriety. In the catalogue to his 1883 show, Whistler had mockingly quoted various criticisms of his work, making it difficult for such criticisms to be used again. On this occasion, in a section he entitled *L'Envoie*, he listed a number of the aphorisms that were to be included in his famous Ten O'Clock lecture and the meaning of these, and their relevance to the works on show, was hotly debated.[146] Menpes recounts how journalists, who came to Press Day that were hostile, were torn to shreds by Whistler amidst great roars of laughter from his followers, whilst those who showed some sympathy were told precisely what to say in their reviews, Whistler having anticipated all possible criticisms and complaints about the slightness of the works. However, he seems to have made little headway, as, if one reads the reviews of the exhibition, it seems to have been considered at the time to have been a complete disaster.[147] The Private View was admittedly packed, but most people there seemed more interested in viewing Whistler's guests from the theatrical world, such as the actress Mrs Bernard Brere, Henry Irving and Squire Bancroft, than the pictures themselves. Reviews talk of "much irreverent tittering" and of men making "boisterous jokes" about the exhibits, coupled with "noisy brayings that they would not take any of them as a gift".[148] The critic from the *Kensington News*, who had rated Whistler's Venetian work highly, dismissed this "arrangement" as "flat, stale and unpredictable from an artistic point of view". In the main, the works were "little momentary impressions which a more modest artist would keep from the public gaze".[149] The reviewer from *Society* called it "an extraordinary collection of pictile nightmares" whilst the *Sunday Times* commented, "The only fine thing in the whole Gallery is Mr Whistler's footman....whose beautiful appearance outshines any of the strange so-called paintings on the walls".[150]

Certainly, if one turns from the concepts behind the exhibition to the works themselves, particularly the paintings of St Ives, it is hard not to be profoundly disappointed. In truth, a number are rather dull sketches and the watercolours are poor. Whereas, for instance, the low tonal range of *Grey and Silver Mist - Life Boat* does gives it a somewhat unusual ethereal feel, it is far from being one of the master works referred to in Sickert's eulogy about Whistler's small panels. Admittedly, Sickert was writing about Whistler's total output and not merely about the works included in this exhibition but art historians have, not surprisingly, picked up on his reference to Whistler's ability to "give you in a space nine inches by four an angry sea, piled up, and running in, as no painter ever did before" and assumed that Sickert was referring to his St Ives painting *The Angry Sea*. Ironically, this uninspiring painting is singled out in reviews for particular opprobrium; indeed, it was one of three St Ives paintings (the others being *The Pier - A Grey Note* and *Pink and Opal Harbour*) criticised by *The Morning Post* as exhibits that "have no more claim to be accounted pictures than an acorn to be described as an oak, or a heap of bricks a house."[151] Whistler, however, did three similar depictions of sand, sea and sky at St Ives and it is likely that Sickert was, in fact, referring to *Violet and Silver - The Great Sea*, which is, by some distance, the best of the St Ives marine scenes due to an impressive sky, filled with vivid storm clouds.

Some of the most highly rated works in the exhibition were Whistler's depictions of shop fronts, with *An Orange Note : Sweet Shop*, a depiction of a Chelsea shop, receiving the most plaudits. In his book, *Whistler As I Knew Him*, published in 1904, Menpes talks about a painting of a shop in St Ives entitled *The Blue Band*, which Whistler considered "a supremely fine work". He records how, at the dinner at the Arts Club the night before the exhibition opened, Dowdeswell had suggested that this be priced at £40 but how Menpes and others of Whistler's followers had talked the work up throughout the evening, as the drink flowed, so that, in the end, the painting was priced at £120. It is felt that Menpes was referring to a work called *Blue and Orange: The Sweet Shop* (Isabella Stewart Gardner Museum, Boston - Fig. 3.5), which was, in fact, only exhibited at the later 1886 show at Dowdeswell's (priced at £100) and is now in poor condition. However, one St Ives shop front painting was included in the 1884 show. This was *Little Shop : Grey Note* (aka *A Grey Note: Village Street* - Hunterian Art Gallery, Glasgow). The foreground of this dull work puzzled the critic from *The Standard*. "Is the white object a cat, a hen in the first pride of maternity, or a newspaper blown by the winds?".[152] Indeed, not a single one of

146 An example is "To say of a picture, as is often said in its praise, that it shows great and earnest labour, is to say that it is incomplete and unfit for view". A number of critics also debated why 'L'Envoi' had been misspelt.
147 The reviews are collected together on a microfiche at Glasgow University Library - GB 0247 MS Whistler PC.
148 *Society*, 22/5/1884.
149 *Kensington News*, 29/5/1884.
150 *Sunday Times*,28/5/1884.
151 *Messrs Dowdeswell's Gallery*, *Morning Post*, 24/5/1884. *The Academy* and *Kensington News* were also singularly unimpressed with *The Angry Sea*.
152 *Mr Whistler's Gallery*, *Standard*, 20/5/1884.

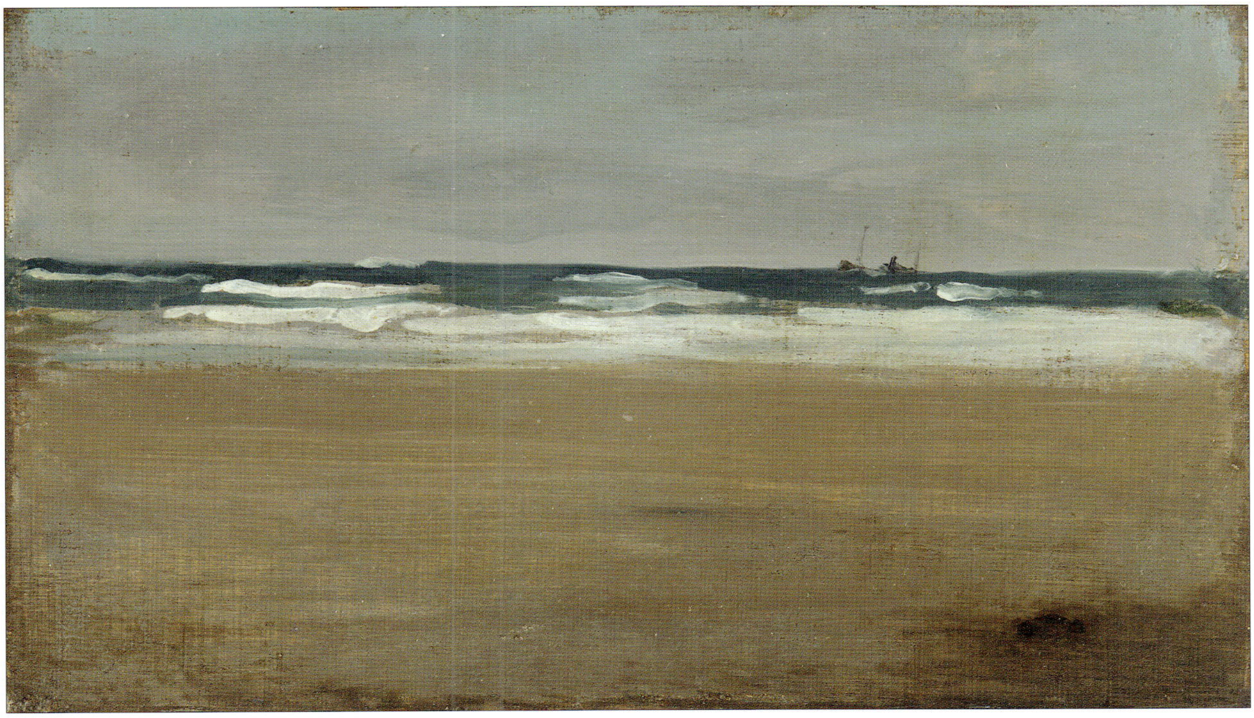

Fig. 3.3 J M Whistler *The Angry Sea*
(Freer Gallery of Art, Smithsonian Institution, Washington, D.C., Gift of Charles Lang Freer, F1904.76a-c)

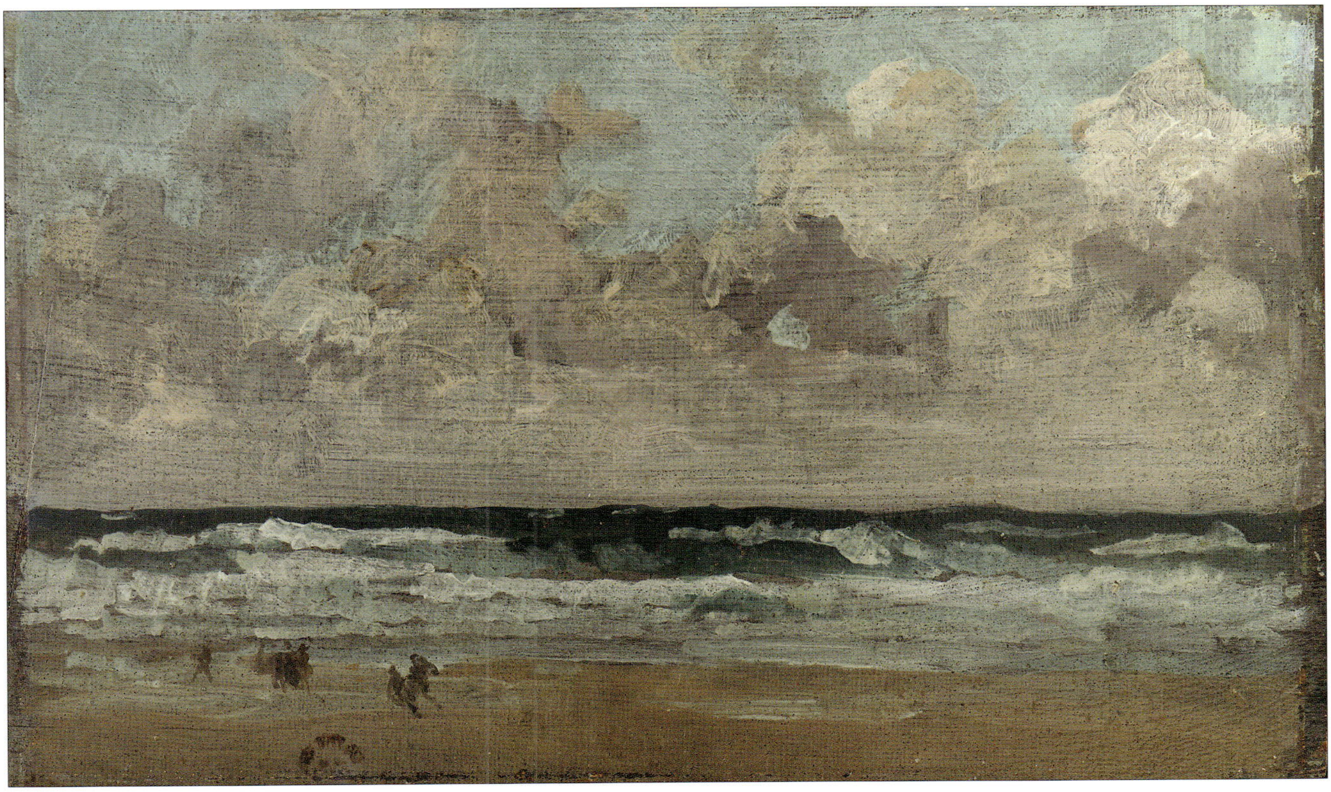

Fig. 3.4 J M Whistler *Violet and Silver - The Great Sea*
(Freer Gallery of Art, Smithsonian Institution, Washington, D.C., Gift of Charles Lang Freer, F1902.148a-b)

the St Ives paintings was singled out for favourable comment. If the exhibition was a failure from the critical standpoint, it was also a failure commercially, as, despite all the expense and publicity, very few works sold during the show.[153]

Whatever importance the 1884 Dowdeswell exhibition may be considered to have in a general art historical context, its importance in relation to St Ives art is a completely separate issue. The proximity of Whistler's visit to the formation of the colony has led historians to assume that either his paintings of the town, the publicity surrounding the exhibition or the mere presence of such a personality in the town led artists to flock to St Ives. However, I can find no evidence to support this. Even those who contend that his St Ives works are important avant-garde paintings cannot dispute the fact that they do not in any way advance the attractions of St Ives. His depictions of sand, sea and sky, or even of shop fronts, could have been of anywhere, as is proved by the disputes that have continued over the past hundred years as to whether works are, or are not, from his St Ives period. Certainly, no artist later came to St Ives because of Whistler's depictions of its scenic attractions.

The Dowdeswell exhibition certainly attracted publicity - there are some forty separate reviews of it - but this will not have impacted on St Ives, for there is no mention of the town in any review. Firstly, the St Ives works formed only a small section of the exhibition, which included paintings executed in Holland, Venice, London, Southend and Purfleet, and, secondly, the words "St Ives" did not appear in any of the paintings' titles. The reviews tended to concentrate on the figure studies included in the show, with only an occasional general comment on his "Cornish" pieces. Individual comments on the St Ives subjects were sparse and, as seen above, when made, were not favourable. The identity of the town depicted, however, was never revealed.

Although Whistler's stock was soon to rise significantly so that by the time of his death in 1903, he was widely proclaimed a genius and one of the nineteenth century's greatest painters, there were many in the mid-1880s, such as Stanhope Forbes, who could not abide the man. The "Whistler Followers", as Menpes termed them, might have been sickeningly sycophantic but they were few in number - never more than a dozen. Many others would have sympathised with the sentiments expressed by his former principal patron, Sir Frederick Leyland, who told him, "The fact is your vanity has completely blinded you to all the usages of civilised life, and your swaggering self-assertion has made you an unbearable nuisance to everyone who comes in contact with you."[154] However, it is only by actually analysing which artists came to settle in St Ives over the next couple of years that one can determine to what extent Whistler played a part (if any) in the colony's formation. Most of these came from Brittany, and so will have missed Whistler's exhibition entirely, and Whistler's overseas trips during this period were confined to Holland. Accordingly, there seems little to connect any of the early settlers, with the possible exception of Edward Simmons, with him. What emerges, in fact, is that his pupil, Mortimer Menpes, may well have played a more important role, but that the real credit lies elsewhere.

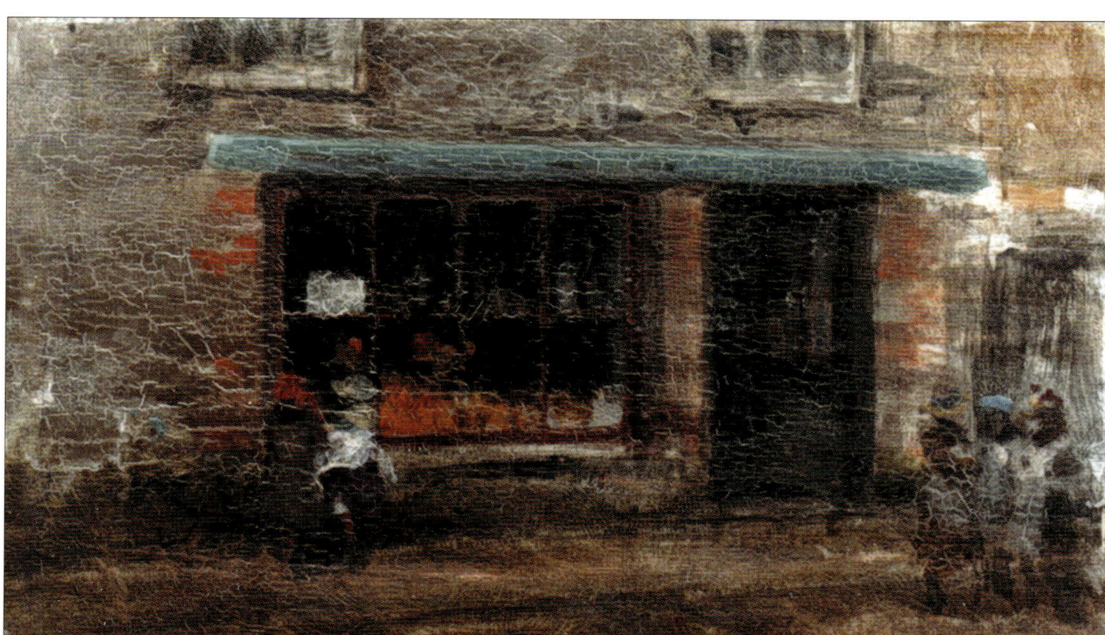

Fig. 3.5 J M Whistler *Blue and Orange: The Sweet Shop* (Isabella Stewart Gardner Museum, Boston)
This is of a shop front on Fore Street.

153 Whistler and Dowdeswell will have been immensely relieved when on 1/7/1885, the London barrister, Sir Henry Stubbs Theobald purchased a large number of works from the 1884 show and these formed the vast majority of the 31 works bought off Theobald by Charles Freer in 1902.
154 Quoted in Frances Spalding, *Whistler*, Oxford 1979 at p.50.

3.2 Émile-Louis Vernier - the artist who was "really the discoverer of St Ives"

The American artist, Howard Russell Butler, in a letter home in August 1887, described the French artist, Émile Vernier (1829-1887), as the person "who was really the discoverer of St Ives".[155] Such a statement, from someone who was intimate friends with some of the most important early settlers in St Ives and who himself spent extended periods in the colony in 1886 and 1887, demands to be given serious consideration and yet, astonishingly, it has been completely ignored by previous historians of the colony. The reason is not difficult to determine as, compared with the visit of Whistler, there are few, if any, sources - and certainly none in the United Kingdom - upon which to base even a speculative reconstruction of Vernier's visits to the town. However, my discovery of a catalogue for a sale of Vernier's paintings held at the Hotel Drouot in Paris on 9th February 1886 gives some base to work from, for of the ninety-four works offered, a truly astonishing number - more than forty - are of St Ives. All were stated to be paintings (tableaux) either on canvas or on wood and so presumably they were all oils. This clearly indicates that Vernier spent a considerable period of time in St Ives in the preceding years, although unfortunately none of the works are dated.

Born in Lons-le-Saulnier, Vernier was a pupil of Colette and worked for the majority of his life as a lithographer. Famous artists whose work he reproduced as lithographs include Corot, Gustave Colin, Jules Joseph Lefebvre, Gustave Courbet and Benjamin Constant. However, in 1872, he took up painting and specialised in coastal landscapes and fishing scenes, working in Brittany, Normandy and Holland. Depictions of the Thames in London were exhibited by Vernier at the Paris Salon in 1884 and in Glasgow in 1885, but an illustration of a view of shipping on the Thames in the Hotel Drouot catalogue is dated 1882, placing Vernier in England several years earlier. Could Vernier perhaps have seen Edwin Ellis' depictions of St Ives at the SBA in 1882? He might even have come down to Cornwall on that visit, as a place such as London was an unusual subject for his brush. Coastal fishing ports were his forté. Nevertheless, it is still not possible to place Vernier definitively in Cornwall until October 1884, for I have found no dated Cornish work and no Cornish exhibits prior to the Paris Salon in 1885 where two Cornish scenes were hung. One of these, entitled *Grande Marée d'Octobre, en Cornwall*, clearly suggests that he was in Cornwall at least by October 1884. The Hotel Drouot catalogue does, however, support the view that he will have come to St Ives on this occasion, and that the scene will have been in the St Ives locality, as there are no other Cornish towns, apart from Hayle, depicted in the works included in that sale.

The sheer quantity of depictions of the town included in the Hotel Drouot sale suggests that Vernier must have spent a good proportion of the years 1884 and 1885 in St Ives, even if he cannot be placed in the town earlier. For him to be labelled the true discoverer of St Ives, however, it is necessary to speculate on how he may have influenced some of the early settlers of the colony to pay the town a visit. There would be two principal ways in which this could happen. Either those artists would have met Vernier and heard his accounts of the plethora of paintable subjects in the town, or they could have seen his work exhibited locally in Brittany or at the Paris Salon. We have already seen, from Arthur Hoeber's account (see p.43), that Vernier was in Pont-Aven in the summer of 1883. He will, therefore, most likely have met Alfred Conquest, a Pont-Aven veteran. A dated work places Conquest in St Ives in 1884, and he was to return to the town frequently over the next decade, renting studios firstly in St Andrew's Street and then on the harbour beach. It is impossible to say, however, whether or not Conquest's first visit resulted from his acquaintance with Vernier. In fact, it is more likely that it was prompted by a friendship with Mortimer Menpes, with whom he would have fraternised much more. The subsequent visit of another Pont-Aven veteran, Melicent Grose, who exhibited a St Ives scene at the SBA in 1885, could, therefore, have been due to a friendship with Conquest, rather than any acquaintance with Vernier or Menpes.

If Vernier's influence on the artists of Pont-Aven is dubious - and it is perhaps worth noting that I have found no reference to any depictions of Pont-Aven by him - , there is a much stronger case for him to have made an impact on the artists of Concarneau, who included Harry Robinson, Dorothy Webb, Frank and Emma Chadwick, Edward Simmons as well, of course, as Howard Butler. In the years 1881-1885, Vernier seems to have paid repeated visits to Concarneau. Musée Quimper have a Concarneau scene dated 1883 and he exhibited depictions of Concarneau at the Paris Salon in 1884 and at Glasgow in 1882 and 1885.[156] There were also thirteen Concarneau scenes in the sale at Hotel Drouot, more than of any other town apart from St Ives. Vernier must, therefore, have met Edward Simmons, one of the principal artists in the Concarneau colony during those years, and there is a very good chance that he will have met the others as well, discussed with them his time in St Ives and showed them some of his Cornish work. Perhaps the key question is whether he influenced Harry Robinson and his fiancée Dorothy Webb to visit St Ives in 1885, for they were the first of the 'Concarneau School' to settle in Cornwall. Whybrow indicates that Robinson came to St Ives because he had seen a painting of the town.[157] Although I have not been able to verify this claim, artists often chose sketching destinations on the basis of other artists' work. Indeed, Butler commented, "It is under the inspiration of one Salon that the subjects for the next

---

155 Letter from H.R.Butler to his mother 20/8/1887. Archives of American Art, Smithsonian Institution, Washington DC, Howard Russell Butler papers, Reel 1189.

156 Other Concarneau scenes are held by the Ateneum, Helsinki and the Museums of Morlaix and Narbonne.

157 M Whybrow, *St Ives 1883-1993 - Portrait of an Art Colony*, Woodbridge, 1994, at p.21.

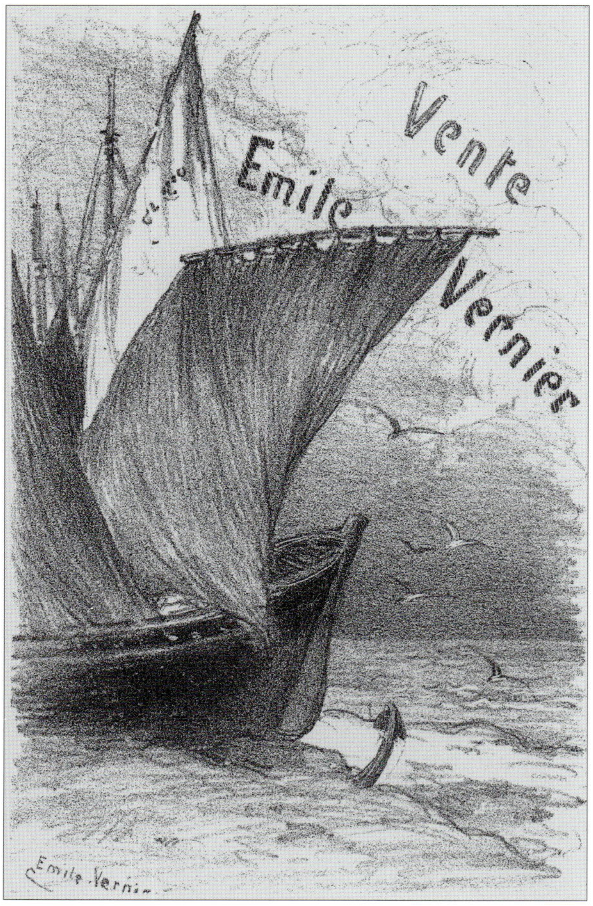

Fig. 3.6 Frontispiece from Hotel Drouot Sale catalogue

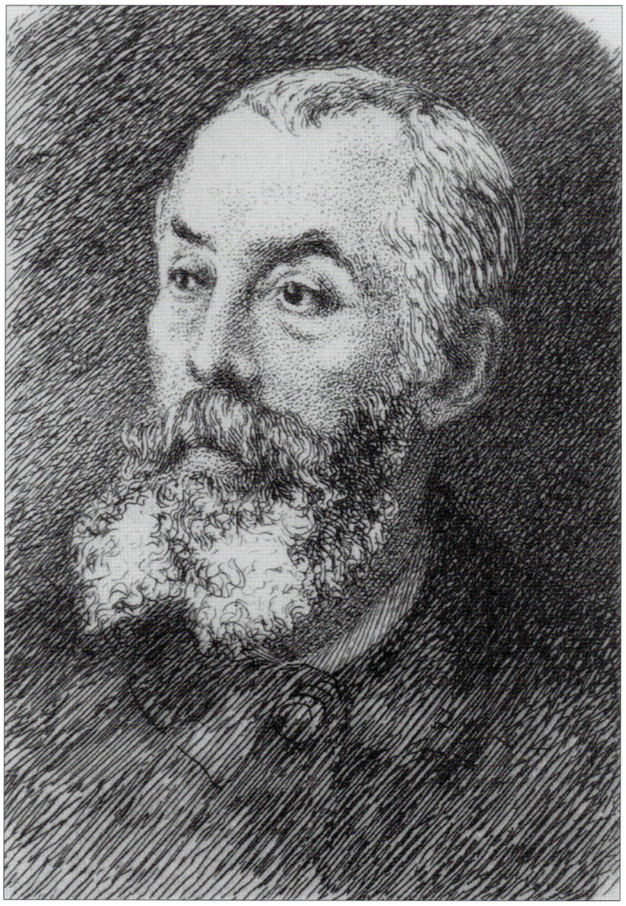

Fig. 3.7 Félix Bracquemond
Émile Vernier, peintre et lithographe

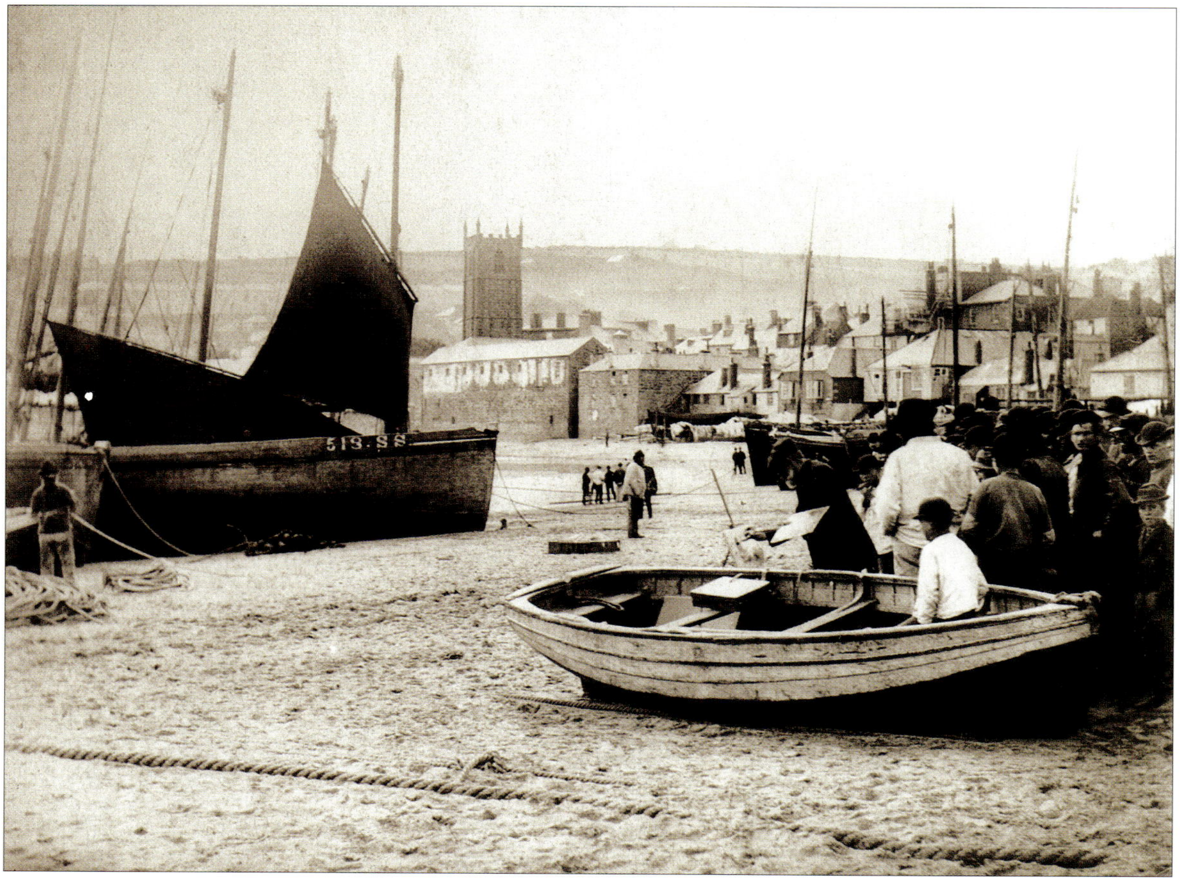

Fig. 3.8 An elderly bearded artist, painting on the harbour beach, attracts a crowd.
Could this possibly be Vernier? (St Ives Museum)

are chosen".[158] If the claim is correct, it is hard to see where in Concarneau or in Paris Robinson could have seen a depiction of St Ives by an artist other than Vernier and, even if Vernier did not take to Concarneau any of his Cornish work, Robinson will surely have seen the two Cornish paintings by Vernier that were hung at the Paris Salon in 1885, for his fiancée was successful at the Salon that year as well.[159] Robinson was certainly an admirer of Vernier's work, as he later referred to him as a "well-known French artist of great talent" [160]

This is all speculation, of course, but given that Butler, who became close friends with Robinson, attributed the discovery of St Ives to Vernier, rather than to Robinson or Simmons, one can fairly safely assume that it was Vernier's depictions of St Ives that persuaded the first settlers to visit the town initially. The subsequent sale of over forty depictions of St Ives at the Hotel Drouot in February 1886 must also surely have had an impact on the plethora of foreign artists who flocked to St Ives in 1886 and 1887.[161] As Table D demonstrates, nearly every aspect of the town was depicted by Vernier - Smeaton's Pier and its lighthouse, the old wooden pier, the church, some old houses and streets, including an old mill, the fishermen's shelters and various scenes in the harbour featuring seine boats and pilchard boats, schooners and coal boats, fishermen mending their nets and fish sales on the beach. He also depicted the town in varied weather conditions - on stormy or misty days as well as fine ones and with the sun rising or setting. Apart from a couple of depictions of Hayle and some local tin and copper mines, he was happy to devote his entire energies to the immediate environs of St Ives, so captivated was he by the scenes around him.

It should also be pointed out that Vernier did not paint exclusively in oils and he is also likely to have done quite a number of watercolour sketches of the town. Indeed, one of these was in the collection of Robert Glanville, the Truro based property agent, who administered Lord Cowley's properties in St Ives. This work, entitled *The Bay of St Ives* (Fig. 3.10), depicts the view across to Godrevy, with the seaward side of the houses of The Warren and the imposing mine engine house of Pednolva Mine on the right hand side. With its rocky promontory, wheeling gulls, distant sailing boats and cloudy skies, through which a shaft of light plays on the waters of the Bay, it is very typical of his low-toned naturalistic style. Vernier himself returned to St Ives in the spring of 1887, when he could have completed further paintings, but he died in Paris on 26th May that year. It is not known whether there was a studio sale of his work but one can imagine that any unsold St Ives paintings at the time of his death

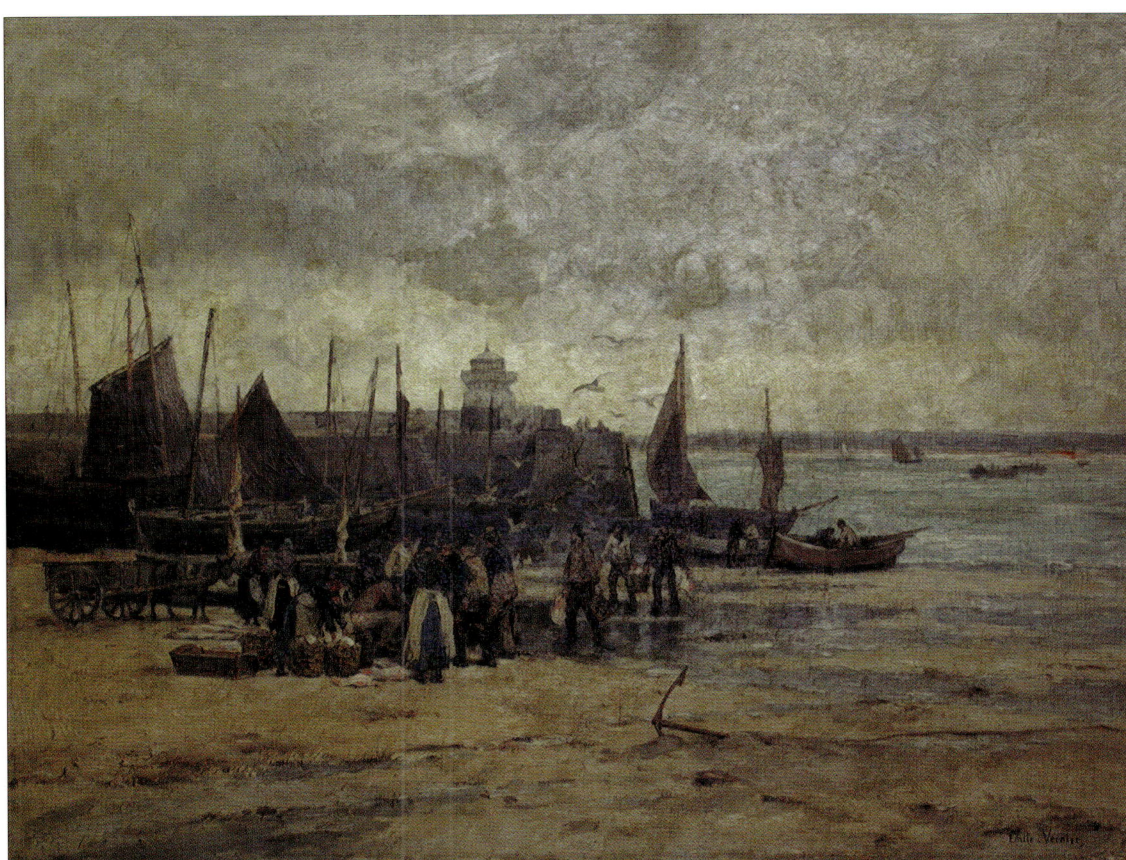

Fig. 3.9 Émile-Louis Vernier *Le Retour de Pêche, Saint Yves* (Musée Arras, Normandy)

158 Letter from H.R.Butler dated 3/7/1885, Archives of American Art, Smithsonian Institution, Washington DC, Howard Russell Butler papers, Reel 1189.
159 I do not believe that Alfred Conquest returned to Brittany after his visit to St Ives and therefore it is unlikely that Robinson will have seen any of his depictions of the town.
160 *St Ives as an Art Colony* in William Badcock's *Historical Sketch of St Ives and District*, St Ives, 1896.
161 The sale realised 25,000 francs - *Magazine of Art*, 1886, Art in March.

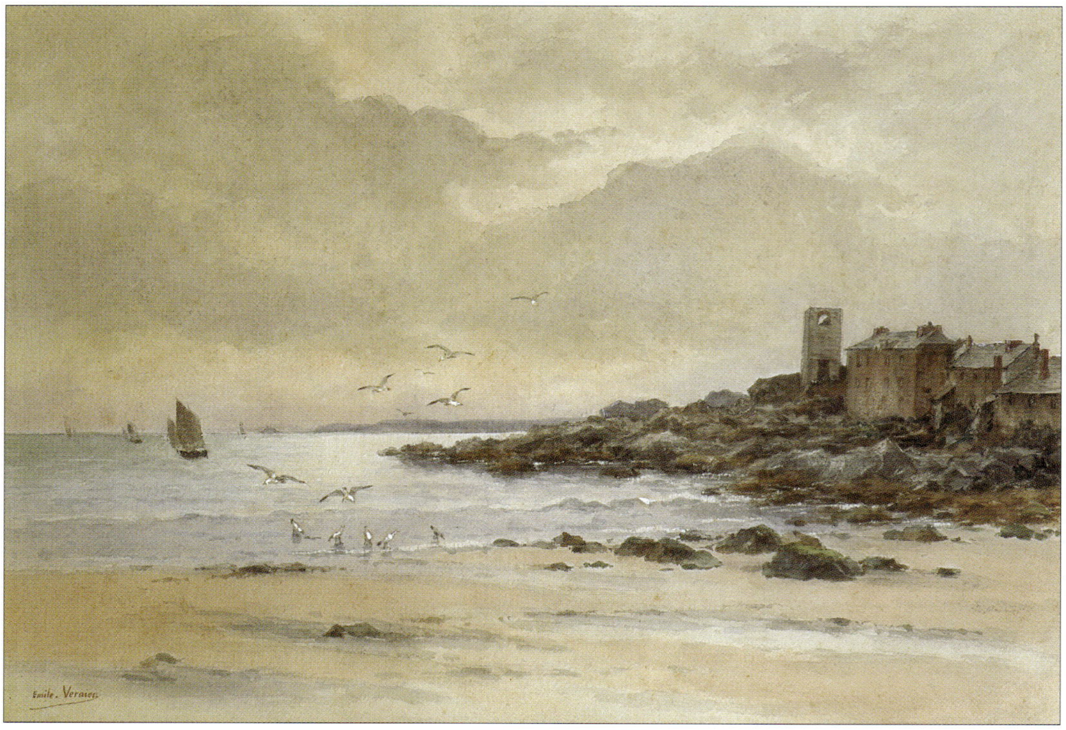

Fig. 3.10 Émile-Louis Vernier *St Ives Bay* (Private Collection)

would have been offered for sale later that year, resulting in additional interest in the colony. It is a little difficult to pass judgement on the quality of Vernier's work, when so few of his St Ives paintings have been located. André Theuriet, in his introduction to the Hotel Drouot catalogue, not unsurprisingly, makes significant claims as to his status as an artist. Vernier, he states "est, par excellence, le peintre préféré de ces amoureux de la mer." He goes on to extol his ability to capture, in whatever location he has chosen, the movement, attitude and physiognomy of those who earn their living from the sea, the particular characteristics of the coastline and the vagaries of the climate. Careful study enabled him able to render spiritually all aspects of the coast - "séveres ou gais, humbles ou grandioses, intimes ou bruyants" - with a simplicity of design, a freshness of touch and a certain "charme du mystère". Certainly, when he exhibited at Tooth's Gallery in 1883, the critic at the *Magazine of Art* was most taken with his work. "M. Émile Vernier has a delightful method and his [exhibit] is full of truth and quiet charm; such faithful, delicate and altogether pleasant work is rarely seen."[162] It has to be said, though, that those St Ives works located so far are a trifle disappointing, but there are some good paintings of other subjects in French and American Museums.

To describe Vernier as the "discoverer" of St Ives is clearly misleading, as many other artists had been advertising its delights for decades. It is not even possible to contend that he was the first foreign artist to discover the town for William Trost Richards had painted it as early as 1878. However, what was unique about St Ives, in comparison with any other art colony of the period in Britain, was the sheer number of foreign artists drawn to its charms. Vernier's paintings may well have acted as the catalyst for this extraordinary phenomenon.

3.3 Other Visitors in 1884-5

There were, of course, other visitors to St Ives in 1884 and 1885, whose presence in the town probably had nothing to do with either Whistler or Vernier, but merely continued the long-term trend of summer sketching trips to Cornish beauty spots. Indeed, the Guide of the town produced by John Hobson Matthews in 1884 is directed, in large part, at the artist visitor. For instance, he commented, "Picturesque as is the aspect of the town of St Ives viewed from a distance, the artist need not fear that closer inspection will be a delusion, particularly if he loves to depict what is quaint in architecture or in character and costume." The quaintness of the town had already "given weeks of work to a considerable number of eminent artists", and he mentioned, in particular, a painting of the picturesque houses in Bunker's Hill by "a well-known artist", that had been much admired. Realising that painters attracted to different genre would be interested in other scenes, he also highlighted that "The Island and Godrevy are the favourite subjects with the landscape painter, and indeed, bid fair to cover, in the course of time, as much canvas as St Michael's Mount itself, but the parish of St Ives is not lacking in other kinds of scenery, besides that in which the sea is a prominent feature."[163] Clearly, artists were already a distinct presence in the town.

162 *Magazine of Art*, 1883, Art in November.
163 John Hobson Matthews, *Guide to St Ives*, 1884.

TABLE D - ÉMILE VERNIER - ST IVES PAINTINGS INCLUDED IN THE SALE AT HOTEL DROUOT ON 9TH FEBRUARY 1886

(Key: T = Tuile (canvas) B = Bois (board) Dimensions in cms)

1. Grande marée d'octobre, [Cornwall] (Salon 1885) (T) (100 x 170)
2. Marée basse, à Concarneau (Salon 1884) (T) (90 x 150)
3. Vue de la Tamise, à Londres (B) (27 x 35)
4. Mine d'étain, en Cornwall (T) (53 x 80)
5. La vieille église de St-Ives (T) (61 x 81)
6. Un Seine-boat, à St-Ives (T) (59 x 73)
7. Les Dunes, à Hayle (Cornwall) (T) (54 x 73)
8. Rochers, à marée basse, St-Ives (T) (70 x 42)
9. Mine de cuivre, en Cornwall (T) (60 x 50)
10. Bateau au rebut, en Cornwall (B) (46 x 70)
11. Le matin, par un temps de brume, à St-Ives (T) (46 x 70)
12. Vielles maisons en Cornwall - soleil couchant (B) (46 x 70)
13. Saloir pour le pilchard, à St-Ives (B) (46 x 70)
14. Bateau en réparation, à St-Ives (T) (45 x 65)
15. La Baie de St-Ives (B) (46 x 70)
16. Vieux bateau, à St-Ives (B) 46 x 70)
17. Déchargement d'un bateau de charbon, à St-Ives (B) (47 x 65)
18. L'arrivée du poisson, à St-Ives (B) (47 x 65)
19. Marchande de poissons, à St-Ives (B) (46 x 70)
20. La vente du poisson, à St-Ives (B) (47 x 65)
21. Rochers au bord de la mer, à St-Ives (B) (41 x 61)
22. Soleil levant, à St-Ives (B) (41 x 61)
23. La Brume, le matin, à St-Ives (B) (41 x 61)
24. L'Estacade, à St-Ives (T) (42 x 70)
25. Maisons de pêcheurs, à St-Ives (B) (41 x 62)
26. Ville et port de St-Ives (B) (41 x 61)
27. Bateau chargeant des pierres (T) (40 x 70)
28. Bateau de pilchards, à St-Ives (B) (41 x 61)
29. Les Mouettes, à St-Ives (B) (41 x 61)
30. Vue de port, le soir, à St-Ives (B) (41 x 61)
31. Le Schooner 'La Clara', à St-Ives (B) (41 x 61)
32. Marée basse, Gros temps, à St-Ives (B) (41 x 61)
33. Le petit port de Hayle (Cornwall) (B) (41 x 61)
34. Abris pour les pêcheurs, en Cornwall (B) (41 x 61)
35. Vieilles maisons, à St-Ives (B) (40 x 27)
36. Rue, à St-Ives (B) (35 x 27)
37. La Jeté en bois, à St-Ives (T) (41 x 61)
38. Pêcheurs de St-Ives préparant leurs filets (T) (33 x 55)
39. Le Quai du port, à St-Ives (B) (35 x 27)
40. Rue, à St-Ives (B) (35 x 27)
41. Un vieux moulin, à St-Ives (B) (27 x 35)
42. Le Phare de St-Ives (B) 27 x 35)
43. Le Port de St-Ives (B) (27 x 35)
44. Pêcheurs embarquant leurs filets (T) (33 x 55)

The other towns featured in works included the sale were Anvers (3), Amsterdam (4), Dordrecht (5), Zaandam (1), Wissant (1), Grand-Camp (7), Cancale (2), Concarneau (12, making 13 in all), Marseille (1), Martigues (1), Villefranche (1), Cannes (6), Menton (1), St-Raphael (2) and Venice (3). Another St Ives subject *Le Retour de Pêche, St-Ives* was exhibited at the Museum of Arras in 1886 and bought for its permanent collection.

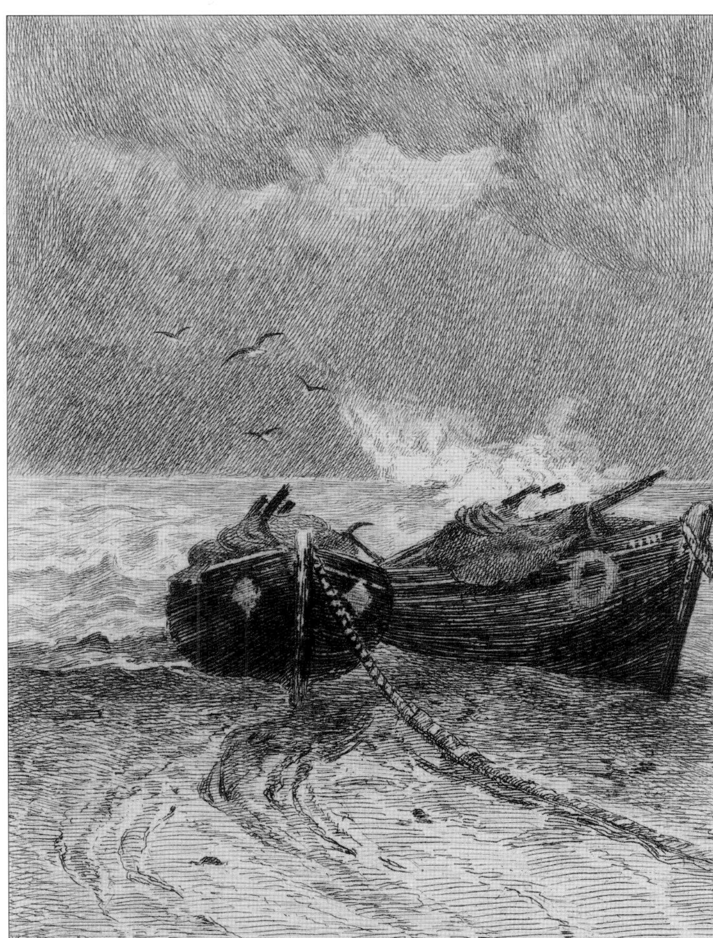

Fig. 3.11 Émile-Louis Vernier *Bateaux, marée basse, Cornwall*
This is one of the illustrations in the Hotel Drouot Sale Catalogue but, as with some other illustrations, its title does not match up to any works included in the sale and it is probably a reproduction of a print issued by Vernier.

The most acclaimed depiction of St Ives in 1884 was not anything produced by Whistler but *Hauling Launces* by William Henry Bartlett, the London-based landscape and marine painter, who had studied under Gérôme and at the Julian School in Paris and painted in the Forest of Fontainebleau in 1879-80.[164] The painting was shown at the Grosvenor Gallery and illustrated in the review of that exhibition in the *Magazine of Art*. Neither the title nor the image nor the review indicate the location of the scene in St Ives but this is made clear by the inclusion of an illustration of the work in a piece written by Bartlett entitled *Summer Time at St Ives, Cornwall*, published in the *Art Journal* in September 1897, in which he also provides a description of this activity.[165] "During the summer months, the launce or sand eel fishing becomes the most familiar sight, it being almost of daily occurrence. After all the necessary preparations have been made in the harbour, the long white boat, containing generally about four men, pulls away for the strand under Tregenna Castle [i.e. Porthminster Beach]. Here, after landing one of the crew, the remainder pull away for about fifty yards from the shore, where the net is cast, and to which the man on the shore has a line attached. Hauling then begins from the boat and from the shore, and the boat gradually draws nearer the shore, until, in about half an hour's pulling, the net bag containing the results of the catch comes into view, and, re-embarking their man, a return is made to the harbour. The whole incident is a picturesque one, and as the main portion of it takes place so close to the shore, one has every opportunity of studying all the varied effects of movement, both of the crew as well of the sea and sky."[166] The painting was hailed in the *Magazine of Art* as Bartlett's finest work to date. "The motionless clouds hang in the calm sky, the sea and the boat with its fishermen glow under the warm sun, and all things suggest a good haul....The life and movement of the sea are capitally suggested, the incident is set forth with vital force and fulness, and the figures are excellent; the men who are engaged in the hauling, and the boy who keeps the stern of the boat off and prevents her drifting ashore, are well contrasted and full of character and truth."[167] The indication by Bartlett that launce fishing was a summer activity suggests that he probably visited the town and painted the work in 1883. His Royal Academy exhibit of 1884, *A Bad Wind for Fish*, which was described by Henry Blackburn in *Academy Notes* as a Cornish coast scene, is also likely to be a St Ives subject.

Louis Grier claimed to have paid his first visit to St Ives in 1884 and the well-known Scottish marine painter, Robert Weir Allan, was in the town that year as well.[168] When noting Allan's success at the Royal Academy in 1892, the local paper referred to him as an ex-St Ives artist, implying that his stay was more than just a cursory visit, and he is referred to as "an old frequenter" in an account of the colony written in 1896, but I have not been

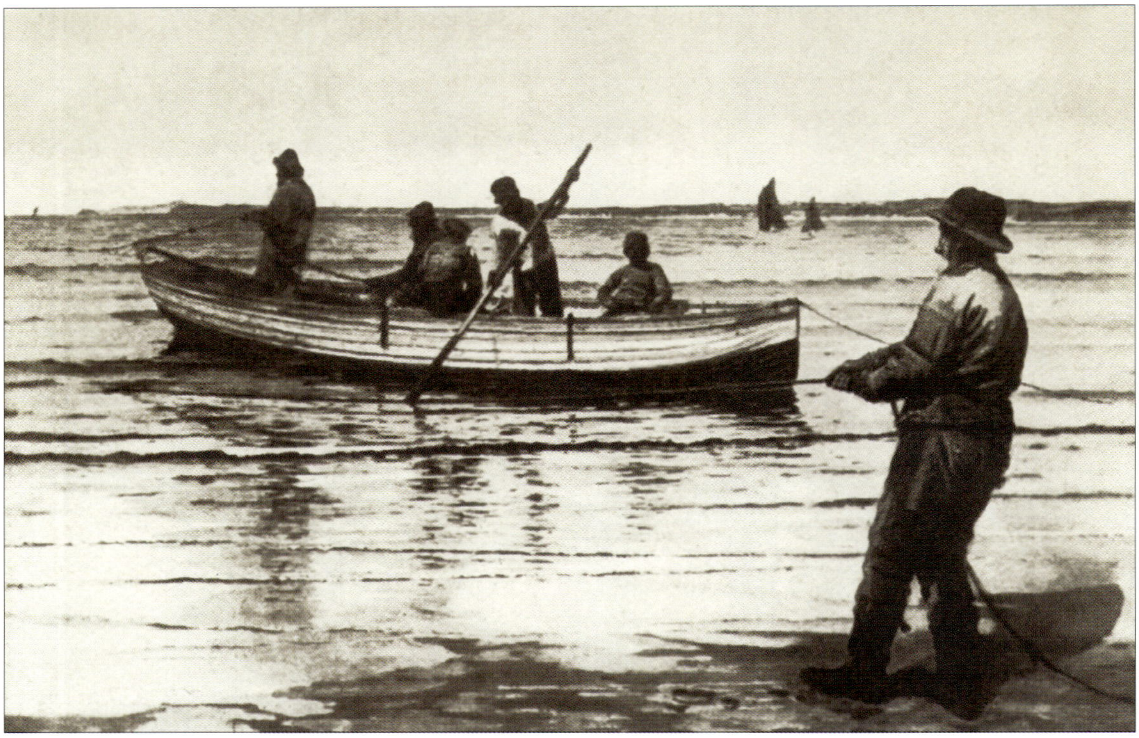

Fig. 3.12 William Henry Bartlett *Hauling Launces* (*Magazine of Art* 1884)

164 His exhibit at the SBA in 1881-2 was *A School of Painting under the direction of M M Bougereau and Tony Robert Fleury during a rest of the Model.*
165 Despite James Clarke Hook having exhibited *Hauling Sand-Launces* at the RA that year - a scene set in Gorran's Haven - , this activity was clearly unknown in London circles as the Grosvenor Gallery indicated the title of Bartlett's painting was *Hauling Cants* and the *Magazine of Art* suggested that the catch was a great influx of "mackerel or whiting or some smaller fry"!
166 W.H.Bartlett, *Summer Time at St Ives, Cornwall*, *Art Journal* September 1897 at p.293.
167 *Magazine of Art*, 1884, at p.446.
168 This is confirmed by a dated watercolour - McTear's, Skypark, 8 Elliot Place, Glasgow - sale dated 25/04/03 Lot 317.

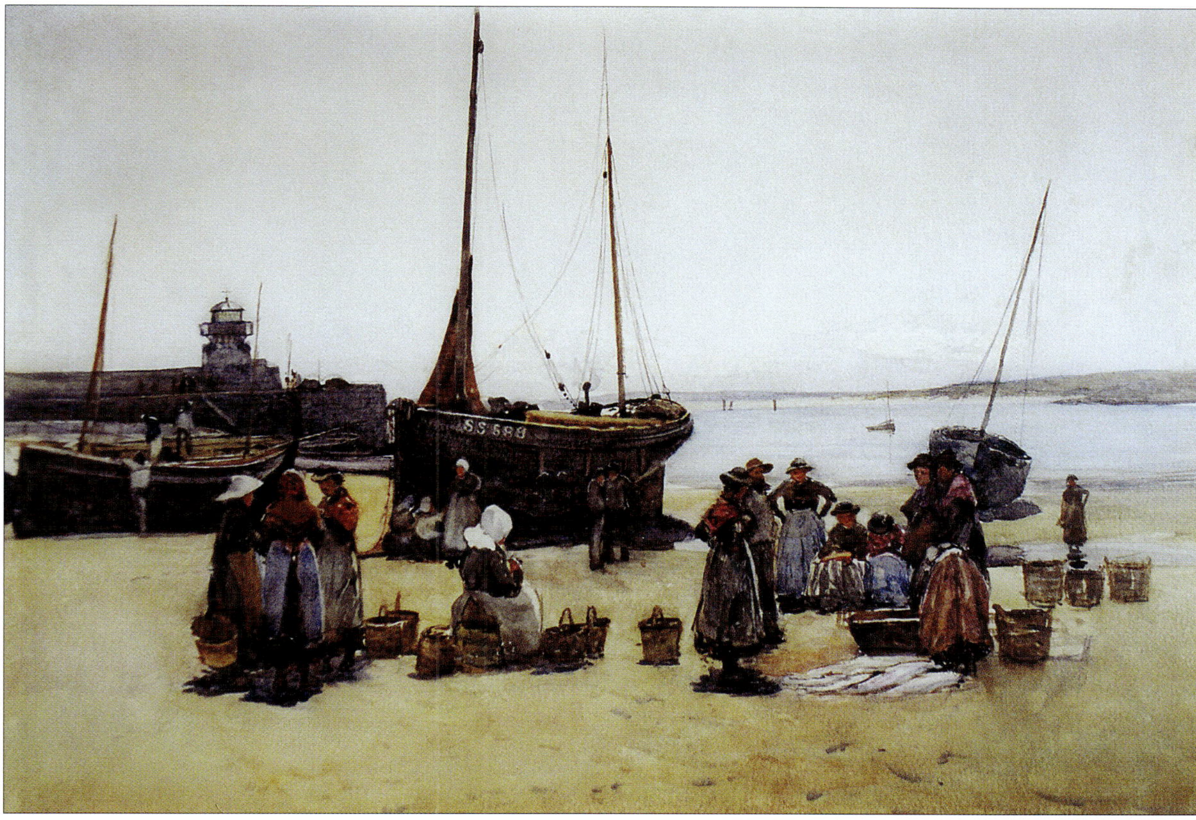

Fig. 3.13 Robert Weir Allan *Sorting the Catch, St Ives* (W H Lane & Son)

TABLE E - SOME DEPICTIONS OF ST IVES EXECUTED OR EXHIBITED IN 1884-5

Year	Artist	Location	Title	Venue
1884	Mrs Val Bromley	London	Bunker's Hill, St Ives	RBSA (S)
	Richard Harry Carter	Truro	A Wild Shore near St Ives Head	Penzance
	Richard Harry Carter	Truro	Dead Low Water, St Ives	Penzance
	James Clarkson Uren	Penzance	Seine Fishing, St Ives	Penzance
	William Henry Bartlett	London	Hauling Launces	Grosvenor Gallery
	Agnes Gardner King	London	A Sunny Evening, St Ives	BAPFA (A)
	Robert W Allan	London	St Ives	Dated Work
	Alfred Conquest	Woodford	On the Quay, St Ives	Dated Work
	James Whistler	London	various - see Table C	Dowdeswells
	Walter Sickert	London	Clodgy Point	Hunterian, Glasgow
	Émile Vernier	Paris	various - see Table D	Hotel Drouot sale

Louis Grier and Ayerst Ingram are also known to have painted in St Ives this year.

Year	Artist	Location	Title	Venue
1885	Émile Vernier	Paris	Grande marée d'Octobre, Cornwall Le matin, en Cornwall see also Table D	Paris Salon Paris Salon Hotel Drouot sale
	Mrs C J Woodward	Birmingham	Nature's Flower Garden, St Ives	RBSA (A)
	John R Reid	London	St Ives, Cornwall	RBSA (A)
	Richard Harry Carter	Truro	Barking Nets, St Ives	RBSA (A)
	Edith Hume	Petersfield	Preparing the Tackle	RA
	Arthur Quartley	London	Evening, St Ives	SBA
	Melicent Grose	Oxford	A Corner of St Ives, Cornwall	SBA
	Harry Robinson	St Ives	A Sunlit Sea, Cornwall	SBA
	Edwin Hayes	Bristol	St Ives Bay	SBA
	Joseph Moseley Barber	London	St Ives Fishermen Preparing for the North On the Quay, St Ives	SBA Liverpool (A)
	John Mogford	London	A Break in the Clouds - Crossing the Bar, St Ives	Liverpool (A)
	J S Rawle	London	The Quay at St Ives, Cornwall, constructed by Smeaton 1770	BAPFA (A)
	Miss M E Hillier	Bristol	The Moorlands, St Ives	BAPFA (A)
	E T Daniell	Bristol	After Sunset - St Ives Old Pier	BAPFA (A)

William Eadie and Dorothy Webb Robinson are also known to have painted in St Ives this year.

able to discover any further details.[169] However, an oil painting, *Sorting the Catch, St Ives* (Fig. 3.13), was sold in Penzance in 2003.[170] The same 1896 account indicates that the Hon Duff Tollemache, who had studied at the Royal Academy Schools, in Paris at Julian's and in Brussels under the sea painter Francois Musin, stayed in the town for an extended period in 1884 as well and created a studio at Carn Crowse. Meaning "the heap of rocks with a cross", this was on the extreme point of The Island. Matthews, in his 1884 Guide, mentions an old barn-like building, known as the 'Briton's House', erected originally for the use of Breton sailors, on the Island, and it may be part of this building that served as Tollemache's studio.

Another artist who exhibited a number of Cornish scenes at this time was the London-based coastal painter John Mogford and, in 1885, the year of his death, he sent *A Break in the Clouds, Crossing the Bar - St Ives* (£63) to the Liverpool Autumn Exhibition. Another artist who sent a St Ives subject, *On the Quay, St Ives* (£25-0), to that exhibition was the London-based genre painter, Joseph Moseley Barber (1836-1892), who also sent a major work, *St Ives Fishermen Preparing for the North*, to the SBA show that year. Other St Ives subjects in the same exhibition were contributed by the London-based landscape painter, Alfred Quartley (1839-1886), and two of the new arrivals from Brittany, Melicent Grose and Harry Robinson. The RBSA Autumn show in 1885 also included some depictions of St Ives by John Robertson Reid, the highly regarded figure painter, who settled in Polperro, and Mrs C J Woodward, who exhibited *Nature's Flower Garden, St Ives*. Richard Harry Carter may also have returned to the town that year as he exhibited a significant painting *Barking Nets, Early Morning, St Ives* priced at £150 and *Breaking up the Wreck*. However, what was different about the 1885 crop of visitors was that three - Harry Robinson and his fiancée, Dorothy Webb, and the Scot William Eadie - decided to settle in the town over the winter months and stayed on. As such, they earn the title "first settlers" but no artist later came to St Ives because of their presence in the town. The reputation of St Ives had already spread far and wide and, although 1885 has to be taken as the date of the formation of the colony, the local populace will not have noticed much difference between the summer of 1886 and that of, say, 1882. In fact, as is quite clear from the accounts of Whistler's visit, which indicate that other artists were working in the town at the same time, winter visitors were not uncommon either.

---

169 William Badcock's *Historical Sketch of St Ives and District*, St Ives, 1896.
170 W H Lane & Son, 2/10/2003 Lot 110.

~4~

THE EARLY YEARS (1885-1889) – FOCUS ON PARIS

4.1 The First Settlers

The starting point for any review of the early development of the colony has always been *St Ives as an Art Colony*, a section in William Badcock's *Historical Sketch of St Ives and District* published in 1896. This was written by Harry Robinson and, in it, he claims that his wife, Dorothy, and himself and William Eadie were the first settlers, having decided to overwinter in the town in 1885.[171] Unlike some of the early Newlyn settlers, who tended to come and go, the Robinsons stayed in St Ives for the rest of their lives and Eadie for nearly twenty years. If the visit of the Robinsons can tentatively be attributed to Vernier, the reason for the decision of William Eadie (1846-1926) to settle in St Ives is not known. Eadie was a figure and portrait painter, who was born and brought up in Paisley in Scotland and who studied at the local School of Art. However, by 1871, he was living in St John's Wood, and, during the 1870s, he had some success with genre scenes at the Royal Academy. In the early 1880s, though, his work does not feature in any exhibitions. Whether this was due to rejections or to the fact that he married in 1880 and fathered five children in six years is unknown but it was clearly a brave decision to relocate his large family to the depths of Cornwall, even if the cost of living was considerably cheaper. The move, however, seems to have been a success, as he began to be hung again at the Royal Academy and won some local portrait commissions.

The text in Badcock continues, "The following summer a number of painters swooped down on St. Ives with the intention of making it their abode and field of labour. Mr. and Mrs. E. E. Simmons, Mr. Louis Grier (followed by his brother, Mr. E. Wyly Grier), Mr. Howard Russell Butler, Mr. and Mrs. Chadwick, and afterwards, in quick succession, Mr. and Mrs. Adrian Stokes, Mr. and Mrs. Grönvold, Mr. Julius Olsson, Mr. Lowell Dyer, Mr. Zorn (whose picture of St. Ives in the Luxembourg Gallery has contributed no little to the popularity of St. Ives), Miss Schjerfbeck, Mr. Blomefield, and Mr. W.H.Y. Titcomb." How does this account, written a decade or so afterwards, match up to the other extant sources?

4.2 The Ramblers' Dining Club, Paris

If the reasons why the first settlers came to St Ives are not crystal clear, at least the ensuing influx of foreign artists can be explained, for the manner in which this came about is set out in the unpublished autobiography of Howard Butler. In this, he speaks of a dining club, called 'The Ramblers', composed of English speaking artists in Paris.[172] "These dinners take place at different restaurants and are very enjoyable affairs."[173] At one dinner in the late spring of 1886, Butler records, "the question came up regarding the best place for summer work. It was agreed that the guests present should start out in different directions and visit the coast towns of France, Belgium, Holland and England and that on their return they should compare notes."[174] Butler, in company with his fellow American, the illustrator, Charles Stanley Reinhart, left for Holland, Belgium and northern France and reported back, after a whistle-stop tour of eleven days, that their favourite venues were Treport and Honfleur. However, Edward Simmons had chosen to go to St Ives. There are a number of reasons why Simmons might have selected St Ives. He might have heard of its attractions from Harry Robinson, his old friend from Concarneau. He might also have recalled Émile Vernier's descriptions of the town or seen the numerous paintings of St Ives by Vernier included in the sale of his work at the Hotel Drouot that February or, possibly, but less likely, he might have been told of the town's charms by Whistler, with whom he was acquainted.[175] In any event, Simmons was very taken with St Ives and Butler commented that "the photographs that he brought back and his enthusiastic descriptions led me to decide against Honfleur and in favor of St Ives."[176] After a short stay with the Reinharts, who were unmoved in their selection of Honfleur, Butler settled in St Ives towards the end of July and, shortly afterwards, wrote to his sister comparing St Ives with the places he had seen on his rapid tour of Continental coastal towns. "But the most

171 In the book, the name of the writer of the article is not mentioned but Robinson's authorship is confirmed in the review of the book in *St Ives Weekly Summary* 6/6/1896.

172 The Ramblers' Club at this juncture seems to have comprised some 15-20 English and American artists. In a letter to his sister, Mary, dated 8/12/1886, Butler comments, "Last evening we held the second meeting of the season of the 'Ramblers' Club'. Only six members were present. I think about ten of our number have returned to their respective English or American homes since last season." Letter from H.R.Butler to Mary Butler 8/12/1886. Archives of American Art, Smithsonian Institution, Washington DC, Howard Russell Butler papers, Reel 1189.

173 H.R.Butler, Unpublished Autobiography, p.150, Archives of American Art, Smithsonian Institution, Washington DC, Howard Russell Butler papers, Reel 93.

174 H.R.Butler, Unpublished Autobiography, p.165, Archives of American Art, Smithsonian Institution, Washington DC, Howard Russell Butler papers, Reel 93.

175 Whistler, however, did not go to Paris between 1884-6 and there is no evidence that Whistler and Simmons wrote to each other. On the other hand, one of Whistler's followers, Sidney Starr, stayed with Simmons in St Ives in 1886. The two became friends for Simmons helped Starr, when he later emigrated to the States.

176 Letter to Mary M Butler dated 8/8/1886, Archives of American Art, Smithsonian Institution, Washington DC, Howard Russell Butler papers, Reel 1189.

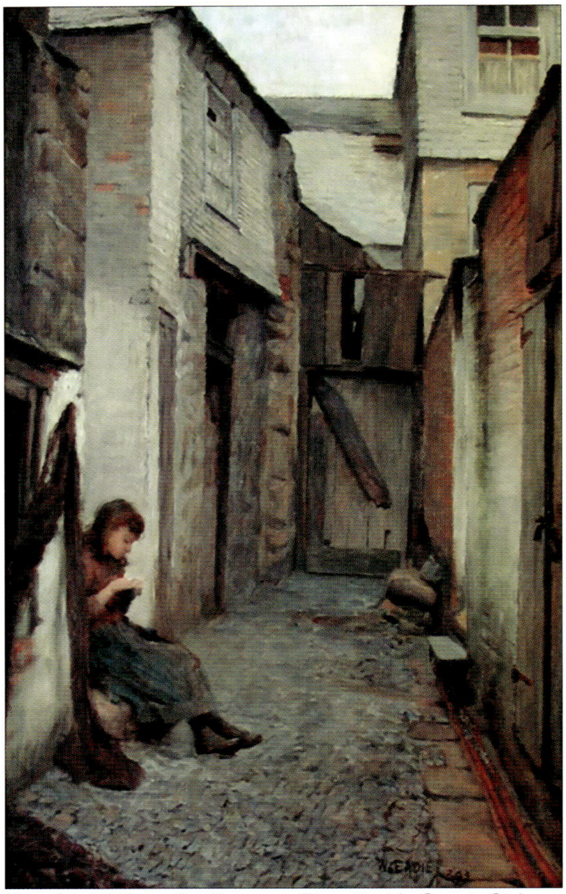

Fig. 4.1 William Eadie *Flamanck's Court, St Ives*
(dated 1893) (Private Collection)
This is the only known depiction of this court

interesting feature of that coast to me is the change of key and color from Holland to Brittany. Holland is beautiful in color. Belgium commonplace though higher in key. Brittany is dark in key and with no color except delicate greys. Normandy is more like Holland, suggesting about the same palette; rich in color and high enough to give a chance for beautiful decorative effects. Of the entire coast I think the most paintable portion is the half dozen miles between Honfleur and Villeville. The only drawback is in the color of the water which is sullied by the muddy outflow of the Seine. But the French coast cannot boast of a single spot as beautiful as St Ives. Here the water is pure and clear as crystal. The old town is fully as picturesque as Honfleur; the fishermen are splendid models: the coast is rugged and the sea heavy. Color exceedingly rich. The only drawback is...liability to sea-fogs".[177]

Butler was not the only artist persuaded by Simmons' enthusiastic recommendations and he records that "Our party consists of Simmons and his wife, Chadwick and his wife, Harry Robinson and his wife and myself."[178] Butler, of course, knew Simmons already, as he had worked with him during the summer of 1885 in Concarneau, and he had met the Bostonian, Frank Chadwick, and his Swedish wife, Emma Lowstadt in Grez that spring. Emma Chadwick and the Robinsons also knew Simmons from time spent in Concarneau, whilst the friendship of Frank Chadwick and Simmons went back to Harvard days.[179]

Simmons commented in his autobiography, "When I went to St Ives, it was unknown as an art colony, the place where they gathered being Penzance about ten miles away. Whistler had been there two years before, but Robinson was the sole representative of the clan upon my arrival. When I left, five years later, there was an Art Club of one hundred members."[180] Neither Simmons nor Butler, therefore, makes any mention in these accounts of William Eadie, one of the first settlers, probably because he was not considered a painter of the first rank, but Butler does refer to him in one of his letters as a permanent resident and comments that, in 1886, he used to visit Eadie's children most Sunday afternoons.[181]

---

177 Letter to Mary M Butler dated 8/8/1886, Archives of American Art, Smithsonian Institution, Washington DC, Howard Russell Butler papers, Reel 1189.
178 H.R.Butler, Unpublished Autobiography, p.166, Archives of American Art, Smithsonian Institution, Washington DC, Howard Russell Butler papers, Reel 93.
179 It appears that images of St Ives may well have been seen by some of the American artists in America even before they came to Europe. A note on the imminent demolition of the George and Dragon Inn in October 1886 comments, "there are certain artists in St Ives at this time who saw photographs of it in America before they knew that there was such a place as St Ives in the civilised world." *Cornish Telegraph* 21/10/1886.
180 E E Simmons, *From Seven to Seventy*, New York and London, 1922, p.164-5.
181 Letter from H.R.Butler to Harriet Butler 11/7/1887. Archives of American Art, Smithsonian Institution, Washington DC, Howard Russell Butler papers, Reel 1189.

4.3 Stanhope Forbes and Elizabeth Armstrong in St Ives in 1886

One of the first artists Simmons met in St Ives was the Canadian, Elizabeth Armstrong (1859-1912), whom he had also known in Brittany. She and her mother arrived in Newlyn in November 1885, where she met Stanhope Forbes. They were engaged in the spring of 1886 and, with their respective mothers, spent July and August that year in St Ives, staying initially in the White Hart Hotel before renting 6, Barnoon Terrace from a Mrs Rodd, with whom they became friendly. It may not have been an easy period for Lizzie, as no girl was likely to be good enough, in the eyes of Mrs Forbes, for her Stannie, particularly one without wealth and with artistic ambitions of her own. Whilst in St Ives, Lizzie did a painting, which Forbes in his letters, refers to as her 'School' painting and which was much admired by all who saw it, including that severe critic, Emma Chadwick.[182] Forbes also refers to a work called *Buzz-z*, which he liked but which was badly hung at the ROI, and a painting with a goose in it which Forbes did not care for. This might well be *The Critics*, a small work that Elizabeth exhibited at the SBA in the winter of 1886 and which Mrs Lionel BIrch, in her biography, confirmed was painted in St Ives. It depicted a boy drawing a stick man on an old door, watched by his two siblings and a goose. Perhaps Elizabeth herself had experienced the unwelcome attentions of a goose, as well as the usual crowd of children, when she was out sketching. When this work was shown at the *Impressionism in Britain* exhibition held at the Barbican Art Gallery in 1995, Kenneth McConkey observed, "The composition of the work, the full-length, close-up depictions of the figures as well as the emphasis on a diagonal arrangement of forms, reveal the influence of Bastien-Lepage, as does the handling and the use of the square brush technique."[183]

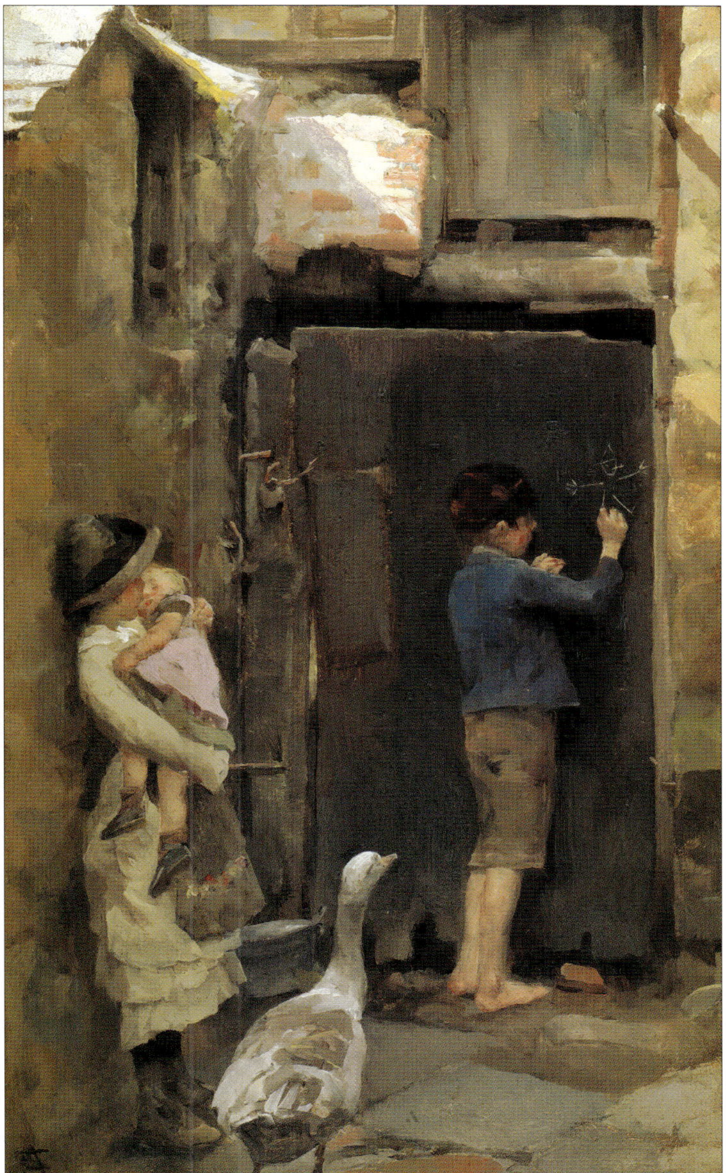

Fig. 4.2 Elizabeth Armstrong *The Critics* (Richard Green, London)

182 The only compositional clue that Forbes gives is in his letter of 23rd September 1886, "The School ought to be a great success if you get those two front figures very strong" -Tate Gallery Archives 9015.2.2.5. It is not therefore an early version of one of her most loved paintings, *School is Out* (RA 1889), which was set in Paul Schoolhouse, but might be a version of a work entitled *Off to School*, which shows two children turning round to have a last word with their mother, as they set off with their satchels. However, she did not complete this until after her marriage.
183 Kenneth McConkey, *Impressionism in Britain*, London, 1995 at p.126.

Frustratingly, with the normal recipients of his letters staying with him, we do not get Forbes' usual blow by blow account of his activities during this period but, when the others left in mid-September, he stayed on, moving to 7, Barnoon Terrace for the rest of the month. In his letters to Lizzie in late September, he mentioned several paintings. "Narrow escape the boys picture had yesterday, the moral of which is don't paint in a field where a game of football is being played. The ball just skewed the top of the picture and flattened the painter on the ground." He also made reference to a painting of a sweet shop - most probably the same shop that Whistler had painted - and was most annoyed to find his friend, Langton Barnard, had utilised an almost identical composition. He did complete this but mentioned that he had been forced to give up his picture of "the pink house". "This morning we found another artist at work there and I fear the comparison might so damage my reputation that it is wiser to give it up at once."[184] As a pink house features in *Their Daily Bread*, he may, in fact, have decided to continue subsequently. This painting shows a little girl returning to a simple home in Digey Square with a large loaf of bread, whilst her mother, with another infant, calls to her from an upstairs window. Two fish shown hanging on the cottage wall are probably intended to give the painting biblical associations and there are a number of other beautifully observed items in the picture.[185]

Bristol Art Gallery have a sketch by Forbes done on the beach at St Ives in 1886. He may have intended to develop this further, for he tells Lizzie on 23rd September, "I went down on the sands but had to return. The sea was quite the wrong colour and everything else different. So I cussed and came home again."[186] The sketch, though, reveals a totally different side to Forbes' work. It is broadly painted, of course, but the composition is most unusual, for two-thirds is merely a depiction of sand, whilst the sea, the beach tents and the circle of sitting figures are all placed in the top third of the painting. If he had decided to keep such a composition and style for a major work, it would have challenged the work of Philip Wilson Steer (1860-1942) for novelty.

The main painting that Forbes worked upon, however, was *Their Ever-Shifting Home*, which was painted partly in St Ives and partly in Newlyn. His letters give a full account of his concerns as this picture developed and all the problems that he faced and demonstrate the enormous amount of effort that went into producing a major exhibition piece - see Special Feature B - Diary of a Picture.[187] Writing about the picture in her biography of the Forbeses in 1906, Mrs Lionel Birch commented that the old road featured, with its gnarled leafless sycamores, which had provided a charming and somewhat melancholy background, had "long since been tidied up out of recognition into parklife propriety".[188]

Fig. 4.3 Stanhope Forbes *Beach Scene, St Ives*
(Bristol's Museums, Galleries and Archives)

184 Letters from Stanhope Forbes to Elizabeth Armstrong dated 14 & 15/9/1886 - Tate Gallery Archives 9015.2.2.2 & 3.
185 When sold at Christies, King Street on 23/11/2005 Lot 116, it was wrongly stated to be a Newlyn street scene.
186 Letter from Stanhope Forbes to Elizabeth Armstrong dated 23/9/1886 - Tate Gallery Archives 9015.2.2.5.
187 In a letter to his mother dated 25/10/1887, Forbes mentions that he has ordered a frame for "a little landscape ...the background to Their Shifting Home. I have now put in a navvy [?], a bulldog and two little frightened kids". Tate Gallery Archives 9015.2.1.452.
188 Mrs Lionel Birch, Stanhope Forbes and Mrs Elizabeth Forbes, London, 1906.

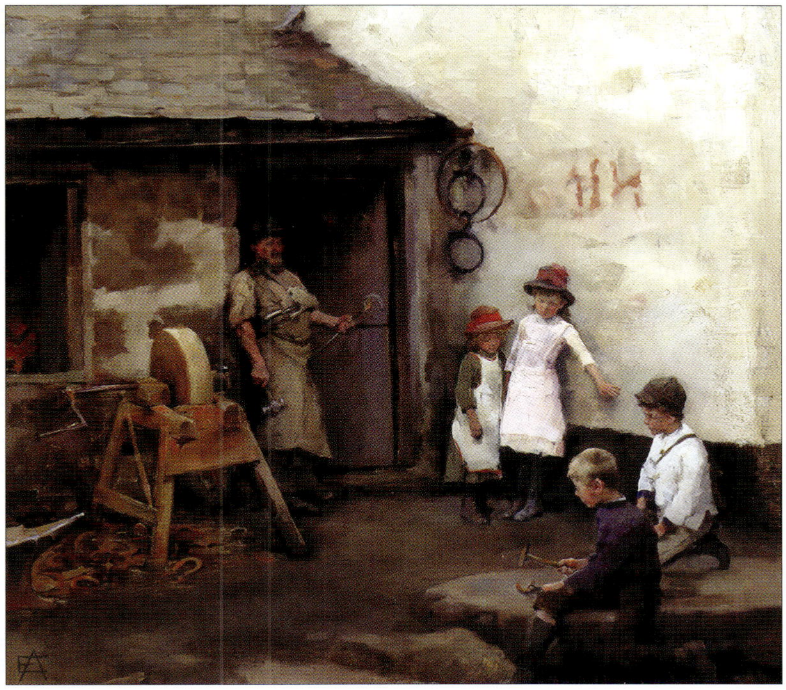

Fig. 4.4 Elizabeth Armstrong *The Forge* (1885-6) (David Messum Fine Art Ltd)

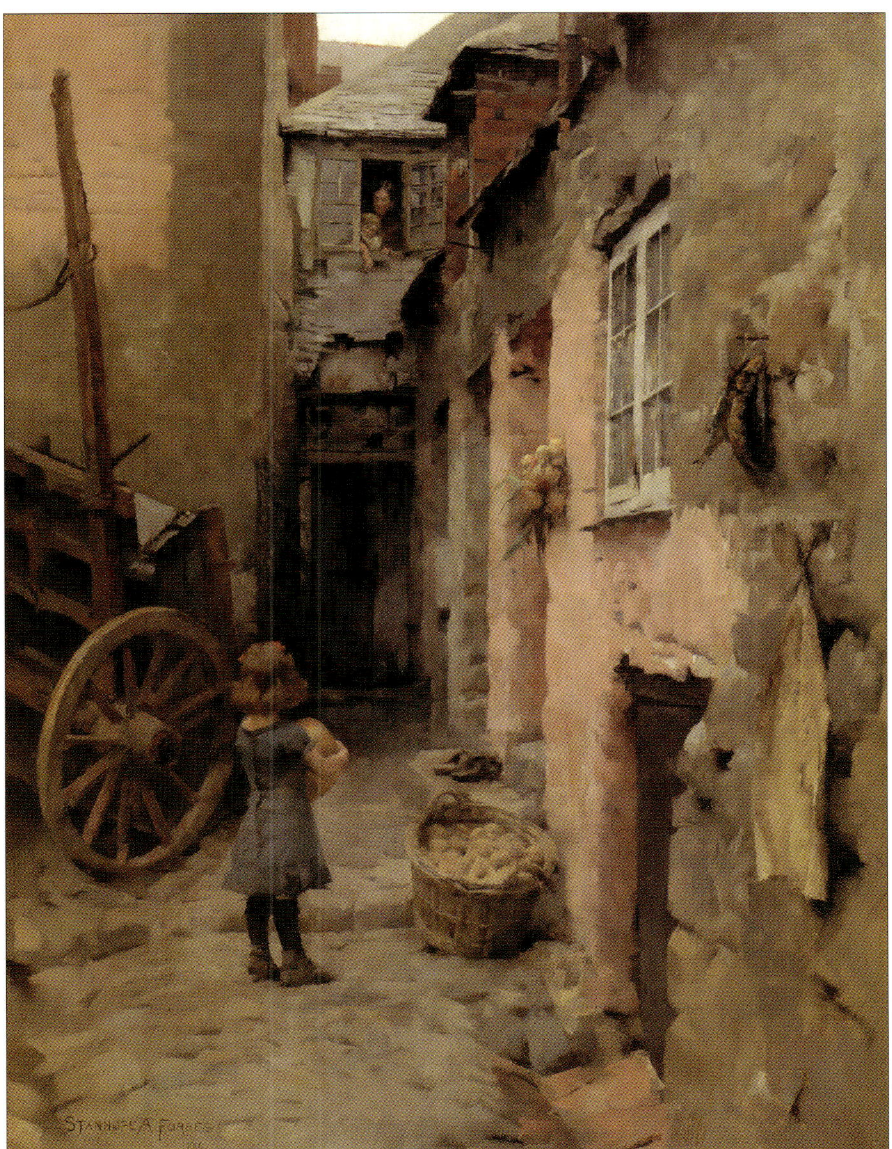

Fig. 4.5 Stanhope Forbes *Their Daily Bread* (Richard Green, London)

Special Feature B

Diary of a Picture - *Their Ever-Shifting Home* by Stanhope Forbes

The following extracts from Forbes' letters to his mother and Elizabeth Armstrong ("EA") tell of the development of this painting.[189] During his time in St Ives with his mother, Forbes had been working on the preliminary sketch and, on 6th October, he writes to tell her that he has sent for it from St Ives.

8th October 1886 - "Do not alarm yourself about my little picture. It's almost finished and I have just started a six foot replica of it with figures. I think you will be glad to hear this for I know you like the subject. I am going to have a gipsy woman and child in the foreground about half life-size and the caravan coming down the hill. I feel very much like making a good thing of it. It will necessitate going to St Ives of course occasionally but my sketch is almost enough to do the background from." [377]

9th October 1886 - "Shall probably go to St Ives tomorrow. I think it promises well. The model for the gipsy woman is very fine but unfortunately there is a most serious difficulty confronting me. She is a married woman and it is only too evident that there will be an increase to her family circle before long. I am in great dread. Perhaps she will hold out until I have got the head and shoulders painted. *Il faut espérer*. She is the finest model I have found down here and nobody has painted her yet. The gipsy van will be a very great difficulty but I hope to overcome it somehow. I feel happier now I have something really on the way." [378]

13th October 1886 - "I went [to St Ives] on Monday and did a sketch which I have since utilised. I think you will like this picture. It is quite a new thing for me. Perhaps a bit like my Breton pictures." [379]

15th October 1886 - "I went to St Ives yesterday and did some more to my background. It is cruel work running over there for a few hours work like that. However, I like the picture. I think it will march all right. The wind is blowing all my leaves off the trees worse luck." [380]

24th October 1886 - "Picture advancing. The background is all but finished...It is better than the small picture although so much larger. And it is also a little difficult for the leaves are all gone now. So that is all for the best. More wintry and desolate looking now. The figures still to come. They will give me trouble of course but I think I see my way." [382]

2nd November 1886 - "A fearful accident yesterday. My model fainted and came down an awful whack in the studio on some glass cutting herself poor woman rather badly. I was regularly scared for I thought she was not in a condition for much tumbling about but oddly enough I find I have been quite mistaken... She is not seriously hurt or shaken and sitting again today." [384]

30th November 1886 to EA - "You want to know what I have been doing at St Ives - only the background. I have almost finished my roofs, keyed up the sky & repainted the trees but hardly touched the ground for I can get better roads than the one I have over there. It has no nice wheel ruts in it & that I must go for on Paul Hill I expect. You should have heard Simmons talking about my picture in Robinson's studio. He excelled himself & criticised it in several languages but principally in French and American. It was something to listen to him on what he called the game of the colouring, which I afterwards found out meant the *gamme* (French - scale or key I think). I said nothing and he talked for half an hour after which I had my revenge for I went round and saw his work." [9015.2.2.15]

1st December 1886 - "It is very tiring work going over [to St Ives] and coming back every evening but I have nearly done now." [390]

12th December 1886 to EA - "A whole week & nothing done. Yes, I had one day & painted the head again, the result of which was a scrape. I suppose I shall get it eventually but it is all wrong now." [9015.2.2.22]

20th December 1886 to EA - "I am done for - Mrs Cattran has caught the measles, so my picture is at present at a standstill... She will not be able to stand again for at least a month or six weeks...I have so far done nothing but groan at this fresh piece of ill-luck." [9015.2.2.24]

2nd February 1887 - "I spent all day yesterday hunting gipsies at Marazion and over on the St Just Road at both of which places I was disappointed and then lo and behold when I got back in the evening to Newlyn found a whole lot of caravans winding up Jack Lane - the very thing I wanted. I interviewed them and found out where they were going to camp out." [395]

6th February 1887 - "I think I told you that I met the vans on Paul Hill and ascertained they were going to camp out near Sheffield. Well I went up there the next day and made a bargain with them. But I hardly believed they would keep their word - however they have done so well. The weather has been exactly what I want and I am most extraordinarily fortunate for I have all but done the caravan and it quite makes the picture. I think now there is no longer much fear of not finishing it and I am quite certain it will go well. It is very telling this old van at the top of the hill. I have not yet got my gipsy people about but there will be a few tramping of course alongside. "On the Tramp" - S.A.F. 500£ - that will be the catalogue of 1887. I have had to shell out pretty freely. 10/- per diem but then I need the whole caravan over - just at the top of Paul Hill near the board school in the little lane running up from Bellevue. I should think I must have had three hundred spectators to see the van. Tomorrow, if fine, I hope to finish with them for of course they will soon be on the move again." [396]

---

189 Tate Gallery Archives, 9015-2-1-377-417.

c.1st March 1887 (after a preliminary showing of the work) - "..my subject picture looks as if it wanted a lot to finish it. Mrs Cattran is however anxious to sit again & comes up tomorrow to sit." [408]

6th March 1887 - "Yesterday brought my picture back from St Ives, the background quite finished." [409]

13th March 1887 - "Picture nearly finished. The grey weather we have had recently has been most fortunate for me." [412]

23rd March 1887 - "The [Newlyn] private view is over. We have had 90 people. If our friends in London think as highly of my picture as they do down here, it will do very well." [417]

? March 1887 - "I want you also to arrange with your greengrocer or one of your tradespeople to meet me at the station with a cart of some kind for my picture. It is too large for a four wheeler....You may tell them the case is 6ft by 4ft but very light - it is merely the bulk that makes it impossible...A tarpaulin to go over it in case of rain will also be necessary."[416]

28th March 1887 to EA - "The [London] private view has been a great success again - nearly 50 people on Saturday and yesterday 80. Almost everybody that I would have liked to see turned up except oddly enough the Sickerts and the Morleys - but I am sorry to say my picture is going in unsold....I forgot to mention that Detmold christened my picture very successfully 'Their Ever Shifting Home'. [9015.2.2.32]

26th April 1887 to EA re the RA - "My picture it seemed to me fell flat. I heard very few complimentary remarks & it seemed to astonish nobody." [9015.2.2.33]

The reviews for the painting were, indeed, not over-abundant with praise, that in *The Daily Telegraph* in particular disgusting Forbes' mother. The review that most pleased Forbes was that in *The Building News*, but he did admit that sections of it reflected what he had told the reporter to say. This, though, gives us an indication of Forbes' objectives in painting the work. The review ran as follows, "Few pictures in the present exhibition please us more than *Their Ever Shifting Home* by Stanhope A Forbes. There is nothing in the picture like trickiness - the woman is no mere pretty gypsy girl but an ordinary Cornish tramp, to whom the trials of life are but too familiar, teaching, by the experience of adversity, the necessity of self-reliance. She heads the cavalcade and, no doubt should occasion require, could hold her own against most comers. Yet how lovely is her face, unsullied by an ignoble action; and though chequered be her lot, there remains no doubt as to her purity as, weary with the "ever-shifting", tramping life thus led, she clasps her child in her arms and marches on. The scene depicted is a common one in English lanes, here painted in a harmony of greys and the wintry landscape against an evening sky is in sympathy with the desolate appearance of the wayfarers, who trudge on selling straw chairs, brooms and basket wares."[190]

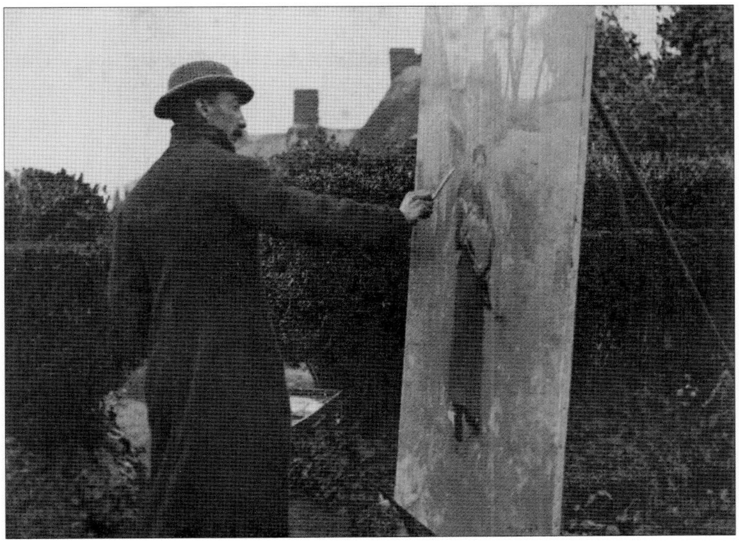

Fig. 4.6 Stanhope Forbes painting *Their Ever-Shifting Home* (Cornish Studies Library)

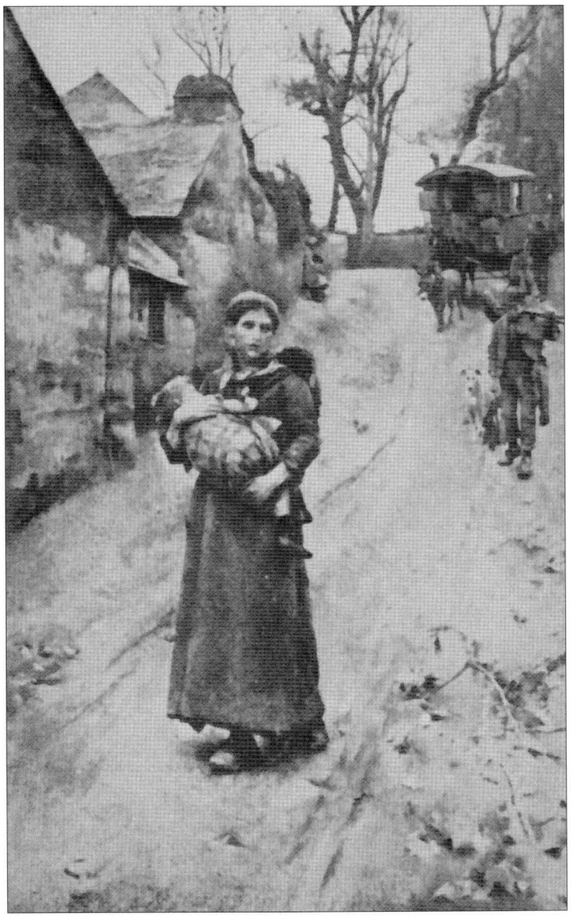

Fig. 4.7 Stanhope Forbes *Their Ever-Shifting Home* (Art Gallery of New South Wales, Sydney)

190 *The Building News*, 3/6/1887 at p.832.

4.4 Fraternising with the Newlyners

During the time that he was based in St Ives in the summer of 1886, Forbes was visited by many of his Newlyn colleagues - he mentions by name Fred Hall, Frank Bramley, Henry Detmold, William Fortescue, Fred Millard, Norman Garstin, Arthur Bateman and his brother, Jack. The Batemans actually rented a cottage in St Ives that autumn.[191] These visits immediately established links between the two colonies and Forbes' need to return to St Ives constantly to continue with his major exhibition piece of the year, *Their Ever Shifting Home*, which he kept in Harry Robinson's studio, meant that he was indebted to a number of the St Ives artists for their hospitality. Two fellow visitors, who entertained him with some frequency, were friends from London - John Langton Barnard, a London-born domestic genre painter, and his wife, Catherine (née Locking), whom he had married in 1880. Catherine, or Kate as she was always known, was also an artist and Forbes expressed the view that the work that she produced during their stay was far better than that of her husband. Kate's sister, Leonora Locking, who was also an artist and who later married Alfred Hartley, was also with them but she seems to have attracted attention at this juncture more for her looks than her art. Forbes was also entertained by the Robinsons, with whom he got on well. Howard Butler joined them on occasion and Forbes went to see his work, which he mentioned to his mother was "certainly very fine".[192]

This hospitality elicited invitations over to Newlyn and Forbes reported on 6th October 1886, "We had a busy day on Sunday...I trotted the Barnards and Butler round the studios and showed them everything and they went away delighted with their day and all they saw. Butler was very enthusiastic, especially about Suthers' picture, which I too saw for the first time on Sunday. Very fine indeed."[193] The Barnards came over the following Sunday as well, just before their departure from St Ives, and the Robinsons later that month. As a result, when a Ball was organised in St Ives in February 1887, an invitation was extended to Forbes and he was also asked "to bring as many dancing men" as he could."[194] The event went very well, as he reported to his mother. "Last night we had what [Chevallier] Tayler calls a punching time. We had accepted the invitation to the dance at St Ives after a great deal of considering & now I am very glad for we had an awfully good time of it. I hired a capital trap in Penzance large enough for our party of five consisting of Lizzie, Tayler, [Fred] Millard & Jack Bateman. The dance was given in the Hall where the entertainments are held. Mrs Robinson kindly acted as Lizzie's chaperone so of course we drove first to their house. Little Robinson was on the committee of the dance with a large rosette in his button hole & the old lady looked as you might imagine - but her *costume de bal* was not very *décollette*. We found a very large muster of ladies & very few men, so our little party was hailed with delight. There was Mr and Mrs Simmons, the little woman looking rather interesting, Mr and Mrs Chadwick, he in a more singular costume than ever - white waistcoat, black page-coat, as the tailors call it, & a gibus which puzzled the damsels of St Ives very much.[195] ...Mrs Chadwick talked a great deal to me, but what with the music and her pronunciation, I cannot tell you what she said."[196] He returns to the theme in his next letter, "I really must take lessons in dancing. Lizzie is evidently so fond of it that I shall have to go. I did not know how much she enjoyed it... Millard and Tayler both tell me she is a craik dancer.... Little Mrs Chadwick was dragged away about 12-30 by her spouse & the Simmons also left early as little Mrs Simmons does not dance. It was immense to see Mr and Mrs Robinson dancing together - but they are very nice folk - both of them."[197]

In March, the accord between the artists was temporarily broken. The Newlyn artists had organised a lottery, for which many of the artists, from both colonies, had donated paintings as prizes. There were thirty prizes in all and six hundred tickets had been sold but Norman Garstin had only added 370, rather than 570, blank tokens in the prize drum, so that all the prizes had been won before the last 200 names were drawn out of the ticket drum. Frank Chadwick, in particular, caused quite a scene. Forbes, who had been unable to get back from St Ives in time, was quite glad to have missed the furore and was delighted that his brother, Bill, had won Simmons' sketch, which he called "a very jolly little view of St Ives pier".[198] He himself had also been successful, winning Henry Detmold's sketch. However, he called this "unfortunately not a good specimen of that great artist".[199] In the same letter, however, he records another trip across the peninsula. "Found all well at St Ives. Chadwick's wrath quite appeased. Very hospitably entertained by the Robinsons, Eadie etc."[200]

---

191 During 1888, Arthur Bateman gave his exhibiting address as 6, The Terrace, St Ives and exhibited a couple of St Ives scenes at the RBA.
192 Letter to his mother dated 3/10/1886 - Tate Gallery Archives 9015-2-1-375.
193 Letter to his mother dated 6/10/1886 - Tate Gallery Archives 9015-2-1-376. Suthers' painting was probably *Finery* (Atkinson Art Gallery, Southport), which was exhibited at the NEAC in 1887.
194 Letter to his mother dated 7/2/1887 - Tate Gallery Archives 9015-2-1-397.
195 A gibus is an opera hat that folds up and can be held under one's arm. The following tries to make Forbes' attempt to reproduce the conversation passing between Chadwick and a damsel of St Ives more understandable. "What is that you in got under your arm?" "A hat." "A what a hat?" Chadwick proceeds to make it fly open, causing screams from the damsel of St Ives.
196 Letter to his mother dated 8/2/1887 - Tate Gallery Archives 9015-2-1-398.
197 Letter to his mother dated 13/2/1887 - Tate Gallery Archives 9015-2-1-400.
198 Letter to his mother dated 6/3/1887 - Tate Gallery Archives 9015-2-1-409.
199 ibid.
200 ibid.

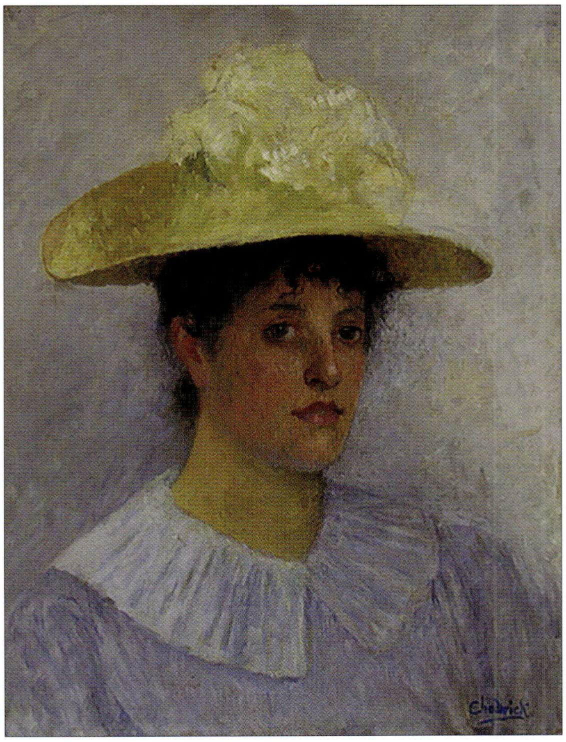

Fig. 4.8 Frank Chadwick
Portrait of Emma Chadwick
(CRN Auctions, Cambridge, Massachusetts)

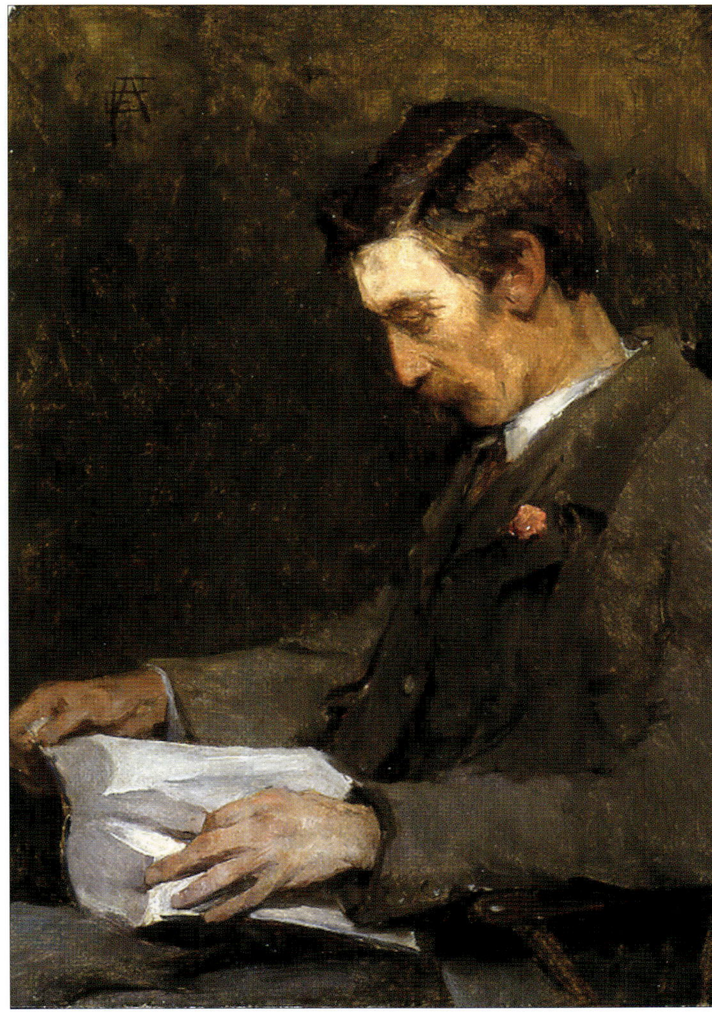

Fig. 4.9 Elizabeth Armstrong
Portrait of Stanhope Forbes
(David Messum Fine Art Ltd)

4.5 Early Impact in Paris

Stanhope Forbes described the 1886 Royal Academy exhibition as the "triumph of Newlyn" and, in 1887, he commented, "Newlyn has come off wonderfully".[201] The newly established art colony in St Ives, however, was nowhere in evidence at the Royal Academy in either year. The first settlers, William Eadie and the Robinsons, had been Royal Academy exhibitors previously but, in 1886, only a Breton scene by Harry Robinson was hung and, in 1887, if one discounts Forbes' own *Their Ever-Shifting Home*, two works by Ellis Wilkinson seem to have been the only St Ives contribution. Wilkinson, the son of the headmaster of a Harrow board school, was a landscape and genre painter, who had settled in the town during 1886, having lived previously in Ashburton and Bath, and he was probably rather pleased with his success, as, when he had asked Emma Chadwick for some advice, she had unkindly replied, "Give up painting"![202]

The foreign artists, who came to St Ives in 1886, did not arrive with the intention of settling in England but merely of locating suitable and different subject matter for their submissions to the next Paris Salon Exhibition and so the major works executed in St Ives in 1886 by Edward and Vesta Simmons, Howard Butler and Frank and Emma Chadwick were sent to the Paris Salon, not the Royal Academy. Butler submitted two works - "one a moonrise with sheen over the sea and sandy shore with three small boys in the foreground playing at jackstones; the other a breaking wave crossed by the sheen of the afternoon sun".[203] He told his sister, "Last year was devoted to Western skies but this year I have chosen to study the more subtle effects of the Eastern horizon." However, he encountered a number of difficulties as the moonlit scene progressed and mentioned that "opinions here differ as to its merits".[204] Having failed to finish it under the September moon, he readied himself to complete it on the occasion of the full moon in October, only to be thwarted by that date witnessing a total eclipse of the moon! He then, much to the amusement of Forbes, had to dash off to America with the work unfinished, as he had accepted an invitation to dinner in New York on a certain day, and so he had to

201 Letters to Elizabeth Armstrong dated 27/4/1886 (Tate Gallery Archives 9015.2.2.1) and 25/4/1887 (TGA 9015.2.2.33) respectively.
202 Letter from Stanhope Forbes to his mother - 3/1887 - Tate Gallery Archives 9015-2-1-414.
203 H.R.Butler, Unpublished Autobiography, p.167, Archives of American Art, Smithsonian Institution, Washington DC, Howard Russell Butler papers, Reel 93.
204 Letter from H.R.Butler to Mary M Butler dated 30/9/1886, Archives of American Art, Smithsonian Institution, Washington DC, Howard Russell Butler papers, Reel 1189.

be there![205] Nevertheless, the painting, which he called *Moonrise, St Ives*, was hung on the line at the Paris Salon and labelled Mention Anterierement. "Everyone tells me it looks remarkably well though there are a hundred things that I should like to do on it now that I see it in the great exposition", Butler told his sister.[206] When it was shown at the American Art Association in 1887, it was hailed as "a charming sea-shore view, with some fishing boats drawn up on the beach and a group of children playing on the sands in the immediate foreground. It is a large canvas .... and is remarkable for breadth and skilful painting. There is no forcing of the effect - boats, children, the long, white pier jutting out into the sea at the left, the quiet evening sky with the full moon half revealed above a bank of clouds at the horizon, are all truthfully rendered, and the canvas bears throughout the impress of sincerity and true artistic feeling. It is subdued and refined in colour."[207]

Butler also considered the paintings of Edward Simmons and Emma Chadwick, which were hung in Paris, to be "perfectly splendid." Simmons' work, *Youth and Age*, depicted a seated old sea dog holding his newly-born grandson on his knee, whilst Emma Chadwick's *Five o'clock* depicted three old women having tea. When he saw it in November 1886, Forbes was not overly impressed, "It was the usual kind of thing, some nice quality in it but I fancy due to frequent scraping and to the fact that nothing absolutely was in the least finished. [sic] But I daresay she will make a good thing of it."[208] This she certainly did for it was awarded a medal, thus becoming the first St Ives scene to be accorded this honour in Paris. As regards her husband, Forbes commented, "Chadwick is still at his experiments but he is going to set to soon & will astonish you I daresay."[209] He too came good and had two works hung - *Un Coup de Lune* and *Meditation*. Vesta Simmons was also represented by a work, *Paysage*, but, unfortunately, none of these works have been traced. With such a good representation at the Salon of 1887, it is perhaps not surprising that most new visitors that year came from France rather than Britain.

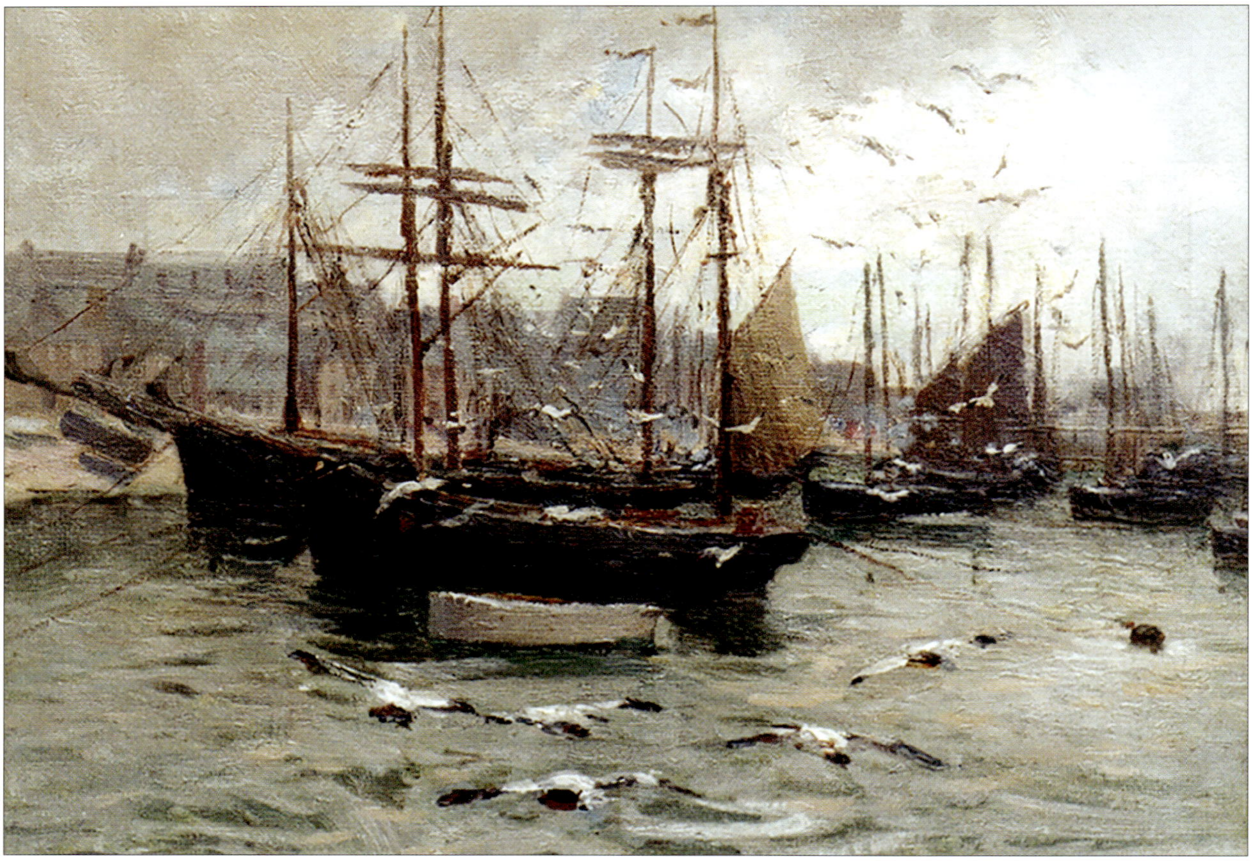

Fig. 4.10 Edward Simmons *St Ives Harbour* (Private Collection)

205 Letter from Stanhope Forbes to Elizabeth Armstrong dated Thursday (15/9/1886) - Tate Gallery Archives 9015.2.2.3.
206 Letter to Harriet Butler dated 3/6/1887, Archives of American Art, Smithsonian Institution, Washington DC, Howard Russell Butler papers, Reel 1189.
207 *The Nation*, Issue 1172, 15 December 1887.
208 Letter from Stanhope Forbes to Elizabeth Armstrong dated 30/11/1886 - Tate Gallery Archives 9015.2.2.15.
209 ibid.

4.6 A Foreign Influx

In March 1887, Forbes tried to persuade his mother to take a house in St Ives again, not just for the summer but for as long as six months, pronouncing, "I like St Ives and it likes me".[210] He even suggested that she let out her house in London, and she did offer to exchange this with Mrs Rodd in Barnoon Terrace, but that lady was not interested.[211] By June, though, after Elizabeth Armstrong had decided to take rooms in St Ives with her mother, Forbes had changed his mind. "I have almost made my mind not to go there too. With my prospects as they are just now, it will be better for both of us to work apart."[212] This seems a slightly lame excuse and it may be that he was put off by reports that there would be many more foreigners in the town that year, for not long after he tells his mother, "St Ives will be crowded this year with people from all parts of the world. Plenty of new Americans... There will be many more people there than there were last year."[213] Artists, whom he specifically mentioned, were Butler's friends, the Reinharts, and Adrian and Marianne Stokes, who were in fact due to arrive the very next day (6th June). They had not only met Forbes before but, as Pont Aven/Concarneau veterans, would have known most of the fledgling colony. The vast increase in numbers was subsequently confirmed by Butler, who returned in early July. Writing to his sister, Harriet, he reports, "The colony at St Ives has doubled. There are to be twenty artists here this summer." Aware of his own enthusiastic recommendations, he adds, "I understand I am to blame for the increase in numbers."[214] The following month, when writing to his mother, he is more specific. "There are many artists here - lately there has arrived a young lady from Finland - she has a wonderful talent and is a most interesting person altogether, although unfortunately lame - there is also a Russian lady here - neither speak any English, but both are fluent in French. We have in our colony in addition to the Finn and the Russian, an Austrian, a German, a Norwegian, a Swede, an Irish, a Scotch, a Canadian, four Americans and several Englishmen - we had a Greek whom we are glad to have got rid of and the only Frenchman, Émile Vernier, who was really the discoverer of St Ives, died a few months ago."[215]

Not all of these artists have been able to be identified. The Finn was Helene Schjerfbeck, who had been invited to St Ives by Marianne Stokes, when she heard that she had won a travel scholarship. The Swede was, of course, Emma Chadwick. The Norwegian was the landscape painter, Bernt Grönvold (1859-1923), who stayed until 1888. Little is known about his art, but later arrival, Anders Zorn, described him as "a pleasant and original human being".[216] The Scot was William Eadie and the Irish was probably Dorothy Robinson, although Stanhope Forbes mentions that Norman Garstin also 'emigrated' to St Ives that summer.[217] The Austrian was Marianne Stokes and the Canadian Elizabeth Armstrong. The four Americans, that Butler was referring to, were presumably himself, Frank Chadwick, Edward Simmons and Charles Reinhart, although he should have included Vesta Simmons as well, as she was producing some highly regarded work at this time, although she later turned to writing novels. Reinhart was clearly persuaded by Butler to make the trip this year, having declined the previous one. Born in Pittsburgh in 1844, he worked on the railways and in a steel factory before coming to Europe in 1882, where he studied art in Paris under Dagnan-Bouveret, who painted his portrait, and at the Munich Academy under Straehuber and Otto. He was best known as an illustrator - Forbes tells his mother that she will have seen his work in *Harper's* - and he contributed illustrations in black and white and colours to a number of leading American periodicals. However, in the spring of 1887, the year that he came to St Ives, he was awarded an Honourable Mention at the Paris Salon. A number of his later exhibited paintings and drawings have titles that might possibly be St Ives scenes but, so far, I have only identified the gouache *Fishermen Conversing* (Fig. 4.11) as a definitive St Ives subject.[218] Although, at the 1889 Paris Exposition, he won both a gold and silver medal and, in 1890, his work *Rising Tide* was bought by the French Government, his untimely death in 1896 has clearly impacted on his reputation.

---

210 ibid.
211 ibid.
212 Letter to his mother dated 1/6/1887 - Tate Gallery Archives 9015-2-1-428.
213 Letter to his mother dated 5/6/1887 - Tate Gallery Archives 9015-2-1-430.
214 Letter from H.R.Butler to Harriet Butler 11/7/1887. Archives of American Art, Smithsonian Institution, Washington DC, Howard Russell Butler papers, Reel 1189.
215 Letter from H.R.Butler to his mother 20/8/1887. Archives of American Art, Smithsonian Institution, Washington DC, Howard Russell Butler papers, Reel 1189.
216 From extract from Autobiographical Notes kindly supplied by Zorn Museum, Mora. In a letter to Elin Lamm, Emma Zorn comments about Grönvold, "He is working on a large painting which I do not like. But it may get better before he has finished." - Letter dated 9/11/1987 (translated by Bjorn Benckert). Nevertheless, he had four works included in the 1893 World Colombian Exhibition in Chicago including *Heartsick* and a portrait of Henrik Ibsen. He was then living in Bergen. In 1896, he edited the autobiography of the noted German academic artist Friedrich Wasmann.
217 See letters to his mother dated 12/6/1887 & 2/10/1887 - Tate Gallery Archives 9015-2-1-433.
218 He held an exhibition of over 150 drawings at the Art Institute of Chicago in 1891. Titles such as *The Fisherman's Funeral*, *The Artists' Ball* and various depictions of fisherfolk are intriguing. There are also several drawings of Sussex.

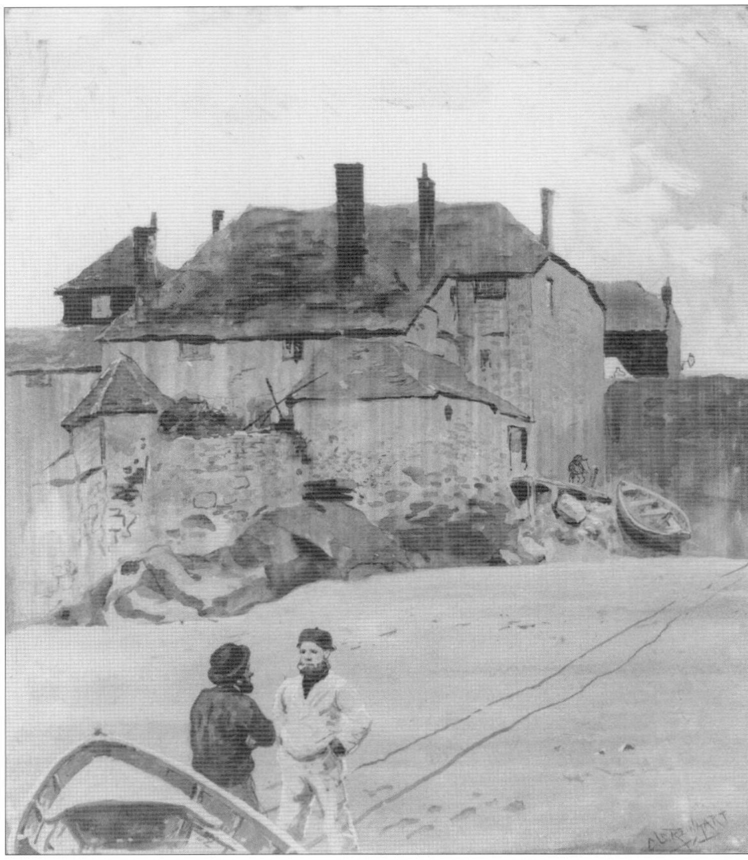

Fig. 4.11 Charles Reinhart *Fishermen Conversing, St Ives*
(Robert C Eldred Co. Inc, East Dennis, Massachusetts)

The scene can be compared with James Bingley's depiction (Fig.1.9)

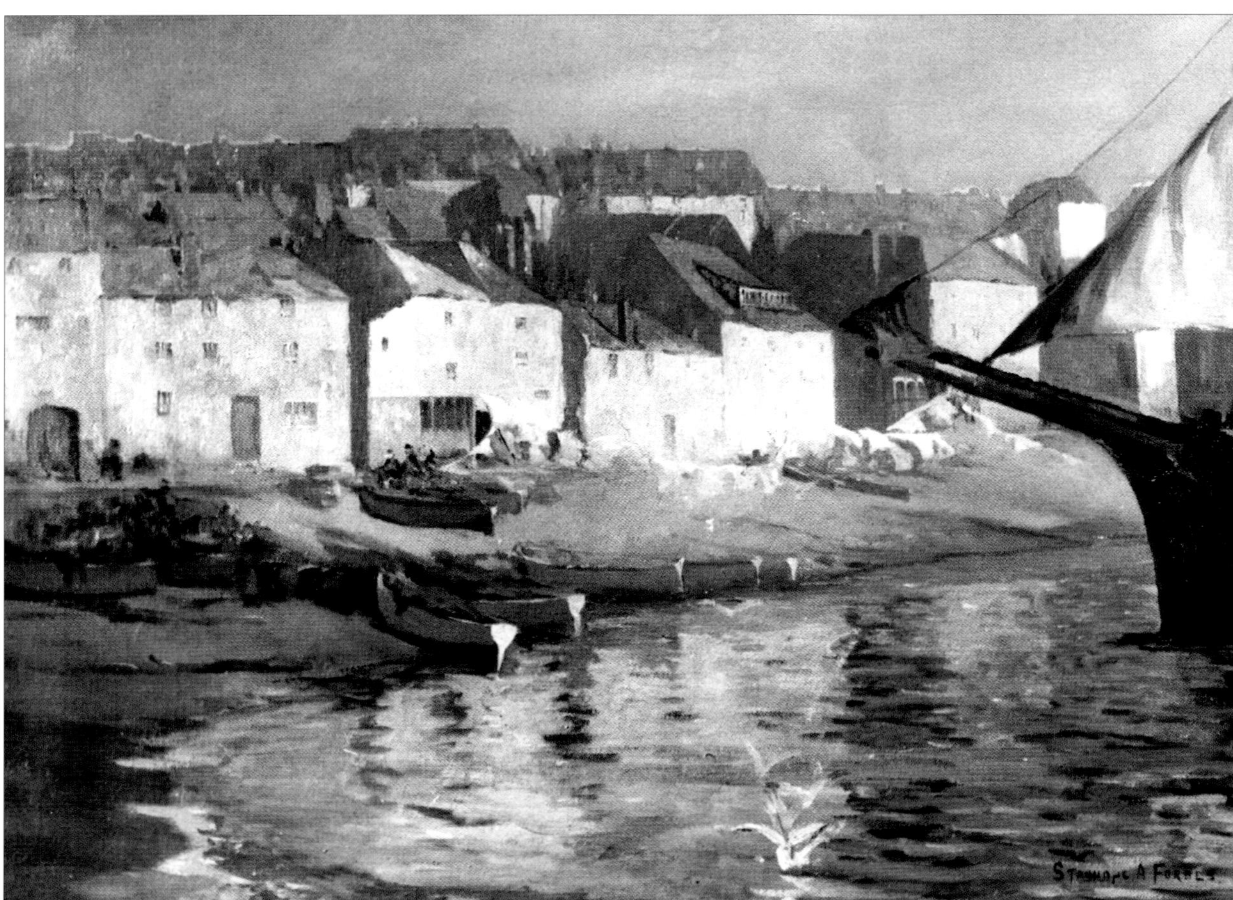

Fig. 4.12 Stanhope Forbes *Morning Sunshine, St Ives* (David Lays Auctions, Penzance Auction House)

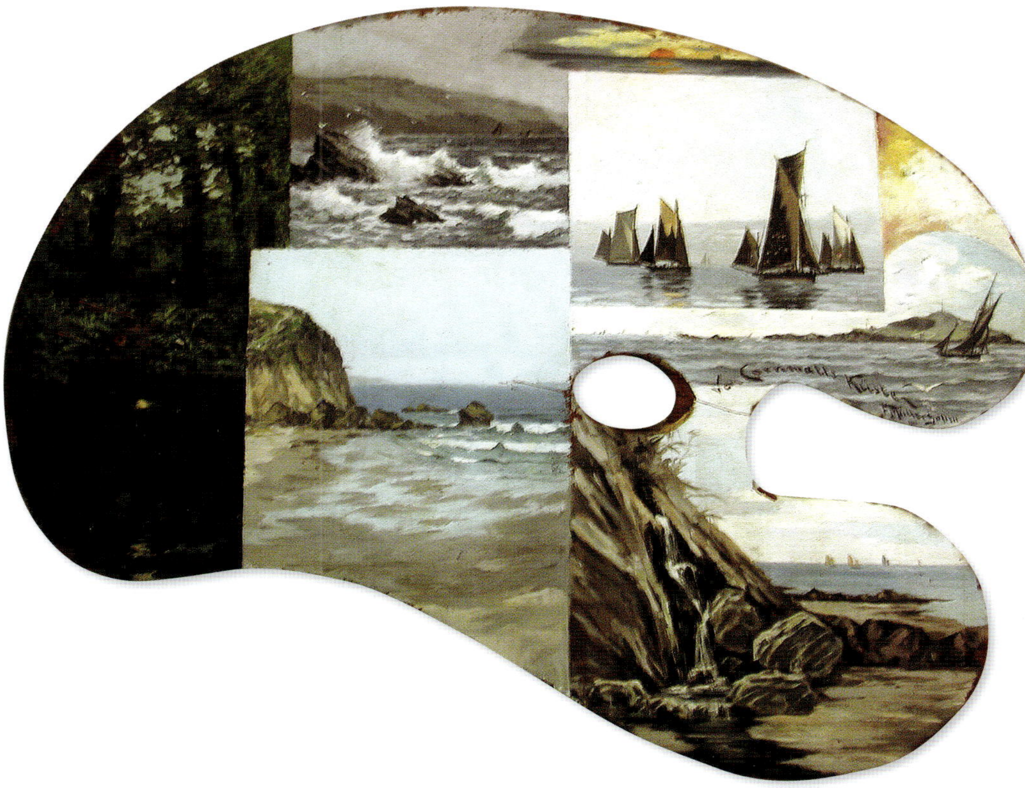

Fig. 4.13 Palette of Franz Muller-Gossen (St Ives Arts Club)

The Frenchman mentioned by Butler - Émile Vernier - died in Paris in May that year - well before Butler's arrival - and so must have been in St Ives in the spring. The identity of the Greek misfit and the Russian lady are not known, but Butler records having dinner with the latter, a young art student, who described herself as "an atheist, a Nihilist and a Home Ruler".[219] The identity of the German is also uncertain. The only German artist known to have visited St Ives at around this time is Franz Muller-Gossen (1871-1946), the son of a successful Monchengladbach industrialist, who owned several loom-making factories. He is normally considered not to have visited St Ives until 1890 following the completion of his training at Dusseldorf, for that is the year noted on an old palette, which he decorated with views of Porthmeor, Tregenna Woods, French crabbers in the Bay and the Longships Lighthouse at Land's End, which was donated to the St Ives Arts Club by his daughter in 1990. However, he may have paid visits during his student days as well. He certainly came to regard Cornwall as "essential for his art and happiness" and, for the majority of his life, he maintained homes in both Cornwall and Munich, living for periods in Penzance, St Ives and Sennen.

By comparison, the English contingent was small. This would have comprised permanent residents Harry Robinson and Ellis Wilkinson and new arrival Adrian Stokes, whilst Newlyner Percy Craft, on Forbes' recommendation, rented Mrs Rodd's property in Barnoon Terrace for three months between July and September. The Barnards were back as well, staying until 9th October. It is not certain whether Butler will have classified Louis Grier as English, Canadian or Australian, as Grier had been born in Australia, but had left that country when he was just two and had been educated in both Canada and England. However, as he had arrived in time to contribute a St Ives scene to the WCAU exhibition in September, he is likely to have been one of the group as well. In fact, his painting, *Among the Seine Boats, St Ives* (Fig. 4.15), is dated 1886, confirming that Grier had paid several visits to St Ives before settling in the town.

Howard Butler, recalling this second sojourn in St Ives, commented, "The weather this summer was glorious, my health was superb and how I did enjoy it."[220]

219 H.R.Butler, Unpublished Autobiography, p.175, Archives of American Art, Smithsonian Institution, Washington DC, Howard Russell Butler papers, Reel 93. This conversation led Butler to write home "There must soon come a terrible struggle in Russia. In fact, it would take little to draw all of Europe into a war...The war would have to be a horrible sanguinary one" This was a prophesy written some 30 years before the Russian revolution and 27 before the First World War that Butler was proud of when putting together his autobiography.
220 H.R.Butler, Unpublished Autobiography, p.175, Archives of American Art, Smithsonian Institution, Washington DC, Howard Russell Butler papers, Reel 93. As regards his work that summer, Butler reported to his mother that he had painted a large picture for a Mrs Cochran and two smaller pictures, which had turned out so successfully that he had decided to enlarge them for the Salon of 1888 but he does not appear to have exhibited there that year - Letter from H.R.Butler to his mother dated 20/8/1887, Archives of American Art, Smithsonian Institution, Washington DC, Howard Russell Butler papers, Reel 1189.

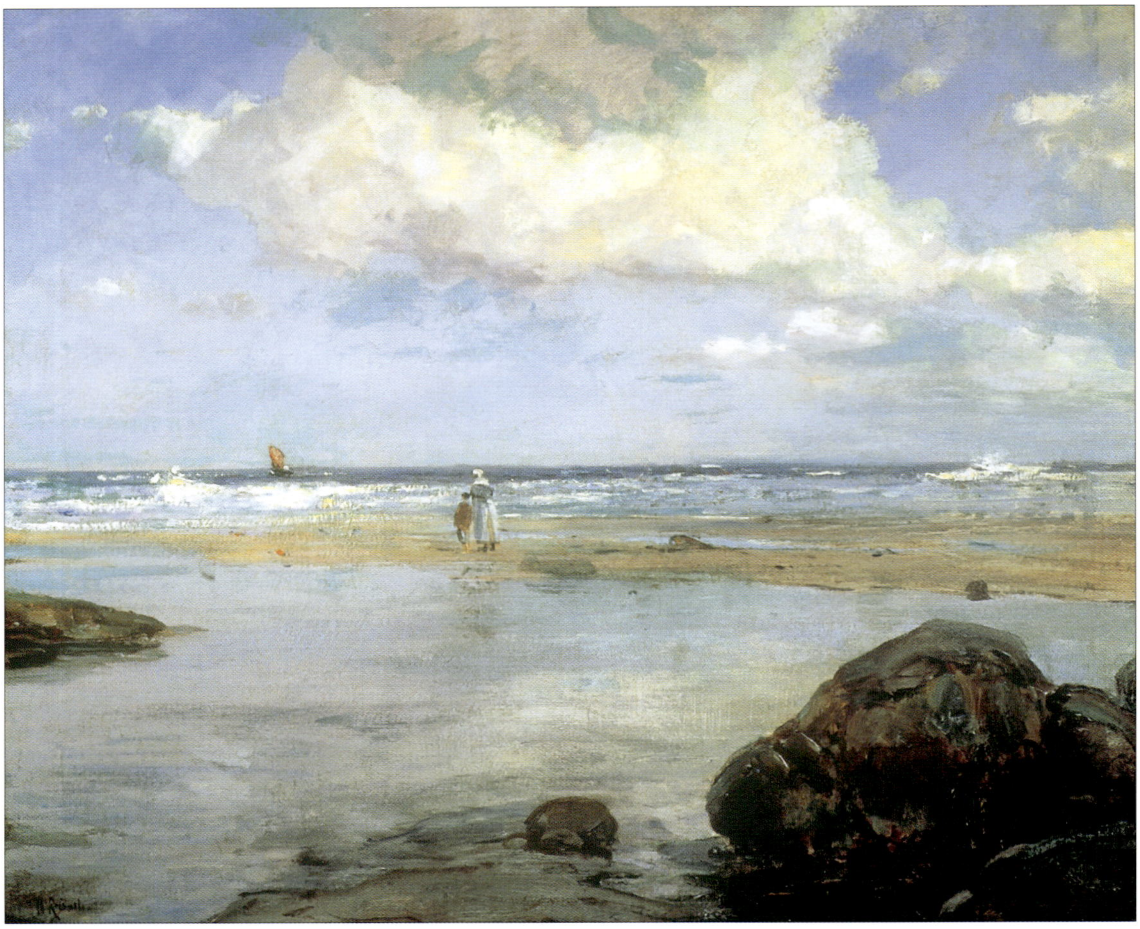

Fig. 4.14 Howard Russell Butler *Gone - On A St Ives Beach* (1886) (National Arts Club, New York)

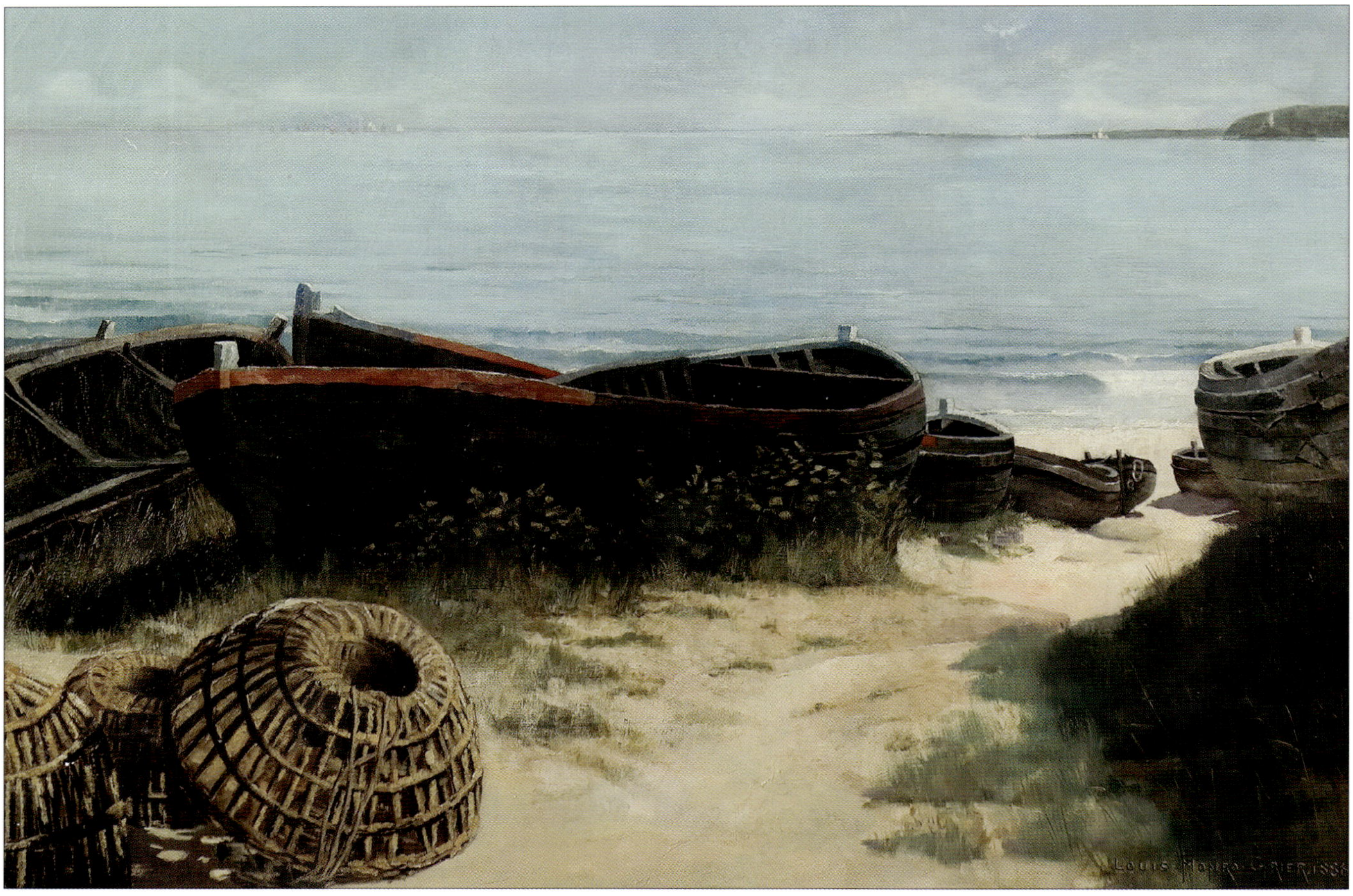

Fig. 4.15 Louis Grier *Among the Seine Boats, St Ives* (Newlyn School Gallery)

4.7 The First Inter Colony Cricket Match

With the Newlyners Percy Craft and his family, Elizabeth Armstrong and her mother and the Garstins and their new born child all lodging in St Ives during the summer of 1887, there was again a steady stream of visitors from Newlyn. Forbes, in fact, spent most weekends in St Ives. This further close fraternisation led to a challenge that the St Ives artists should take on the Newlyn artists at cricket, the idea seemingly being that of Henry Detmold.[221] Butler records the encounter, played at Tregenna Castle, which involved high drama. "September 5th [1887]. We have had a most exciting day. The artists of Newlyn (where there is a colony of young English artists known as the "Square-touch School" hopefully trying to climb into the kingdom of art without going through the straight and narrow path) challenged the artists of St Ives to play them at cricket. Notwithstanding that our team was made up largely of Americans, we beat them 86 to 50. Chadwick made the highest score."[222] However, the day had a sad ending. "It was not during the game but while we were on the field that the ball was tossed into the air and two of the Newlyn men sprang forward to catch it at the same instant neither seeing the other. They came together face to face. It was a most remarkable accident. Scully's nose must have gone into Millard's mouth for it was badly cut by Millard's teeth, several of which were crushed in and the jaw was so strained that he has hardly got the use of it yet. Both fell like dead men. Poor Millard striking on the back of his head and receiving a slight emission of the brain. It was awfully sad. We had been having such a delightful day. Some ran for water, others ran into the town for the Doctor. I held the poor fellow in my arms for fully twenty minutes while others wiped the blood away from his eyes, nose and mouth. None of us knew whether he would die or come to life again."[223] Millard was eventually carried about a mile, with a door being used as a stretcher, to Simmons' house on The Terrace, where he took care of him for three or four days, until friends arrived who hired a house for him to stay in until he recovered. The doctor anticipated this would take at least a month. Scully, however, recovered more quickly. Butler concluded, "The Englishers are very much cut up over their defeat and we have agreed to play a return match tomorrow. We will probably let them win". Whether or not intentionally, the St Ives artists did indeed lose the rematch and Butler lamented that "there is no prospect of a rubber now that the damp weather has arrived."[224]

4.8 The First Exhibition with the Newlyn Artists

That month, September 1887, the artists from the colonies of St Ives, Newlyn and Falmouth exhibited together for the first time. The occasion was the biennial exhibition of the West Cornwall Art Union ("WCAU"). Before the colonies of professional artists in Newlyn and St Ives had been established, there had been regular exhibitions staged by the West Cornwall Art Union in Penzance (and also by the Royal Cornwall Polytechnic Society in Falmouth ("RCPS")). These exhibitions were part of the initiatives encouraged by the South Kensington Museum and contained a strange mixture of mechanical devices and inventions, scientific apparatus and artistic productions. Works from the collections at South Kensington were often included in the exhibitions but the local artistic input tended to be from amateurs, particularly students at the local schools of art, and there was as much emphasis on needlework and crafts as there was on painting.[225] The WCAU Exhibition of 1887 was different, however. It was held for the first time in the new Penzance Art Museum, which had been built next to the School of Art in Morrab Road. The establishment of a prestigious Art Gallery in the town had been the dream of Henry Malcolm Geoffroi, the initial headmaster of the Penzance School of Art, that had been founded in 1853. Accordingly, on this occasion, professional artists submitted work to the WCAU exhibition and this gathering of works of fine art in the new Museum was the highlight of the exhibition, attracting considerable interest and comment. Without doubt, it was the finest exhibition yet staged in Cornwall.[226]

From St Ives, contributions came from Harry and Dorothy Robinson, William Eadie, Louis Grier, Adrian and Marianne Stokes, Edward and Vesta Simmons, Helene Schjerfbeck, Elizabeth Armstrong and her American friend, Rosalie Gill, Ellis Wilkinson, G.H.Forth and two amateurs, Frederick Massey and Miss Ida Jennings.[227]

---

221 Letter from Stanhope Forbes to Elizabeth Armstrong dated 27/8/1887 - Tate Gallery Archives 9015.2.2.60. Forbes, who was in Wales with his family, regretted not being able to take part.

222 H.R.Butler, Unpublished Autobiography, p.168, Archives of American Art, Smithsonian Institution, Washington DC, Howard Russell Butler papers, Reel 93. This diary note is inserted in Butler's autobiography in 1886 and Jacobs in *The Good and Simple Life* gives this date. However, the *Cornish Telegraph* of 1/9/1887 records the injuries to Millard and Scully.

223 Letter from H.R.Butler to Harriet Butler 5/9/1887 but mistakenly dated 1886. Archives of American Art, Smithsonian Institution, Washington DC, Howard Russell Butler papers, Reel 1189.

224 Letter from H.R.Butler to Mary Butler 18/9/1887. Archives of American Art, Smithsonian Institution, Washington DC, Howard Russell Butler papers, Reel 1189.

225 The WCAU exhibition in 1885 predated the establishment of the St Ives colony but does not appear to have attracted any of the Newlyn artists. In 1886, an Art Union exhibition was held at Hayle but none of the St Ives artists exhibited.

226 WCAU exhibitions were bi-annual and the 1889 show did not gain such a good response from the St Ives artists. Although the Newlyn artists were represented in force, works from St Ives were only sent by Louis Grier, Harry and Dorothy Robinson, William Eadie and Julius Olsson. It seems as if the major artists in the colony had directed their attention this year to Paris.

227 G H Forth was living in Fish Street, when he applied, probably unsuccessfully, on 13/1/1892 for the tenancy of 2, The Terrace - Mornington Estate Papers, County Records Office, Truro, GHW/12/3/6/1/57/19. Massey's two watercolours were, in fact, considered some of the most striking in the show. *Daydreams* showed a young girl lying on a clifftop whilst *Waiting for Father* showed two girls looking expectantly out of a cottage window. However, he was still classed as an amateur in the RCPS Exhibition the following year. He then moved to Penryn and exhibited at the RBA, Liverpool and at the RI in the years 1892-3. However, he continued to exhibit large numbers of inexpensive works in both oils and watercolours to the RCPS shows until the War. St Ives Museum have his oil painting, *Catching Pilchards*, which is not without merit.

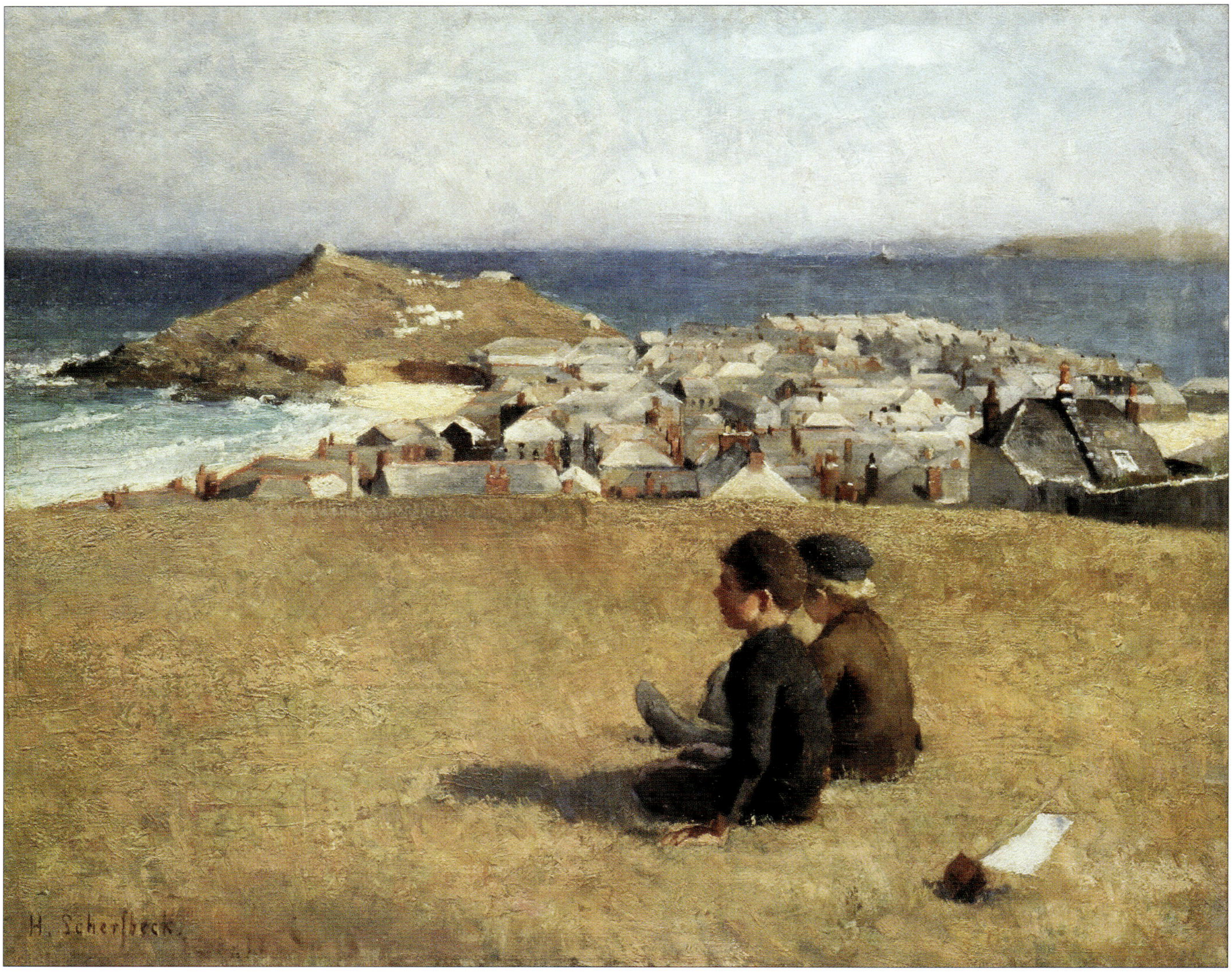

Fig. 4.16 Helene Schjerfbeck *View of St Ives* (Private Collection, Helsinki)
(Photo: Central Art Archives/Hannu Aaltonen)

Helene Schjerfbeck's *View of St Ives*, her well-known painting of two boys sitting on a grassy hillock overlooking the town, was considered one of the best works in the exhibition. Its attractions have endured, for just over one hundred years later, David Brown, the curator for the Tate Gallery of the seminal exhibition, *St Ives 1939-1964*, considered it "one of the most beautiful landscapes of St Ives ever painted".[228] Edward Simmons' *Lunch, Elche, Spain* was also highly regarded. Simmons had been much taken with Elche, which he had visited whilst based in Concarneau, commenting "I realized I had quietly stepped back four or five hundred years in the history of the world".[229] The painting showed an old dame, who had seated herself on the shady side of a wall to enjoy a frugal meal, and had already been hung at the Paris Salon. The reviewer commented, "There is no picture in the Exhibition which will better repay careful study than this".[230] Other successes included *From the Foresand, St Ives* by Adrian Stokes, *The Afterglow* by Dorothy Robinson and *Messmates* by Ellis Wilkinson, which all found purchasers quickly. The latter depicted an old fisherman wringing out a garment in a cottage interior, whilst keeping a keen eye on the welfare of a youngster who had been allotted the task of cutting some bread with a knife. Its sale will have boosted Wilkinson as, in June that year, Forbes told his mother, "Poor Wilkinson has been very ill. I fear he has not many months to live now."[231] However, he did recover for a while and continued to play a part in the colony until 1890. He died in the Isle of Wight in June 1891 aged only 36, leaving his widow, Martha, to bring up four children on her own, one of whom, Norman Wilkinson, later studied in St Ives and became a leading marine painter.[232]

228 David Brown, Introduction to M.Whybrow, *St Ives 1883-1993 - Portrait of an Art Colony*, Woodbridge, 1994 at p.10.
229 E E Simmons, *From Seven to Seventy*, London, 1922, p.152.
230 *The Cornish Telegraph*, 22/9/1887.
231 Letter to his mother dated 5/6/1887 - Tate Gallery Archives 9015-2-1-430.
232 Norman Wilkinson CBE was aged 13 when his father died and yet he makes no mention of him in his autobiography or of the time that his family spent in St Ives in the late 1880s. In fact, he dismisses his early years, with the words, "My childhood was of no particular interest and I remember little of it." N.Wilkinson, *A Brush with Life*, London, 1969 at p.1.

One of the fascinating aspects about this exhibition is that the review of the show in the *Cornish Telegraph* uses the term 'the Newlyn School'.[233] Historians of the Newlyn colony have puzzled over when this term first came into being and it is often thought to derive from Alice Meynell's seminal article on the colony in the *Art Journal* in 1889. This reference shows that the term was in use at a much earlier juncture. Although the exhibition did include such classic 'Newlyn School' works as Walter Langley's *"But men must work and women must weep"*, Frank Bourdillon's *1887* (now called *The Jubilee Hat*) and Leghe Suthers' *Dame Trimmer*, what is particularly ironic, however, is that a number of the artists considered to be leading lights in the 'Newlyn School' were in fact exhibiting St Ives subjects. Stanhope Forbes exhibited *Their Daily Bread*, a depiction of Digey Square in St Ives, and a portrait of Percy Craft's wife, whilst Craft himself showed two oils *In the Valley, St Ives* and *The Old Seine Boats, St Ives*. Elizabeth Armstrong's *The Pot Bunny*, noted for its bright colours, is likely to have been painted in St Ives whilst Norman Garstin's *September* might also be a St Ives scene, given that he had been based in the town that month.

Other likely summer visitors to St Ives that year are the future Academician, Ernest Waterlow, who sent to the exhibition *Field path to the Stennack*, and Ayerst Ingram, whose contributions included *Breakers, St Ives*. Ingram, who had lodged with Forbes in Newlyn for some time that year, may well have spent some considerable time in St Ives during 1887 as he contributed paintings of St Ives to the RCPS exhibitions in both 1887 and 1888 and to an exhibition of Cornish paintings held at the Fine Arts Society jointly with Alfred East and Thomas Gotch in April 1888. Although not contributing to the WCAU show, Alfred East is also likely to have been around that summer, as his exhibits at the Fine Art Society included *A Glimpse of St Ives Bay on a Blue Day*, a sketch of a fish market on St Ives pier, a moonrise over Trencrom and various paintings of Lelant, Carbis Bay, Hayle, Phillack, Gwithian and St Erth.[234] This Fine Art Society exhibition probably ranks as the first ever exhibition devoted just to Cornish Art in London

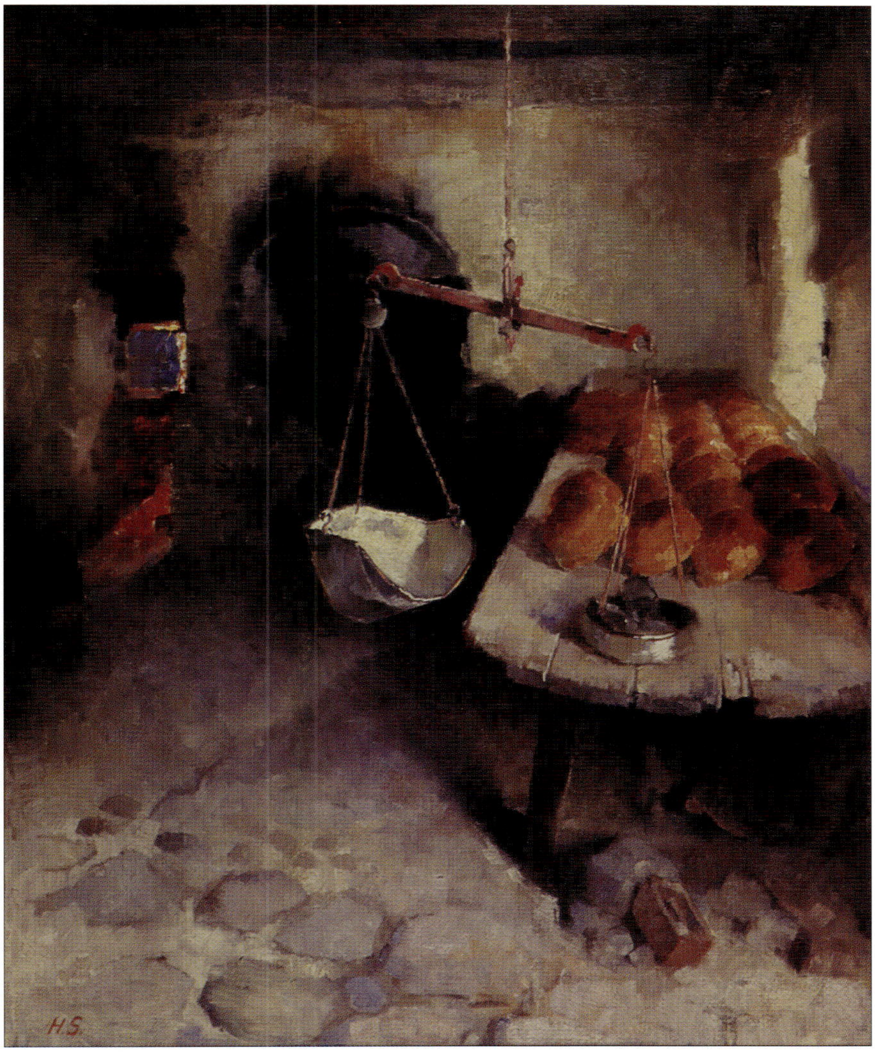

Fig. 4.17 Helene Schjerfbeck *Bakehouse Interior*
(Osterbottens Museum, Vasa, Finland)

233 After dealing with the watercolour exhibits, the critic turns to the oil paintings and comments, "The 'Newlyn School' is well represented, most of its principal members being represented. Mr Simmons sends a work which has hung on the walls of the Paris Salon, and his accomplished wife is also represented." *The Cornish Telegraph*, 22/10/1887

234 Other Cornish towns visited included Truro, St Austell and Fowey and there were also paintings of Mount's Bay and Land's End. *A Glimpse of St Ives Bay on a Blue Day* was also exhibited at RGIFA in 1888.

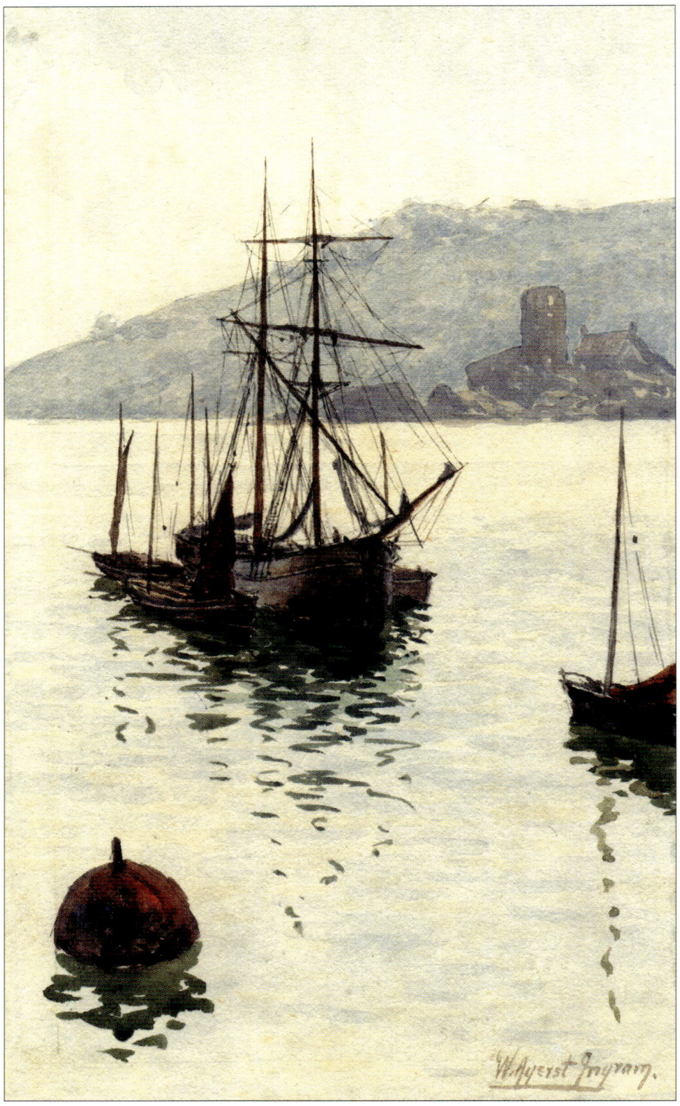

Fig. 4.18 Ayerst Ingram *St Ives* (Private Collection)
The old mine building can be seen on the rocks of Pednolva Point in the rear

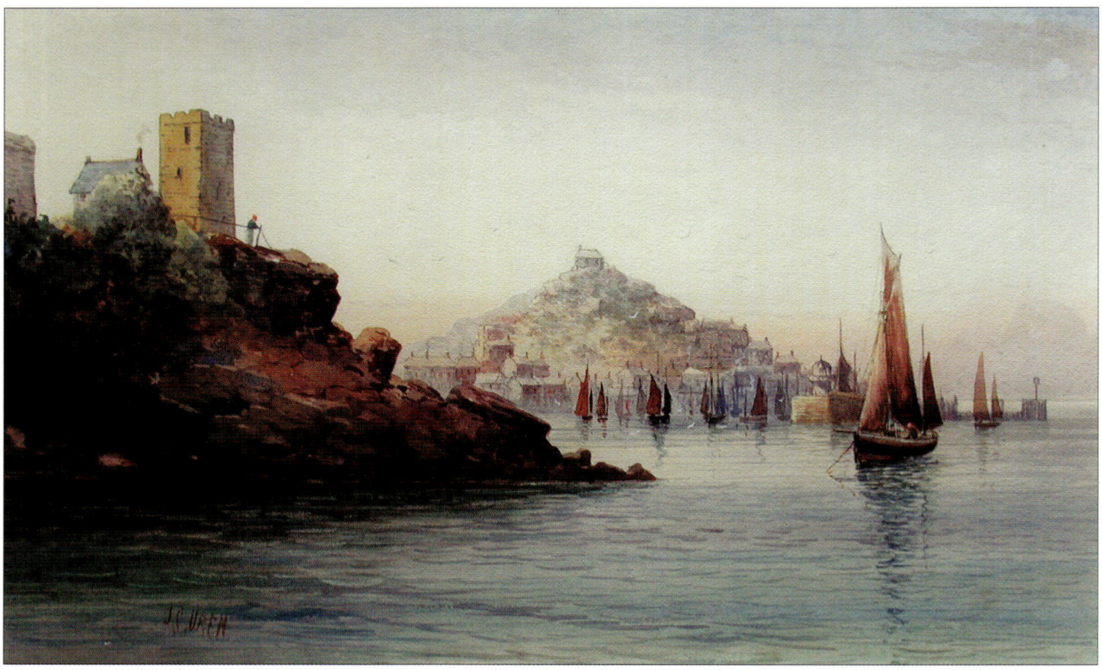

Fig. 4.19 John Clarkson Isaac Uren *St Ives* (Private Collection)
Note the artist sketching on the rocks by the old mine building, which the artist has castellated, in this rather fanciful depiction. Smeaton's Pier is shown prior to its extension and so the work will be pre-1890

4.9 The First Exhibition in St Ives

The interest aroused by the WCAU show led to it being reassembled, with some additions, in Redruth in October. It also led Harry Robinson to propose that there should be an 'Art Exhibition and Union' in St Ives in November. This, however, was to be for the express purpose of clearing the debts of the Choral Society, of which the Griers and himself were members, and, accordingly, works were to be provided *gratis* by the artists. Apart from Adrian and Marianne Stokes, the same group of St Ives artists who had exhibited in Penzance kindly offered work to this show, along with Frank Chadwick, Wyly Grier, Louis's elder brother, who arrived after him, and another new arrival, Moffat Lindner. Contributions were also sent by Walter Langley and the Penzance marine watercolourist, John Clarkson Uren (1845-1932). Uren too may have spent the summer in St Ives, as he exhibited at the Plymouth Arts Club at the beginning of September a work *Baiting the Hooks, Pudding Bag Lane, St Ives* and it was this work and a view of St Ives pier that he contributed to the Choral Society show. The event was held in the Public Hall and Harry Robinson led the way by contributing one of his best known works, *On the Foresand, St Ives*, depicting a fisherwoman holding her basket, which was later owned by the Queen's Hotel, Penzance. This painting shows the clear influence of Stanhope Forbes' *A Fish Sale on a Cornish Beach* and Robinson, therefore, may have benefitted from Forbes' time in St Ives. Other exhibits included a portrait of William Eadie by Ellis Wilkinson and a self-portrait by Wyly Grier.

Helene Schjerfbeck's exhibit, *Bakehouse Interior* - also known as *The Bakery* (Fig. 4.17) - is now in the collection of Osterbottens Museum in Vasa, Finland. This is the same bakery that is featured in Adrian Stokes' work *Bakehouse in a Cornish Village*, which was reproduced in the *Illustrated London News* in August 1888 (see Fig. 4.35). Schjerfbeck often painted similar subjects to the Stokeses, as she had little English. Jacobs considered this work one of the most advanced paintings of her early career, calling it "a work of extreme subtlety and near abstract simplification."[235] It is clear, though, that she contributed to the show out of a sense of duty to the landlord of her tower studio, Harry Robinson, who was promoting the event, rather than out of regard for the work of the Choral Society, as she later confided to her brother, "When the English sing, it sounds as if they

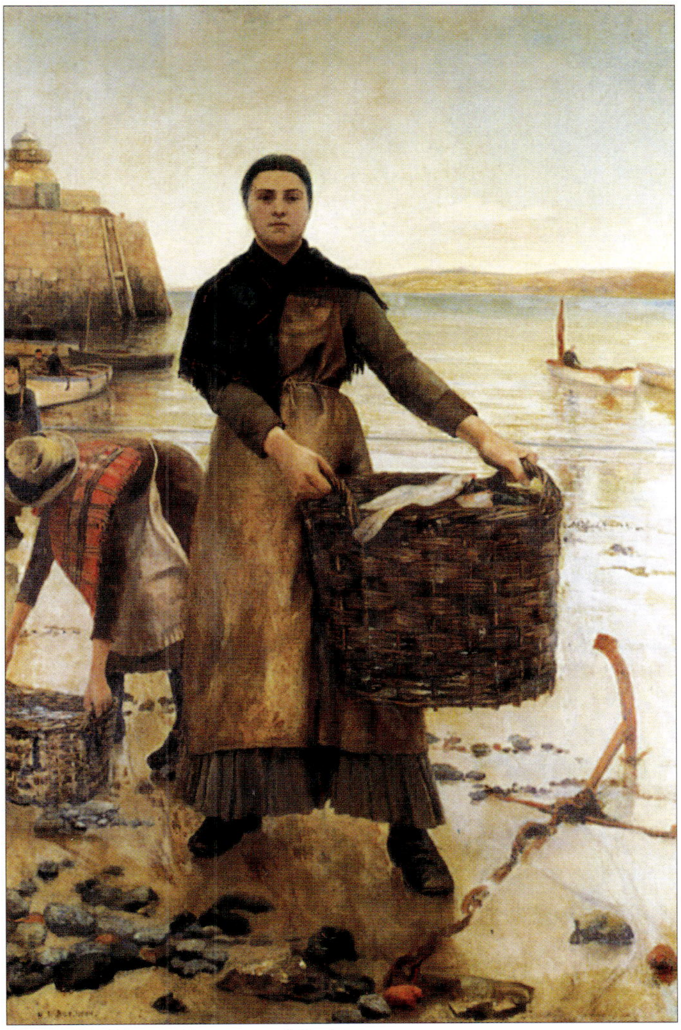

Fig. 4.20 Henry Harewood Robinson
On the Foresand, St Ives (Phillips)

235 M. Jacobs, *The Good and Simple Life*, Oxford, 1985, p.160.

are about to throw up!"[236] However, the most remarkable picture in the collection was considered to be Moffat Lindner's *Old Pier*, a moonlit scene on a wild night in St Ives harbour. Lindner is one of the few artists, whose initial presence in St Ives may be due to his friendship with Whistler. The son of a wealthy Birmingham merchant, he was to become a central figure in the art colony for most of his long life. However, he only managed to escape from the family business in 1874, at the age of 22, and he then took lessons from a pupil of David Cox, during which he "learnt to look at nature broadly... I had many opportunities of seeing the Master's work and, to this day, I have always looked upon those lessons as the foundation of my present success."[237] Initially, his work was very intricate but he came to reject detail and search instead for an object's essence or truth. At the time of his visit in 1887, Lindner had become part of Whistler's circle and he was, in fact, elected a member of the RBA during Whistler's ill-fated Presidency the following year. He was also elected a member of the NEAC in 1889 and the prevalence of moonlight scenes in his output at this time - for instance, his exhibits at Liverpool in 1888 were *Moonlight at St Ives* and *The Moonlit Bay* - led to him being labelled 'the moonlighter'.

Given the beneficiary of this charitable endeavour, it is not surprising to learn that musical evenings were held on each of the four nights of the show, in which many of the artists participated. The project was a huge success and clearly stimulated the artists to have further musical get-togethers.[238] In fact, it probably inspired the social evenings in Louis Grier's Foc'sle Studio, which led ultimately to the formation of the St Ives Arts Club.

4.10 The visit of Elizabeth Armstrong and Rosalie Gill in 1887-8

After leaving St Ives in mid-September 1886, Elizabeth Armstrong went up to London in November because she wanted to do some further etching. Whilst there, she stayed with her uncle. The sale of one of her pictures at the ROI to Mrs Walter Sickert meant that she again fraternised with the Sickert/Whistler set, something that alarmed Stanhope Forbes. "Gotch has told me much about the Whistler gang lately and really I cannot find words strong enough to show my contempt for them. I feel sure a time will come when you will see it too but my prayers do not go up for those who were instrumental in drawing you into that clique."[239] One might have expected that some of the etchings that she completed that winter would have been of St Ives subjects but, to date, all Cornish etchings by her have been labelled Newlyn scenes.

She returned to Newlyn in late January 1887 but decided that she would like to spend the summer in St Ives again. She found lodgings for herself and her mother in July at The Manor House, Green Court, St Ives. This was described by Matthews as an "unpretentious edifice of the seventeenth century", but worth a visit, as its rooms were "wainscotted and adorned with dim old Italian landscapes". However, it no longer commanded an unimpeded view of the sea. She was soon joined by her old student friend, the American Rosalie Gill (1867-1898), and for a while by a Miss Cheever, probably another American art student.[240] Gill, who was always called Daisy, was born in Elmira, New York but, from the age of seven, was brought up in Baltimore. However, she began studying, when only 12, under William Merritt Chase at the Art Students League in New York, and it was there that she first met Lizzie Armstrong. She was very young then, but they met up again when Chase and some of his students worked at Zandvoort, near Haarlem, in the summer of 1884. She arrived in St Ives in mid-July 1887 and loved the town, staying much longer than she originally intended.[241] Forbes told his mother, "She has had a queer sort of bringing up but comes out of it very well. She has very few friends except a few fellow students like Lizzie and this strange notion of her father's letting her go about the world alone is so contrary to all English notions that I fancy she would scarcely get on with most people in this country".[242] However, her high spirits and vivacity won Forbes over.[243] She was also passionate about the theatre and enjoyed the productions of the Newlyn artists. After her departure, he told his mother, "The shopkeepers here all miss her so much. They say she was a real lady she was."[244]

During her time in St Ives, Gill did a number of paintings and contributed an oil, *Hick's Garden*, to the WCAU Exhibition in Penzance that September. However, Forbes records in October, "Miss Gill is in despair. She has heard from America her pictures arrived there all glued together. She fears they are all spoilt. More telegrams to her father...She keeps them going at the office here."[245] However, her extended stay no doubt resulted in further work being done.

---

236 Letter to Magnus Schjerfbeck, dated 1889, the 26th, Saturday evening (translated by Erkki Toivanen).
237 Notes of a talk given to members of STISA in 1929.
238 Two years later it was reported that the £30 capital of the Society restored by this event had dwindled to nothing, leading to the resignation of both Conductor and Secretary. *Cornish Telegraph*, 3/10/1889 & 10/10/1889.
239 Letter from Stanhope Forbes to Elizabeth Armstrong dated 7/12/1886 - Tate Gallery Archives 9015.2.2.18.
240 Forbes, who was holidaying with his family in Wales, wrote of Miss Cheever, "I am very curious to meet her - your description has raised my expectations very high" - Letter from Stanhope Forbes to Elizabeth Armstrong dated 25/8/1887 - Tate Gallery Archives 9015.2.2.59.
241 In a letter to his mother dated 15/6/1887, Stanhope Forbes writes, "Lizzie and her mother have taken their rooms at St Ives - Miss Gill is coming over to join them early in July." Tate Gallery Archives 9015-2-1-432. When she eventually left at the end of November, she had been paying for some weeks for Paris lodgings that she was not using.
242 Letter to his mother dated 7/12/1887 - Tate Gallery Archives 9015-2-1-470.
243 For instance, she decorated their lodgings at The Manor with Chinese lanterns for his birthday and produced copious presents, most of which were just brown paper and string. Forbes was amused that, on one of her visits to Newlyn, when they went to Eyre Crowe's studio, she believed that he was German and kept on addressing him as Herr Crowe.
244 Letter to his mother dated Sunday (11/121887) - Tate Gallery Archives 9015-2-1-471.
245 Letter to his mother dated 2/10/1887 - Tate Gallery Archives 9015-2-1-443.

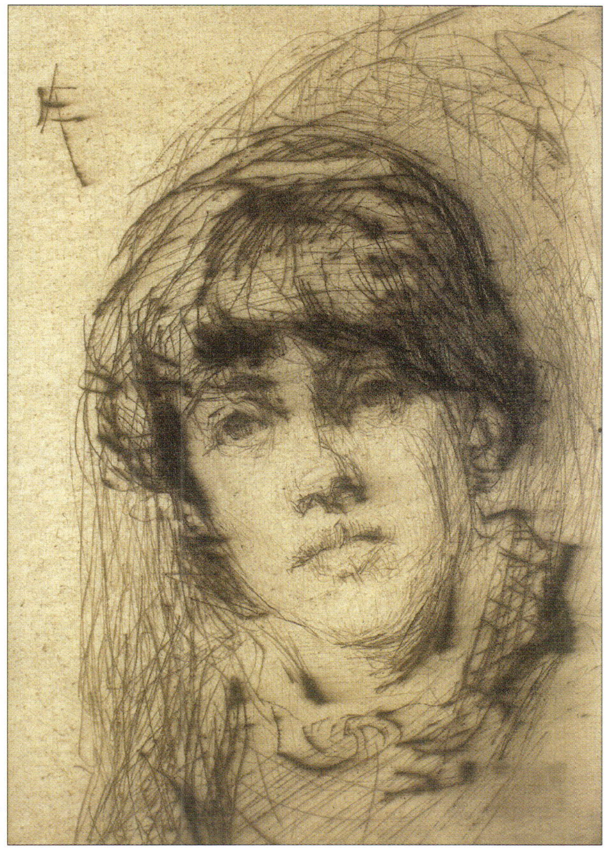

Fig. 4.21 Elizabeth Armstrong *Self-Portrait* (Etching)
(Penlee House Gallery & Museum, Penzance)

Although initially only intending to spend the summer in St Ives, Lizzie Armstrong herself became enamoured with the town and decided to overwinter there. She therefore sublet Percy Craft's studio, probably in St Andrew's Street, telling Mrs Forbes, "I have made up my mind to do several things there before leaving St Ives", but there are few clues in the correspondence as to what these 'things' were.[246] It is often stated that Armstrong preferred St Ives to Newlyn and that she only settled in Newlyn reluctantly, due to Forbes' own strong preference. However, if the full set of correspondence is reviewed, Lizzie's views on St Ives seemed to change with the seasons. In October 1887, she pronounced, "I certainly like the place far better than Newlyn" and told Forbes that it had ten times as many subjects to paint but, in January, when the majority of the foreign artists had left, she commented, "..after Newlyn, it does seem a dull little town".[247] By the time that she returned to Newlyn in March, she was pleased to get away from her bleak, damp studio. However, she did give serious consideration to returning to St Ives for the summer of 1888, for the Crafts were anxious that she should join them there, but she told Mrs Forbes she did not know what to do. "I became a little tired of it last year and yet I am afraid that the summer straight through in Newlyn is not a good thing. So much depends on the weather in this place. Should it be a cold damp summer, St Ives would be too dreary for anything but, if it was like last year, it would be far better than Newlyn". Her decision to remain in Newlyn in 1888 was, in the end, influenced by her mother who felt more at home at Cliff Castle Cottage, Paul because the wives of the Newlyn artists made an effort to visit her. Her mother also seems to have put paid to Daisy Gill joining them again - "Mother has the idea that she is a great responsibility", she tells Mrs Forbes. However, she was soon complaining that life in Newlyn was dull.[248]

Gill subsequently settled in Paris, studying under the Belgian artist, Alfred Stevens, and exhibiting regularly at the Paris Salon. *The Orchid*, a mother and child scene, made a strong impact at the 1889 Paris World Exposition and at many other exhibitions. She returned to St Ives in October 1890, when she was a guest at the Arts Club, and her exhibits at the Chicago World Columbian Exhibition in 1893 included *Twilight on St Ives Bay*. In September 1897, she married René Lara, becoming Comtesse de Chaban, but died the following January from the gripe. Her work is in several Baltimore public collections.

---

246 Letter from Elizabeth Armstrong to Mrs Forbes dated 12/10/1887 - Tate Gallery Archives 9015.4.2/3. As mentioned above, she exhibited an oil, *The Pot Bunny*, at the WCAU show in September, and, for the Choral Society show in November, she contributed a portrait of a young girl and two of her etchings. Other paintings exhibited at the RBA in 1887-8, such as the pastels *Hatching Mischief* and *Cuckoo* and her major work *Matinée Musicale*, priced at £50, might also be St Ives executed work, as might her work *First Love*, which was suspended from the NEAC exhibition of 1887, as her lovers were deemed too young.
247 Letters from Elizabeth Armstrong to Mrs Forbes dated 12/10/1887 and 31/1/1888 - Tate Gallery Archives 9015.4.2/3 & 12. See also 9015.2.2.54.
248 Letters from Elizabeth Armstrong to Mrs Forbes dated 10/6/1888 & 16/7/1888 - Tate Gallery Archives 9015.4.2/8 & 9.

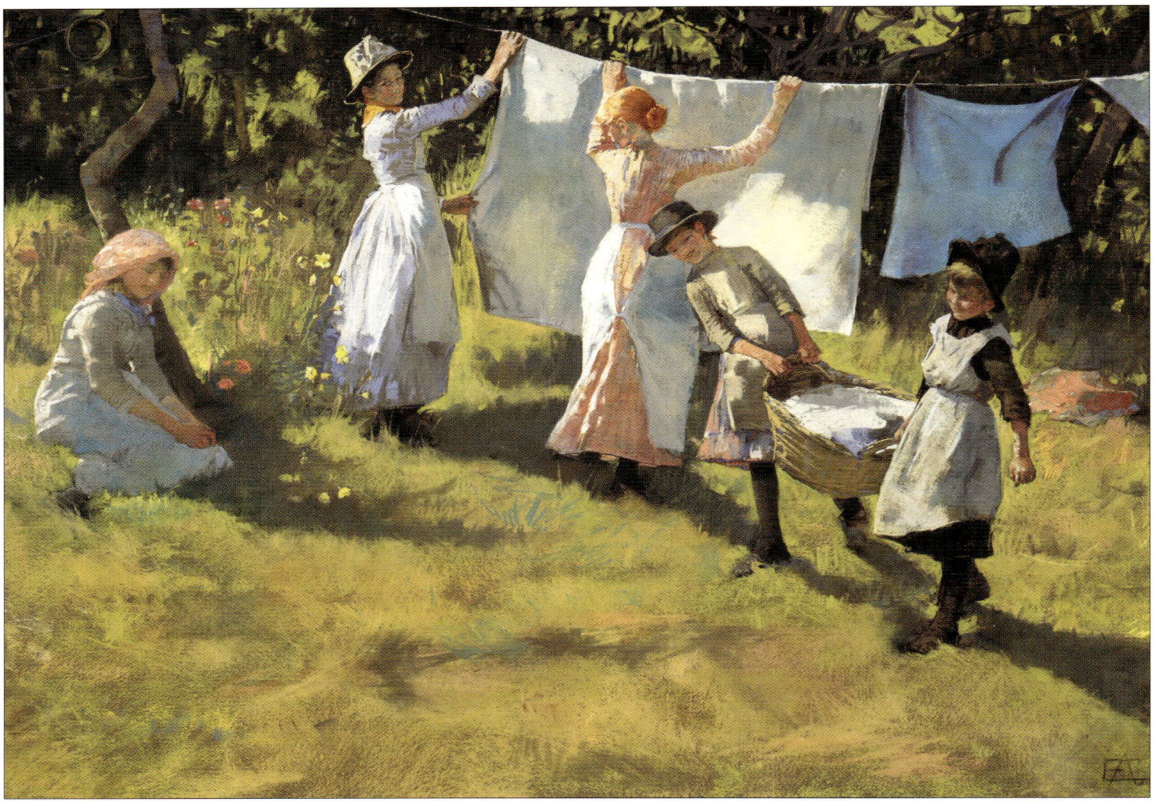

Fig. 4.22 Elizabeth Armstrong *Hanging Out the Washing* (Richard Green, London)

With his fiancée based in St Ives, Forbes continued to visit with regularity and the social inter-reaction of the two colonies continued. In October 1887, he mentions "a grand silhouette evening" in St Ives when he got capital likenesses of many of the St Ives artists, although he felt that the pretty and charming Nora Locking did not come off too well in profile - "Too much beak".[249] Others clearly were not put off for, when Elizabeth Armstrong and Nora came over to see the work of the Newlyn artists in February 1888, Forbes commented that "there was a regular fight between Tayler and Bourdillon as to who should see Miss Locking to the station."[250] Lizzie and Nora became good friends and Nora was her one bridesmaid at her wedding.[251]

In February 1888, Forbes was also impressed that twenty or so St Ives residents had made the effort on a foul night to come across to Newlyn to see two plays - *Turn Him Out* and *Checkmate* - put on by the Newlyn Artists' Dramatic Society. He tells his mother, "I am going up to supper with the Robinsons and we shall hear what the St Ives party thought of it. I hear, however, that they were delighted." The initial favourable report had no doubt got back to him through Lizzie, who had acted in one of the plays, although still living in St Ives. Chadwick, however, was furious that his sketch had been left out of the collection of works shown at the venue and wrote Forbes a strong letter. Reporting the incident to his mother, Forbes commented, "I think he is a fool to kick up a shindy about so little. If you saw the sketch you would smile. It is quite the worst in the collection."[252]

Forbes was a little shocked to hear that Lizzie had decided to stay on in St Ives over the winter. Perhaps in an effort to put her off, he expounded his own views on the competing claims of the two colonies. Whilst he was prepared to agree with Lizzie that St Ives had "ten times as many subjects to paint", there was the issue of lodgings. He did not fancy "a small apartment by myself", which he felt was the only option in St Ives. "The comfort of Mrs Maddern's" - his rooms at Bellevue in Newlyn - "is not to be had elsewhere". He also preferred the milder climate of Newlyn. The clinching point, however, was that he preferred the company in Newlyn. "In my opinion, it is more conducive to work to be living amongst a nice pleasant set of men than with a parcel of foreigners, with whom I have no sympathy."[253] It is quite clear that Forbes had particular difficulty getting on with Americans, for his letters to his mother, whether from Paris or Brittany, are full of complaints about the number of Americans around and their antics.[254] Although happy to socialise with Howard Butler, he makes clear in his letters his dislike for Frank Chadwick and Edward Simmons, whose loquacity he found most trying.

249 Letter to his mother dated 2/10/1887 - Tate Gallery Archives 9015-2-1-443.
250 Letter to his mother dated 1/2/1888 - Tate Gallery Archives 9015-2-1-474.
251 Leonora seems to have socialised as much with the Newlyn artists as with the St Ives ones and, in December 1889, she contributed a work to the Penzance exhibition designed to raise funds for the Newlyn Amateur Dramatic Society.
252 Letter to his mother dated 2/2/1888 - Tate Gallery Archives 9015-2-1-475.
253 Letters from Stanhope Forbes to Elizabeth Armstrong from Wales in August 1887 - Tate Gallery Archives 9015.2.2.54 & 61.
254 See for example Tate Gallery Archives 9015.2.1.56, 57 & 167.

4.11 The visit of Anders Zorn in 1887-8

The fledgling colony at St Ives was considerably enhanced by the arrival at the beginning of November 1887 of the Swedish painter, Anders Zorn. Zorn is now one of Sweden's best known artists on the international stage and a museum in his home town of Mora is dedicated to his work. Born illegitimately, he never met his father, the German brewer, Leonhard Zorn, and was brought up by his grandparents in Mora. At the age of 15, he entered the Royal Academy of Art in Stockholm and, between 1881 and 1885, he studied abroad, mainly in England and Spain. In 1885, he married Emma Lamm, the daughter of a wealthy Stockholm merchant, whose encouragement and critical analysis played an important role in his artistic growth.

When he arrived in St Ives in 1887, Zorn was known principally as a portrait painter in watercolours and had already received commissions from some of the leading members of Stockholm society. In fact, the reason for his trip to England in 1887 had been to paint the portrait of Anna, the niece of the wealthy banker, Ernest Cassel, at his shooting lodge in the north of England. After this, he and his wife had intended to visit Cornwall briefly to look at the scenery before taking a boat from Plymouth to Spain. However, after experiencing a terrible storm in Penzance on 31st October, which caused widespread devastation, they journeyed across to St Ives, fell in love with the place and decided to stay. They were accompanied by a young English female portrait artist, Alice Miller, whom Anders had known for some time and who was recovering from typhoid and other fevers, and they all took lodgings together at 12, The Terrace, where they had their own kitchen. Alice and Emma did the shopping and shared the household tasks and, in addition to her help with the language, Alice's practicality was considered a great boon. Emma, writing to her cousin, commented, "We have the benefit of the refreshing Atlantic winds, serious storms with sky-high waves from time to time, lack of cold due to the Gulf Stream (at least it is attributed to it), beautiful fishermen etc etc. All are benefits apart from one disadvantage - St Ives is a place for artists. Yet we haven't suffered from it. We have only seen a few." Not unnaturally, they made contact with their fellow Scandinavians, but Zorn was rather upset at the cold reaction of Emma Chadwick, with whom he had studied at art school. They liked the Norwegian, Bernt Grönvold, however, although Emma was not too complimentary about his work, and Anders admired the paintings of Helene Schjerfbeck. However, the artists with whom they had most contact, were Adrian Stokes and the American, Edward Simmons, whom Emma described as "clever in chess and conversation" for he came round to have tea and play chess with them on a regular basis. Simmons, whom Anders called "one of America's best painters", was more forthcoming in his autobiography about Zorn than any other artist he met in St Ives. "Zorn had a disposition of sweetness and light, and, although he had inherited a great charm and delicacy from the paternal side of his family, he cared nothing for society and manners, and thought like a simple peasant; therefore, like a child. He was large, fattish, built on a small skeleton - a man who would break easily - and had the head of all the colorists - that is, a square forehead, delicate but square jaw, slight acquiline nose, and enormous pale-blue watery eyes. His drooping yellow moustache was long but not thick, and his hands were of the softest, most personal and interesting character. He was a man with a great hypnotic quality who did not talk much, but dominated without speaking."[255]

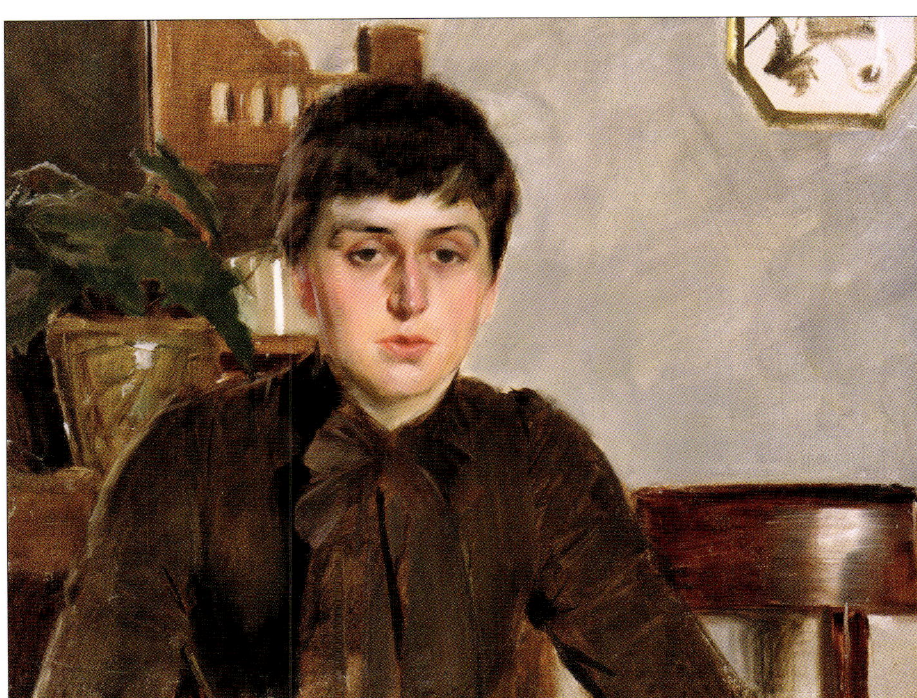

Fig. 4.23 Anders Zorn *Alice Miller* (Zorn Museum, Mora)

255 E E Simmons, *From Seven to Seventy*, New York and London, 1922 at p. 167-8. Simmons also records that Zorn had, at one juncture, planned to be a sculptor and, when bored with the company or the argument, he would often saunter over to a window and carve in wood exquisite small pieces.

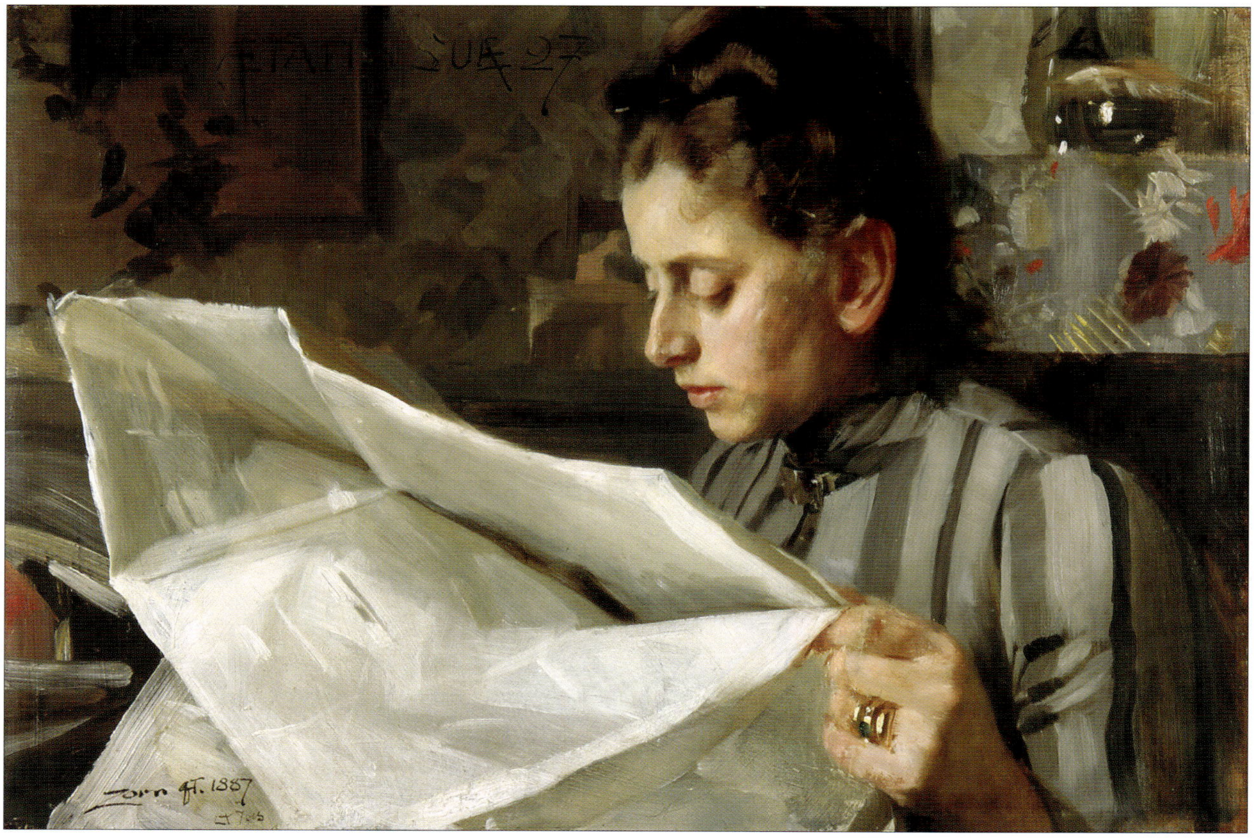

Fig.4.24 Anders Zorn *Emma Zorn Reading* (Zorn Museum, Mora)

With Simmons' encouragement, Zorn decided during his stay in St Ives to start painting in oil. He commented, "I thought I had a few months to spare without having to think of earning my living... I started with a small portrait of my wife in profile reading the paper. I have often seen her lost in her reading and painted her that way. After that, I started a painting *A Fisherman*, who flirts with a girl in a way that I found strange there. They stood side by side leaning over a long wall looking at the moon in the background, the harbour and the red sails that had been pulled up ready for departure. That hour where the setting sun, with its warm full light, still makes the objects glow. This debut in oil was a good debut."[256] Emma Zorn indicated that one of the novel aspects of the picture was that the figures were depicted from behind, but that this had become a favourite motif in St Ives at that time.[257] Simmons mentions that Zorn had jokingly called himself Simmons' pupil, as Simmons had set his palette and told him what materials to buy, but had become "as peevish as a child" when Simmons had criticised the fact that he had put the moon in the due north.[258] The painting, which became known as *Fisherman, St Ives* and which was painted from the window of 12, The Terrace, was indeed a good debut - it won a Mention Honorable at the Paris Salon in 1888 and was bought by the French Government. Although originally hung in the Luxembourg Museum, it is now at Pau in the Pyrenees. Other oil paintings that he completed during his time in St Ives included a portrait of his companion, Alice Miller, (Fig. 4.23) and a head of a fishwife, *Old Anne* (Fig. 4.28). [259]

Zorn worked hard during his time in St Ives and he continued to paint in watercolours. He produced a number of depictions of boats in the harbour and of the waters of the Bay but his principal watercolour was of a fish sale on the harbour beach (Fig. 4.26). He commented, "One day I saw a healthy fisherman's wife inside a house. I requested that I may paint her and I started an aquarelle with her as the main motif, dragging a few six feet long fish on the beach where the catch was auctioned, stowed and sent to Paris or London. The naked reddish arms clearly absorbed the painter's main interest."[260] This is probably the painting about which Simmons tells a number

---

256 From Zorn's autobiographical notes kindly supplied by the Zorn Museum, Mora (translated by Bjorn Benckert).

257 Letter from Emma Zorn to Hugo Greber dated 3/1/1888. She also comments, "It is for the moment very fashionable here to paint two people from behind watching a rising full moon. The difference is only one person's pair is in their sixties whereas the other person's pair is youthful and watching the glowing moon shine etc" Zorn Museum Archives – translated by Bjorn Benckert. The other painting, to which she was probably referring, was Edward Simmons' *John Anderson, My Jo*, which featured an old man kissing his wife goodbye, with neither face being depicted.

258 E E Simmons, ibid, at p.169.

259 Writing in 1920, an unidentified reviewer mentioned a conversation that he had had with Anders Zorn during his time in St Ives. "From what source", I asked him, "does the artist derive the inspiration?" "From the canvas, sir." replied Zorn, with a touch of sarcasm. It takes an artist, perhaps, to appreciate the subtlety of that reply, which not only rebuked a foolish question, but gave three-quarters of the whole truth." *St Ives Times, A Cornish Painter - The Work of Charles Simpson*, 16/4/1920.

260 From Zorn's autobiographical notes kindly supplied by the Zorn Museum, Mora (translated by Bjorn Benckert).

of stories about Zorn's original approach. "I went into his back yard one day" - he records - "and he had a six-foot watercolour leaning against the house, and was throwing pails of water on it - 'bringing it together' ".[261] Having completed the work, Zorn laid it on a box hedge in the garden to dry off. However, the arrival of the loquacious Simmons meant that they failed to notice a gathering storm, which drenched the painting. Everyone thought it was ruined but Zorn had declared "Now I can make a fine picture" and turned the large raindrops in the sands in the foreground into footprints. The painting was a huge success at the Grosvenor Gallery, with the critics praising the naturalness of the footprints![262]

The buxom fishwife, with her chubby arms and rosy cheeks, who was the main model in *Fish Sale, St Ives*, also featured in an oil painting, *In the Kitchen* (Fig. 5.1), where she is shown putting a kettle on to an impressive black range, glowing fiercely. In this beautifully observed interior, which is lit by an unseen window to the left, Zorn has included a backview of her husband sitting on a chair in the foreground, whilst the warm light of the fire reflects off the copper knobs on the range and the pewter plates lining its shelf. There is no story to tell. No sentiment is invoked. It is merely a study of light.

Zorn described St Ives as a beautiful fishing village, "where a little international community had found its ideal place...It was a very pleasant and relaxing time in this community of skilful artists".[263] When it was determined that they had to leave in February 1888 for Paris, as Anders had a portrait commission there, Emma too was sad, "I am not happy to leave this place where I have been very happy and had it so homely, and where we have also found such nice acquaintances."[264]

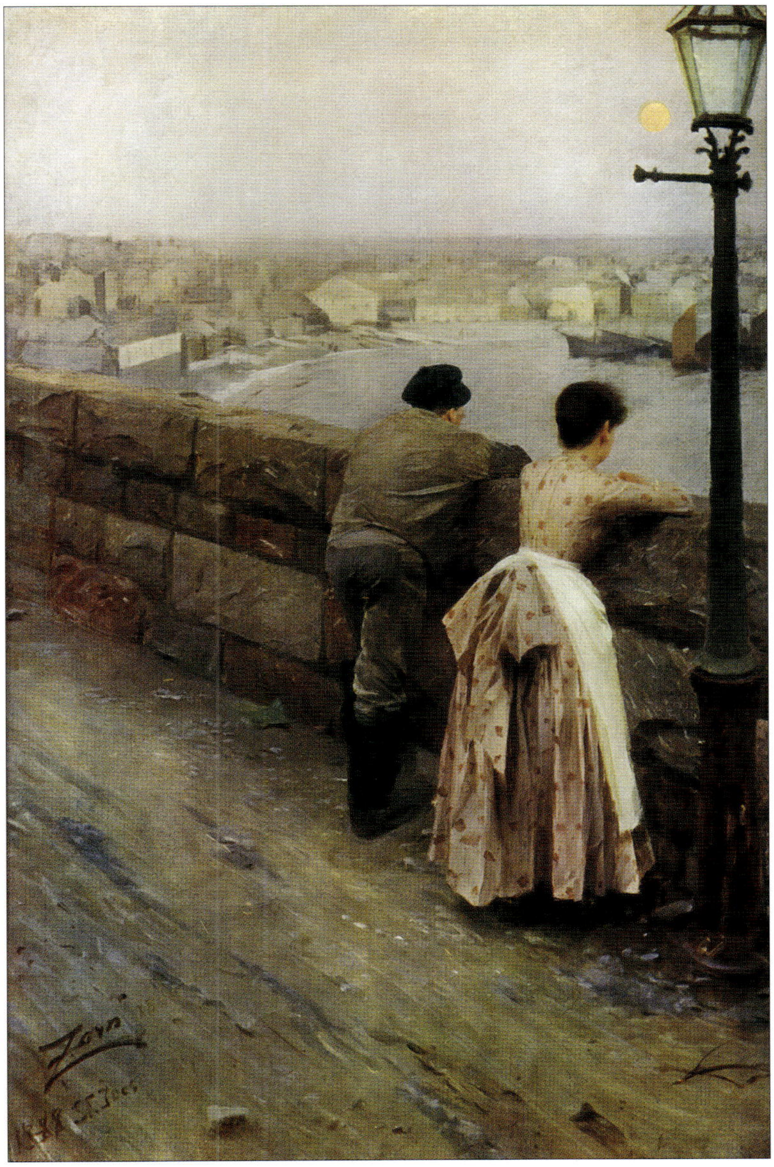

Fig. 4.25 Anders Zorn *Fisherman, St Ives* (Musée de Pau)

261 E E Simmons, ibid, at p.169.
262 E E Simmons, ibid, at p.169-70.
263 From Zorn's autobiographical notes kindly supplied by the Zorn Museum, Mora (translated by Bjorn Benckert).
264 Letter to Elin Lamm 9/11/1887.

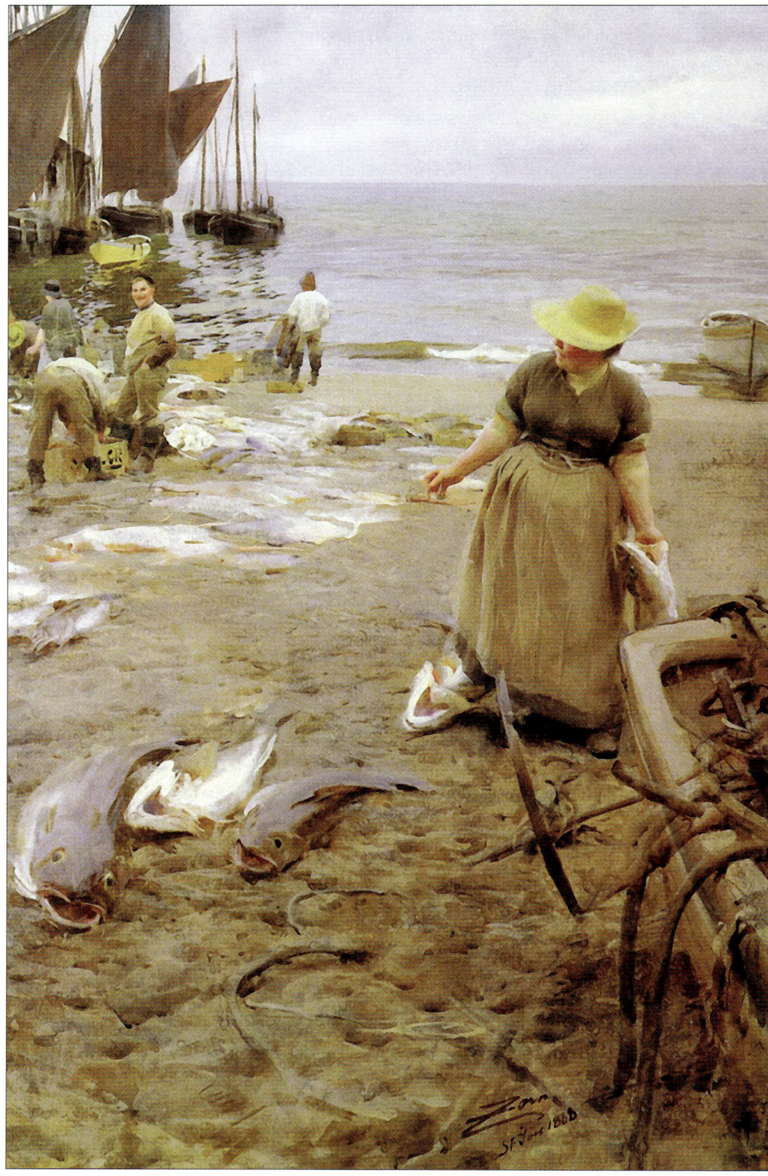

Fig. 4.26 Anders Zorn *Fish Sale, St Ives*

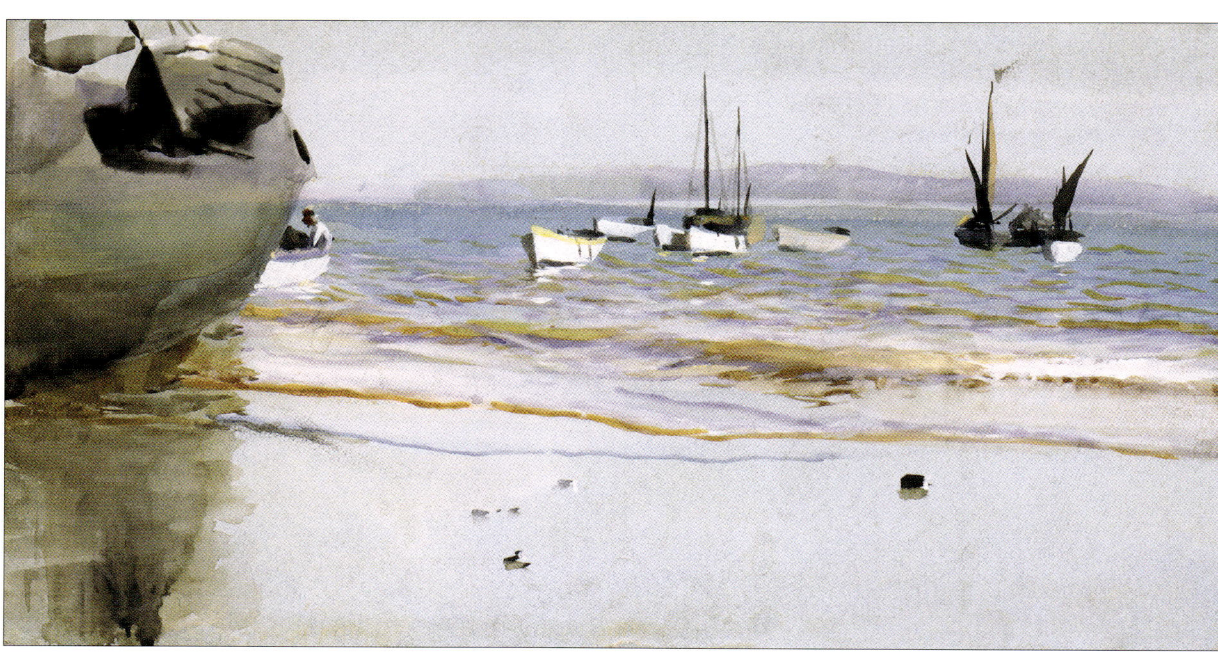

Fig. 4.27 Anders Zorn *Boats at St Ives* (Zorn Museum, Mora)

4.12 Helene Schjerfbeck's *The Convalescent*

At the same time as Anders Zorn was producing one of *the* seminal works of his early career, another Scandinavian, Helene Schjerfbeck, was doing likewise. Despite feeling that the English, unlike the French, made little attempt to make foreigners feel comfortable, she was soon writing enthusiastic letters back to Maria Wiik about the Cornish landscape. "There are thousands of subjects here I would like to paint: the old fishing village down below, the new artists' town on the hills above, a couple of sandy beaches, the harbour with the boats, heaths and grassy pastures browned by the hot summer sun. Cornwall is the most beautiful place I have ever seen - at least the scenery I saw when travelling here from Plymouth by train: hills and inlets, sea and forests....Since I arrived here, I have had this *urge to work*, *urge to work*. There isn't much time. I wish you were here. Today, the sea is so blue and bright, the sky blue, and the light so soft you cannot see the horizon. The sunsets are glorious, either with tremendous clouds or with nothing but a rosy afterglow over the whole world. As you may notice, my impressions of England are only about landscape and nature; fortunately, there is nothing oppressive here."[265]

Helene's letters to Maria also indicate that Adrian Stokes, shortly after his arrival, started up some painting classes. "Two or three times a week there's an evening class at A. Stokes's studio attended mostly by old colleagues from Pont Aven. We draw fishermen in sou'westers and oilskins. Unfortunately, they spend most days at sea fishing and only seldom find time to pose for us. In the summer, it is easy to find models, but now that there's fish to be caught the locals have become uninterested."[266] In the same letter, she commented, "I think you would love it here and like the models, children and old people. Once they are over 17, they all become dull and common. Nowhere have I seen young girls' faces and expressions as dull and impassive as here. Yet, they are often beautiful to look at......... I have found an excellent model, a fine old woman with enough history in her face. She offers another major advantage when I've tired her out - as regularly happens - her identical twin sister can take her place. They are 73 years old. I would like to paint them together."[267] The principal work that she completed featuring this model (or these models) was *Autumn Rose*, a rather grey interior, showing an old maid - in her 'autumn' years - sitting on a chair, with a rose in her right hand. The pose, though, is unconvincing. However, the distinctive headwear worn by the woman does raise the possibility that she was the same model used by Anders Zorn for his sketch Old Anne.

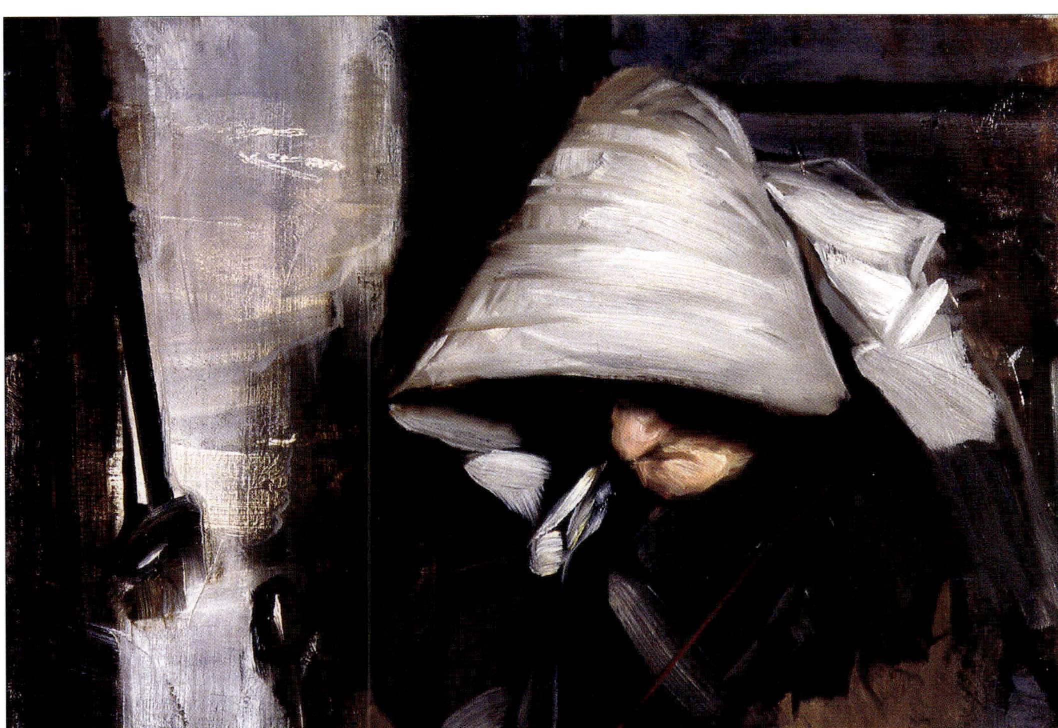

Fig. 4.28 Anders Zorn *Old Anne* (Zorn Museum, Mora)

265 Letter to Maria Wiik, undated, 1888 - reproduced in translation in Marjatta Levanto, *Helene Schjerfbeck - Convalescents*, Helsinki, 1988 at p.46.
266 ibid.
267 ibid.

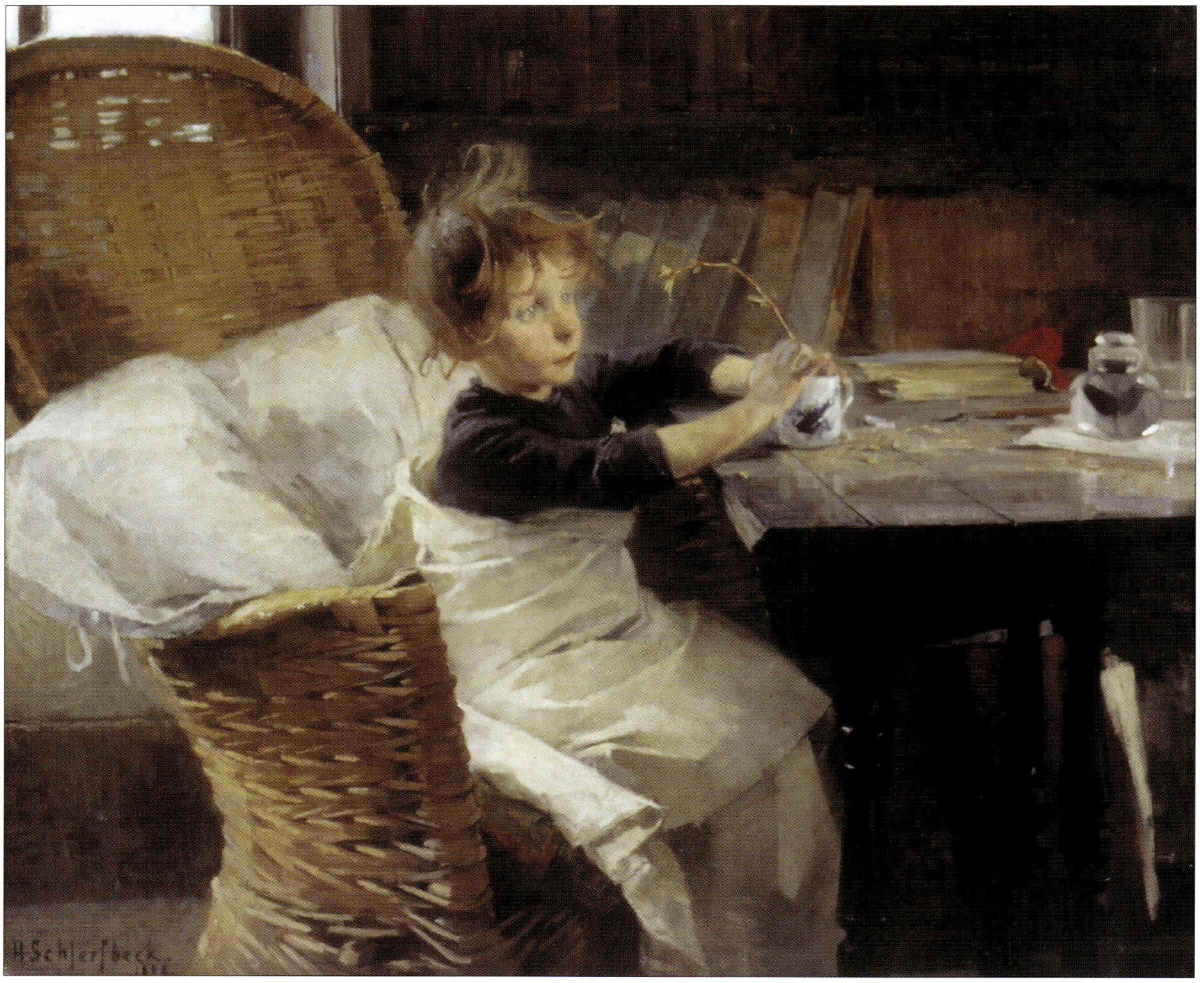

Fig. 4.29 Helene Schjerfbeck *The Convalescent* (Finnish National Gallery, Helsinki) (photo: Central Art Archives/Hannu Aaltonen)

Mention has already been made of Schjerfbeck's paintings *View of St Ives* and *Bakehouse Interior,* but her most ambitious work during her first visit was *The Convalescent*. This is dated 1888 but, as she left St Ives at the end of January that year, it is likely to have been painted mostly during the latter part of 1887. The model was a young Cornish girl, who also featured in Schjerfbeck's *Profile of a Child* (Fig. 7.2) and several works by Marianne Stokes, including *The Red Dress* and *The Tearful Child* (Fig. 7.1).[268] Indeed, she is likely to be the girl to whom Adrian Stokes was referring, when he commented, "The best child model my wife ever had here was a little girl so wicked that her teachers were thankful when she stayed away from school."[269] The picture shows her, well wrapped up, with tousled hair, sitting disconsolately at a table in a room lined with old books. She holds in her hand a twig, which is about to blossom, and this is intended to signify a new beginning. Indeed, the work was called *Premiere Verdure* (The First Greening), when it was first exhibited at the Paris Salon that year The sentimentality of the subject, and the rather unnatural incorporation of the twig, makes it untypical of Schjerfbeck's work and suggests that she had been influenced by the type of subject matter selected by her peers in the colony. Like many 'Newlyn School' interiors, it is the play of light streaming through the window at the rear of the painting that is one of its principal features. It was an enormous success, however, being bought by the Finnish Art Society from its autumn show in 1888, when it was exhibited under the title, *Recovering*, and it was lent to the Paris International Exhibition in 1889 under its current title, *The Convalescent*, where it won a first class bronze medal. Finnish art historians feel that the painting can be interpreted as reflecting Schjerfbeck's own mental state, as she gradually blossoms again following her cruel rejection by her fiancé.

4.13 Edward Simmons' controversial depictions of the Holy Family

Edward Simmons, during his time in Concarneau, acquired a significant reputation both in France and America and he was clearly one of the leading figures in the St Ives colony in its early years, for he was the only one of the initial influx of foreign artists to base himself in the town for an extended period of time. Fellow American, Arthur Hoeber, who worked with Simmons in Paris and Concarneau, later commented, "There are some men...whose natural gifts are most interesting, and whose ability seems simply marvellous. These happy mortals appear to have none of the trials and tribulations that beset the path of their comrades and from the beginning draw and

268 Sotheby's Victorian Painting Sale 30/9/1987 Lot 159.
269 Prefatory Note to the Stokes's Fine Art Society Exhibition, February 1900.

paint dexterously. Such a man is Edward Emerson Simmons. At the schools in his earlier years, his easel was a favourite loafing place for other members of his class...in his studio later on, fellow workers would stand and watch him draw with charcoal or paint with surprising facility; and today, when he has arrived, he finds seemingly none of the perplexities that worry most men."[270]

Simmons' principal work for the 1888 Paris Salon exhibition was *The Carpenter's Son* (66" x 50.5"), which he described as "a simple pose of one of my children in my studio. A blond boy, with a light shining over his head, sat dreaming, instead of sweeping out the shop, whilst his mother, in the back, told his father what a worthless son he had begotten. The shavings had accidentally fallen in the form of a cross and the light seemed to be a halo."[271] By the mere sprinkling of some wood shavings on the floor, Simmons has converted a portrait of his own son in his studio into a depiction of the Christ Child. As Simmons always seemed to be fully aware of market forces, it is not clear whether he was merely pandering to the known fondness of the public of the time for reading storylines into paintings or whether he intended to produce a controversial and novel work secularising the Holy Family. He clearly knew his market, as, when the painting was exhibited at the Royal Academy the following year, he received a formal enquiry from the Chantrey Trustees. *The Scotsman*, however, then came out with a scathing denunciation of the painting, as Simmons had painted the Christ Child in the costume of a French peasant boy! As a result, for the very first time, much to Simmons' chagrin, the Chantrey Trustees reneged on an offer of purchase.[272]

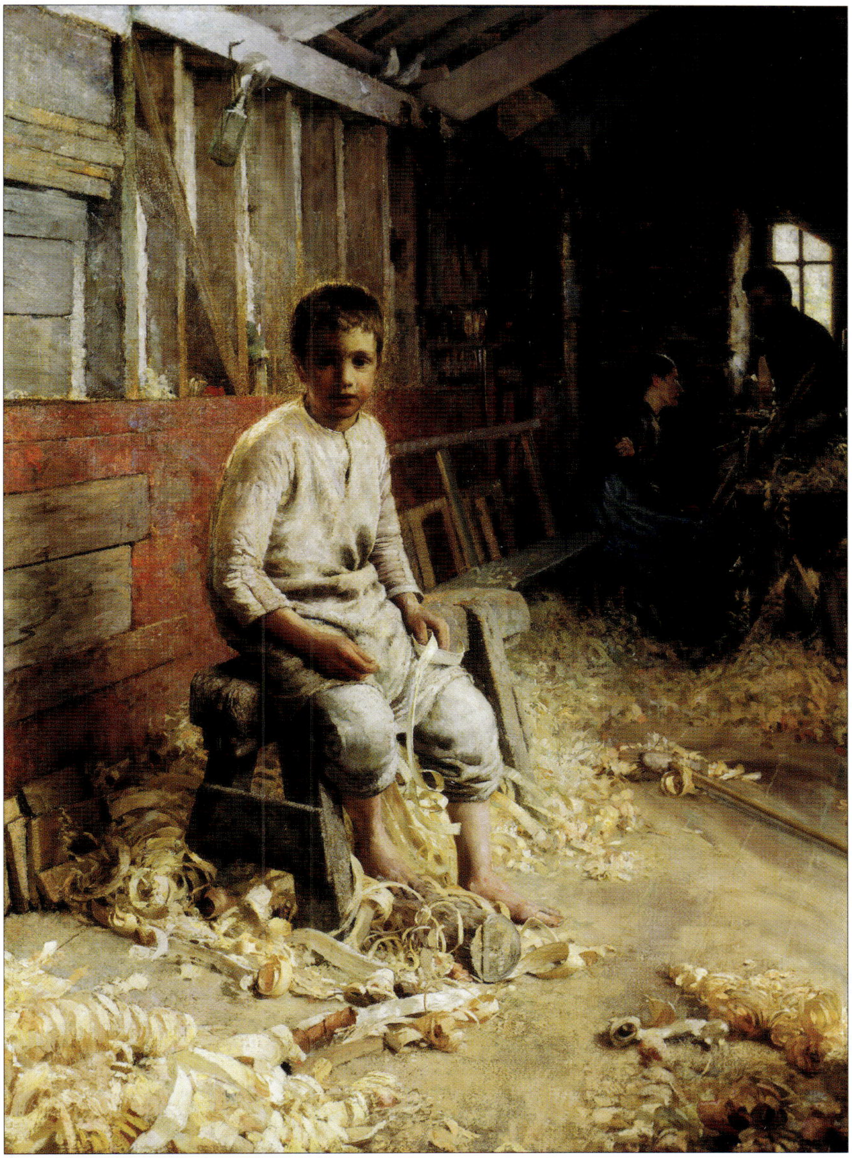

Fig. 4.30 Edward Simmons *The Carpenter's Son*
(New Unitarian Church, New Bedford, Massachusetts)

270 From an article on Simmons dated 1900 quoted by Summer Crane and Susan Lehman in relation to his window *The Light Bearer*.
271 E E Simmons, ibid, p.177-8. Simmons indicates in his autobiography that he painted the work in his Paris Studio but the painting is actually inscribed 'St Ives'.
272 The painting, which in its frame measured 82" x 62.5", was exhibited at the 1893 Chicago World Columbian Exhibition in Chicago and was later bequeathed by Amelia Jones to the First Unitarian Church in New Bedford, Massachusetts. It was included in the Smithsonian Centennial Exhibition in 1993. *Maine Antique Digest*, April 1997.

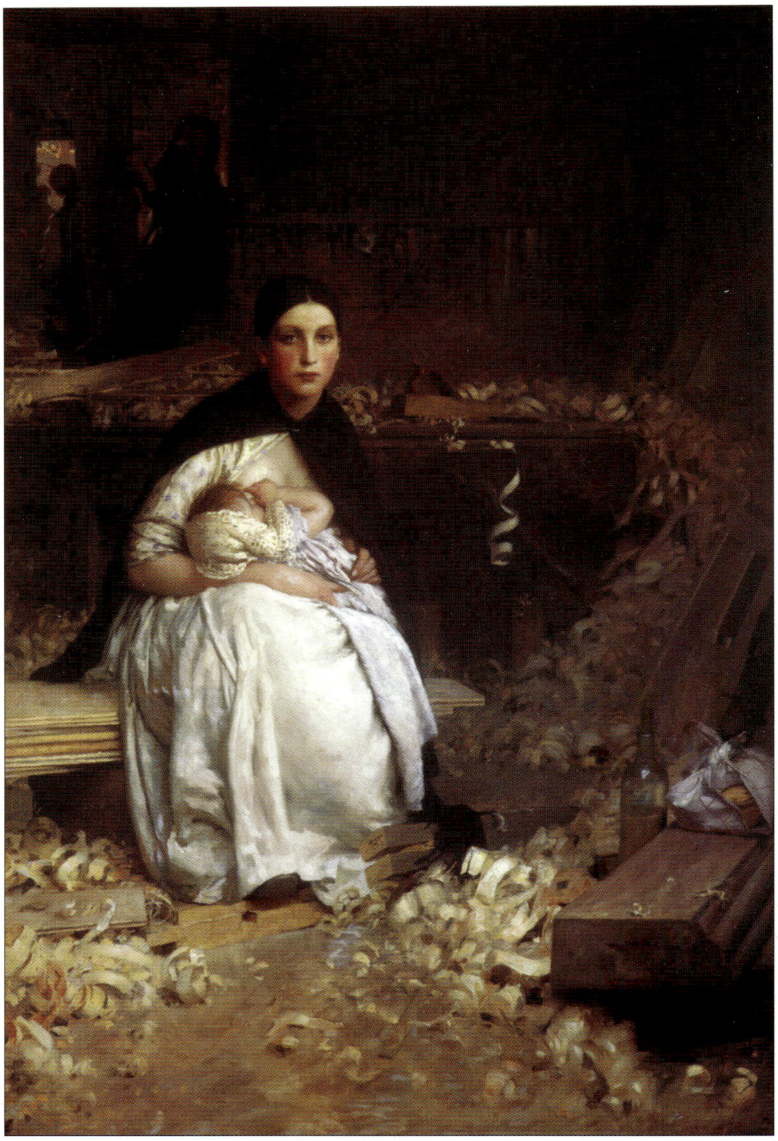

Fig. 4.31 Edward Simmons *The Mother* (Hardwick Simmons)

Simmons' second exhibit at the Paris Salon of 1888 was called *Mother and Child* and it is not clear whether this was the painting, or an early version of the painting, that became known simply as *The Mother*. This featured his wife, Vesta, breast-feeding their second child, with himself in the shadows in the background, but again the spectator was encouraged to think of the Holy Family. *The Cornish Telegraph*, which considered it to be his finest work to date, when it was exhibited on Show Day in 1891, described the scene. "The subject is the interior of a carpenter's shop. It is dinner time and the carpenter's wife has brought the mid-day meal for her husband, and whilst waiting for him to do the needful with the simple repast, she sits and nurses her child. The picture is not only nobly conceived, but the faithful treatment of the accessories is simply perfect, and the beauty and consistency of the colour is in every way worthy of the painter. The chips are painted so naturally and realistically that the observer is almost tempted to stoop for the purposes of handling them. The foreground is occupied by the partially nude figure of the mother, whose natural poise, facial expression and costume, are all beautifully and vigorously treated, and the marvellous execution of the most trifling details is extremely wonderful."[273] The St Ives paper was also enthusiastic "*The Mother* is a magnificent work, the power and intense realism of which is positively startling. It is *only* the interior of a carpenter's shop, *only* a woman nursing her baby, - yet so wonderfully wrought out in every detail that the effect is fascinating in the extreme."[274]

These paintings pre-date Abbott Thayer's more well-known works, in which the Holy Family is humanised, such as *Virgin Enthroned* of 1891 (Smithsonian American Art Museum), and clearly made a considerable impact. The ability of them to continue to shock was sadly demonstrated in November 1996, when *The Carpenter's Son*, which had been donated to the First Unitarian Church of New Bedford, Massachusetts, was badly vandalised, the figure of the Christ Child being cut out of the canvas. The missing portion was only re-discovered in 2005 and the painting, now owned by an insurance company, is apparently in the process of being restored.

273 *Cornish Telegraph*, 9/4/1891.
274 *St Ives Weekly Summary*, 4/4/1891.

The First Sales by St Ives and Newlyn artists to the Chantrey Trustees

The St Ives colony clearly, once again, made a significant impression at the Paris Salon exhibition of 1888, with these major works by Zorn, Schjerfbeck and Simmons, whilst paintings by Emma Chadwick (2), Frank Chadwick, Charles Reinhart (2), Rosalie Gill and Adrian Stokes were also hung. It was the first year, however, that the colony made a mark at the Royal Academy. In fact, it was rather a special year for both Cornish colonies.

On 19th March 1888, a group of St Ives artists were invited over to see the works of the Newlyners. The party included the Robinsons, Nora Locking and Anders Zorn.[275] One of the principal works on view was Frank Bramley's *A Hopeless Dawn*. Forbes, reporting on the day to his mother, commented, "Bramley's picture strikes me more than ever. I cannot describe how beautiful it is...He has got hold of a most wonderful quotation from John Ruskin's writings that fits it exactly. Both picture and quotation are equally fine and full of splendid poetry." [276] This was not the view of Anders Zorn, however. In his autobiographical notes, Zorn records, "One day, we visited another artist community, "The Newlyn School" as it was called and whose prophet was Stanhope Forbes. Amongst other things, I entered an artist's studio and complimented the artist. What I saw was unusually promising. Then he said, "I thought of quoting a few words by Ruskin", followed by something about rolling waves. "Goodbye, Mr...", I said and retreated quickly. This was too much for me, these disgusting English quotations that are glued to their frames to give the painting the mandatory poetry. An Englishman's pleasure derived from a painting is solely based on reading about it in the catalogue."[277] Such diverse reactions to a title typifies the different approaches of British and Continental artists, with the British always needing to pander to the Victorian love of drama, pathos and a story. Frank Bramley's *A Hopeless Dawn* fitted the requirements of the Victorian public to a tee and was bought for the nation by the Chantrey Bequest Trustees. What is often overlooked, however, is that, at the same time, the Trustees bought Adrian Stokes' *Upland and Sky*, his painting of cattle grazing on the Lelant Towans. Accordingly, representatives from both the St Ives and the Newlyn colonies won this honour for the first time in the same year.

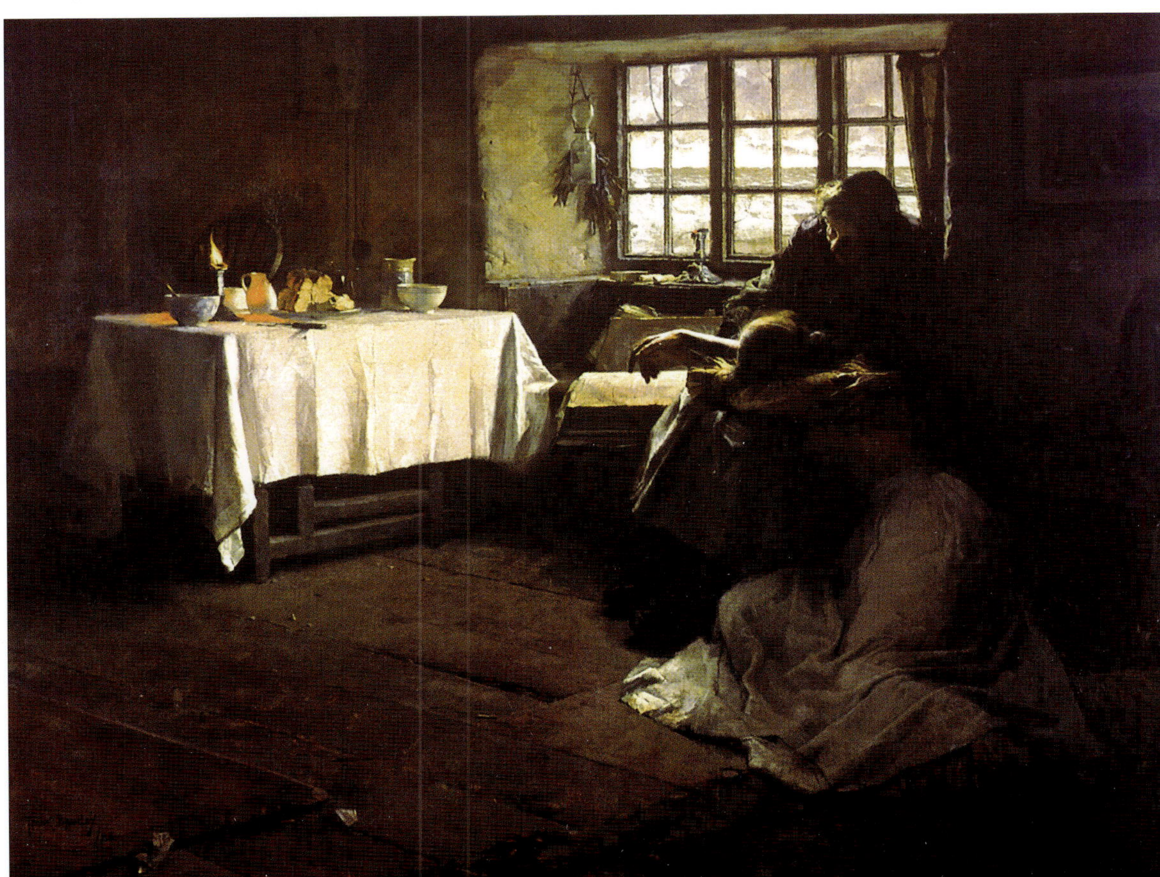

Fig. 4.32 Frank Bramley *A Hopeless Dawn* (Tate Gallery)

---

275 Forbes was rather peeved at Dorothy Robinson's criticism of the figure of the girl in his work *Palmistry* - see letter to his mother dated 19/3/1888 - Tate Gallery Archives 9015-2-1-481.
276 Letter to his mother dated 19/3/1888 - Tate Gallery Archives 9015-2-1-481.
277 From Zorn's autobiographical notes kindly supplied by the Zorn Museum, Mora (translated by Bjorn Benckert).

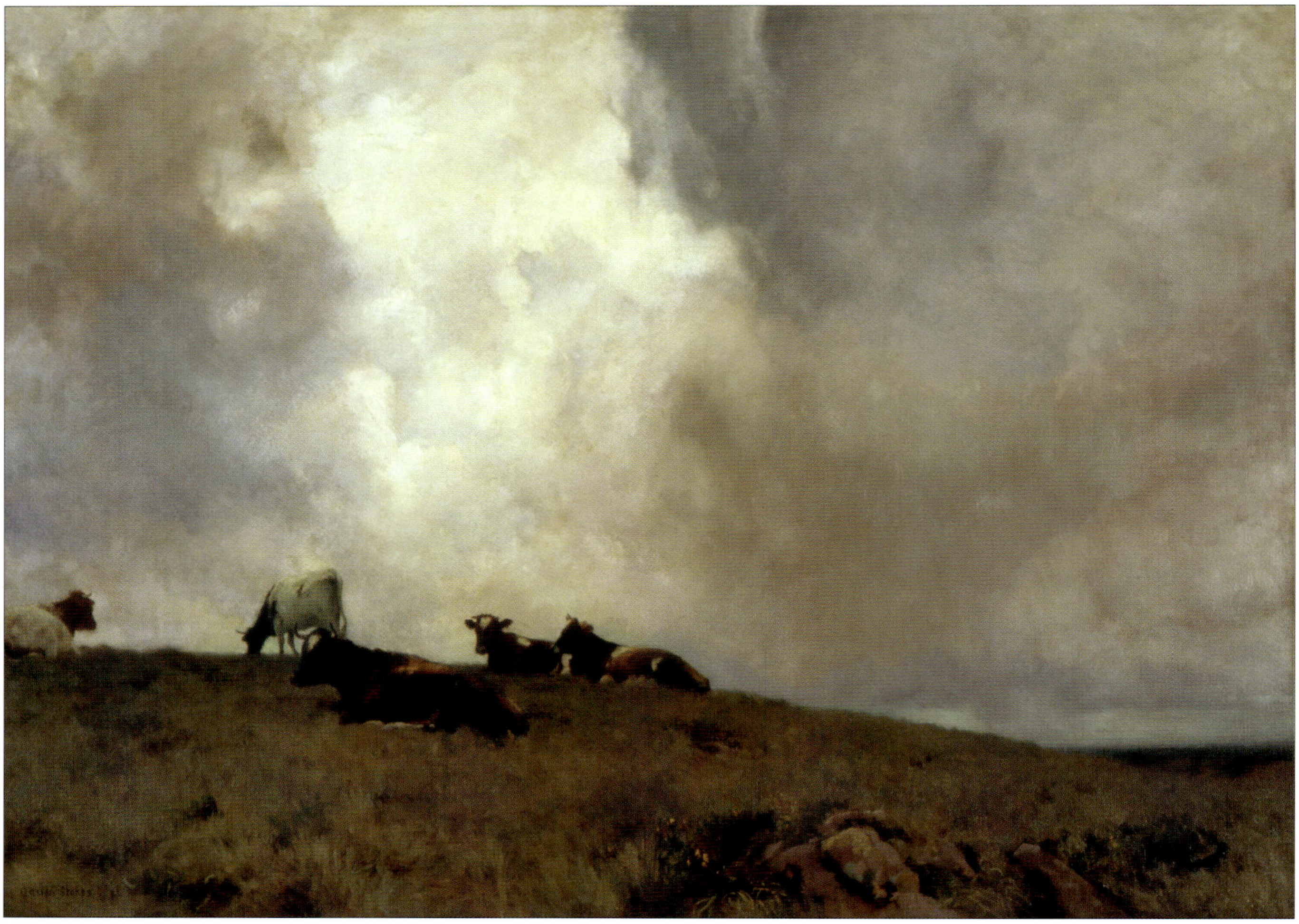

Fig. 4.33 Adrian Stokes *Upland and Sky* (Tate Gallery)

A Hopeless Dawn has become one of the best known images of late Victorian art and certainly one of the most popular early Cornish paintings. Despite this, it can be argued that the completely unknown and rarely exhibited *Upland and Sky* is a much more advanced painting for its time, albeit now, perhaps, it seems unexceptional. The dramatic story of loss and bereavement told in *A Hopeless Dawn* rendered it a typical Victorian narrative painting, with a title drawn from literature, and it followed closely subjects already dealt with by Josef Israels and Frank Holl. It also spawned a whole series of bereavement scenes from other Newlyn artists, who quickly realised the commercial attractions of such a subject when coupled with British romanticised views of seafaring communities. Adrian Stokes' *Upland and Sky*, on the other hand, merely concentrates on an atmospheric effect, with some seventy per cent of the canvas devoted to the sky. In contrast to landscapes of the period, there is nothing dramatic about the scenery - nothing to inspire awe or wonder. Some cows graze on the upland but there is no story to tell, there is no invocation of a rural idyll. It is merely the artist presenting an attractive transient lighting effect that he has witnessed and wishes to share. It seeks to capture and inspire a mood of restfulness. In an article in *The Artist* in 1898, the painting was hailed as "a source of inspiration to lesser men, leading them to the observation of fresh aspects in nature, to new arrangement of material".[278] It was indeed a ground-breaking work and a much braver choice by the Chantrey Trustees than *A Hopeless Dawn*.

Stokes was not the only St Ives artist to be hung at the Royal Academy that year and, for the first time, there was a small group of St Ives work on show, comprising also Edward Simmons' *The Coast of Cornwall*, Ellis Wilkinson's *Jolly Strollers*, Harry Robinson's *Waiting for the Auction*, Dorothy Robinson's *Hard a Port - A Critical Moment* and her Concarneau painting *The Net Menders* (see Fig. 2.14), Marianne Stokes' *Lantern Light*, an exquisite study of light reflecting on glass-ware of different types, as a boy polishes glass under the light of a lantern, and Louis Grier's *A Golden Autumn Eventide*. The latter won high praise when it was exhibited at the 1889 WCAU Exhibition. "St Ives Bay is the scene; the sun has disappeared behind the town; a beautiful afterglow fills the sky, and tinges the fleecy clouds to the north-west; in the middle distance a sailing boat ploughs lazily over the still waters; to the left frown the black weed covered rocks, their irregular outlines mirrored in the glassy sea beneath. We have all seen and admired such a sunset; not often do we see its fleeting glory caught and fixed and placed permanently before us as it is in this picture. The workmanship is bold and free, yet delicate and truly artistic."[279]

278 *Some Landscape Painters in Cornwall, The Artist*, 1898 at p. 141-2.
279 *Cornish Telegraph,* 19/9/1889.

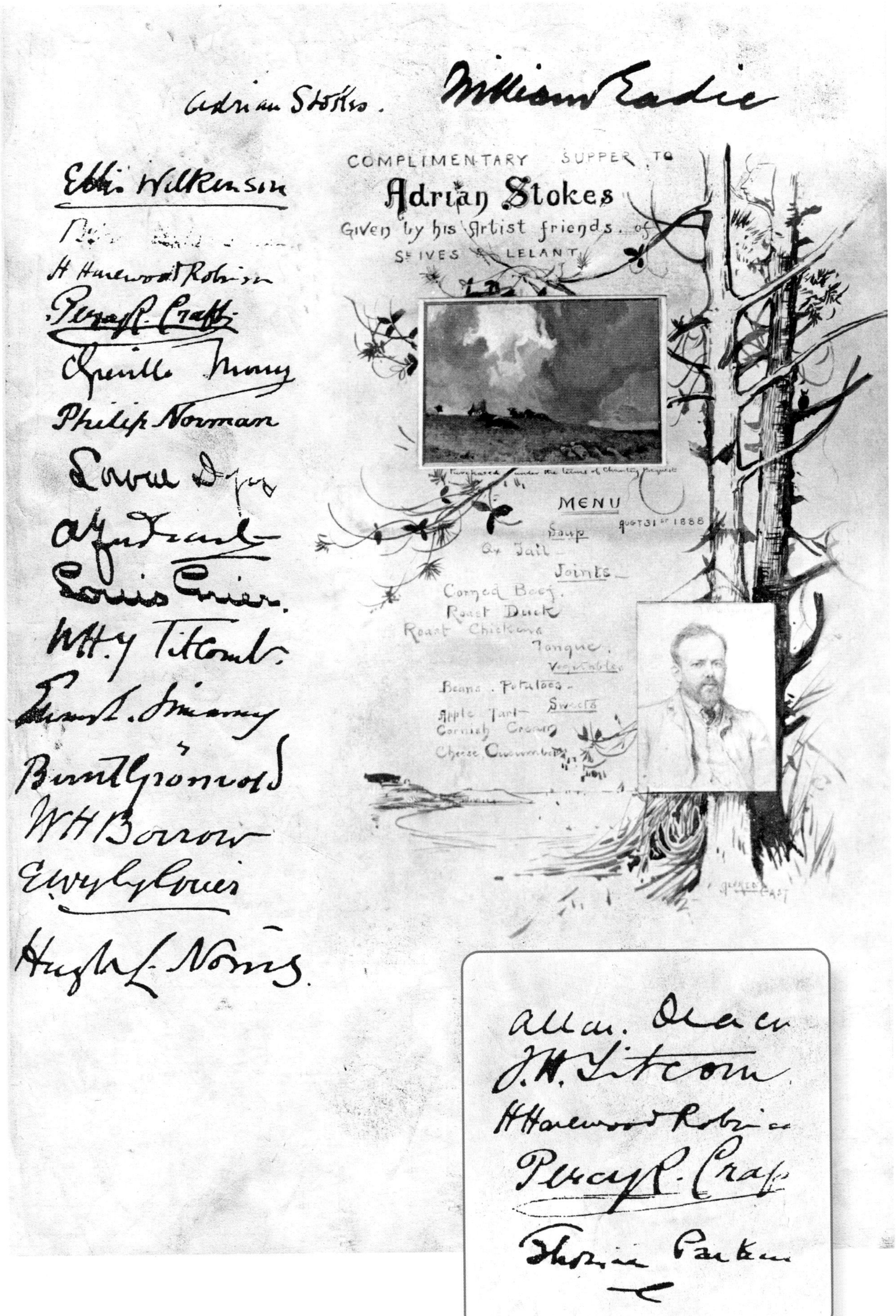

Fig. 4.34 Menu for Adrian Stokes' Chantrey Supper designed by Alfred East (Cornish Studies Library)

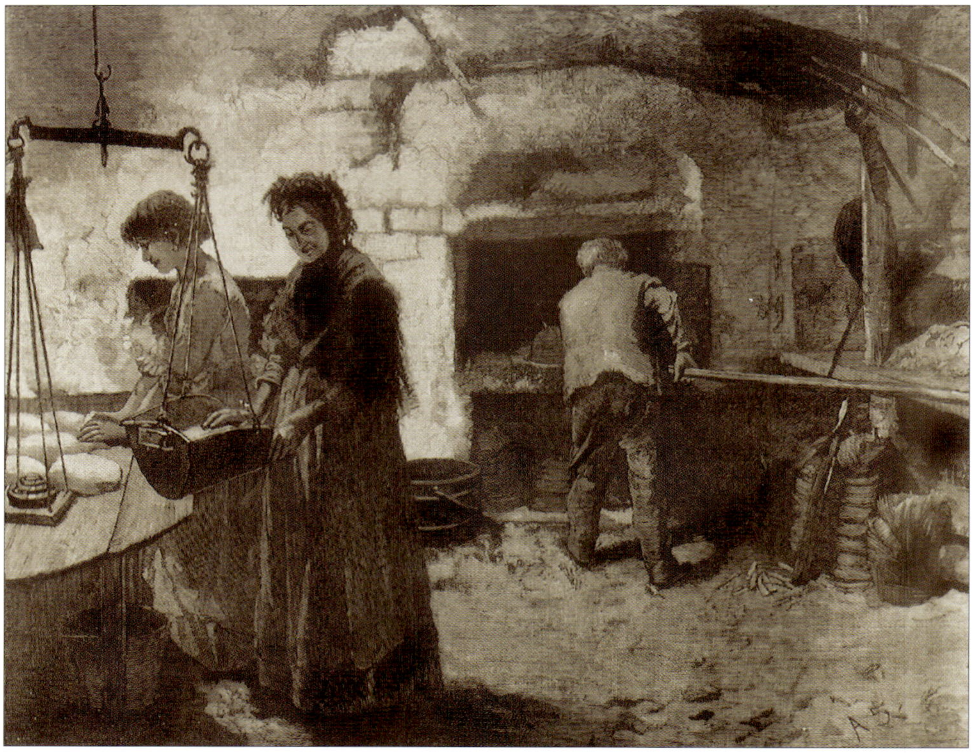

Fig.4.35 Adrian Stokes *Bakehouse in a Cornish Village*
(Illustrated London News, August 1888)

4.15 Adrian Stokes' Chantrey Supper

The menu for the Complimentary Supper thrown in August 1888 to celebrate Stokes' Chantrey success proves to be another useful source for it was signed by some twenty artists.[280] Of those artists already mentioned, Harry Robinson, William Eadie, Edward Simmons, Bernt Grönvold, Louis and Wyly Grier, Ellis Wilkinson, Alfred East and Percy Craft were present in addition, naturally, to Stokes himself. Another signatory was William Titcomb, who claimed to have settled in St Ives in 1887, but this is the first indication that I have found of his presence.[281] His brother and frequent companion, Jack, was also at the Supper but he did not settle in the town until much later. The American, Lowell Dyer, another artist referred to in the list in Badcock's, who was to stay in the town for over fifty years, was also present and other diners, who were to have long associations with the colony, were Greville Morris and Allan Deacon, both of whom were then studying at Bushey. Hugh Norris, on the other hand, although an irregular visitor to St Ives, is perhaps more associated with Newlyn, and his first Royal Academy exhibit in 1890 was a highly acclaimed work, *Washing Day, Newlyn*. Another signatory, William Borrow, was a London-based marine and coastal painter, whose depictions of the activities of the Hastings fishermen are extensively represented in that town's museums. He had been exhibiting paintings of Cornwall since 1863, but he does not appear to have visited St Ives before. A work that he executed during this stay, *A Rough Sea at St Ives, Cornwall*, was exhibited at the Royal Academy in 1889. Philip Norman (c.1843-1931) was also London-based. Slade trained, he specialised in watercolours of old buildings. He clearly revisited the town from time to time as he exhibited a St Ives scene in Falmouth in 1890 and at the Royal Academy in 1897. The signatory Thomas Parker or Parkes seems unknown but I believe that the signature, which is almost indecipherable, is that of Julius Olsson, who has signed himself with the Swedish title, Bror. The date of arrival of Olsson, whose mother was English, but whose father was a Swedish-born timber merchant, is normally given as 1890, but he was clearly in Cornwall in the summer of 1888, for he stated that he was living in Paul, near Penzance, when he married in September 1888. He also appears to have settled in St Ives shortly after his marriage, for he exhibited on Show Day in St Ives in 1889.

From the list in Badcock's, only Eardley Blomefield has not yet been confirmed as present. As Blomefield, the son of a clergyman, had studied in Paris, and exhibited at the Paris Salon in 1885, he may have already known some of the early settlers from his time in France. He is described in June 1889 as one of the artists returning to their studios and so he, too, may well have settled in the town in late 1888, although he did not exhibit on Show Day in 1889.

280 The success of the evening can perhaps be judged by the fact that Robinson and Caft each signed twice!
281 See the biographical note contained in the catalogue to the exhibition of St Ives artists at Cheltenham Art Gallery in 1925.

4.16 Percy Craft in St Ives

The presence of the Newlyner, Percy Craft, at the Chantrey supper is no surprise, as he worked in St Ives quite a bit at this time. Born in London, he was educated privately and studied art at Heatherley's and the Slade (under Poynter and Legros), where he was a gold and silver medallist. He settled in Newlyn in 1885 but his RBA exhibits of 1883 (*Fisherman Mending His Nets*) and 1884 (*Breaking the Tide, Cornwall*) clearly indicate he had visited previously. He soon struck up a friendship with Stanhope Forbes and, in 1887, his wife and himself, accompanied by his mother, rented Mrs Rodd's house at 6 Barnoon Terrace in St Ives - the house where Forbes had stayed the previous year - for the summer. He also took a studio at that time, which he later sublet to Elizabeth Armstrong and then Vesta Simmons. The location of this studio is not certain but there must be a significant chance that it was the loft studio in St Andrew's Street, of which he later took a formal three year lease in August 1888. On this first visit, they seem to have stayed in St Ives until early October 1887, when Forbes reported to his mother that Mrs Craft was back in Newlyn whilst Percy Craft was taking his mother back to Sydenham and "is precious glad to be rid of her".[282] Craft produced a number of works in St Ives during this visit as his two works at the WCAU show in September were St Ives subjects and his RBA exhibits that year included *Among the Old Seine Boats, St Ives*. The following summer, the Crafts returned to St Ives in early June. Elizabeth Armstrong tells Mrs Forbes, "The house they have got for two guineas a week is much larger and more comfortable than Mrs Rodd's."[283] It was during this visit that Craft started work on his best known St Ives painting, *Heva! Heva!* (RA 1889), and he will have returned to his studio in St Ives repeatedly over the coming months. The title derives from the cry announcing a shoal of pilchards in the Bay, and the location is Bunker's Hill, St Ives. Frank Boudillon commented that it was "a good subject, but a little beyond poor old Craft's technical ability".[284] In 1897, Craft produced a sequel, *Tucking A School of Pilchards off the Cornish Coast*, and, whatever their technical failings, both paintings are now enjoyed for their depiction of this fascinating aspect of Cornish history.

Craft continued to rent the studio in St Andrew's Street until February 1890.[285] In August that year, he had eight drawings of St Ives illustrated in *Sporting and Dramatic News* and he continued to visit St Ives from time to time. [286] Indeed, the Rate Books of 1893 and 1894 record him as renting a small studio on the harbour beach from Lord Cowley.

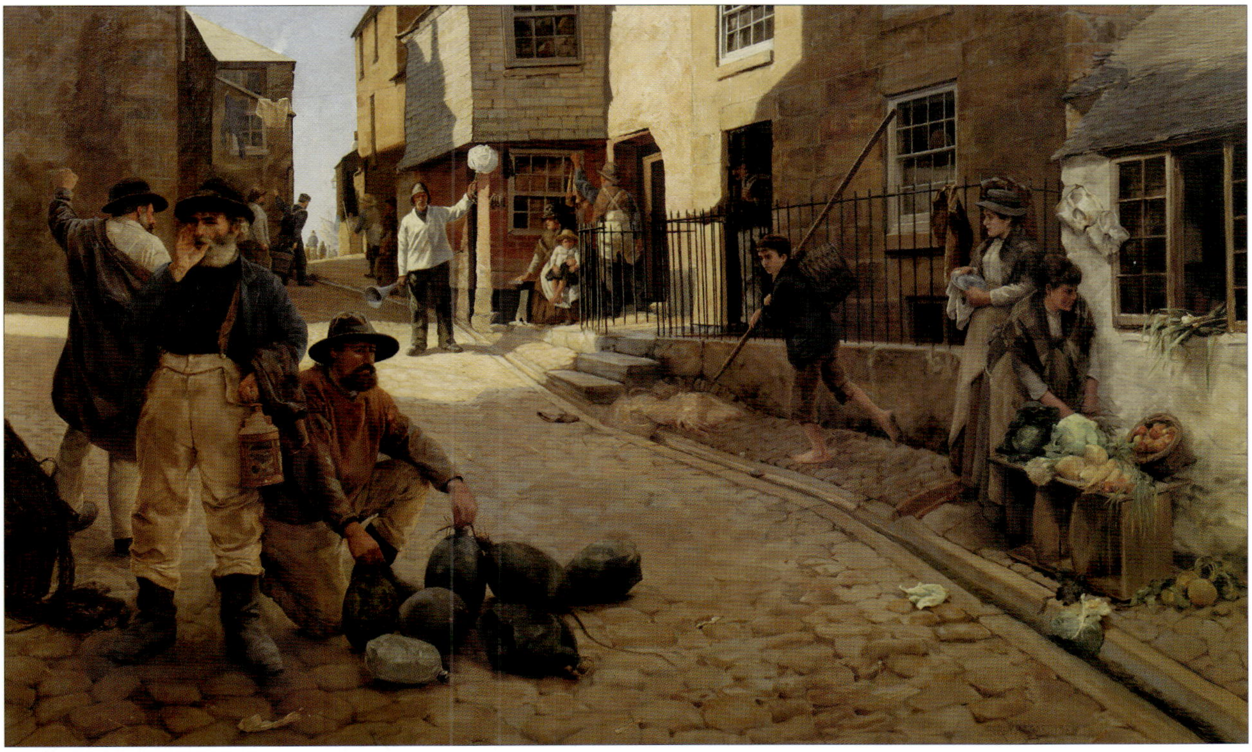

Fig. 4.36 Percy Craft *Heva! Heva!* (Penlee House Gallery & Museum, Penzance)

282 Letter to his mother dated 2/10/1887 - Tate Gallery Archives 9015.2.1.443.
283 Letter from Elizabeth Armstrong to Mrs Forbes dated 10/6/1888 - Tate Gallery Archives 9015.4.2.8.
284 Letter from F Bourdillon to his sister dated 21/2/1889.
285 His departure may be connected with the arrival of the artist, W.J.Hebblethwaite, a serial complainer. In November 1889, W J Hebblethwaite took a lease of the Blue Bell Studio, which included the yard that Craft had been allowed to work in. Hebblethwaite wrote to the property agent, Reginald Glanville, "I do not think Mr Craft and myself will quarrel about the yard but at the same time as well to let him know, as he told me he only had it provisionally." It appears, though, that they did not manage a satisfactory arrangement as, in February 1890, Craft wrote to Glanville, "I am sorry that I shall have to dispense with the Blue Bell yard as I had every intention of working there during the coming season, but of course it cannot be helped." He also arranged for his studio to be taken over by Hebblethwaite.
286 He is, for instance, noted as a visitor in September 1893, when his wife and himself stayed at 1, Bowling Green Terrace.

4.17 Edward Simmons' "ethereal transcripts"

Edward Simmons was not merely a figure painter and, during his time in St Ives, he painted a number of marine and harbour scenes, often in the low grey-blue tones beloved by disciples of Bastien-Lepage. Sand particles lodged in the paint indicate that these were often executed on the spot. Simmons, of course, was a good friend of the marine painter, Alexander Harrison, when they were working together in Concarneau, and was very familiar with his famous painting *The Wave* (Fig. 2.8). It is likely, therefore, that Simmons' approach to marine work was influenced by Harrison. Nocturnes were a particular speciality of Simmons and *The Farmer : Moonrise over St Ives Bay* and *Night, St Ives Bay* were two major works that he exhibited in 1889. The latter was an enormous canvas measuring 50" x 66.5" and depicted the vista looking east from the town across the Bay to Godrevy. Employing a high horizon, the waters of the Bay are bathed in light from an unseen moon. When the painting was exhibited in 1987, it was described as having been painted with a square flat-ended brush in a broad and vigorous fashion, with the edges of the waves blurred in order to create the impression that light was passing through them.[287] This vista seems to have fascinated Simmons, for he returned to it on a number of occasions, despite the fact that it contained a large expanse of sea and sky and little else.[288] He exhibited at the Society of American Artists in 1888 a work called *Bay of St Ives at Evening* and, at the Chicago World Columbian Exhibition in 1893, *The Early Moonlight, Bay of St Ives*. There is a possibility that these are, in fact, other titles for the work *Night, St Ives Bay* but, in 2005, Spanierman Gallery, New York offered for sale a separate work, *Night, St Ives Bay*, which measured 29.5" x 59.5". Although, on this occasion, both Godrevy lighthouse and the moon were visible, it was in much more subdued tones and little light from these sources was reflected on the waters of the Bay. The limited tonal range employed may signify the influence of Whistler's nocturnes of the Thames. The influential American art critic, Clarence Cook, commenting on such works, said, "Mr Simmons' pictures of the

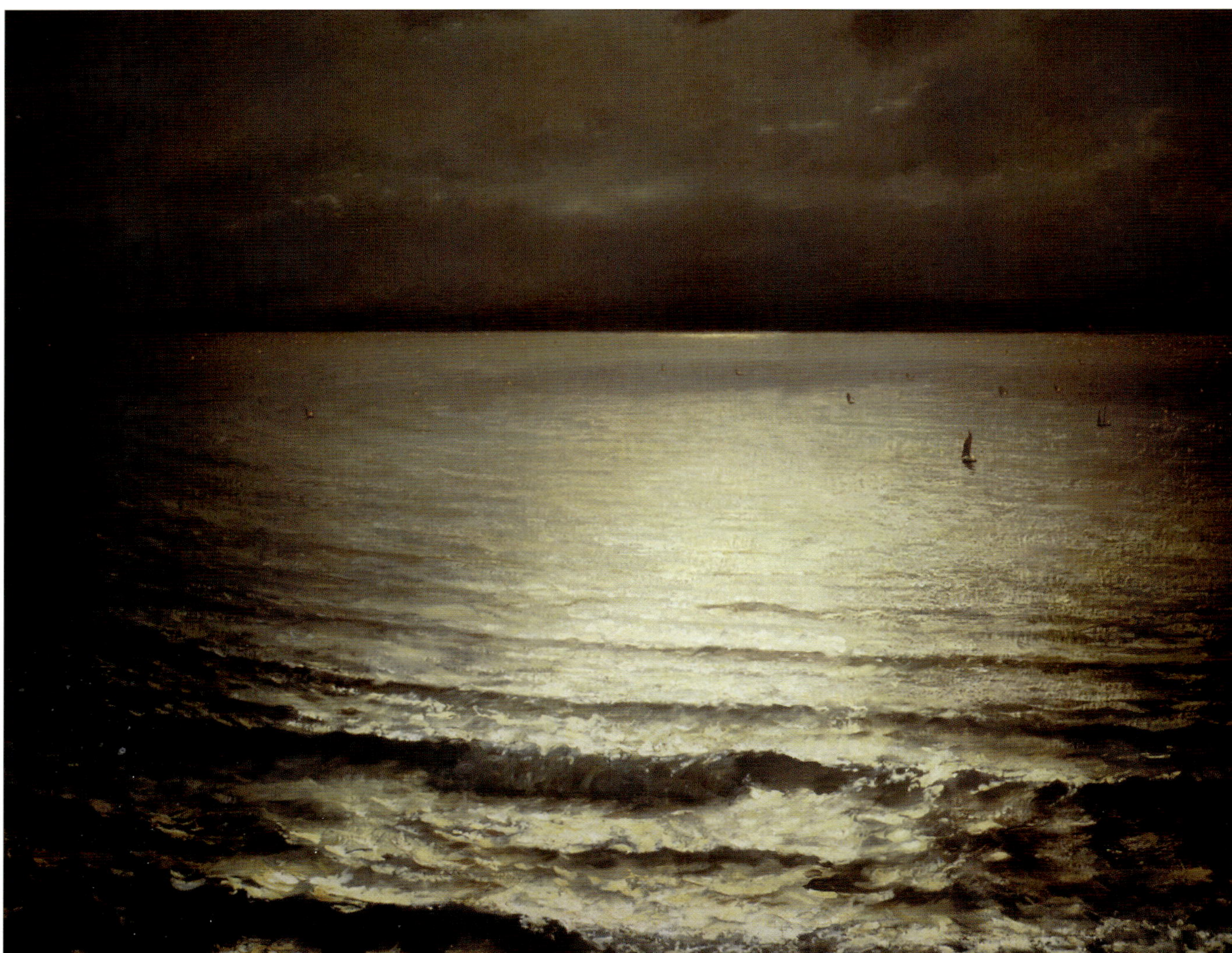

Fig. 4.37 Edward Simmons *Night, St Ives Bay* (Hardwick Simmons)

287 Bruce Weber and William H Gerdts, *In Nature's Ways - American Landscape Painting of the Late Nineteenth Century*, 1987.
288 Works exhibited at the Pennsylvania Academy include *St Ives Bay, Cornwall*, which won a silver medal, and *At Sunset, Looking East* (1890), *Calm Evening After a Shower* and *Night* (1891) and *Bay of St Ives : Early Morn* (1892).

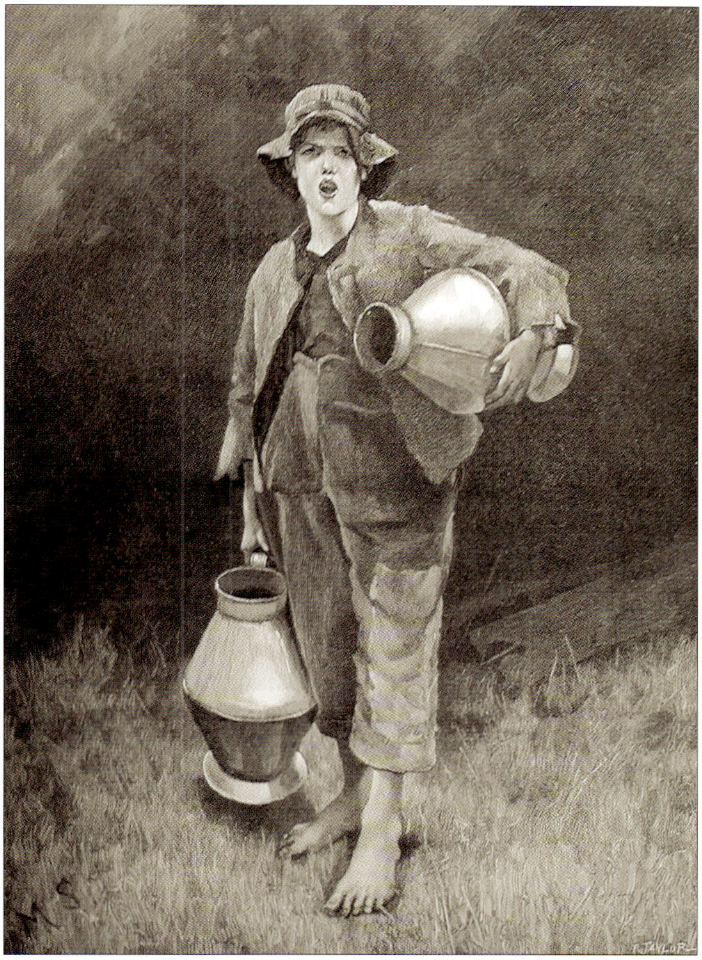

Fig.4.38 Marianne Stokes *Cornish Milk Boy*
(Illustrated London News, May 1888)

Bay of St Ives are among the most beautiful and poetic works of the kind that we owe to any modern artist. The marines of Alexander Harrison are exquisite of their kind, but they are paint and canvas alongside the ethereal transcripts of Simmons."[289]

4.18 The Paris Exposition Universelle of 1889

The 1889 Exposition Universelle in Paris, marking as it did the centenary of the French Revolution, was the major art event of that year - indeed, it was one of the highlights of the decade - and the St Ives artists were well-represented and won high honours. Adrian Stokes won a silver medal with *On the Dunes, Cornwall*, Helene Schjerfbeck won a bronze medal for *The Convalescent*, Edward Simmons, who was on the American selection jury, won a bronze medal for his exhibits which included *The Farmer : Moonrise over St Ives Bay* and *Night, St Ives Bay* whilst Howard Butler won a bronze medal for his exhibits which included *Low Tide, St Ives* and his first great success at the Salon, *The Seaweed Gatherers*. Alfred East, who had spent some months in St Ives the previous year, won a Mention Honorable and Gold Medal (2nd Class) for a Scottish scene. Moffat Lindner was represented by *Autumn Moon*, which may well be a St Ives scene as he exhibited moonlight depictions of St Ives Bay in both Liverpool in 1888 and Falmouth in 1890.

This small group of paintings also highlights the wide range of work already being produced in St Ives, in strict contrast to the numerous figure paintings of the fisherfolk emanating from Newlyn, for in addition to the figure paintings of Zorn, Schjerfbeck and Simmons, there were the Barbizon-influenced landscapes of Adrian Stokes and Alfred East and the Whistlerian-inspired marines of Simmons and Lindner. This diversity in genre, individuality in style and progression in outlook made St Ives an exciting and inspiring place in which to work and the colony retained these qualities for many years.

289 Clarence Cook, *Art and Artists of Our Time*, New York, 1888. In addition, the Mariners' Museum, Newport News have a small work, *Looking East at Sunset, St Ives Bay*, showing a cloud bank over Godrevy reflecting the rays from the setting sun, and one of the works he contributed to the Dowdeswell show in December 1890 was *After the Storm - Looking East*. The Henry Art Gallery at the University of Washington also have a puzzling work *Bay of St Ives, Cornwall* (23" x 30") which is dated 1907. This suggests that Simmons was still fascinated by the subject years after his stay in the town, as it is not believed that he returned at this time Perhaps because it was painted years later, there are aspects about the work that do not ring true. The orb looks more like a sun than a moon and the cliffs are lit up in a way that seems strange with the light source behind them. The Gallery also has the work's title as *Bay of Ives*.

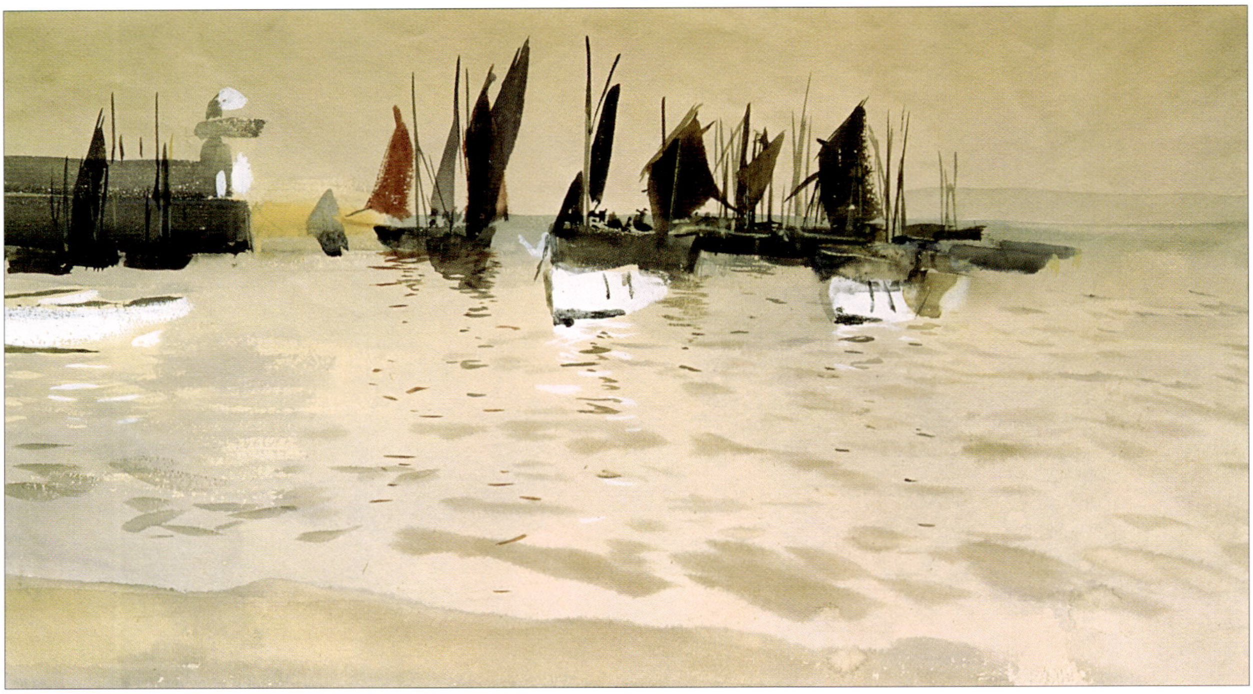

Fig. 4.39 Anders Zorn *Boats in St Ives* (Zorn Museum, Mora)

4.19 The emergence of a settled core

In these initial years, the colony was a transient community, but it had a character that was far removed from the occasional groupings of artists that had come together in the pre-colony period. Although the foreign artists had no intention of making St Ives their permanent home, they still stayed in the town for far longer than any pre-colony visitor, for, during their stays, St Ives became their principal base in England, if not in Europe. Their sojourns, therefore, were measured in months (rather than days, or sometimes weeks, as had previously been the case) and often lasted for periods in excess of six months. By the time of the Paris World Exposition, however, all, with the exception of Edward Simmons, had moved on. The British contingent of the colony was also very fluid in these early years, and the Rate Book for 1888 confirms how few of the artists had yet made a firm commitment to St Ives. Whereas William Eadie had taken a lease for his family of 'Windy Parc' in the Ayr district of town and fellow initial settlers, the Robinsons, had taken a property in Richmond Terrace (also then known as Richmond Place), no other artist was listed as a ratepayer for accommodation, whilst Robinson and the Grier brothers were the only artists shown as ratepayers for a studio.[290] Most artists were still merely taking rooms in boarding houses for sections of the year and tended to use their home, as opposed to a St Ives property, for their exhibiting address. Twenty artists may have taken part in Adrian Stokes' Chantrey Supper in August 1888, but this was at the height of the summer season, and that gathering contained a number of artists that had limited ties to the colony. A much more reliable indicator of the core group of artists, that were at the heart of the emerging colony, is revealed by the participants in the series of studio private views, that were held in March 1889, and which were reviewed in a local paper for the first time that year.[291] This was the event that was to become known as Show Day - the day, or days, when artists opened their studios to the public so that they could view the works that were being sent to the London exhibitions. This became the highlight of the artistic calendar in St Ives, and, as participants tended to have worked in St Ives on these major works over the winter months, the reviews of Show Day are crucial sources for determining the principal members of the colony in any year. In 1889, the artists who invited the public into their studios were Adrian and Marianne Stokes, William Eadie, Harry and Dorothy Robinson, Louis and Wyly Grier, Edward Simmons, Julius Olsson and William Titcomb.[292] Although a good proportion of such artists could only be described as regular long-stay visitors, as opposed to settlers, at this juncture, they did, for some years, represent the core of the colony and that year's display of paintings resulted, not only in Edward Simmons' near miss with the Chantrey Trustees, but medals at international exhibitions for William Titcomb, Wyly Grier and Marianne Stokes, and sales to public collections by Adrian Stokes, with both his works, Wyly Grier and Titcomb.[293] The colony, accordingly, was now making a mark in London, as well as Paris. The winter of 1888 had also seen the initiation of Saturday evening socials in Louis Grier's studio, 'The Foc'sle', and these led in 1890 to the formation of the St Ives Arts Club. The character of the colony was taking shape.

290 Robinson was the only artist recorded in Kelly's Directory for 1889.
291 *The Cornishman*, 28/3/1889. Although such private views had occurred the previous year, the artists featured are not known, as it was not covered in the press.
292 C.Davis, about whom I can find no information, unless he is the American Charles H.Davis, also participated.
293 These works are discussed in the second book in this series, *Pioneers of St Ives Art at Home and Abroad (1889-1914)*.

~5~

THE INITIAL IMPACT OF THE ARTISTS' ARRIVAL

5.1 From occasional curiosity to permanent feature

It seems clear that the town's poor sanitation and drainage, when combined with the overpowering smells of the fishing industry, made artists disinclined to spend lengthy periods of time in St Ives, until some action had been taken to remedy these problems in the 1880s. Accordingly, James Clarke Hook's stay of two-and-a-half months in 1860 was a valiant effort, but, no doubt on Edward Opie's recommendation, the visit was timed to coincide with the lull in the fishing seasons, when many of the boats departed for the North Sea. Fortunately, this lull did tend to fit in with the standard late summer/early autumn sketching tours that artists at that juncture tended to make, but no other artist stayed anywhere near the length of time that Hook did. Whilst John Brett worked in the town for most of September 1872, other artists' visits were much briefer. Accordingly, in the 1870s, the occasional artist visitor was probably still a summer or autumn curiosity.

The opening of the branch line from St Erth in 1877 must have had an impact on the number of artist visitors, as it did on the level of general tourists, but, even so, the 1881 Census does not record a single artist in St Ives, even as a lodger. However, in the early part of that decade, as conditions in the town improved, artists seem to have been prepared to stay longer, and did not mind their visits overlapping with the height of the fishing seasons. Indeed, it was the activities of the townsfolk during the pilchard season that became of particular interest to many artists. No details are known of the visits of Edwin Ellis and Émile-Louis Vernier but, judging from the quantity of work that they produced, they will have stayed in the town for a period of months, rather than weeks. Furthermore, artists were now undertaking winter sketching trips, for accounts of Whistler's visit indicate that his pupils and himself were by no means the only artists in the town that January. Nevertheless, it was only in 1885-6 that artists stayed throughout the winter, and there can be little doubt that 1885 is the year when the colony should be treated as having been established, previous use of the dates of 1883 and 1884 being based solely on the visit of Whistler. Unlike the other Cornish art colonies, the position is not complicated by the presence of any locally-born professional, or keen amateur, painter working in the town before the arrival of outsiders, such as Thomas Hart or James Philp in Falmouth, Richard Harry Carter in Truro or James Uren in Penzance. Furthermore, the initial three settlers, the Robinsons and William Eadie, did, in fact, become permanent residents from the outset and lived in the town for many years.

5.2 Accommodation

The impact of the artists upon various aspects of the town was immediate.[294] With only William Eadie and the Robinsons taking long-term lets of houses, the need for accommodation tended to be met, initially, by the landladies of the town, who were very flexible in the terms that they were prepared to agree. The Zorn party and the Forbes/Armstrong families, for instance, seem to have rented whole houses on a self-catering basis, whilst the Whistler party took a suite of rooms and had their meals cooked for them by their landlady. Howard Butler experienced a range of different regimes. In his first year, he took lodgings and himself bought the food that he wished his landlady to cook, but felt compelled to eat alone, as she made a charge for each item consumed. He was delighted, however, at the easy availability of farm produce, which made "a most agreeable change after the artificiality of Parisian dinners", and was also most impressed with the standard of her cooking, telling his sister, "such baked apples and cream as I get here were never equalled even by the Queen of Sheba herself."[295] The next year, 1887, he took a whole house to himself, but his new landlady, Mrs Dumble, the widow of a fisherman, soon took control of the shopping, pointing out that he was getting very poor deals. Butler, of course, was only too delighted, and the total cost of this house, with all home services provided, was just eleven shillings a week.

The artists tended to take rooms in the higher part of town, away from the noise and the smells of the fishing quarter, and properties on The Terrace and Barnoon Terrace were popular. These afforded good views, and Butler commented that he liked to keep an eye open for weather effects. No 6, The Terrace, which was run by Mrs Pearson, herself an amateur artist, seems to have been particularly popular, as Louis and Wyly Grier, William Titcomb and Eardley Blomefield all spent several months lodging there. The influx of artists completely transformed the profitability of these boarding houses, for not only did the artists stay for much

294 I will deal with the issues discussed in this Chapter in much greater detail in my proposed book Early St Ives Art (1885-1927) - The Artists and the Community.
295 Letter from H.R.Butler to Mary Butler dated 8/8/1886, Archives of American Art, Smithsonian Institution, Washington DC, Howard Russell Butler papers, Reel 1189.

longer than the normal tourist, but they also came and went throughout the whole year - not just during the summer tourist season of July and August. The high percentage of artists amongst the visitors listed in the late spring and autumn Visitors' Lists, in the new local paper in 1889, confirms the significant impact they were already having.

5.3 Studios

Perhaps of more importance to the early colonists, than suitable accommodation at a reasonable price, was a good, cheap workspace, and Harry Robinson, in his account of the fledgling colony, commented, "Old sail lofts and cottages were sought out, and turned into studios, and large skylights appeared everywhere among the grey roofs of the old town."[296] Properties, into which a northern facing skylight could be inserted, were particularly prized, and an astonishing array of different types of building were pressed into service. William Eadie seems to have converted an outhouse in the grounds of his home, 'Windy Parc', whilst Harry Robinson used, initially, a carpenter's shop in Back Street.[297] This was probably where Forbes stored his paintings, when he was working in St Ives. However, in the garden of Robinson's home in Richmond Terrace, there was an old, dilapidated Music Pavilion, with an attractive upper room, decorated with plaster reliefs, which he later rented out as a studio to Helene Schjerfbeck, and so Forbes may have used this. Schjerfbeck called it her 'Tower' and loved its dishevelled state. After her departure, Louis Grier may have used it for a while, as he gave 'Ivy Tower', St Ives, as his exhibiting address in 1888, before moving later that year to 'The Foc'sle', the studio on the harbour beach, with which he was to be associated for the rest of his life.

Howard Butler was the first to see the conversion potential of the town's net and rope lofts and created the first studio on Porthmeor out of a loft previously used for storing ropes from the pilchard fishery.[298] This was possibly the Porthmeor studio now numbered 8, which is believed to be the oldest building in the complex. It had one facility that Butler particularly prized. "This loft was reached by a ladder which entered through a trap-door in the floor. By pulling up the ladder, I was indeed isolated. I found this very serviceable when Simmons, who was an inveterate talker, would come around determined to finish some argument began the night before and I did not want to be disturbed."[299] Other artists, who seem to have created their early studios from net lofts in this area of town, were William Titcomb, who took one in Porthmeor Road, and Julius Olsson, who rented one in Back Road East. Adrian Stokes surprisingly took a studio in a multi-use building in Virgin Street, well away from the sea, whilst Edward Simmons had a studio in a large property in St Andrew's Street, next to the Churchyard. The interior of this can be seen in his paintings *The Carpenter's Son* (Fig. 4.30) and *The Mother* (Fig. 4.31). Harry Robinson also soon took a small cottage on the seaward side of St Andrew's Street (probably No. 3), which was to be his painting base for the rest of his life, whilst Percy Craft rented a building adjoining the yard of the old Blue Bell Inn, the well-known smuggling haunt, on the same street. Another unusual studio was created by Eardley Blomefield from the old Mine Engine House on Pednolva Point, which offered a fine view of the harbour. The decline in the fishing and other industries, that had dominated the town in times past, meant that suitable premises were widely available at cheap rates. At this early juncture, though, artists' workplaces were scattered all over Down-along, and the concentration of studios in the Porthmeor Beach area did not occur until the mid-1890s, when a series of new purpose-built studios were erected. Without the influx of the artists, it seems certain that many of these historic buildings would have been demolished.

5.4 Models and painting equipment

Another important requirement for artists was cheap, but interesting, models and, here again, St Ives could satisfy them, for, even if the working fishermen were too busy to sit, there were a number of extravagantly bearded old salts and elderly fishwives with care-worn features, only too willing to wile away time, earning some additional funds. Names, such as 'Prussian Bill', 'One-Eyed Barber' and 'Old Bull', immediately indicate some fascinating characters. The children too were keen to sit, or do odd jobs, for the artists, and Butler records how he employed the boy, Daniel Lander, whom he called 'Deronda', to carry his things, wash his brushes, clean his studio and generally be on call, from nine in the morning to nine at night, for just five (later six) pence a day.[300]

It is known that both Brett and Whistler, whilst in St Ives, had to order oil paints to be sent from a great distance and, according to the St Ives artist, Arthur White, as recorded by Marion Whybrow, it was Whistler who first suggested to James Lanham, an entrepreneur with a general merchants' store in the High Street, that he should

---

296 Harry Robinson, St Ives as an Art Colony, in Babcock's Historical Sketch of St Ives and District, 1896.
297 See St Ives as an Art Colony in Badcock's Historical Sketch of St Ives and District, 1896 and Letter from H H Robinson to R Glanville dated 21/6/1891 - Mornington Estate Papers, County Records Office, Truro, GHW/12/3/6/1/52/30.
298 Letter from H.R.Butler to Mary Butler dated 8/8/1886, Howard Russell Butler papers as aforesaid, Reel 1189.
299 H.R.Butler, Unpublished Autobiography, p.167, Howard Russell Butler papers as aforesaid, Reel 93.
300 Letter from Howard Butler to his mother dated 20/8/1887. Howard Russell Butler papers as aforesaid, Reel 1189.

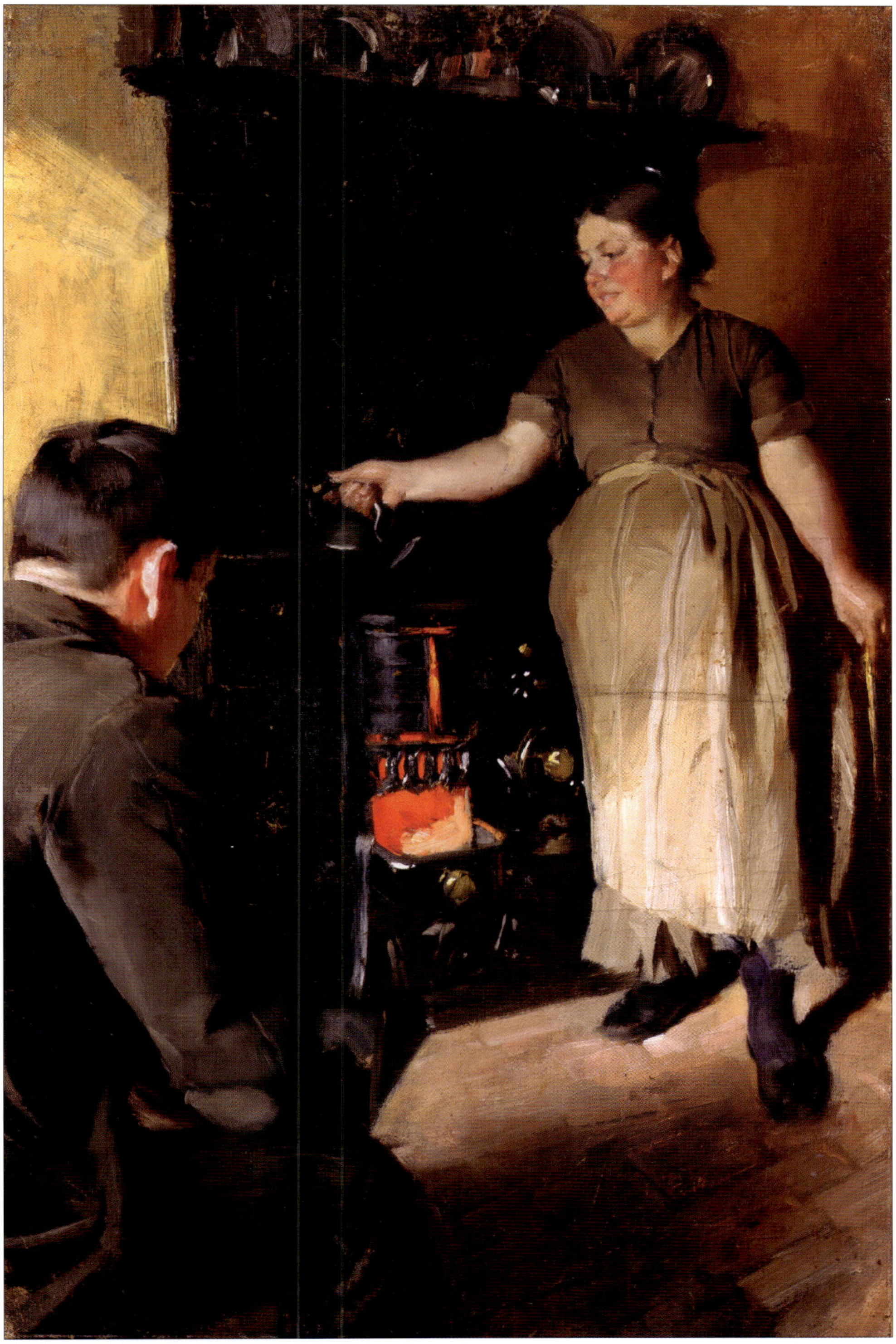

Fig. 5.1 Anders Zorn *In the Kitchen* (Zorn Museum, Mora)

stock paints for use by the artists.[301] Certainly, by 1887, Lanham is including, in local Business Directories, 'Artists' Colourman' among the many areas of business, in which he specialised, and that year, he also made available a room in his High Street premises, in which the artists could exhibit their work for sale. This was re-furbished in 1889, and was to be the principal exhibition venue in the town until 1928, with the selection of works re-hung each month. The services of James Lanham, in relation to a wide variety of matters, came to be indispensable to the artists in the colony and he is the classic example of a local trader becoming extremely successful by pandering to the needs of the bohemian brotherhood.

301 I am indebted to Charles Brett for informing me that Brett, whilst staying at 3 Bowling Green Terrace in September 1872, ordered paints from Roberson's in London, whilst Whistler is reputed to have had to send to Cambridge. See Marion Whybrow, St Ives 1883-1993 - Portrait of an Art Colony, Woodbridge, 1994 at p.39.

5.5 Social life and cultural activities

As many of the early colonists were already friends after shared experiences in Brittany, there was, from the beginning, considerable camaraderie and a healthy communal spirit. Card games and musical soirées were regular features, whilst Butler enjoyed games of logomachy (word duels), as this was one way of keeping Simmons quiet for a while![302] The artists also socialised with some of the leading townsfolk. Simmons records evenings at 'Talland House' with the family of Leslie Stephen, who was then editing the Dictionary of National Biography, and the Stokeses, Titcombs and Olssons also fraternised with the Stephenses.[303] Butler, on the other hand, mentions evenings with Mr Reed, the banker, and the Vicar, John Balmer Jones, and his curate, who was "a pleasant fellow and a capital hand at tennis".[304] Although a Unitarian himself and not a fan of the "high" service at the Parish Church, Butler was most impressed with the conscientious work that these clergy did amongst the poor, even though they were often dissenters or agnostics. William Eadie and his large family were also regular members of the congregation, and his 1889 Royal Academy exhibit depicted Canon Jones preaching in the Parish Church (St Ives Town Collection). William Titcomb, being the son of an Anglican Bishop, will also have been a regular at the Parish Church, but both he and Edward Simmons were fascinated with the fervour of the services at the Primitive Methodist chapel in St Ives. Indeed, the first of Titcomb's trio of paintings of the Primitive Methodist congregation, which were to draw worldwide attention to this sect, caused a sensation at the 1889 Royal Academy show.

The good relations fostered with the Newlyn artists, by the repeated presence in St Ives of Stanhope Forbes, Elizabeth Armstrong and other Newlyners, led to trips across to see the dramas and musicals put on by the artists in Newlyn, whilst the musical abilities of the Grier brothers and Harry Robinson saw them playing important roles, from the outset, in the Choral Society and other cultural groups in the town. Soon, the increasing numbers of artists in St Ives enabled them to lay on entertainments, not only for themselves, initially in Grier's studio, and then, after 1890, in the Arts Club, but also at a variety of venues in the town, for a range of local charitable causes. It was later felt that the artists had contributed immensely to the cultural education of the townsfolk and to the promotion of a greater broadness of vision.

5.6 Burying "the hatchet of ignorant animosity"

It would be wrong, however, to intimate that the arrival of the artists was welcomed in all quarters. The majority of the artists were well-educated, middle class and, compared to the fisherfolk, in any event, well-heeled. Their outlook and beliefs, as well as their daily habits and mode of dress, were very different to those of the locals, and each side needed to adapt to take account of the perceived eccentricities of the other. Howard Butler commented, "I am thrown a great deal with the poor people here. There are carpenters and fishermen and ship chandlers all around me working in similar shops to mine. I often talk with them and if I don't know them all, I am known to all... I like the men and the boys - they are a rough lot, but there are some fine rustic characters among them. But the women all seem to be fiends. They will beat a child of three years old - and the little girls are most insolent. All are slovenly, given to overdressing, lazy and filthily dirty."[305] Emma Zorn was also shocked at the cramped and dirty surroundings in which the fisherfolk lived, which she believed led to low morals.[306] For their part, the fisherfolk, who tended to be devout Methodists, frowned upon some of the 'bohemian' ways of the artists. For instance, they drank too much and sang popular songs at inappropriate times, and the ladies wore too many frills, but the biggest bone of contention concerned the observation of the Sabbath. No work at all was permitted in St Ives on Sundays, and there are several references to artists being dowsed with a bucket of water or, worse, thrown into the harbour, for sketching on the Sabbath. There is also no doubt that the arrival of the artists raised prices for food and some other necessities, which helped local businesses, but annoyed local consumers. Accordingly, in the colony's infancy, "there were occasional loggerheads; surface misunderstandings between two impetuous races, whose idiosyncrasies neither understood", but, before too long, "they mutually respected and comprehended each other, and the hatchet of ignorant animosity was buried."[307]

---

302 Letter from Howard Butler to his father dated 12/8/1886. He adds, "If you spent one hour with Simmons, you would appreciate this".
303 See Marion Dell and Marion Whybrow, *Virginia Woolf & Vanessa Bell - Remembering St Ives*, Padstow 2003.
304 Letter from Howard Butler to his mother dated 20/8/1887, Howard Russell Butler papers as aforesaid, Reel 1189.
305 Letter from Howard Butler to his mother dated 20/8/1887, Howard Russell Butler papers as aforesaid, Reel 1189.
306 Letter from Emma Zorn to Hugo Greber dated 3/1/1887, Zorn Museum Archives.
307 This description of the colony of St Ars in Folliott Stokes' novel is clearly based on St Ives - A.G.Folliott Stokes, A Moorland Princess, London, 1904 at p.86.

~ 6 ~

AN INTERNATIONAL COMMUNITY WITH A COSMOPOLITAN OUTLOOK

Given that St Ives was well-known to British artists, the manner in which the colony was effectively established from France is all the more extraordinary. It is somewhat ironic - at a time in the art world when all things French were applauded and all things English derided, and ambitious English artists were busy populating the art colonies of France - that the premier art colony in England should assume its unique character due to its "discovery" by a Frenchman - Émile Vernier. The initial influx of artists from France, many of whom were foreign nationals, made St Ives, from the outset, a most unusual English colony. Indeed, Butler's description of his fellow colonists in 1887 makes it clear that foreigners outnumbered English artists, and so the St Ives colony came into being as an international community with a cosmopolitan outlook.

The plethora of foreign artists in St Ives resulted in the focus of the colony being very different to any other British enclave. All of the Americans had come to Europe principally to study in France, whilst the other nationalities also viewed French training as the best, and Paris as the centre of the art world. Accordingly, each year, the main objective of all these artists was to be hung at the Paris Salon. Few bothered with the Royal Academy shows at all. This attitude also rubbed off on the British artists in the colony, who made a point of submitting major works to the Paris Salon as well. As the attractions of St Ives were displayed time and again in Paris, the influx of students from France, whether British or foreign, continued apace, and became self-perpetuating. The decision of the French Government in 1888 to buy Zorn's *Fisherman, St Ives*, and hang it in the Luxembourg Museum in Paris, was of considerable importance in this regard. Previous accounts of the early years of the Cornish art colonies have tended to suggest that the St Ives colony took some time to make a mark, and really only came into its own, when the Newlyn colony began to dissipate in the mid-1890s. This view is based solely on an assessment of the relative successes of the colonies at the Royal Academy, and completely ignores the very considerable reputation gained by the St Ives artists in Paris, right from the outset.

The contrast with the reputation of the Newlyn colony in Paris is telling. In Newlyn, Elizabeth Armstrong (later Forbes) was the sole foreign artist and her colleagues, being predominantly British, concentrated each year on the Royal Academy Summer Exhibition and rarely bothered to send works to the annual Paris Salon shows. Newlyn's attractions, therefore, were not constantly being advertised in Paris and, accordingly, the colony received few foreign visitors. Certainly, Newlyn did not seem to strike the same chord with foreigners as St Ives - possibly, its south-facing aspect, which tended to mean that marine paintings had to be executed *contra jour*, was off-putting. In any event, I find it extraordinary that I have not located one painting of Newlyn, or even of that iconic subject, St Michael's Mount, by any of the early foreign colonists in St Ives. Whereas Stanhope Forbes, Elizabeth Armstrong, Percy Craft, Arthur Bateman, Norman Garstin, Henry Detmold, Edward Docker and Thomas Gotch all spent several months painting in St Ives in the colony's early years, not one of the St Ives artists seems to have been inspired to paint in Newlyn.

What impact did this multinational group of French-trained artists have on the type of work produced in St Ives? Naturally, it was transformed. In the pre-colony period, it is not surprising to find that a good proportion of the paintings executed were topographical watercolours, for Cornwall was a fresh subject and there was a demand for such descriptive work. For artists paying short-term visits, during which they were intent on exploring as many new places as possible, the convenience of watercolours would have been an important consideration in their choice of medium. Given the experiences of Brett and Whistler, who had to order oil paints from afar, the availability of materials might have been an issue as well. With the notable exception of Edward Cooke, most artists seem to have been satisfied with their watercolour sketches as exhibition pieces in their own right, rather than using them as a basis for more substantial works. After the formation of the colony, however, with the exception of Anders Zorn, watercolour was hardly employed at all, for the novel painting techniques that the artists had learnt in France were all concerned with oils. Greater emphasis was now placed on bold and more obvious brushwork, with some artists occasionally employing the "square brush" technique. As a result of the enthusiasm for *plein air* work, there was more concern with light and atmosphere, and capturing truth of tone, than with a high level of finish. Accordingly, the hard outlines of artists, such as Edward Cooke, were replaced by soft, fuzzy edges. The overtly sentimentalised depictions of rustic life, as made popular by James Clarke Hook and Edith Hume, gave way to a more objective presentation, in which age, hardship and poverty were more starkly revealed. However, given that most of the artists had shared similar experiences in France to the Newlyn residents, during the period when the cult of Bastien-Lepage was at its height, the output from St Ives was surprisingly different to that from Newlyn. In the case of some artists, it was also surprisingly different from the work that they had done themselves in Brittany, only shortly beforehand.

Anders Zorn, as has been seen, had not painted in oils at all before his arrival in St Ives, but his approach to his subject, as one might expect from his outburst at Bramley's *A Hopeless Dawn*, was very much in accord with that of Bastien-Lepage. His figure paintings do not try to tell a story or to invoke sentiment, and are merely records of interesting scenes or effects that he has witnessed. His "tutor", Edward Simmons, on the other hand, despite his high regard for Lepage, produced, during his time in St Ives, figure paintings that are clearly directed at the Victorian market. Portraits of his family become Biblical stories, quotations from literature are used as titles and appeals to the emotions are commonplace. Such works are far removed from his objective, unsentimentalised depictions of the Breton fisherfolk. Helene Schjerfbeck, whose work had been admired by Bastien-Lepage in Brittany, produced several paintings, such as *View of St Ives* and *The Bakery*, which not only demonstrate continued French influences, but represent a significant advance on her Breton work. However, her major work, *The Convalescent*, is an archetypal Victorian narrative painting, appealing to sentiment. It is astonishing that such a short acquaintance with painters aiming at the British market should have influenced her so markedly, particularly as she did not submit the work to the Royal Academy. Similarly, Maria Wiik, during her brief time in St Ives in 1889-90, which is discussed in the next Chapter, was so infused with the style and approach of her fellow Cornish artists that her painting *Out into the World* can be considered a classic 'Newlyn School' work in subject, style and colouring. Such works demonstrate the dilemma faced by all French-trained artists, irrespective of nationality, who decided to settle in Cornwall - how did they adhere strictly to the principles eagerly adopted during their French sojourns, when trying to earn a living in the Victorian market-place? Very few did so without some significant compromises.

Unlike Newlyn, however, figure painting was not the sole genre practised in St Ives and, even in these early years, the foundations for the colony's later reputation as a centre for landscape and marine painting were laid. In this connection, Adrian Stokes is the key figure and the sale of *Upland and Sky* to the Chantrey Trustees in 1888 led to an extraordinary succession of budding landscape artists, such as Arnesby Brown, Arthur Meade, Algernon Talmage and Greville Morris - all students at the Herkomer School at Bushey, joining the colony and working in a style, based on an intense study of tones and values, that was influenced by Stokes' experiences in Barbizon and Pont-Aven. Landscapes were no longer merely descriptive of an attractive scene; they were intended to evoke a mood or inspire poetic thoughts. The effect became of more importance than the subject.

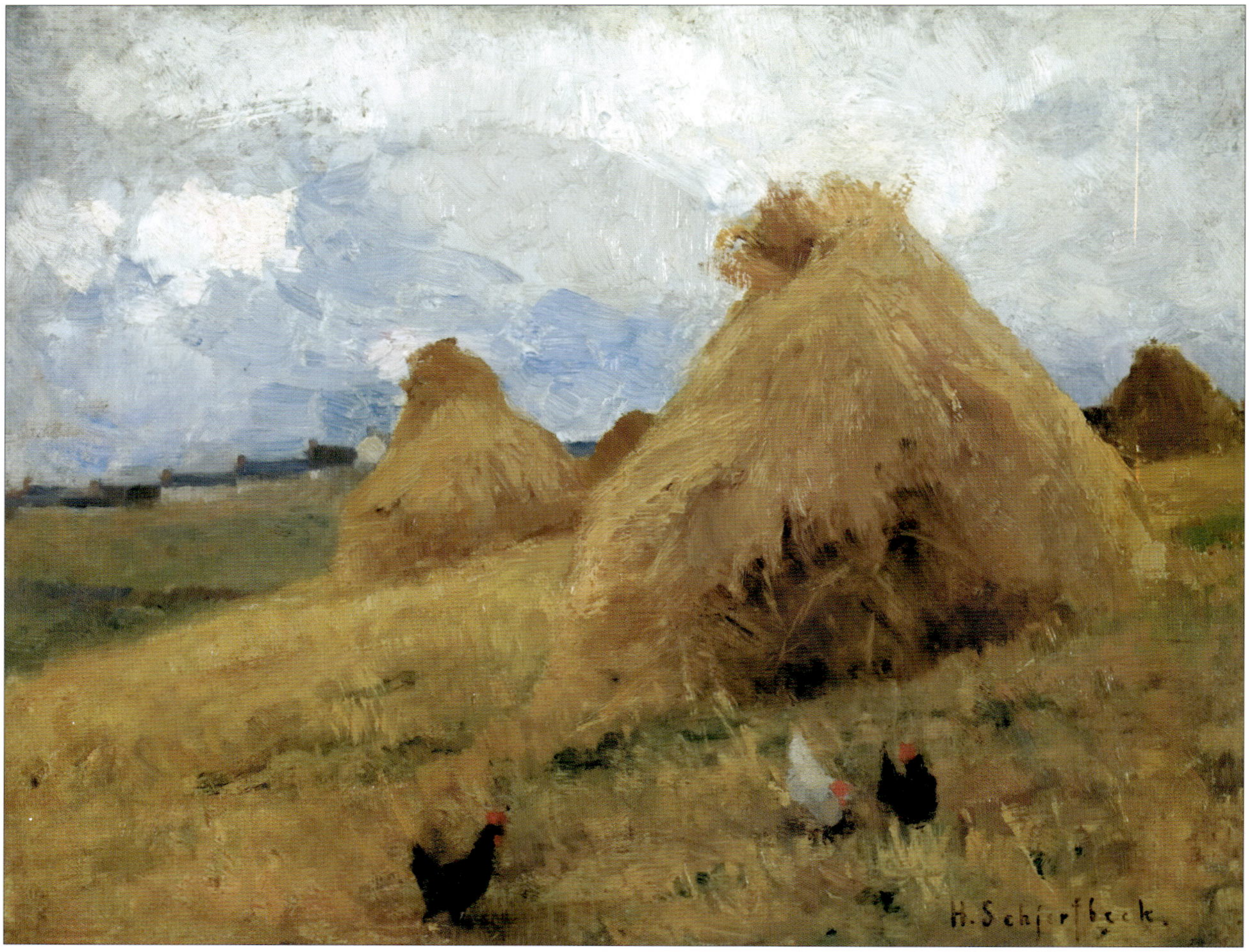

Fig. 6.2 Helene Schjerfbeck *Cornstooks in Cornwall* (Penlee House Gallery & Museum, Penzance)
This work was originally in the collection of Adrian Stokes.

Due to St Ives' north-facing position, which means that the sun, shining from behind the town, lights up the waters of the Bay from dawn until dusk, St Ives has always been popular with marine artists and, as has been seen, in the pre-colony period, it attracted leading figures, such as John Brett, Henry Moore and William Trost Richards. It was the sea that was also the principal attraction for Whistler.[308] When the marine section of the colony was developing in the 1890s, Brett and Moore, as the two leading marine painters in the country, were the principal reference points. Brett's work was derided, for his meticulously detailed approach was considered to be cold and lacking emotion, whilst the broader, more atmospheric approach of Henry Moore was greatly admired, even if, ultimately, it was felt to lack the requisite poetry. With Tonalism a central facet of painting in St Ives after the birth of the colony, certain St Ives artists did pay some regard to the work of Whistler, given his mastery of tonal effects. It is unlikely, though, that they will have seen Whistler's own paintings of St Ives, as the best of these (those now in the Freer collection) had been bought for the private collection of the London barrister, Sir Henry Stubbs Theobald, in July 1885, before the colony was even formed. However, I consider that Adrian Stokes, who produced a series of fine marine paintings in the years 1889-1891, can again be demonstrated to be the key influence on up-and-coming marine artists in the colony, such as Julius Olsson and Louis Grier, for the methods taught at the School of Painting, that they set up in 1895, were again based on Stokes' interpretation of Barbizon School techniques. French painting was again the primary source. However, although Whistler did not do any depictions of St Ives Bay under moonlight, his nocturnes of the Thames may well have had an influence on Edward Simmons' "ethereal transcripts". Simmons' *Night, St Ives Bay* (Fig. 4.37) was the first, large, pure seascape produced in St Ives and this, and his similar depictions of St Ives Bay under the light of the moon, will also have had a major impact on the colony.[309] Its success in Paris, whilst being ignored in England, typifies the Victorian reaction to pure seascapes at that time, for depictions of sea and sky alone were considered to be of little interest. Marine paintings needed to be full of dramatic incident. It would take some years to break down this prejudice but, in due course, it was this same scene - the waters of the Bay converted into a carpet of silver and gold by the light of the moon - that would eventually enable Julius Olsson, who was to become the colony's finest seascape painter, to make his mark in Britain.[310]

Whilst it is always tempting to believe that the early colonists responded to the work that had been done in St Ives previously by artists of the stature of Brett, Moore and Whistler, in reality, they will have had little opportunity of viewing it, and William Titcomb was quite adamant in his speech at the opening of the Cornish Artists Exhibition at Nottingham Castle Museum in 1894 that "they had derived all their inspirations from France".[311]

By 1890, as evidenced by the formation of the St Ives Arts Club that year, the colony at St Ives was well-established and, with more British artists settling in the town, it began to turn its attention towards gaining a reputation in London art circles as well. 1890 saw the first joint exhibitions with artists from the other Cornish art colonies in London, first as a special feature in the last Summer Exhibition at the prestigious Grosvenor Gallery and, then, in the dedicated show at the New Bond Street dealers, Dowdeswell and Dowdeswell. However, as their Newlyn colleagues had already won a reputation at the Royal Academy before the St Ives colony had even been formed, the St Ives artists found it difficult in the early 1890s to establish, in Britain, a separate identity. Labelled Newlyners and their work, even when it was of marine and landscape subjects, as of the 'Newlyn School', their contribution to the reputation of that School has been overlooked. By the late 1890s, though, the St Ives art colony had won a worldwide reputation as a centre for both the practice and the teaching of marine and landscape painting. This story - and much else - is told in the second book in this series *Pioneers of St Ives Art at Home and Abroad (1889-1914)*.

I trust that this account of the establishment of the art colony has dispelled some of the myths that have grown up about early St Ives art. The true story is, in any event, far more interesting than the myths, for it demonstrates that the St Ives colony, from the outset, was quite unique.

---

308 From the number of seascape sketches in the Zorn Museum, it also clearly attracted Zorn as well.

309 I have discounted John Brett's St Ives Bay (Fig.1.11), as this contains a number of boats.

310 Having won numerous awards in Paris and Pittsburgh, Olsson finally received recognition in Britain, when his work Moonlit Shore, a depiction of St Ives Bay from Carbis Bay, was bought by the Chantrey Trustees in 1911.

311 Nottingham Express, 29/9/1894.

~7~

FOREIGN ARTISTS' EPILOGUE

As some of the early foreign artist visitors to St Ives later became internationally acclaimed figures in the art world, it may be of interest to record how their careers developed and to assess the importance or influence of their sojourns in St Ives.

Without doubt, the artist who achieved the highest honours on the international stage was Anders Zorn. After leaving St Ives in the spring of 1888, Zorn made an immediate impression in Paris and his success at the 1889 World Fair led to him being awarded the French Legion of Honour. He was also asked to paint his self portrait for the Uffizi Gallery in Florence. Although he settled in Paris for the next eight years, he returned to Sweden each summer and, in 1888, painted the first of his outdoor nudes, a motif for which he became well-known. In 1893, he supervised the Swedish section at the Chicago World Columbian Exhibition and made a number of important American contacts, resulting in seven visits to the States during which he undertook portrait commissions. In 1896, the Zorns moved home to Mora in Sweden and played an important role in many aspects of the town's cultural heritage. After Anders' death in 1920, Emma, who died in 1942, worked towards creating a museum to honour his memory. This opened in 1939 and holds some fifteen of his St Ives works. A number of these are watercolour studies of the sea in various moods, often under the light of the moon, and there are two fine watercolours of boats in the harbour. There are also four figure paintings in oils - his very first work in the medium, *Emma Zorn Reading*, his portrait of Alice Miller, their companion in St Ives, and his paintings *In the Kitchen* and *Old Anne*. The fact that this group of paintings by such a distinguished artist is completely unknown to Cornish Museums aptly demonstrates the neglect that early St Ives art has suffered, particularly as it can be argued that St Ives played a key role in the development of Zorn's art. It was in St Ives that Zorn first started to paint in oils, a medium in which he became highly accomplished, and the fact that he was assisted in his initial experiments by Edward Simmons demonstrates the kind of mutual support that must have been commonplace in the colony. His success at the 1888 Paris Salon with only his second oil, *Fisherman, St Ives*, which he later reproduced as an etching, was his major breakthrough in France and it was in France that he really established his reputation. It is also interesting that, apart from this painting and his large watercolour of a fish sale, Zorn seems to have made no attempt to sell any of his St Ives work, as if it held tender memories for him.

Another Scandinavian, Helene Schjerfbeck, also went on to win international acclaim, but only at the end of her life. Schjerfbeck, in fact, revisited St Ives in the summer of 1889, this time with her Finnish friend, Maria Wiik, as a companion, and they stayed at 8 Bellair Terrace with Mrs Henry Williams.[312] Helene did a number of portraits of Cornish girls and some still life work during this sojourn and exhibited *Wild Flowers* and *A Hard Lesson* at the ROI in 1889. She spent a lot of time with the Stokeses. Adrian looked after her finances - "acting as my personal secretary" - whilst she linked up with Marianne in the evenings when Adrian was out. She did not produce, however, any work to compare with *The Convalescent*, which is now considered one of the seminal works of her early career, for, after her second visit to St Ives, Schjerfbeck's progress came to a stuttering halt. She was eventually forced to take a job as senior teacher of the life class at the Finnish Art Society's drawing school, which she hated, and was repeatedly struck down with illness. The little self confidence that she had drained away, and she resigned herself to looking after her mother - what she saw as a woman's lot. In 1902, she moved with her mother to Hyvinkaa, a secluded place, and there lived in isolation for twenty-four years. The much later resurrection of her career was due to friendships with a forester, Einar Reuter, who organised her first solo exhibition in 1917 and published a biography of her in the same year, and the journalist turned art dealer, Gosta Stenman, who directed much of her later output. This included returning to the theme of *The Convalescent*, which she did on a number of occasions, and these works were the subject of a special exhibition in 1988. She also completed a haunting series of self portraits at the end of her life, the works for which she is now best known.[313] For many artists, the loss of control over selection of subject-matter would have been abhorrent, but Schjerfbeck commented, "So many years I have been out of the world and now somebody needs me! - it is marvellous and heavy and I feel responsible."[314] She was also much more concerned about *how* she painted than *what* she painted.

---

312 In one of her first letters to Maria on her first visit in 1887, Helene had exclaimed, "Think if we could come here together! Yet I am still too inexperienced and dependent on others to be able to make your stay enjoyable, however much I would like to have you here." (Translated by Erkki Toivanen). Clearly, in 1889, she now felt more confident.

313 See Marjatta Levanto, *Helene Schjerfbeck's Convalescents*, Helsinki, 1988.

314 Letter to Helena Westermark, with whom she studied at Colarossi's, dated 16/12/1937, reproduced in Levanto, ibid, at p.57.

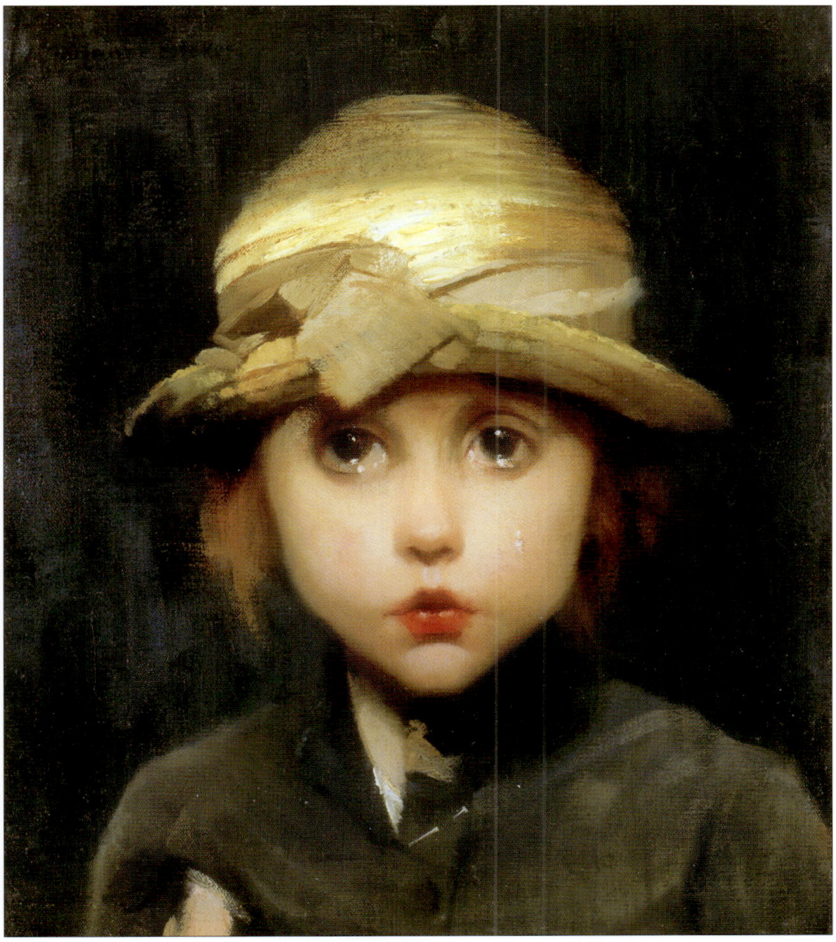

Fig. 7.1 Marianne Stokes *The Tearful Child* (David Messum Fine Art Ltd)

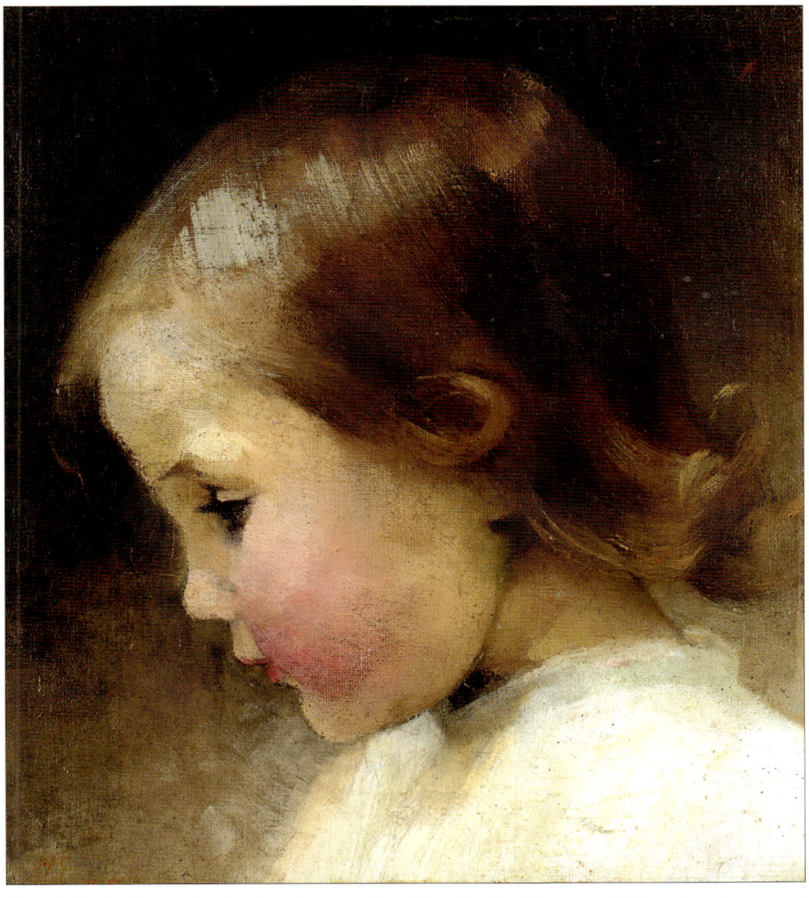

Fig. 7.2 Helene Schjerfbeck *Profile of a Child* (Christies Images)

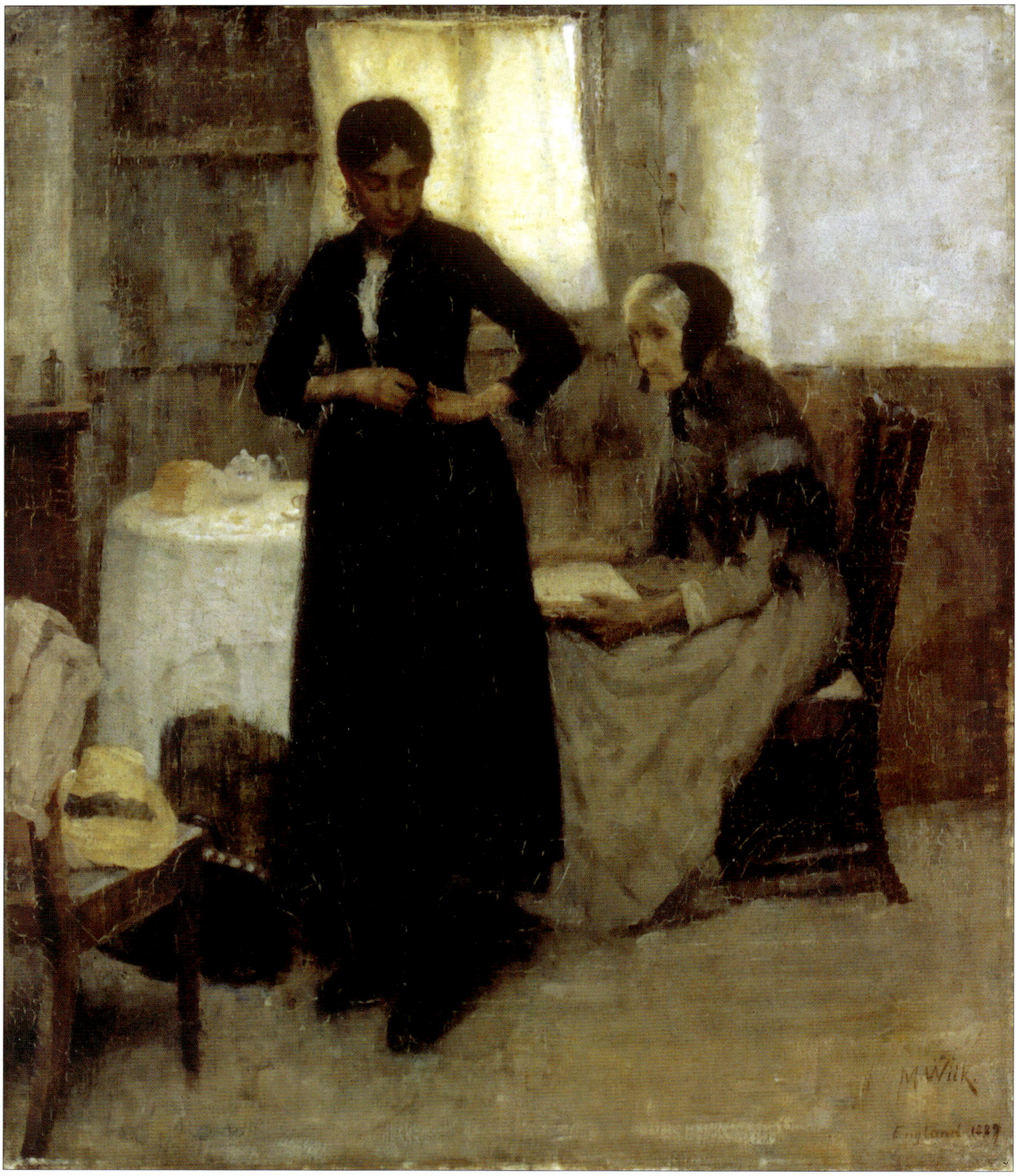

Fig. 7.3 Maria Wiik *Maailemalle* (*Out into the World*) (Finnish National Gallery, Helsinki) (photo: Central Art Archives/Hannu Aaltonen)

Schjerfbeck might not have produced a major work on her second visit in 1889-90, but her friend, Maria Wiik, was inspired to produce one of the most celebrated paintings of her career. Its Finnish title, *Maailmalle*, is not adequately expressed by the normal English version, *Out into the World*, as it connotes a special ceremony when young girls leave the family home. The painting is, in fact, a classic 'Newlyn School' style interior scene, lit by a window at the rear and painted in the low blue/grey tones that were so much in fashion in Cornwall at the time. Mother and daughter have been sharing their last meal together, but now it is time to go. The old woman is shown sitting sadly by the table, contemplating her impending loss, whilst her daughter's back is turned as she puts on her coat. Her hat and bag are ready and she is about to embark on a new life. For the old woman, loneliness beckons, as her clothes indicate that she is already a widow. A book in her hands, most probably a bible, has not provided the comfort desired. Several charcoal sketches show the artist trying out different positions for the two figures before selecting one that emphasized the impending split. The daughter has turned her back on her mother, giving rise to the suggestion that the mother has been cast off, whilst, unseen by her daughter, the mother need not try to keep up appearances but can let her despair show. The painting proved a great success and is now owned by the Atenaeum in Helsinki and has featured prominently in numerous exhibitions devoted to the talented group of Finnish women artists, of whom Schjerfbeck and Wiik were part.[315]

315 A painting of a young girl sitting on a chair is one of several other works known to have been executed by Wiik on this trip.

The other Scandinavian female artist among the early colonists, the Swedish-born Emma Lowstadt Chadwick, and her American husband, Frank, settled in France, dividing their time between Grez and Paris. However, they returned to St Ives on a very regular basis and remained members of the West Cornwall Golf Club until 1932.[316] Indeed, they were resident in St Ives at the time of the 1901 Census and Emma exhibited on Show Day in 1902 and was represented by *Moonlight, St Ives* in the Whitechapel exhibition devoted to the Cornish artists that spring. She also exhibited three etchings, including *Old Paris* and *Old Houses in Brittany*, on Show Day in 1922. Tracking down paintings by her has not proved easy and, to what extent, she produced further major works during her St Ives visits is not known, particularly as she started to concentrate on paintings of mystical female nudes, for it is difficult to tell precisely where these were painted. One such work, *Moses discovered by Pharaoh's daughter*, is owned by the Chateau-Musée, Nemours. Frank's work, so often derided, is, in fact, represented not only in the Musée d'Orsay, which has an attractive, sunny picture by him of Grez bridge, entitled *River in Springtime*, but also in the National Gallery of Art, Washington, which has a drawing by him dating from 1895, entitled *Destiny*.

I have already made mention of the return visits to Cornwall of William Trost Richards, including that in 1905, the year of his death. William John Whittemore, the other American artist known to have visited St Ives before the formation of the colony, also returned on several occasions. In 1891, he was accompanied by the New York based marine painter, Carlton Theodore Chapman (1860-1925), who had also studied at the Julian School. They stayed for several months at 3 Tregenna Terrace and, accordingly, Whittemore's watercolour *Coast of Cornwall after a Storm*, priced at $200 when exhibited in Chicago in 1892, and Chapman's watercolour *Toilers of the Sea* shown that year in Philadelphia, might well be local scenes. A painting by Whittemore, entitled *Evening, St Ives*, has also passed through the salerooms.[317] Whittemore returned to St Ives again, this time with his wife, in September 1893 and his exhibit at the Pennsylvania Academy in 1894 was a watercolour of the Parish Church in St Ives. I can find no reference to Chapman accompanying them but he too exhibited a St Ives scene in Philadelphia that year, whilst a further return visit by Chapman is suggested by a St Ives scene shown at Chicago in 1902. Chapman, who won medals in Boston in 1892, Chicago in 1893 and Atlanta in 1894, became well-known for his marine paintings and reconstructions of naval engagements, whilst Whittemore enjoyed a long career, becoming best known for his portraits and his oil paintings of girls in landscape settings filled with blossom.

Two other American members of the 'Concarneau School' of 1885, Alexander Harrison and Arthur Hoeber, also visited St Ives. By the time the party-loving Arthur Hoeber came to St Ives in 1893, he was married and he stayed with his wife and family and a nurse at Barnoon Villa from early July until mid-October that year.[318] A painting entitled *Cornish Rocks* has appeared in the American auction rooms and he also exhibited at the 1893 RCPS show, *The Fisherman's Daughter*, a work priced at £30 which he had presumably executed that summer in St Ives. On his return to the States, he did exhibit at the Pennsylvania Academy of Fine Arts but became better known as an art critic for *Harper's Weekly* and *New York Globe*.

One might have imagined that a marine painter, such as Alexander Harrison, would have been tempted to visit St Ives by the Cornish seascapes that he saw exhibited in Paris in the late 1880s by his old acquaintances, Edward Simmons and Howard Butler, but there is no convincing proof that he visited St Ives until 1899.[319] This followed a month's stay in Sweden with Anders Zorn, with whom he had been "living simply and making sketches".[320] Zorn presumably encouraged Harrison's visit to St Ives and, shortly after his arrival, he recorded in a letter, written from the Tregenna Castle Hotel on 20th September, that he had met in the town "numerous old chums and acquaintances".[321] The only one that he mentions by name is fellow American, William Dana (1833-1927), but he will certainly have known Harry and Dorothy Robinson from their days together in Concarneau.[322] As Harrison rarely reveals in his titles the location depicted, it has proved impossible to determine whether he did any significant work during his time in St Ives.

---

316 In October 1898, a Mr and Mrs Chadwick from Paris are staying at 14 Richmond Terrace. In March 1899, Emma Chadwick attended the funeral of Lucy Lanham. In 1900, Frank Chadwick subscribed to the St Ives Volunteer Artillery Corps. In 1901, they are living in The Terrace at the time of the Census. In March and May 1901, both Frank and Emma played in golf competitions at Lelant and in December 1901, Frank attended the Golf AGM. In 1902, Emma exhibited on Show Day. In 1903, Chadwick played golf with the artists. In October 1905, they are listed as staying at 10 Sea View Terrace, along with Mr Alphonse Isaac, and, in November 1907, they are signed in as guests at the Arts Club by Kate Deacon. In August 1908, they are staying with Mr and Mrs Vitry from Paris at the Carbis Bay Hotel. Frank is signed in at the Arts Club by Allan Deacon in February 1910. They were clearly back in 1922, when Emma exhibited on Show Day, and, in December 1924, Frank seems to be a member of the Arts Club again as he signs in a Mrs C C Chadwick from Paris.

317 Sloan's, Bethesda 27/10/2000.

318 It will be recalled that the English artist, Tom Trythall Rowe, lived with Hoeber in Quimperlé. They clearly remained friends, as Rowe used Hoeber's address when he exhibited in Philadelphia in 1892. I had expected Rowe to visit Hoeber in St Ives but can find no evidence of this, although Rowe was clearly around shortly afterwards as he exhibited with the St Ives artists at Nottingham in 1894.

319 Marion Whybrow in *St Ives - Portrait of an Art Colony*, 1883-1993, Woodbridge, 1994 at p.21 indicates that Harrison stayed at the Tregenna Castle Hotel in 1889 but I can find no mention of his name in the Visitors' Lists that year and I believe that she has mixed up 1889 with 1899. A Mr and Mrs Harrison, with son, daughter and maid lodged at Hendra's Hotel in Carbis Bay in September 1896 and August 1897. Frustratingly, and unusually, no address is given for their home and, with Harrison being a common name, there is little likelihood that this is Alexander.

320 Letter from A. Harrison to "Morris", dated 20/9/1899 - Archives of the Pennsylvania Academy of the Fine Arts, Philadelphia.

321 ibid.Harrison's visit was probably quite short, as he expected to be in Paris in early October.

322 Frustratingly, 1899 is the one year where no copies of the local paper are extant and so there is no list of visitors in the town to work out to whom Harrison will also have been referring. He may have overlapped with William Wendt and George Gardner Symons but his visit seems to have preceded by some weeks the return that year of Howard Butler, who is not signed into the Arts Club until December.

The careers of the two American artists, who played the most prominent roles in the establishment of the colony, - Howard Butler and Edward Simmons - took unexpected directions. Howard Butler's artistic activities rather took second place after his return to the States as, by 1893, he was immersed in an extraordinary undertaking - the founding of the American Fine Arts Society and the erection of a Fine Arts Building for use by the Society's members. This was an attempt to bring together the younger American artists, who had studied in Europe and who had formed various disparate societies. As ever, high ideals and commercial logic made rare bedfellows but Butler pulled it off, with the help of George Vandervilt and many other important patrons of art. Andrew Carnegie penned this tribute to Butler, who was elected President of the new Society. "We know of no undertaking that shows the character of the American more thoroughly than this - such effort, enthusiasm, organising power, general ability and self-devotion".[323] These qualities appealed to Carnegie, who employed Butler to sort out the finances of the Carnegie Hall and to perform many other tasks for him over a nine year period.

Butler returned to St Ives several times over the next few years. In 1895, Andrew Carnegie paid for his wife and himself to come over to Europe so that they could visit him at his property, Cluny Castle, in Scotland. Butler took the opportunity of showing his wife some of the haunts from his student days and they came down to Cornwall in August and September 1895. They stayed at 1 Carrack Dhu Road, having "hired the house of my friend, Harry Robinson", and Butler worked hard in a studio adjoining that of Julius Olsson, whom he called "a marine painter of great talent".[324] A painting, *Coast of Cornwall*, exhibited in Philadelphia in 1898 might be one of the results, as might his other exhibit that year, described as *Portrait of W B F*. Could this be of William Banks Fortescue? During this trip, he utilised his experiences with the American Art Association to advise the Newlyn artists on the constitution that they should adopt now that they had their own Gallery.[325] The Butlers returned to the States in October on the same steamer as the Carnegies.

The Butlers are also signed in to the Arts Club in December 1899, but they did not stay long enough on these occasions to take part in Show Days or other exhibitions. On returning to America, Butler was elected to the National Academy in 1902. He is best known for his landscape and marine paintings. He had a particular affinity for the desert landscapes of California, where he lived from 1905-7 and, again from 1921-26. However, from 1911, he was primarily based in Princetown. His keen interest in astronomy also resulted in a number of paintings of solar eclipses. Unfortunately, as his major St Ives works from 1886 and 1887 have not been located, it is not possible to judge their quality against the work that he produced over the rest of his career, but it would be no surprise to find, with his greater involvement in commercial activities back in the States, that his Cornish work is his best. Certainly, his later work does not have a large following.

Edward Simmons, who along with Anders Zorn, was the most talented of the early foreign colonists, stayed based in St Ives for much longer than any of the others and continued to play an important role in the colony until 1892. On his return to the States, he was immediately commissioned to construct a stained-glass window for Harvard and, in 1893, he was chosen to decorate the domes at the Manufacturer's Building for the World Columbian Exhibition in Chicago. His exhibits at that Exhibition were all St Ives works - *Early Moonlight upon the Bay of St Ives*, *Darby and Joan* and *The Carpenter's Son*. Vesta Simmons is recorded back in St Ives in 1895, at the same time as Howard Butler, and it is likely that Edward also returned then, although they did get divorced a few years later. In 1898, he joined the celebrated 'The Ten American Painters' to exhibit independent of juries and he became very famous. However, for the rest of his career, Simmons devoted himself principally to murals of American life, rather than painting canvases "to hang on strings in the wrong light". Accordingly, his paintings of Concarneau and St Ives represent the height of his career as a painter of oils on canvas.

St Ives can truly claim to have provided inspiration for some of these artists' career highlights.

---

323 A Carnegie, *Triumphant Democracy*, 1893, p.221.
324 H.R.Butler, Unpublished Autobiography, unpaginated section, Archives of American Art, Smithsonian Institution, Washington DC, Howard Russell Butler papers, Reel 93.
325 See Speech of Stanhope Forbes at the opening of the Passmore Edwards Gallery, in which he expressed his indebtedness "to Mr Howard Butler, an American artist, who had given them a vast amount of useful information and advice" - *Cornish Telegraph* 24/10/1895

ACKNOWLEDGEMENTS

I am, of course, deeply indebted to numerous people for most valuable assistance with my research for this book and I offer my warmest thanks to all that I have not been able to mention below.

First, I must thank various Scandinavians, without whose help, I would have been powerless to research the lives of Helene Schjerfbeck, Maria Wiik and Anders Zorn. Leena Ahtola-Moorhouse most generously supplied me with extracts from her ground-breaking books on Finnish women artists, whilst Erkki Toivanen kindly translated for me Schjerfbeck's letters. Various staff at the Zorn Museum were unfailingly helpful in providing information about their collection and in supplying copies of Zorn's autobiographical notes and letters written by Emma Zorn. For their translation, I am indebted to my good friend, Bjorn Benckert.

In relation to the American artists, I am deeply indebted to Wick Simmons, Edward's grandson, and to his relative, Willa Harris, for the provision of photographs and other information. Judy Lund of the New Unitarian Church of New Bedford also kindly arranged for me to have a duplicate transparency of Simmons' *The Carpenter's Son*. Linda Ferber was most helpful concerning her specialist subject, William Trost Richards, and William Vareika Fine Art kindly let me have images of his St Ives works.

Following my failure to get funding to visit the Archives of American Art at the Smithsonian Institution in Washington DC, I am deeply indebted to the Gloucestershire Library Service (and, in particular, the staff at Tewkesbury Library), for organising and funding a never-ending succession of inter-library loans of microfilms.

Kenneth Myer's book on Whistler's 1884 exhibition was a major source for this artist and I am also grateful to Patricia de Montfort at the Hunterian Gallery, Glasgow. Juliet McMaster, a Canadian academic, was most helpful concerning her relative, James Clarke Hook, and kindly supplied me with images.

I was lucky to meet Catherine Puget at Musée Pont-Aven shortly before her retirement and am indebted to her for allowing me to go through the Museum's records. I am grateful for the feedback of Melissa Hardie concerning Elizabeth Armstrong and I look forward with great interest to the forthcoming exhibition and book on Adrian and Marianne Stokes by Magdalen Evans, who has been most helpful.

I am also most grateful to Kate Morgan at the Royal West of England Academy for allowing me to look through all their old catalogues. Similar thanks are due to the Royal Society of Birmingham Artists and to Moira Lindsay at the Walker Art Gallery, Liverpool.

John McWilliams in St Ives has, as always, been immensely helpful on numerous occasions in passing comment on the vessels and old buildings included in paintings and on much else besides. Brian Stevens at the St Ives Museum was also a fount of knowledge, alerting me to the Rate Books and the Mornington Estate Papers, and the constant encouragement and assistance of Janet Axten, the head of the St Ives Archive Centre, has been most welcome.

I am particularly grateful to everyone not already mentioned who has supplied me with images free or at a discount to normal commercial rates. Particular thanks are due, in this regard, to the art dealers David Messum of David Messum Fine Art Ltd., Victoria Law of Richard Green, London, John Biggs of John Collins Fine Art, Bideford and Sue Freeman of Godolphin Fine Art, Devon, and the auctioneers, David Lay of Lays Auctions, Penzance, Graham Bazley of W.H.Lane & Son, Penzance, CRN Auctions, Cambridge, Massachusetts, and Robert C. Eldred Co. Inc., East Dennis, Massachusetts; also to Lou Van de Vel of booksonfriday.com and Fausto Manara. With a self-funded publication such as this, such gestures are much appreciated.

I am delighted to have been able to work with Tate St Ives on the Dawn of a Colony exhibition and the input of Alison Bevan, the Director of Penlee House Gallery & Museum, was of crucial importance as well. As always, Adam Allen-Foord at Rowe the Printers has been brilliant in ensuring that the book and, in particular, its illustrations look good. I am so lucky to have such an artistic eye at work.

At a time when most people were questioning my sanity, I am deeply grateful for the support of Sir Geoffrey and Lady Carol Holland, who read the manuscript and agreed that the story just had to be told in all its detail. Their encouragement was immensely uplifting. However, it is my wife, Sherry, who deserves the greatest vote of thanks. I promised after producing three books in three months in 2003 never to do it again and yet here we are once more. It was never intended - the story just took off. So thank you, my dear, for all your support, patience and understanding, and apologies for all those ridiculously early mornings and disturbed nights when my brain refused to switch off!

SELECTED BIBLIOGRAPHY

Archives of American Art, Smithsonian Institution, Washington DC, Howard Russell Butler papers
Archives of American Art, Smithsonian Institution, Washington DC, W.T.Richards Papers
William Bartlett, *Summer Time at St Ives, Cornwall*, *Art Journal*, 1897
Beacon Hill Art, *American Painters on the French Scene 1874-1914*, New York 1996
Mrs Lionel Birch, *Stanhope Forbes and Elizabeth Forbes*, London, 1906
Annette Blaugrund, *Paris 1889 - American Artists at the Universal Exposition*, New York, 1989
Charles Brett, M. Hickox and C.Payne, *John Brett - A Pre-Raphaelite in Cornwall*, Bristol, 2006
J. Cooke, M. Hardie and C. Payne, *Singing from the Walls : The Life and Art of Elizabeth Forbes*, Bristol, 2000
Tom Cross, *The Shining Sands - Artists in Newlyn and St Ives 1880-1930*, Tiverton, 1994
Linda Ferber, *Tokens of A Friendship: Miniature Watercolors by William T Richards*, New York, 1982
Caroline Fox and Francis Greenacre, *Artists of the Newlyn School, 1880-1900*, Newlyn, 1979
Archibald S Hartrick, *A Painter's Pilgrimage Through Fifty Years*, Cambridge, 1939
Arthur Hoeber, *A Summer in Brittany*, *The Monthly Illustrator*, vol IV, no 2, 1895
Allan Hook, *Life of James Clarke Hook RA*, privately published
Blanche Willis Howard, *Guenn,* London and New York, 1883
Peter Howard, *Landscapes - The Artists' Vision*, London, 1991
W.H.Hudson, *The Land's End*, London, 1908
Michael Jacobs, *The Good and Simple Life*, Oxford, 1985
J.Johnson and A Greutzner, *The Dictionary of British Artists 1880-1940*, Woodbridge, 1980-8
Pia Katerma, *Maria Wiik*, Helsinki, 1954
Marjatta Levanto, *Helene Schjerfbeck - Convalescents*, Helsinki, 1988
Nina Lubbrens, *Rural Artists' Colonies in Europe 1870-1910*, New Brunswick, 2001
A Ludovici Jnr, *An Artist's Life in London and Paris*, London, 1926
S. MacDonald, *History and Philosophy of Art Education*, London, 1970
Juliet McMaster, *Woman Behind the Painter - The Diaries of Rosalie, Mrs James Clarke Hook*, Edmonton, Alberta, 2006
Frank Maclean, *Henry Moore RA*, London, 1905
Dorothy Menpes, *Brittany*, London, 1905
Mortimer Menpes, *Reminiscences of Whistler*, *The Studio*, 1903, Vol 29
Mortimer Menpes, *Whistler as I Knew Him*, London, 1904
Wilfred Meynell, *Mr and Mrs Adrian Stokes*, *Art Journal*, July 1900
Leena Ahtola-Moorhouse, *Helene Schjerfbeck*, Helsinki, 1992
Leena Ahtola-Moorhouse, S. Sarjas-Korte and S. Sinisalo, *Mallerinder Fra Finland*, Statens Museum, 1983
John Munday, *E.W.Cooke (1811-1880) RA, FRS, FSA, FLS, FZS, FGS - A Man of his Time*, Woodbridge, 1996
Musée de Pont-Aven, *Artistes Finlandais en Bretagne*, Pont-Aven, 1995
Musée de Pont-Aven and Julian Campbell, *Peintres Irlandais en Bretagne*, Pont-Aven, 1999
Musée de Pont-Aven and Julian Campbell, *Peintres Brittaniques en Bretagne 1818-1939*, Pont-Aven, 2000
Kenneth John Myers, *Mr Whistler's Gallery : Pictures at an 1884 Exhibition*, London 2003
F Newlin Price, *Howard Russell Butler*, Princeton, 1936
Cyril Noall, *Beloved St Ives*, St Ives, 1958
Cyril Noall, *The Book of St Ives*, Buckingham, 1977
Cyril Noall, *Yesterday's Town - St Ives*, Buckingham, 1979
A G Robins, *Walter Sickert; The Complete Writings on Art*, 2000
Henry Harewood Robinson, *St Ives as an Art Colony* in *Babcock's Historical Sketch of St Ives and District*, 1896
David Sellin, *Americans in Brittany and Normandy (1860-1910)*, New York, 1982
W. Sickert. *The New 'Life of Whistler'*, *The Fortnightly Review*, December, 1908
E E Simmons, *From Seven to Seventy*, London, 1922
Frances Spalding, *Whistler*, Oxford, 1979
F.G.Stephens, *The Life and Work of J C Hook RA*, London, 1888
Adrian Stokes, *Landscape Painting*, London, 1925
M Sturgis, *Walter Sickert - A Life*, London, 2005
Tate Gallery Archives, Forbes papers
André Theuriet, Essay in *Catalogue de Tableaux Marines et Paysages par Emile Vernier*, Paris 1886
André Theuriet, *Jules Bastien-Lepage and his Art*, London, 1892
Walter H.Tregellas, *Artists' Haunts: Cornwall - the Cliffs*, *Magazine of Art*, 1878, pp.8-11 and 141-146
Walter H.Tregellas, *The moorlands and glens of Cornwall*, *Art Journal*, 1883, pp.314-316
Gabriel P Weisberg, *Beyond Impressionism - The Naturalist Impulse in European Art 1860-1905*, London, 1992
Marion Whybrow, *St Ives 1883-1993 - Portrait of an Art Colony*, Woodbridge, 1994
Norman Wilkinson, *A Brush with Life*, London, 1969
Anders Zorn, Autobiographical Notes, Zorn Museum, Mora

INDEX